THE ASCENDANT ORGANISATION

By the same author

THE ROAD TO NISSAN
MANAGEMENT IN THE FAST TRACK
LEAN PRODUCTION AND BEYOND

The Ascendant Organisation

Combining commitment and control for long-term, sustainable business success

Peter D. Wickens, OBE

First published 1995 by
MACMILLAN PRESS LTD
Houndmills, Basingstoke, Hampshire RG21 2XS
and London
Companies and representatives
throughout the world

ISBN 0–333–61130–6

A catalogue record for this book is available
from the British Library.

10 9 8 7 6 5 4 3 2 1
04 03 02 01 00 99 98 97 96 95

Copy-edited and typeset by Povey–Edmondson
Okehampton and Rochdale, England

Printed and bound in Great Britain by
Mackays of Chatham PLC, Chatham, Kent

*To **Brian** and **Gaye***
Who cared
When it mattered

Contents

List of Tables xii

List of Figures xiii

Acknowledgements xiv

Introduction xv

PART I 'KNOWLEDGE'

1 The ascendant organisation **3**

2 Our changing industrial society **8**
International competition 8
Technology 11
The collective to the individual 12
Restructuring 13
Employment 17
Conclusions 18

3 Rising to the ascendant **20**
The 'controllers' 20
The 'behaviouralists' 23
Elton Mayo 23
Frederick Herzberg 24
Douglas McGregor 24
Abraham Maslow 26
Eric Trist 26
Victor Vroom 27
William Ouchi 28
Conclusions 29

4 The Japanese – right or wrong? **31**
The standard operation 33
Kaizen 34

The elimination of waste 36
Japanese manufacturing and lean production 37
Automation 39
The critics of Japan 40
The Japanese critics 41
The German critics 43
The Canadian critics 45
The British critics 48
The American critics 49
Responding to the challenges 51
The Swedish experience 58

5 Conclusions – and beginnings **63**
Conclusions – so far 63
Prescribed and discretionary work 70
The Nine Alpha Organisation Map 71
The axes 73
The organisation types 74

PART II 'KNOW-HOW'

6 Culture, vision, mission – whatever you call it **81**
Culture 81
Mission 85
How to establish a culture 'statement' 87

7 Leading the ascendant organisation **91**
Leadership at the top 91
How to lead the ascendant organisation 95
Personal attributes 95
Strategic perspective 97
Communication 98
Achievement 99
Managing 102
Leadership in the front line 104
The supervisor in the ascendant organisation 106
How to change to 'teambuilding supervisors' 113

8 Ascendant behaviour **115**
'Everyone a first-class citizen' 115
Teamworking 119

How to introduce teamworking 123
Communication 126
Involving people 130
Kaizen in practice 140
How to involve people 144
Flexibility 147
Commitment in an 'insecure' environment 154

9 The processes and practicalities 157
Cell manufacturing 157
Autonomous work groups 160
Total productive maintenance 162
Changeover times 164
Inventory reduction 165
Material supply 167
Level scheduling and distribution 169
The five 'S's 171
Visible management 172
Operator care 174

10 Beyond TQM – integrating quality 178
The changing nature of quality 178
Customer focus 180
Design for quality 183
Building for quality 187
Poka yoke 189
Commitment to quality 190
Involving all of the organisation 192
Club Med 193
How *not* to introduce an integrated quality culture 195
How *to* introduce an integrated quality culture 195
Strategy 196
Planning 196
The process 198

11 Partnership sourcing 205
Adversarial relationships 205
Japanese suppliers 206
Partnership sourcing 208
Supplier development 213
How to introduce partnership sourcing 216

12 Every worker a knowledge worker **219**
The fundamentals 219
A job with training – Germany 223
A job with training – Japan 225
Continuous development 227
Beginning at the bottom 231
How to introduce continuous development 232
The learning organisation 235

13 The long and the short of the finances **238**
Corporate finances 238
Non-financial indicators 244
The principles of pay 245
Performance-related pay (PRP) 249
Skill-based pay 251
Salary progression 253
Performance bonuses 259
Pay at the top 262
Top pay in the ascendant organisation 265

14 Trade unions in the ascendant organisation **268**
The decline of trade unions 268
The new agenda 271
Trade unions in the ascendant organisation 279

15 Becoming ascendant **286**
How not to change 286
BP 288
IBM 290
Jaguar 293
Imposing change – Ford 294
The Rover Group 296
How to become an ascendant organisation 298
Understand the concept 299
Determine the strategy 300
Involve the people 301
Implement the change 305
Sustain the gain 308

16 Two sides of the coin lead to an edge **310**
The special contribution of Japan 310

The special contribution of the west 312
The two sides of the coin 313

17 The end of the beginning 320

References 337

Index 348

List of Tables

4.1 Wage Gradient: Japan v. UK 43
4.2 CAMI Attitude Survey 47
11.1 Automotive Suppliers' Performance 207
11.2 Suppliers' Attitude to Partnership 215
13.1 Salary Progression Systems 253
13.2 Financial Performance: Profit-Sharers v. Non-Profit-Sharers 261
14.1 Summary of Benefits and Risks Associated with Options for Trade Union Response 272

List of Figures

1.1	Organisation Types: The Simple Model	4
4.1	The Interdependence of Japanese Management Practices	32
5.1	The Nine Alpha Organisation Map	72
7.1	The Nissan Skill Matrix	109
8.1	CBI Statement of Principles on Employee Involvement	133
9.1	The 3 'S' Rating System	172
10.1	Design Changes over Time	185
12.1	The SCANS Report: a Three-part Foundation	221
12.2	The SCANS Report: Five Competencies	222
13.1	Non-Financial Indicators	246
13.2	Performance Evaluation Factors	256
13.3	Performance Ratings	257
16.1	The Occidental/Oriental Synergy	313

Acknowledgements

This book was researched over a three-year period and written mainly at weekends. My greatest appreciation must therefore go to my wife, Helga, for her tolerance of the considerable disruption to family life.

A number of people have commented on individual chapters and I thank Terry Hogg, Keith Jones and Peter Hill for their comments on Chapters 9, 10 and 11. Helen Murlis made fundamental contributions to my thinking about reward structures and these are incorporated into Chapter 13. I spent a week with Barry Venter, Dieter Lange, Deon Fourie and Owen Viljoen of Organisation Development International in Johannesburg at Easter 1994 and together we challenged many of the concepts and learned much in the process. I owe special thanks to Barry whose idea it was to change the original simple, two-axes model to the more complex but much more meaningful four-axes model. We spent a great week refining it. Pam Coates typed the manuscript through numerous revisions and not only retained her sense of humour but kept pushing me along when the spirits flagged. Pam gave much of her personal time to this and I am eternally grateful. It was also her idea to lay out the references in tabular form – so much easier to follow!

Many others have contributed, often unknowingly, but I wish in particular to mention Werner Sengenberger of the International Institute of Labour Studies whose summary paper, 'Lean production: the way of working and production in the future', prepared for an experts' seminar in 1992, helped crystallise many emerging thoughts. Dr Anne Wright, Vice Chancellor of the University of Sunderland offered me the University's first ever Honorary Professorship which caused me to prepare an inaugural lecture 'Lean production and beyond: the system, its critics and the future', which formed the foundation for much of Part One. Dan Jones, co-author of *The Machine That Changed the World* has often shared platforms with me and I have learned much from him.

Of Toshiaki Tsuchiya, Nissan's first Managing Director, all I can say is that I owe him a great deal. He had the wisdom to appoint people who had independent minds but an empathy with the Japanese way. He then created the environment in which these people could build a company which hopefully pulls together the best of the Orient and the Occident, and rejects that which is not transferrable. Few have had such a privilege.

Camberley, Surrey, England PETER D. WICKENS, OBE

Introduction

In the last ten years thousands of business executives have visited Nissan in Sunderland looking for a magic formula. Every European car manufacturer, virtually every British company of significance and hundreds who wish to be of significance have joined with visitors from all continents in wanting to learn the secrets. It is not difficult for them to see the practical details, but echoing Sun Tzu, the Chinese militarist of some 2500 years ago, 'All men can see the tactics whereby I conquer, but what none can see is the strategy out of which great victory is evolved.'

I have long had a concern about this failure to separate strategy and tactics. But it is not only practising business executives who do not make the distinction. Academic analysis, by itself, achieves very little but neither do practical recipes with a narrow focus and little real understanding of the underlying principles. Biographies of transformational leaders can inspire but most of us are not transformational leaders and only rarely are the lessons transferrable. Descriptions of national cultures and practices are often based more on prejudice than reality and consultants' panaceas last only as long as it takes for the next one to be thought up. In short, much writing is by thinkers who can't do and doers who can't think!

The Ascendant Organisation is an attempt to pull 'knowledge and 'know-how' together. It incorporates practical experience gained over 30 years with British, American and Japanese companies, understanding gleaned through academic research and lecturing, and knowledge accrued by working with academics, trade unionists and from advising business executives from all over the world. It takes a multi-dimensional approach – theory and practice, strategy and tactics, hard and soft issues, historical and contemporary analysis, examples from a variety of nations and examines the perspectives of both advocates and critics.

It is structured like an open-ended egg timer. Into the top half, Part I, I pour knowledge – an overview of the macro changes taking place in established industrialised societies, and the work of the 'controllers' and 'motivators'. I look at the Japanese way in its ideal form but also at criticisms, and how Japanese society is responding to the challenges of the late twentieth century.

This knowledge leads to the neck of the egg timer in which I draw twenty-five conclusions from Part I which in turn lead to the central concept of the ascendant organisation which seeks to combine high levels of commitment of the people and control of the processes to achieve a synthesis between high effectiveness and a high quality of life leading to long-term, sustainable business success. All of these now seem to me so obvious that it is a wonder that they took so long to determine.

Part II, 'Know-how', is the bottom half of the egg timer. It also contains 'knowledge' but is more concerned with practices, and because it is open-ended offers numerous indications as to the paths readers may take if they choose to move their organisations to the preferred state. In keeping with the overall philosophy I emphasise that the directions are indicative rather than prescriptive. There is no magic formula. All any of us can do is what we believe is right for our organisation based on our own history, personalities and culture. But, continually, I emphasise the need to understand before acting; for action without understanding leads to but short-lived success.

The central thrust of *The Ascendant Organisation* is about people. An organisation or company as such, achieves nothing. Machinery, computers and tools left alone for long, deliver nothing. Managerial concepts, theories, systems and procedures are produced by people for people. Leadership cannot exist without followers. Culture is about relationships between people. Only when people are brought into the equation does anything come to life. Without people there are no organisations, no problems, no solutions and no need for managers – nor authors!

However, I reject the hypocritical statement, 'Our people are our greatest asset' often uttered by senior executives who, in any case, rarely act in such a way. The words subconsciously imply that 'our people' are something separate from 'us', that somehow they belong to 'us' or to 'our company'. They do not. While the legally defined company has an employment relationship with individuals, the real company is just as much the people who work in it and give their time as those who are outside and invest their money. Indeed, when most such investments are through the large financial institutions, interested primarily in the balance sheet, it could be argued that the people have more right to be called 'the company' than any other grouping. Therefore, 'our greatest asset' is not 'our people'. When 'all people' are genuinely part of the company, '*Our* greatest asset is *our* customers'.

I also choose the word, 'people' throughout, rather than the more fashionable 'human resources'. People are people when they get up in the morning, eat in the evening and relax in whatever pastime they enjoy. They do not suddenly change to human resources for that one-third of the day during which they are at work!

Most ascendant organisations are not new companies with all the advantages of a greenfield site, nor are they necessarily Japanese. Indeed by the end of Part I readers may conclude that very few are Japanese. Most are established companies which have realised that 'there must be a better way', have learned from many sources and have taken a strategic view of their businesses.

The common element is not a greenfield site but a greenfield mind!

PART I

'Knowledge'

1 The Ascendant Organisation

The ascendant organisation combines high levels of commitment of the people and control of the processes to achieve a synthesis between high effectiveness and high quality of life leading to long-term, sustainable business success.

The basis of what I have come to call 'the simple model' of the ascendant organisation was initially developed during a bar room discussion one late evening in Düsseldorf in 1992. I still have the scrappy piece of paper on which I first drew the quadrant with its two axes and four organisation types. It took many months, though, for the term 'ascendant' eventually to emerge.

However, having suffered from a plethora of panaceas, I have never seen the ascendant organisation as yet another miracle cure nor as a brand new concept breaking entirely new ground. It recognises that business managers have to attend to a host of issues, many of which conflict with each other. It forms part of a continuum, preceded by many eminent thinkers and, no doubt, will be followed by many more.

For example, several years ago I was much influenced by Richard Walton's *Harvard Business Review* article, 'From control to commitment in the workplace', in which he explained the shift from the Taylorist 'control' model to the human relations 'commitment' model as a main reason for the significantly improved performance of a number of American companies. Under his commitment model:

> Jobs are designed to be broader than before, to combine planning and implementation and to include efforts to upgrade operations, not just maintain them. Individual responsibilities are expected to change as conditions change and often teams, not individuals, are the organisational units accountable for performance. With management hierarchies relatively flat and differences in status minimised, control and

lateral coordination depend on shared goals and expertise rather than formal position-determined influence. (Walton, 1985)

Walton was essentially correct in his analysis and that article, coming at the time when we were establishing the Nissan culture in Sunderland, greatly reinforced my thinking. However, having worked with American, Japanese and British companies for some thirty years and having experienced the problems and successes of each of them I am now convinced that Walton went too far in his rejection of the 'control model'. *If we are to achieve long-term, sustainable success we need the right balance between the commitment of the people and control of the processes.*

This is the essential concept of the ascendant organisation. During the course of the next three chapters I shall present the 'knowledge' which led me to this conclusion and then discuss the more complex model. Let me though at this stage introduce 'the simple model' (see Figure 1.1).

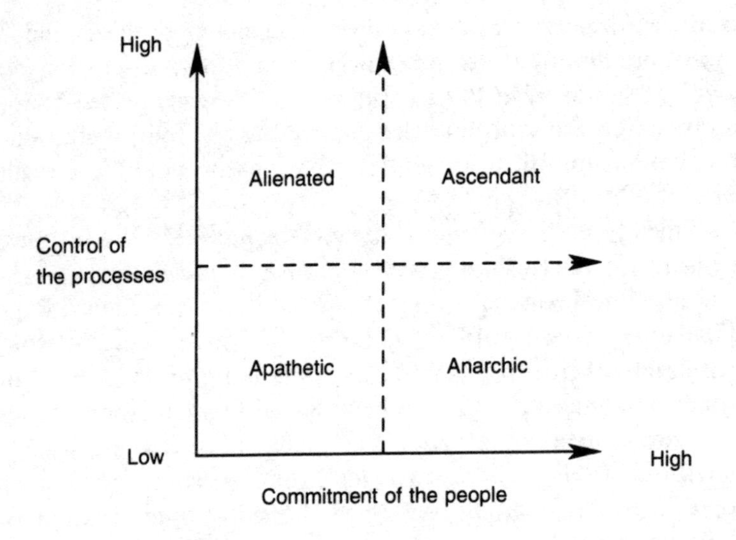

Figure 1.1 Organisation Types: The Simple Model

Most writers, with the honourable exception of Eric Trist (see Chapter 3), concentrate on just one axis; the 'scientific management' school on controlling the processes and the 'behaviouralists' on commitment of the people. Many believe that the Japanese strength lies in the latter but, as we shall see, they are also the most effective of 'controllers'.

'Control' is, essentially, externally imposed. It is the top down imposition of standards, rules and processes. Command and direction are the normal methods of determining behaviour and achieving results. 'Commitment', however, is internal with people believing in their own values. Committed people are highly motivated to work to achieve their own goals and, hopefully, those of the organisation.

As with all such models, it is probably too simple and for this reason I subsequently developed a more complex model, the Nine Alpha Organisation Map, which, following the detailed analysis in Part I, will be fully explored in Chapter 5. However, in order to put the analysis into a framework I briefly discuss the simple model in this first chapter.

The first quadrant I describe as *anarchic* – high levels of individual commitment combined with low levels of control which at the extreme can lead to people doing what they, individually, think is right for them and/or the organisation.

A classic example of this was the selling of personal pension plans in Britain in the late 1980s and early 1990s. A basically good product was released on to the market and the enthusiastic sales people either had no guidelines or, if they did, were allowed to ignore them. As a result personal pensions were sold to thousands of people already in excellent occupational pension schemes and who lost out as a result. An investigation by the Securities and Investment Board (SIB) found only 9 per cent of cases complied with industry guidelines on giving best advice and 83 per cent of records examined were unsatisfactory. The sales agents had simply failed to enquire properly into the benefits of the customer's existing pension scheme (SIB, 1993). As a result the insurance companies are now faced with bills running into millions of pounds either to buy back their customers into their old schemes or to pay compensation. Such a practice can be described as *anarchic*.

But anarchic organisations are not usually in the staid insurance industry. Commission only brokerages and creative businesses in which it is everyone for themselves are much more typical.

The opposite effect, high control and low commitment results in the alienated organisation. Douglas McGregor's Theory X company was based on the view that the average person dislikes work, and the company therefore had to rely on control and coercion to generate effort. Brains were left at the door. The classic example is the traditional, line paced car assembly plant but it may just as easily be any low wage, mass production facility based on piece work or any organisation in which low calibre management cares only about results and little about people.

The lower left segment is low commitment and low control and applies to the type of organisation in which management has given up trying, has abdicated its responsibility or is simply of low calibre. People broadly do what they want but without any shared objectives or sense of direction. It may be the large, fat, private sector company, comfortable in its markets and sure of its profits; or the public sector organisation which does not really have to try. 'Low commitment, low control' is the *apathetic* organisation. In such an organisation neither management nor the people really care what happens and generally if you do not care what you get, you are not disappointed! In discussing this model I was surprised how many university audiences placed their institutions in this lower left quadrant.

The objective must, therefore, be to progress to the upper right quadrant, a high level of commitment of the workforce and high control of the processes. In such an organisation the best of scientific management combines with the behavioural scientists and the subsequent work of the Japanese engineers, Taiichi Ohno and Shigeo Shingo, plus a significant amount of practical experience, understanding and plain common sense.

I spent a long time trying to determine the right word for that upper right quadrant. My conclusion was 'ascendant'. The *Concise Oxford Dictionary* defines 'ascendant' as:

Rising towards the zenith

and 'zenith' as:

The highest point, time or place of greatest power, or prosperity or happiness.

This was my first 'Eureka' moment – a definition which is so right that afterwards it seemed amazing that it took such a struggle.

Translating these dictionary definitions into a business context:

The ascendant organisation combines high levels of commitment of the people and control of the processes to achieve a synthesis between high effectiveness and high quality of life leading to long-term, sustainable business success.

In my definition, the word 'effectiveness' combines productivity, quality and profitability. It reaches out to suppliers and to the market place. It requires high quality investment, engineering, research and product development. Above all, it requires high calibre, highly motivated people but it also needs a culture and leadership committed to these goals. 'Quality of life' is deliberately chosen to take us beyond the workplace. Many in the West would regard the Japanese quality of life as low, both in the workplace and beyond but if all we do is concentrate on the workplace we are missing something. It is no good working hard to achieve prosperity if you are unable to use that prosperity in the way you prefer, whatever that might be.

The quadrant is, however, simplistic. There is no room for the maverick organisation, or for the autocratic, the authoritative nor the numerous other organisation types. The more complex model in Chapter 5 has four axes, not two, allowing nine organisation types, not four, to be developed.

However, before exploring the complex model it is necessary to explain in more detail how I arrived at this concept and in the next three chapters I will discuss the fundamental long term changes taking place in Western industrial society, the influence of the 'thinkers' and the impact of Japan.

2 Our Changing Industrial Society

Almost 40 per cent of the companies which comprised the Fortune 500 a decade ago no longer exist. Of the 1970 Fortune list, 60 per cent have gone, either acquired or out of business . . . of the 12 companies which comprised the Dow Jones Industrial Index at the turn of the century, only General Electric survives as a giant.

(Christopher Lorenz, *Financial Times*, 22 September 1993)

My lead quotations tell us that little is permanent (except, perhaps, General Electric). Virtually all industrialised, market economies have in the last twenty to thirty years experienced fundamental, long-term changes. These changes permeate all we do, the way we manage our organisations and the demands made on the people in those organisations. In turn, they impact on every facet of society. These pressures for change are numerous but I will limit discussion to those central to the theme of this book:

- the growth of international competition
- the impact of technology on the nature of work
- the shift from the collective to the individual
- the restructuring of organisations
- structural changes in employment

INTERNATIONAL COMPETITION

In the last thirty years the whole basis of international competition and the determinants of competitive advantages have changed. Without great exaggeration one can say that until the 1960s manufacturers demanded more and more volume, being able to sell everything they produced. As manufacturing capacity developed throughout the world and competition intensified, price often became the determining factor – this in turn impacted on costs and eventually led to the transfer of low-level assembly work to low-cost countries. The 1970s was characterised as the era of quality, particularly as high-quality but low-priced Japanese products entered western markets in significant numbers. During the 1980s production capacity exceeded demand and manufacturers offered an ever widening range of products. In the 1990s the basis of competitive advantage has become even more complex. Today's market place demands that manufacturers compete on price *and* quality *and* innovation *and* delivery time *and* customisation *and* service.

Manufacturing industry in the advanced, high cost, industrialised economies faces increasing competition from the lower wage, lower social cost economies. The newly industrialising countries with employment costs a fraction of the West's are able to manufacture standardised products more cheaply, and compete successfully on price despite the established economies' productivity advantages. Bankers, Morgan Stanley estimate that hourly labour costs in manufacturing in Germany are almost $25, in America and Japan $16–17 but in South Korea the cost drops to $4.90, it is $2.40 in Mexico and less than $1 in China and Thailand. This effectively expands the world supply of unskilled workers.

International trade used to be in the basics – food and primary products. Now, there cannot be a product or service which is not traded and the once precious natural resources can even be a disadvantage when national politics demands the protection of a local, high cost, low quality resource. Japan and Singapore have no natural raw materials and are able, therefore, to trade on the world market seeking, for example, the highest quality iron ore at the lowest cost. Indeed, what Lester Thurow (1993, p. 45) has called the seven key industries of the next few decades (micro-electronics, biotechnology, the new materials industries, civil aviation, telecommunications, robots plus machine tools and computers plus software) could all be located anywhere, depending not on where the natural resources are located, but where market growth is happening and where brainpower and practical skills can best be utilised. Already, the process has taken a further step. The previous 'new' nations, such as Singapore, which built products designed in Japan now have their own managerial and design capability and get some of their manufacturing done in Sumatra or the Philippines. Singapore calls itself the Intelligent Island; it relies not on natural resources but on applied intelligence. What really count are knowledge, capability and motivation.

In the financial sector there are no longer separate markets for Europe, North America and Asia. Electronic transfer of funds, whether from your supermarket to your bank or across the world, facilitates international trade and investment, allowing investors to take advantage of the most favourable interest rates wherever they occur and wherever they wish to invest. Lack of funds is no longer the limiting factor when the world capital market is ready to lend to a Third World entrepreneur who can demonstrate sales commitments from a First World customer. The result is that for most manufactured products there is now virtually a global market and, as important, global manufacturers.

Transnational companies are able to operate in those countries which best suit them, ensuring that all are exposed to the latest production technologies, materials and costs. All companies in all economies are exposed to the standards established by the most successful. There are now few captive markets, few people who are prepared to wait, few companies which can now say, 'This is what we produce or provide – this is all you can have.' We have for the most part changed from a producer-led to a customer-led market place in which the ability to respond rapidly to changing customer demands has become one of the key competitive advantages.

Globalisation, however, does not necessarily mean selling the same products in different markets. Ford is moving to a co-ordinated management, product and manufacturing strategy. But there are numerous permutations ranging from central control with no national structures to national autonomy with little or no co-ordination between decentralised units, which may even compete with each other. The extremes are rare. More likely is some form of central direction or co-ordination, looser, less formal co-ordinating committees and systems or informal co-operation.

The distribution of increasingly sophisticated but user-friendly technology aids this process – it facilitates decentralisation to a level not previously thought possible. Shell UK used to design its North Sea oil and gas platforms in its London and Glasgow design offices. Now, using modern IT systems it can specify precisely what is required to Indian design teams who are able to do the work and return the results at ten per cent of the cost with no loss of quality. The more sophisticated use of financial information enables improved monitoring of the work of suppliers and contractors, thus allowing outsourcing of previous in-house services. Automobile manufacturers are expert at manufacturing motor cars. They are not caterers, security specialists, gardeners, cleaners, vehicle transporters or waste removers and now, instead of high levels of vertical integration, encourage the development and use of niche companies, and purchase systems rather than components. They have always been there but the provision of such services is now a growth point in the economy. One of General Motors' biggest suppliers is Blue Cross–

Blue Shield health insurance and, even before its move into credit cards, one of its biggest products was financial services, in the form of loans and insurance to dealers and customers. Suppliers of sophisticated manufacturing systems now offer sophisticated training packages and after-sales service, and can earn more money this way than from the initial sale. *Manufacturing and service are becoming both fused and diffused.*

TECHNOLOGY

In the 1960s computers were large, expensive machines used for number crunching, located in secure, air-conditioned rooms. Today they are small, cheap and, while in large organisations the central processing unit remains in a secure custom-built room, for the most part they are a desk-top or lap-top tool. The key to the rapid expansion was the microchip. Engineers developed the integrated circuit – a miniature circuit produced within a single piece of semi-conductor – and changed the world.

Technology, by eliminating much routine processing and giving more power to the fingertip, allows companies to offer a better service to the customer and at the same time eliminate vast numbers of managers, supervisors, staff and departments whose previous task was to process that paperwork. Computers, when first introduced, created highly specialised centralised departments with highly specialised staff. Now, computing power can be distributed throughout an organisation. Those people who were initially afraid of a computer terminal now welcome it for what it is: a tool which helps them do the job better – a sophisticated screwdriver!

Retailers are demanding higher degrees of sophistication in marketing, layout, design of goods and packaging. New technology is used in functions such as warehousing, stock control, cash balancing and ordering. Electronic point of sale terminals (EPOS) allow automatic cash and inventory recording, and laser scanning is now facilitating such activity without manual input. IT allows functional specialisation at head offices which in turn allows for a high degree of integration between functions such as finance, pricing, marketing and distribution.

Within manufacturing, computerisation has transformed the processes. Numerically controlled machines first hit the shop floor forty years ago. Now, flexible manufacturing systems facilitate not only the integration and control of the manufacturing processes but also the movement of work between the machines. Technology, combined with highly motivated and properly trained people, allows a rapid response to changing customer demands. Twenty years ago it took car manufacturers four hours to change the dies in the power presses. Now this can be done in less than ten minutes. The movement is to achieve 'one of a kind' production on a large scale, in which consumer durables will be engineered to meet the specific needs of a customer. Product differentiation will be demanded and fully responsive manufacturing systems will be able to manufacture the product to order and deliver it to the customer in days at a quality and price that makes it attractive. The trick to achieve this is to design-in flexibility, by having a large number of parts in common but so designed that many permutations are possible and the very specific requirements can be uniquely produced.

People speak of the dark factory, believing that manufacturing jobs will come to an end. However it should not be supposed that the dark factory is the ultimate. This was, perhaps, the view two decades ago when advocates of automated systems caused many manufacturers, particularly General Motors in the United States and Fiat in Italy, to invest too much money in capital intensive, inflexible technology. The result was that in order to recoup their investment they needed lengthy production runs at a time when rapid response to the market was becoming critical to competitive success. One of the reasons for Japanese success was their realisation that properly selected, well-trained, highly motivated workers are far more flexible and capable than inflexible automation dependent on unreliable technology.

It is people, not robots, who continuously improve both products and processes.

THE COLLECTIVE TO THE INDIVIDUAL

The third long-term trend is the shift of influence from the collective to the individual. There are many obvious signs ranging from the break-up of the Soviet bloc to declining membership of trade unions in almost all industrialised market economies.

But individuality goes deeper – more fundamental is the expression of individuality and the exercise of individual choice. The lack of respect for established authority; improvements in education which convince people that they can develop through their own efforts; the view that you have to earn respect rather than automatically receive it; and the fact that more people now expect work to fit in with their lives rather than their lives with their work are all fundamental changes which question not only the employer–employee relationship but also the total motivation pattern.

As we shall see when examining the work of the behavioural scientists, the highest 'needs' were thought to be self-actualisation or fulfilment and for social contact and acceptance. For many, traditional paid employment is failing to satisfy these needs and, perhaps, a combination of dissatisfaction, alternative opportunities, increased leisure time and the ability to pay has led to a dramatic growth in 'new age' life styles whether they be of the contemplative type or engaging in challenging physical activities. All, in their various ways, are seen as expressions of individualism and are attempts to use leisure time in a satisfying manner. The greater the satisfaction outside work the less need there is to seek satisfaction inside it. Perhaps there is now evident in many an even higher need, a need to contribute unselfishly to society.

My own thinking in this area was influenced very much by a conversation I had in the mid–1970s with the late Danny Connor, then the Communist trade union leader of the Ford Dagenham Body Plant where I was Industrial Relations Manager. While no one could ever suggest that our relationship was good, we did have a few conversations which were slightly removed from total confrontation. During one such discussion he said, 'Your trouble is that you don't realise the talent you've got on the shop floor. If you'd only listen to the lads and use them properly most of your problems would be resolved.' The fact that Danny Connor was the first person to try to stop us doing just that did not detract from the basic truth of what he said, even though trade union militants thrived on the very conditions they professed to abhor, and often sought to prevent a *real* improvement in those conditions. People who are encouraged to contribute as individuals, thrive and grow; those who are not, stagnate at work and find the outlet for their talents elsewhere.

RESTRUCTURING

In the face of growing internationalisation of competition, established companies throughout the world found themselves with organisational structures which had developed to meet the circumstances of an earlier era. They had frequently grown through merger and acquisition; resulting in conglomerations of unrelated businesses, with multi-layered, inflexible management structures, and headquarters, regions, divisions and operating groups, each reporting masses of detailed information to the next layer up. Complex matrix structures had become the norm, with people having several bosses, perhaps in the national company, the product group and the functional chimney. The areas of discretion were rapidly reduced the further the organisational unit was from the centre.

The indirect areas of the organisation expanded both in size and authority at the expense of the direct. Functions such as finance, personnel and marketing, which in the early years of industrialisation barely existed, acquired high status and higher salaries, particularly in the Anglo–Saxon countries. This process, combined with so-called scientific management, led to an approach in which it was thought possible to define jobs rigidly, breaking them down into the simplest elements requiring from the majority little skill and no discretion. Workers were a factor of production to be hired and fired according to demand. Rules, procedures, prerogative, authority and status symbols were the order of the day. Labour was paid to 'do', not 'think' and the manual worker was a second-class citizen. Information was retained at the centre and the masses 'knew their place'. Relationships in the workplace were based on the assumption of a natural conflict of interests between workers and their bosses and in assessing the priority of interests between the owners, shareholders, customers, suppliers and workers, the workers came a poor last. Not everything has since changed!

To compete successfully at the end of the twentieth century changes have had to be made. Jack Welch, CEO of General Electric, recognises this:

> The old organisation was built on control, but the world has changed. The world is moving at such a pace that control has become a limitation. It slows you down. You've got to balance freedom with some control, but you've got to have more freedom than you ever dreamed of. (Tichy and Sherman, 1993, p. 21)

After the growth through merger and acquisition phases of the 1960s and late 1980s many organisations have refocused, that is they have sold off their peripheral businesses to concentrate on their core activities. As a result of this and a realisation that they were just too top-heavy, there has been a dramatic reduction in the number of people employed, often by eliminating whole layers of the organisation and by dramatically slimming the central staff overhead. Decision-making has been passed down the line to points much closer to the market place. The power of indirect departments over the direct is being drastically reduced. Response time to market place changes has speeded up. Responsibility, authority and accountability have been passed to diversified, autonomous profit centres with some organisations almost becoming federations of semi-independent companies or business units working in loose networks, connected only as far as it makes business sense. Within these new autonomous units there has been a shift of emphasis towards the people actually in the front line, whether the business is building motor cars or selling insurance policies. It has been realised that people have brains as well as hands. Companies are changing their emphasis from centralised control to devolved responsibility.

This is far more than 'empowerment'. Empowerment implies management giving something, with the ability to take it back again. We are not discussing some wet and soggy theory about how to be nice to people or how to get the best out of them. The whole concept recognises that it is wrong for the centre to hold all power unto itself. There are many tasks, actions, decisions that are best *taken away from the centre* as opposed to *given to the periphery* and the distinction is much more than semantic. The logical extreme is to argue that real power should lie where the action is and that these 'action centres' should delegate upwards those responsibilities they believe can best be handled on a centralised or co-ordinated basis, or where there are clear cost advantages, for example in centralised purchasing of commodities.

Perhaps we need a sort of corporate 'Yellow Pages' directory in which the 'action centres' can dial up the resources they need!

We should not, however, suppose that all change points inexorably in the direction of restructuring, refocusing, decentralisation and delayering. Constantinos Markides of the London Business School has found that of the top 850 American corporations, 398 have restructured but, 'more than half of these firms have failed to improve their competitive positions or create significant shareholder value' (Markides, 1994). He also found that many firms which refocused, actually destroyed value and argues that it can only work when it is an 'integral part of the company's long-term diversification strategy.' This is, or ought to be, common sense. First, develop the strategy and then decide if acquisitions or divestments achieve the correct balance between the economies and diseconomies of scale, the gain or loss of technology, the acquisition or loss of product range.

One company which has significantly changed its approach is Shell UK. In 1980 Shell employed 20 000 people and then for all the right reasons decided to decentralise. It did all the 'right' things. It established a framework of guiding principles, values and standards; and introduced a strategic planning system aimed at sensitising managers to recognise significant external changes and trends quickly and to respond rapidly. All the time it maintained its financial conservatism to counter-balance uncertainties in the oil industry.

As a result of its delayering, decentralisation, networking and empowering Shell, by the mid–1990s, had halved its staff while significantly extending its activities. However, top management began to realise that these efforts to loosen the organisation were adversely affecting its current performance and operational reliability. Management of current projects was causing concern.

John Whybrew, Shell's Director of Public Affairs and Planning told me in February 1992 that while many of the recently adopted organisational concepts and HR initiatives were individually sound, their implementation together had eroded the functional integrity, professionalism and coherence on which Shell's decentralised culture depended. In the UK they saw that Britain's individualistic culture added to the problems. Some of these problems resulting from a loosening of the organisation were:

- fragmentation
- removal of the checks and balances implicit in a matrix organisation
- removal of management layers with the result that *the custodians of the values were no longer there*
- weakening of functional integrity and authority
- weakening of the feel for the health of the organisation – they were becoming too dependent on the software
- poor communications – senior managers did not have time to get around
- mismatch of values
- too many distractions

John went to great lengths to emphasise that it is the managers in an organisation who are responsible for maintaining and constantly reinforcing its values. People easily revert to type and if the responsible cadré of the 'keepers of the faith' is significantly reduced it can have a debilitating effect on the culture. They were also greatly concerned about losing the 'feel' of the organisation; computer-generated information is no substitute for managers walking the job, *knowing* what is going on.

As a result of this experience Shell embarked on a programme which, while not undoing everything it had achieved, sought to reassert functional authority and integrity, re-establish professional standards and competence, improve communications, plan and manage the whole organisation, change its heroes and remove distractions.

Shell found that without control as well as commitment things began to fall apart.

The experience of Shell, and the globalisation of Ford, bring out a number of interesting points. Despite the view that 'small is beautiful', big need not be ugly. The critical issue is not about size but about whether or not the organisation, be it large or small, is well managed. The potential problems with large organisations are that they can become fat, bureaucratic, self-indulgent and inefficient, and they do tend to diversify too widely to be effectively managed. This need not necessarily be the case. BMW has purchased Rover, Ford is re-organising into global divisions, 3M is structured as though it were scores of small businesses and there are numerous examples of big businesses which are fleet of foot.

The trick is to get rid of superfluous activities which do not add value or benefit, concentrate on what you are good at, devolve responsibility and accountability to the business units but then ensure that potential economies of scale are fully exploited in those areas in which it is meaningful to do so. This will vary from business to business. It may be in research, purchasing, distribution or service. It will certainly be in people development. It then becomes a balancing act. How do you co-ordinate the network, define those areas where economies of scale can help, and devolve responsibility and accountability without incurring unacceptably high costs?

There is no absolute answer but I hope the theme of this book, control of the processes combined with commitment of the people, is one way.

EMPLOYMENT

All of these changes are having a major impact on the employment market. For the majority, employment in a large company with a virtual lifetime commitment has always been the exception but the statistics are staggering. In Britain in 1992 there were over 2 million businesses employing just one or two people and only 2000 businesses employing more than 500. Any growth in employment will be in the managerial, professional and technical jobs – at least in the formal economy. The Institute for Employment Research (IER) estimates that the last decade of the twentieth century will experience 1.7 million additional jobs in these categories but a decline of 1.3 million manual jobs (IER, 1993).

We are experiencing a long-term trend in which long-term employment with a single employer is no longer the most common experience, if indeed it ever has been. The ability to stay in work will depend more than ever on possessing and continuously updating a skill which remains in demand. *Employability* is the watchword. For those who do not possess a marketable skill the probability is that they will move to the ranks, not of the unemployed which suggests a chance of future employment, but to the non-employable which implies that there is no chance of a job.

There does, however appear to be an emerging consensus as to the broad direction that needs to be taken. The OECD *Jobs Study* published in June 1994 produced some sixty recommendations for putting people back to work. The consensus formed around measures designed to achieve the high quality education and training found in much of Europe and the dynamic labour mobility, wage flexibility and ease of setting up new businesses found in the USA. The *Jobs Study* also advocated reductions in non-wage labour costs and a removal or reduction of provisions in the structure of tax and social security contributions that discourage hiring and part-time employment. Those countries with the strongest employment protection legislation, perversely, discourage employment creation because once you hire it is difficult to fire.

The critical point is that we can educate and train all we want but unless there are jobs waiting for the people, much of the money and time will be ill-spent.

CONCLUSIONS

We are all affected by the impact of these changes but they place a major conundrum before managers of organisations. While always subject to the pressures of the market place, the private sector is now having to change at a pace previously unheard of, and the public sector is going the same way. In the era when full employment was regarded by many governments as a key goal and when there were unskilled jobs for the taking, the vast majority of males were able to look forward with confidence to a lifetime of employment, either with a 'career' in the large organisations or by moving frequently between employers with but short periods of unemployment. The skills acquired during the first few years of an individual's working life were sufficient to take *him* through a further forty to forty-five years.

The old certainties are no longer with us. The key themes now include rapid response, flexible employment structures and development of individualism, but the conundrum is that within this new way, employers become increasingly dependent on the skills, flexibility and commitment of the people in the organisation. How can you achieve commitment to your organisation when people know that they will be with you for but a short time? Or was it that in the past this very security gave rise to complacency? Is it perhaps better that we recognise the realities and simply wring everything out of our transient workers while they are with us?

As we progress through Part I, the need to focus on the totality of these interrelating issues will become clearer. Whether our organisation is in the private or public sector, large or small, seeks to employ permanent, temporary or contract staff, the fundamentals remain the same and we are all subject to the same pressures, both internal and external.

The answer is the ascendant organisation!

3 Rising to the Ascendant

No number of men, when once they enjoy quiet, and no man needs to fear his neighbour, will be long without learning to divide and sub-divide their labour.

(Mandeville, *Fable of the Bees*, 1729)

Add the fact that to have conscientiously studied the liberal arts refines behaviour and does not allow it to be savage.

(Ovid, 43BC–17AD)

THE 'CONTROLLERS'

Since Adam Smith wrote in 1776 of his celebrated pin factory, 'The greatest improvement in the productive powers of labour, and the greatest part of the skill, dexterity and judgement with which it is anywhere directed, or applied, seems to have been the effects of the divison of labour', the debate over what makes for effective work organisations has ebbed and flowed.

F. W. Taylor argued against the waste of human effort; sought to gather in, 'the great mass of traditional knowledge which in the past has been in the heads of the workmen' (Testimony to House of Representatives Committee, 1912) and reduce it to laws, rules and formulae so as to produce more work of better quality. He sought to select his workmen scientifically, and systematically train them, and then separated thinking, planning and control from doing. His concept that the workman was simply a pair of hands with no real need to use his brain formed the basis of the time warp in which much of manufacturing industry has lain throughout the twentieth century.

Taylor not only separated planning and control from doing; he also split up planning and control. 'Detailed written instructions as to the best way of doing each piece of work' (Taylor, 1911, p. 22) were prepared by the planning department which comprised specialists in tooling, motion study and time study.

His principles of scientific management pre-dated both the Japanese concept of *kaizen* (continuous improvement) which recognises that the people doing a job know more about that job than anyone else, and their emphasis on the one best way, the standard operation. While wrong in his emphasis on separating planning from doing, it is not insignificant that Taiichi Ohno, the genius behind much of modern Japanese manufacturing techniques, expressed his debt to the work of F. W. Taylor.

Henry Ford's great contribution was his insistence that the components needed to build a car be easy to fit and made to a rigorous specification so as to make the job easy for a recently immigrated workforce who had, he thought, little ability to think and high potential to get a complex job wrong. Once that had been achieved, Charles Sorenson takes the credit for inventing the moving assembly line:

> It was then that the idea occurred to me that assembly would be easier, simpler and faster if we moved the chassis along, beginning at one end of the plant with a frame and adding the axles and the wheels, then moving it past the stockroom, instead of moving the stockroom to the chassis. . . . We did this simply by putting the frame on skids, hitching a tow rope to the front end and pulling the frame along. (Sorenson, 1956)

Life is circular. Modern concepts of just in time are now moving stock from the stockroom to the workplace.

With the basic building blocks in place, Ford introduced the moving assembly line in 1913 at Highland Park, Detroit. With the requirement to minimise the learning time of what was a largely casual workforce he reduced the job cycle time to 1.9 minutes. The training time was then about ten minutes. He gave the planning and control to specialist functions and in order to get as much control as possible over his components sought to maximise in-house production. Using dedicated machinery and dedicated workers he created an environment in which the assemblers were not paid to think or contribute, simply to undertake the short-cycle repetitive task. Foremen became progress chasers and disciplinarians, and engineers were divided into '57 varieties' .

The combination of Taylor's division of labour, the insistence on using 'the best way', the separation of planning from doing, and Ford's moving assembly line provided a working environment in which brains were either left behind at the factory gate or used within the workplace to gain control of the shop floor. The idea of the well-educated man working in industry was unthinkable, particularly in Britain where manufacturing was not seen as an appropriate occupation for an educated gentleman, and even those who progressed up the managerial chain very quickly sought to distance themselves from what happened on the shop floor, which became a battleground between the shop stewards and the foremen.

The brainpower of the workers went into finding ways of beating the system, of scoring points over their foreman, of doubling up and getting additional rest breaks. Mike Judge, Personnel Director of Peugeot, told me of his early days as a personnel officer in a car assembly plant:

> We only needed two men to fit the roof lining, but as it was a difficult job at some time someone had agreed to four: two on and two off. One day we had a claim that they needed two more and if they didn't get them there would be a stoppage. Those were the days when we needed all the cars we could get, so we gave in. We subsequently found that they needed two more because they had become enthusiasts at playing bridge and always needed four off the job at any one time to make sure the game continued! Anyway we eventually designed a rigid roof liner and put a stop to that!

Such stories are legion throughout the automobile industry and are mild compare to those coming out of the USA.

The work of Taylor and Ford led to top-down control and coercion, the enforcement of standards and people leaving their brains at the gate. The result was restriction of output, a conflict culture and alienation, and while the gathering in of the knowledge of the workforce was potentially beneficial for all, the alienation and control culture led to an atmosphere in which this came to be regarded as expropriation of workers' knowledge. One aspect of the system precluded another aspect from being achieved. Taylor's concept of the 'one best way' also had great potential, but when responsibility for defining it belonged to the foreman or engineer there was no ownership by the people who were subject to it. Therefore, there could be no working together to improve it.

By the late 1920s, the intellectual basis of 'control' was in place and while its practice varied widely there is no doubt that in mass production industries it was becoming the conventional wisdom. The division of labour, the moving assembly line, functional specialisation and the controlling foreman touched most organisations and in turn created the inevitable reaction. From one direction came militant trade unionism and from another came the thinking of the behavioural scientists.

THE 'BEHAVIOURALISTS'

The forty years from the mid-1920s when Elton Mayo conducted his investigations into the behaviour of people employed at the Hawthorne Plant of the Western Electric Company were the golden years of the behavioural scientists. Much of the work of Mayo, Douglas McGregor (Theory X and Theory Y), Frederick Herzberg (motivation-hygiene), Abraham Maslow (needs hierarchy) and so on, has been criticised as being non-provable and simplistic. Many practising managers, however, have some knowledge of their thinking, believe there is 'something in it' and behave accordingly. The great Japanese engineers, Taiichi Ohno and Shigeo Shingo, knew of the work of at least some of the Human Relations School and it influenced their own thinking. Most important, it is not possible to understand the concept of the ascendant organisation without knowing something of the underlying principles. (It is for this reason that I briefly describe what to many will be common knowledge, though, perhaps, a little revision will not be unrewarded!)

Elton Mayo

The celebrated studies undertaken at the Hawthorne Plant of the Western Electric Company in Chicago from 1927 to 1932 had begun with attempts to study the relationship between different intensities of illumination and their impact on productivity. Whatever they did, increasing or reducing the light either in the test room or the 'control' room, production went up. Said Mayo, 'What actually happened was that six individuals became a team and the team gave itself wholeheartedly and spontaneously to co-operation in the experiment . . . they were happy in the knowledge that they were working without coercion from above or limitation from below' (Mayo, 1949).

Mayo also discovered that the cohesiveness of the group could work against the employer. In studying male employees in the Bank Wiring Room he found that they restricted their production levels to a norm established by the group. Just as with the first group, it was the informal social culture that determined the behaviour pattern. The difference was that the first group knew that management was interested in them and they had greater control over their own environment; the second group was just as effective a team but had no motivation to work for the interest of the company. If this insight into the importance of the informal group had been properly understood by succeeding generations of managers they might have been saved much fruitless effort when seeking to achieve teamworking and commitment simply by changing organisation structures or physical layouts.

Frederick Herzberg

Herzberg's seminal book, *The Motivation to Work* (1959), was based on interviews with 200 engineers and accountants working in Pittsburgh. He sought to discover when and why they felt good and when and why they felt bad about their jobs. He classified events into those which caused satisfaction and those which caused dissatisfaction. He found there were five strong determiners of job satisfaction – achievement, recognition, work itself, responsibility and advancement. The dissatisfiers most frequently mentioned were: company policy and administration, supervision, salary, interpersonal relations and working conditions. However, other factors were also mentioned, though less statistically significant. He found 'possibility of growth' to be a task-centred motivator and, 'status, job security and effect on personal life' as potential dissatisfiers.

Those factors which caused satisfaction he termed the motivators. However, the other factors served only to bring about dissatisfaction and were rarely involved in events that led to positive attitudes. They seemed to Herzberg to be related to the environment in which the job was done and he borrowed a medical term, 'hygiene' factors, meaning preventive and environmental. Just as a lack of hygiene will cause disease but the presence of hygienic conditions do not in themselves produce health so lack of adequate job hygiene causes dissatisfaction but its presence will not necessarily cause satisfaction.

Herzberg's theory led him to the view that, once the basic policies and conditions are in place, jobs need to be enriched, and he advocated an industrial engineering approach to job design. But, instead of Taylor's division of labour and the mere adding of one simple, boring job on to another, he proposed a model in which enriched jobs led to enhanced job satisfaction and motivation and the psychological growth of the individual.

Douglas McGregor

Without doubt the most widely-known term coined by the behavioural scientists is Douglas McGregor's 'Theory X and Theory Y'.

Theory X represents the traditional view of direction and control as reflected in the practices of scientific management:

- The average human being has an inherent dislike of work and will avoid it if he can.
- Because of this characteristic, most people must be coerced, controlled, directed or threatened with punishment to get them to put forth adequate effort towards the achievement of organisational objectives.
- The average human being prefers to be directed, wishes to avoid responsibility, has relatively little ambition, wants security above all.

Theory Y represents the integration of individual and organisational goals. This 'modest beginning for a new theory' put forward the following assumptions:

- The expenditure of physical and mental effort in work is as natural as play or rest.
- External control and the threat of punishment are not the only means for bringing about effort towards organisational objectives. People will exercise self-direction and self-control in the service of objectives to which they are committed..
- Commitment to objectives is a function of the rewards associated with their achievement.
- The average human being learns, under proper conditions, not only to accept but seek responsibility .
- The capacity to exercise a relatively high degree of imagination, ingenuity and creativity in the solution of organisational problems is widely, not narrowly, distributed in the population.
- Under the conditions of modern industrial life the intellectual potentialities of the average human being are only partially utilised.

McGregor said that his Theory Y assumptions had major implications for the way people are managed, stressing growth and development rather than control, and that the limitations were not those of human nature but of, 'management's ingenuity in discovering how to realise the potential represented by its human resources'. Management is to blame if workers are lazy, indifferent, or unwilling to take responsibility. He argued that, 'The organisation must take account of the individual's needs and not make unilateral decisions.' The principle of integration demands that, 'both the organisation's and the individual's needs be recognised'.

He did not see Theory Y as a soft option. Theory Y assumes that people will exercise self-control in the achievement of organisational objectives *to the degree that they are committed to those objectives.*

> If that commitment is small, only a slight degree of self-direction and self-control will be likely, and a substantial amount of external influence will be necessary. If it is large, many conventional external controls will be relatively superfluous and to some extent self-defeating. Managerial policies and practices materially affect this degree of commitment.

Throughout this book the concept of 'ownership' will loom large. McGregor's work provides the intellectual underpinning.

Abraham Maslow

Abraham Maslow used the term 'hierarchy of needs' (Maslow, 1970) to describe his theory of motivation, postulating that basic needs have to be satisfied before an individual can move to a higher need, and that when a need is satisfied it decreases in strength as a motivator. His hierarchy begins with physiological needs (food, water, air, shelter); and moves on to social needs (belonging, acceptance, giving and receiving friendship); esteem needs (self-confidence, achievement and recognition and respect from others) and self-actualisation (self-fulfilment, realisation of one's own potential, continuous self-development).

If the needs hierarchy has any meaning it must be that it becomes a managerial responsibility to facilitate the development of individuals.

Eric Trist

Eric Trist's key studies related to the impact of increased technology and the resultant changes in working arrangements on British miners (Trist and Bamforth, 1951). The pick and shovel process in which a group of two or three men worked closely together and engaged in multiple tasks was replaced by the mechanised long wall method which needed forty to fifty workers and supervisors. Formality replaced informality, mutual support was replaced by division of labour, and self-direction by the close presence of the supervisor. Because the trust associated with the previous system had gone, Trist found a growth of anti-social practices: competition for the best workplaces, always blaming the other shift, increased absenteeism, and so on. This led him to the view that the working group is neither a technical system nor a social system but an interdependent socio-technical system in which the social and technical requirements are mutually interactive and dynamic, not only within the group but also externally in relation to the changing environment within which it operates. He recognised that the hard and soft issues of managing businesses are inextricably related and that management ignores this link at its peril.

What was important however was that subsequent technological developments combined the efficiency of the new method with the social benefits of the old. The group became responsible for the whole task, could allocate themselves to shifts and jobs and were paid a group bonus. This led to, 'Greater productivity, lower cost, considerably less absenteeism and accidents, and greater work satisfaction since it was a socio-technical system which was better geared to the workers' social and psychological needs for job autonomy and close working relationships.' Maybe the beginning of a synthesis between the hard and the soft issues.

Victor Vroom

Victor Vroom's expectancy theory (Vroom, 1964) seeks to bring us into the real world, believing that the work of the classicists is somewhat simplistic and that people are motivated by a wide variety of factors all of which interact with each other. It makes four assumptions about behaviour:

- It is a combination of individual and environmental factors that determine behaviour.
- Individuals make their own decisions about their behaviour in their organisation (whether to come to work, how hard to work, and so on).
- Different individuals have different needs, wants and goals.
- Individuals decide on how they will behave depending on their perception of how likely it is that that behaviour will lead to a desired outcome.

In the jargon, the amount of effort an individual will put into a task depends on expectancy (whether the individual believes the effort will produce a better performance) instrumentality (whether the better performance will pay off in terms of outcomes) and valence (the extent to which the possible outcomes are attractive). In short, if my effort is likely to result in a desirable outcome I will be prepared to make that effort. If not, I won't.

Vroom's theory, unlike the thinking of the other behavioural scientists, puts the horse before the cart. They argue that managerial efforts should be aimed at achieving high levels of satisfaction and as a result task performance will improve. Vroom, however, basically says, 'Get the task right and satisfaction will follow'.

William Ouchi

In 1981 William Ouchi's *Theory Z* was published. Ouchi sought to combine some elements of Japanese practices with some elements of American. Theory Z, 'Quite simply, . . . suggests that involved workers are the key to increased productivity and the first lesson of Theory Z is trust. Productivity and trust go hand in hand.' The other important lessons are subtlety, 'A foreman knows his workers well, can pinpoint personalities, decide who works well with whom and thus put together work teams of maximal effectiveness' and, in Japan, 'The caring, the support and the disciplined unselfishness which makes life possible come through close social relations' (Ouchi, 1988, pp. 4–8).

Ouchi concentrated very much on the people aspects of Japanese management: lifetime employment, the seniority progression system, non-specialised career paths, participative decision-making, collective values and the holistic concern for people. He contrasted this with the American concentration on short-term employment, merit based progression, specialisation, individual decision-making and individual values.

For Ouchi, however, the big breakthrough came when he realised that some American companies had many of the Japanese characteristics; IBM, Proctor and Gamble, Hewlett-Packard, Eastman Kodak and the US military were repeatedly mentioned. These were his Theory Z companies; those which had developed naturally in the USA but had many characteristics similar to firms in Japan. Z companies had all the modern mechanisms and systems but rarely allowed them or the numbers to dominate in major decisions. The managers were agreed on their central objectives and way of doing business; the decision-making process was typically a consensual, participative one although responsibility was clearly defined (unlike Japan). Z companies show a broad concern for the welfare of all staff, relationships are informal and egalitarian implying, 'that each person can apply discretion and can work autonomously without close supervision because they can be trusted' (Ouchi, p. 81). The Type Z organisation, 'is a consent culture, a community of equals who co-operate with one another to reach common goals. Rather than relying exclusively upon hierarchy and monitoring to direct behaviour, it relies upon commitment and trust' (Ouchi, p. 83).

Time and again Ouchi returns to his central concept of trust. It manifests itself in his call for a redirection of attention to human relations, for management by walking around, for an emphasis on a long-term relationship with customers and on value rather than efficiency. The problem with Ouchi's analysis is not what he included, but what he left out. He virtually ignored the very strong 'control' culture of the Japanese.

CONCLUSIONS

What then do we make of these theories? How do they relate to the work of Taylor and Ford? Do they complement or replace them? Without doubt they are different in tone; but in intent? Both Taylor and Ford sought in their own way to liberate the workforce, but they were both primarily concerned with the process. They were, in fact, practising managers concerned with getting a job done and making a profit. Their perspective was different from that of the academics who, without the encumbrance and pressure of having to achieve a daily schedule, were able from the outside to observe the behaviour of people in organisations. But the external observer often sees the wood while the internal practitioner may be lost in the trees.

Despite the internecine, academic criticism of the improvability of the work of the classic behavioural scientists their importance is that they *have* written and they *are* read. There is much overlap in their work and common threads are readily discernible.

- Any group which is given special attention will respond positively.
- Individuals who are regarded as having low-level needs and are controlled in that way will behave accordingly. They will develop their own norms of behaviour and at best switch off and at worst use their capabilities against the organisation.
- There are higher-level needs which become increasingly important once lower-level needs are satisfied.
- Most managers fail to develop and use the talents of individuals, but if people are properly stimulated and given the freedom to use their judgement there will invariably be a positive response. If managers fail to stimulate, people are just as likely to slip backwards.
- Different people have different goals and respond in different ways depending on whether they see the effort as being worth it.
- People who are not trusted will behave accordingly.
- Individuals who are able to participate in setting goals are more likely to be committed to them and motivated to work to achieve them, particularly when they receive effective feedback.

- The basic pay and conditions have to be right and equitable but do not in themselves cause satisfaction at work.
- Work which is physically and/or mentally stimulating and over which the individual can have influence is more likely to be satisfying that work which is not.
- When subordinates' jobs are enriched supervisors become free to develop different aspects of their own job.
- Recognition of achievement in whatever way, whether a simple, 'Thank you' or a financial payment is greatly valued.
- The link between the social and technical factors in the workplace is profound, as is their link with the external environment.
- Technical determinants of behaviour should be kept to a minimum.
- Individuals will quickly develop informal groups even if the formal structure and management style opposes them. The norms of these groups will usually be stronger than anything imposed by the organisation.
- Tasks which are perceived as having significance, either within the organisation or beyond, will be more satisfying.
- Externally imposed change is invariably resisted.

These conclusions are generalisations and probably not complete, and there will always be exceptions, but based on the work of the theorists and my own personal experience, they are not far out. If we are to move towards a synthesis between high efficiency and high quality of life *the* critical point is that both the physical and social structures are important. The lessons for leaders and managers will emerge.

4 The Japanese – Right or Wrong?

The Japanese out-Taylor us all.

(Richard J. Schonberger, *Japanese Manufacturing Techniques*, 1982)

Individual Japanese industries are efficient, but not to the degree the world has been led to believe. Much of their advantage is based on unsavoury practices. Japan has 'borrowed' or copied foreign technology . . . resorted to bribery, industrial espionage and outright theft . . . [It] is winning the trade war because it refuses to play by the rules.

(Marvin J. Wolf, *The Japanese Conspiracy*, 1982)

Taylor's *The principles of scientific management* was translated into Japanese in 1912 and sold 1½ million copies as *The secret of saving lost motion*, and Taiichi Ohno acknowledged his debt to Henry Ford, arguing that Ford's successors failed to fine tune his system and did not adapt it properly to changing times. Said Ohno, 'I, for one, am in awe of Ford's greatness. I think that if the American king of cars were still alive today he would be headed in the same direction as Toyota' (Ohno, 1988b, p. 97).

In comparison with Taylor and Ford, the names of Ohno and Shigeo Shingo are less known in the West, but between them these two engineers, working for Toyota in the 1950s and 1960s, developed virtually all the techniques that are now the very stuff of contemporary manufacturing. The Western visitor on a ten-day study tour of Japan, or one who reads some of the thousands of superficial books and articles written about that country, could do well by starting with the writings of these two gentlemen (all available through Productivity Press). They will find that Japan is not some sort of industrial Lourdes, but that success comes from attention to the basics of manufacturing, and that the so-called sacred treasures of lifetime employment, seniority progression and enterprise unions are not all that there is. There are many elements which together comprise what has become known as the Japanese production system but at this stage I wish to discuss just three – the standard operation, *kaizen* (continuous improvement) and the elimination of waste – because they are at the heart of Japanese manufacturing and lead to a discussion of lean production and automation. They are also subject to major criticism.

Japan has not done away with the division of labour; indeed one of the lead quotations states that, 'The Japanese out-Taylor us all.' Shingo argues that among its benefits are the facts that it reduces operations to a single task, eliminates unnecessary motions and that in allowing work to become a reflex action raises skill levels ('skill' in this sense means the ability to perform the simple, repetitive task without mistakes). Disadvantages include a resulting imbalance in the use of muscles leading to fatigue, boredom and the fact that a failure at one point spreads rapidly through the system. But, surprisingly, Shingo came down, on balance, against division of labour, at least as far as its impact on people is concerned, 'Considering its net effect the value of the division of labour runs counter to human nature' (Shingo, 1988, pp. 240–2).

The interdependence of Japanese manufacturing practices is illustrated in Figure 4.1. In the outer ring are the so-called 'sacred treasures'; life time employment, seniority progression, consensus management and

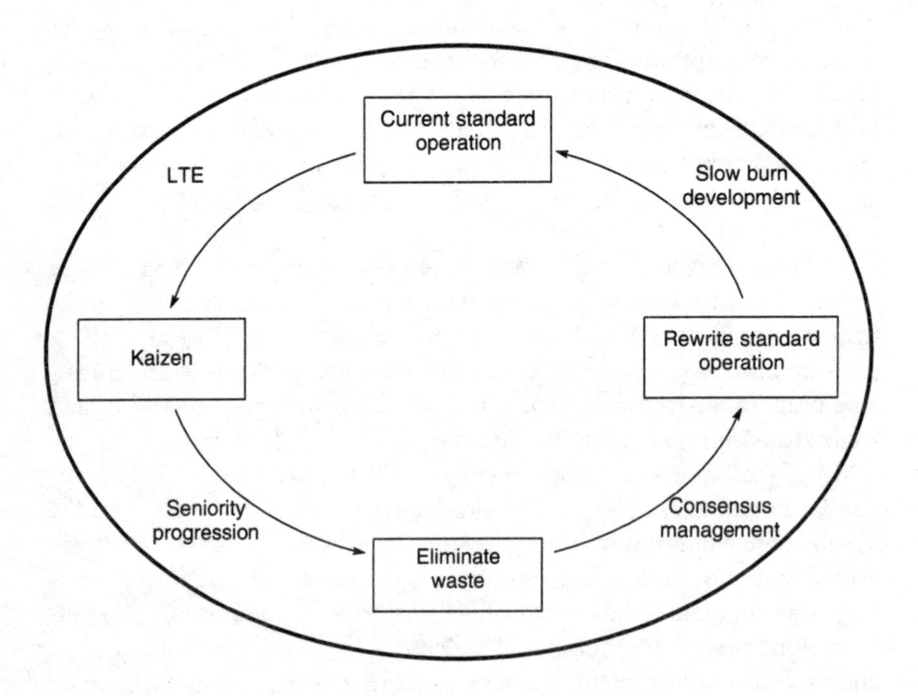

Figure 4.1 The Interdependence of Japanese Management Practices

slow-burn development. These 'treasures' are discussed and criticised later in this chapter but it is important to recognise that they were not the *cause* of Japanese success, despite what many authors, including Japanese, would have us believe. To use Herzberg's term, we should regard them as the hygiene factors and to paraphrase, hygiene factors do not cause success but their absence can result in lack of success.

As, if not more important for Japanese manufacturing success was the virtuous, continuous circle of improvement of the standard operation, Taylor's 'one best way'.

THE STANDARD OPERATION

If there is one element which is pivotal to Japanese manufacturing techniques it is the standard operation, that is: *the best current work method for achieving quality, cost and delivery time in a safe manner*. It is F. W. Taylor's 'best method' of doing a job, adhered to in a way far beyond anything he conceived.

The standard operation is formalised in a written document which includes all information about a task including its description, main steps in the right order, key points and the reasons for those key points. It details the required protective clothing, the jigs and tools used, the necessary checks for quality and safety and the training needed. It states the time allowed to do the job. Because it details the currently known best method for doing a job, then, by definition, any deviation from it will result in a reduction in quality, productivity, ease of working or safety and will create waste. It must be adhered to.

Once a task has been standardised it can be improved. Therefore the standard operation is the starting point for all improvement activity. Even in processes where there is inevitably some variation, such as in food preparation, the standard operation is necessary. In such instances it allows provision for check and adjustment.

Most Western manufacturing companies have something similar to the standard operation. Work study and method study have been around for a long time but no Western company emphasises its importance and insists that it is followed to the same degree as the Japanese. Many Japanese companies have regular checks to ensure that the standard operation sheets are complete and up to date, that the operator understands the best method and is using it, and that the sheets are not static but are being continuously improved. Supervisors are assessed by their boss and receive a big black mark if they or their staff are delinquent. The standard operation is the centrepiece of Japanese *genba kanri*, workshop management, but it does not mean the total absence of discretion as well shall see when discussing prescribed and discretionary work – Chapter 5.

KAIZEN

Adam Smith thought of *kaizen*! Writing of the division of labour he said, 'It is naturally to be expected, therefore, that someone or other of those who are employed in each particular branch of labour should soon find out easier and readier methods of performing their own particular work, wherever the nature of it admits of such improvement' (Smith, 1776, p. 13).

When I wrote *The Road to Nissan* the concept of *kaizen* was there but it by no means had the importance I now attach to it. The Japanese word is made up of two *Kanji* characters *Kai* – 'modify' and *zen* – 'goodness', but it is now generally translated as continuous improvement. The simple definition of improvement belies, however, the deep philosophical approach.

At its heart the concept of *kaizen* recognises that the person doing a job knows more about that job than anyone else and it is the management's task to motivate the workforce so that this knowledge can be utilised to the benefit of both the workers and the organisation. In most Western organisations such knowledge is at best withheld and at worst is used against the company. It is about the hundreds of 0.01 per cent improvements that, added together, can significantly enhance quality, productivity, safety and ease of working, and at the same time greatly improve motivation.

Japanese contrast the Western concept of innovation with the Japanese concept of continuous improvement. The West, they argue, is concerned with top-down innovation in large incremental steps often as the result of capital investment in new facilities. Having done that, Western management is content to sit back and expect the improved results to be maintained. However, this does not happen. First, the incremental change has frequently not included any input from the workforce and therefore is not as effective as it might be; and secondly, if there is no continuing input, the benefits will decay.

Although through effective maintenance the period of decay can be delayed, it is only through the direct involvement of the people doing a job that continuous improvements can be achieved. It is then the responsibility of the supervisor to create the environment in which the operators are able to contribute effectively. This is achieved not through some vast bureaucratic process but in the simplest way possible – by, for example, an operator saying to the supervisor, 'If we shifted the pallet one metre to the left I wouldn't have to walk so far.' Responds the supervisor, 'That's a great idea. Will you make sure the opposite shift are happy with it. If they are, you can re-mark the pallet position on the floor and we can then modify the standard operation sheet.'

Within that simple example lie the key ingredients of continuous improvement: it came about as a normal part of the operator's job, it was nothing special; the supervisor had the authority to agree readily and did so; the individual concerned made sure other affected people were happy with it and then undertook the actual physical change; and finally, together, they amended the standard operation sheet which then becomes the revised 'best way' until a further improvement is made. The change was initiated, owned and implemented without reference to any authority outside the group and there was no specific reward although it would be noted in the supervisor's log book for the next overall performance assessment.

But individual initiative and *kaizen* are not restricted to production tasks. The principle that a person doing a job knows more about that job than anyone else applies everywhere: from offices to airlines, from mail delivery to retailing. The problem is that managers have not been prepared to create the environment and equip people in a way which brings this knowledge out. It is never the individual's fault that this knowledge is withheld. It is always the boss's.

For the Japanese the process is as important as the results. It is the fact of contributing rather than what is achieved that counts. It is long-term and long-lasting and seeks to involve everyone in the organisation in low-cost improvements. It can be top-down or bottom-up. Top-down it is management asking a work group to examine a problem to see if they can come up with a solution; bottom-up it is an individual or small group coming up with an idea. It is also important that employees feel secure. Under no circumstances should any *kaizen* activity result in any person losing their employment. If it does, then any future activities will dry up.

It would be foolish though to pretend that *kaizen* activities do not result in productivity improvements. The ideal *kaizen* makes life easier for the worker and at the same time increases productivity and quality. But productivity does not increase if the time saved is not used for other value adding work. What normally happens is that an individual's non-productive time is increased for a while but when a sufficient number of individual savings have accumulated the work schedule is reassigned and the savings accrue to the company. If this is not done, the company receives no benefit.

THE ELIMINATION OF WASTE

The motivation of Ohno and Shingo was their constant urge to eliminate *muda*, waste, of all types and in all activities. Within this the most widely known, though not widely understood, concept is that of just in time (JIT), aimed at eliminating inventory waste, particularly between the supplier and the customer. For the Japanese, though, that is but one element. Waste can occur at any stage of the process. It includes excessive work in progress, buffer stocks, time spent waiting for stock or work, the transportation of partly finished products between the manufacturing stages, non-productive movements and actions by the operators, breakdowns and subsequent idle time, defective products and subsequent reworks, unnecessary processing, over-engineering, excessive stocks of finished goods and delays in getting those goods to the market.

The ideal state of non-waste is one in which every machine and every person spends 100 per cent of available time adding value to the product. But one of the great problems is that it is not always easy to identify waste, particularly of human effort, where non-essential work usually increases to use up the available time. Spare time, for example, allows for mistakes to be rectified during the build sequence, however they are often corrected without any records being kept, hence the real cause goes undetected. Operators accept the rework as part of the job, out of good intent, but in reality fail to address the causes of the problem and incur unnecessary costs. The effect of removing spare time makes more problems surface, which then have to be solved.

A clothing manufacturer explained to me why they had large buffer stocks of work-in-progress between the various manufacturing operations. 'They are there to assist the work flow. If there is a problem upstream, then downstream operators can draw from the buffer stock. If there is a problem downstream, then upstream operators can feed into the buffer stock.' Like most manufacturers he created the buffers 'just in case'. But in doing so he failed to identify the *real* cause of the problems. The Japanese response would be, 'Eliminate the buffer stock, highlight the problem, find the real cause and fix it!' – an extreme position which only a few can reach, but it is the target.

Shigeo Shingo believed that searching out waste was an unrelenting task:

> Plant improvements demand an unrelenting keen eye and persistent efforts to identify problems. Maintaining this attitude and timelessly observing the job at hand to find problems makes it possible *to wring water even out of dry towels* [my emphasis]. This is how we have to think about total waste elimination. (Shingo, 1988, pp. 27–8)

After, through the *kaizen* process, waste is reduced the standard operation is revised and then used as the control mechanism. Shortly after the next *kaizen* activity begins again and the improvements continue.

JAPANESE MANUFACTURING AND LEAN PRODUCTION

A central element of Japanese manufacturing success is built on emulating Taylor's and Ford's control of the process. Shingo wrote that W. Edwards Deming, long considered by many to be a major contributor to Japanese success, 'seems to ignore the effectiveness of the control function' (Shingo, 1988, p. 228).

In the Japanese environment, therefore, Taylorism and Fordism are not dead but neither are the influences of the behavioural scientists. In their comprehensive study of the world's car manufacturers, *The Machine that Changed the World*, James Womack, Dan Jones and Daniel Roos (Womack *et al.*, 1990) popularised the term 'lean production' to highlight the elimination of waste in Japanese companies:

> Lean production is 'lean' because it uses less of everything compared with mass production – half the human effort, half the manufacturing space, half the investment in tools, half the engineering hours to develop a new product in half the time. Also it requires keeping far less than half the needed inventory on site, results in many fewer defects and produces a greater and ever growing variety of products. (Womack *et al.*, p. 13)

Mass production aims for 'good enough'. Lean production aims for perfection: continually declining costs, zero defects, zero inventories and endless product variety. They see lean production as a further development along the path from craft production and mass production. It combines:

> the advantages of craft and mass production while avoiding the high cost of the former and rigidity of the latter. Towards this end lean production employs teams of multi-skilled workers at all levels of the organisation and uses highly flexible, increasingly automated machines to produce volumes of products in enormous variety. (Womack *et al.*, p. 13)

According to Womack *et al.*, Japanese lean production has two key organisational features, 'It transfers the maximum number of tasks and responsibilities to those workers actually adding value to the car on the line, and it has in place a system for detecting defects that quickly traces every problem, once discovered, to its ultimate cause' (Womack *et al.* p. 99). But you cannot have a dynamic work team undertaking these responsibilities unless there is a genuine sense of reciprocal obligations. Management must value its workers, make sacrifices to retain them in the difficult times and be willing to delegate responsibility. In contrasting lean production with mass production Womack *et al.*, say, 'While the mass production plant is often filled with mind-numbing stress, as workers struggle to assemble unmanufacturable products and have no way to improve their working environment, lean production offers a creative tension in which workers have many ways to address challenges' (p. 101).

But they warn, 'Lean production is fragile . . . to make a lean system with no slack–no safety net work at all it is essential that every worker try very hard . . . if management fails to lead and the workforce feels no reciprocal obligations are in force, it is quite predictable that lean production will revert to mass production' (Womack *et al.*, p. 103). They argue that while a properly organised lean production system does indeed remove all slack, 'it also provides workers with the skills they need to control their work environment and the continuing challenge of making the work go more smoothly.' It is in this area that the fingers of the critics begin to prod.

So impressed with this concept was Louis Hughes, then President of General Motors Europe, that he said, 'The mass production of Henry Ford has no future. Lean production is the second great industrial revolution after the invention of the assembly line' (*Financial Times*, 24 September 1992).

AUTOMATION

However, it must not be supposed that it is automation that makes lean manufacturing more efficient. The *most* automated plant in the world (with 48 per cent automation) required 70 per cent *more* hours to build a car than the most *efficient* plant, which had only 34 per cent automation. The most automated plant, which was in Europe was, in fact, less efficient than the *worst* Japanese plant. Womack *et al.*, estimated that automation accounts for about one-third of the total difference in productivity. Their conclusion is that, 'High-tech plants that are improperly organised end up adding as many indirect technical and service workers as they remove unskilled direct workers from manual assembly tasks' (p. 94). Further, they found that the frequent breakdowns of the complex machinery, 'reduce the fraction of the total operating time that a plant is actually producing vehicles' and conclude that, 'Lean organisation must come before high-tech process automation if a company is to gain the full benefit.'

They are right. The love affair with automation and high technology for its own sake is long over, often as the result of expensive mistakes such as General Motor's $50 billion investments in the first half of the 1980s, and the failure to recognise that the Japanese use the most *appropriate* technology, not necessarily the most advanced. Visitors to Japan are often amazed to find a mixture of high technology and machines which are years old but have been lovingly maintained and continuously updated. The Western visitor fails to see that the Japanese use robots for simple, not complex tasks.

This does not mean that the basic thinking behind automation and flexible manufacturing systems is wrong, but many of the extreme advocates have failed to follow the Japanese adage of simplification before automation. The real problems with automation, as with division of labour, arise when it is introduced in an unthinking way, without taking account of the views of the workforce and the impact of the process upon the people who will work within it. If the writings of the behavioural scientists have taught us anything, it is that human beings thrive best when they are able to have an influence on what they do and the environment in which they do it. If workers are not able to have control over what they do then it is absolutely certain that they will seek to gain control of the workplace in other ways; by restricting output, by scoring points over their supervisors, by doubling up, working ahead, taking more rest time, by excessive absenteeism, by resisting change. There is no end to the techniques a frustrated workforce can use to ensure that the frustration they cause to management exceeds that which they feel.

Ohno, Shingo and the subsequent proponent of the Japanese system suggested that they had found the answers to the ills of mass production. The combination of manufacturing techniques with the sacred treasures of lifetime employment, seniority progression, consensus management and enterprise unions brought about a highly motivated workforce, committed to the success of the enterprise. They had satisfying jobs and economic success. What could be better?

THE CRITICS OF JAPAN

The stereotyped view of Japanese management practices is just that, a stereotype. Like all such views it contains an element of truth, but reality is much more complex. Perception remains, long after reality has changed. In any case the stereotype applies to about 20 per cent of the working population, usually to adult, male, full-time, permanent employees working for a blue chip company. There are as many, if not more, varieties of management practices in Japan as there are in the West. One of the criticisms of Japan is that the maintenance of the sacred treasures of the blue chip companies is only possible because of the poor conditions in the dependent companies but we shall see that the stereotyped practices were changing even before the bursting of the Japanese financial bubble accelerated the process.

Much of Japanese success over the last thirty years was due to the undervalued yen, low rates of interest, excessive lending by banks against over-inflated assets and an internal distribution system which deters the potential new entrant.

What is amazing, however, is that with the bursting of the financial bubble many of the objectives of Japanese business, once considered central, have been rapidly sidelined. Market share was considered to be *the* business objective and all the time Japanese companies were experiencing rapid rates of growth that objective could be maintained. As long as they were certain of profit they did not have to worry about it. Once that certainty had gone, it very quickly assumed an importance not dissimilar to that in the West. The long-term view is fine as long as you are certain of the long term. When you are not, short-term actions rapidly assume great importance.

Even the great concept of *kaizen* is being questioned. Revolutionary change in business processes as advocated by Hammer and Champy are now regarded by some as the order of the day but one of the great difficulties for the Japanese is to make the really big *conceptual* changes or, in the jargon, achieve a paradigm shift. They are able to change their objectives but have difficulty with changing the means of attaining those new objectives. The truth, as with so many things, lies somewhere in the middle. By continuous improvement the need for revolutionary change is reduced but every now and again the fundamental questions have to be asked.

The Japanese critics

Much of the criticism of Japanese working practices has its emotional origins in Satoshi Kamata's account of his experiences as a seasonal worker with Toyota in the mid-1970s. His book *Japan in the Passing Lane* was published as *Automobile Factory of Despair* in Japan. Kamata, a left-wing, freelance journalist sought employment to obtain material for his writing and was hostile from the start:

> Almost as soon as I begin, I am dripping with sweat. Somehow I learn the order of the work motions but I'm totally unable to keep up with the speed of the line . . . Some skill is needed, and a new hand like me can't do it alone. I'm thirsty as hell, but workers can neither smoke nor drink water. Going to the toilet is out of the question. Who can have invented a system like this? (Kamata, 1983, p. 22)

While Kamata's work is somewhat dated it remains for Japanese workers to display the 'right' attitude, to work overtime and not take their full holiday entitlement. It was, however, still surprising that in February 1992 the Japan Auto Workers Union (JAWU) published, *Japanese Automobile Industry in the Future*, in which they highlighted what they called the triple sufferings of the Japanese automobile industry, 'The employees are exhausted, the companies make only little profit and the automobile industry is always bashed from overseas' (JAWU, 1992).

While many commentators commend the high level of competition within the domestic market as a factor contributing to Japan's success, the JAWU argues that the resulting constant demands for innovation with the associated high costs place unacceptable demands on the companies and their workforces. In particular it emphasises the length of the individual's working year and asks, 'How competitive will we be when we shorten our 2200 hours to 1800?'

These figures for Japanese working time do not tell the whole story. Many companies have traditionally relied on 'voluntary' overtime to meet their production requirements. Often this is unpaid and rarely does it appear in the statistics. A Ministry of Labour Report in July 1991 showed that the average Japanese had 7.1 days holiday in 1990 and in a survey of nearly 1200 companies, 76 per cent were good enough to say that they would allow employees to take consecutive holidays of three days or more in July and August!

But if the Japanese are stressed in their work they accept it. The archetypal Japanese salaryman, the male university graduate destined to stay with one company for life, professes to enjoy himself. I have asked the same question to various salarymen, 'Do you enjoy yourself?'. 'Yes', is the inevitable reply. They know they work hard and long but it is in a good cause. To them it is *seishinshugi* – the victory of the spirit over the material, meaning that their spirit triumphs over adversity.

In his annexe to the JAWU report Professor Haruo Shimada, who was also a contributor to *The Machine that Changed the World* and works long hours in his campaign for shorter hours, said of the Japanese automobile industry:

> There is competition for competition's sake and everything is sacrificed to it, wages, working hours, profits, suppliers, traders, the welfare of Japanese employees and job prospects of workers overseas . . . If competition becomes an end in itself and people compete whatever the cost then it will grow into a monster which can destroy life, society and even the economy.

A Japanese survey of parental attitudes asked 'Would you advise your children to work in the automobile industry?' Only 4.5 per cent answered 'Yes' (Nomura, 1992) with the most frequent reasons being:

	%
Pay too low for intense work	43
High work intensity	41
Onerous shift system and nightshift	40
Much work on holidays and overtime	36
Unfriendly personnel practices	33

Clearly, in Japan there is a perception of the automobile manufacturing industry that is different from that presented overseas by the most extreme enthusiasts.

The German critics

Criticism of Japanese working practices is also coming out of Europe. In particular, the International Metalworkers Federation (IMF) in addition to citing the long working hours, untaken holiday, unpaid overtime and high workloads, emphasises what it sees as other reasons for Japanese success, including major outsourcing of final assembly to subsidiary companies which pay considerably lower wages, supportive government policies and success, 'based on a young and steadily growing market, whereas the North American producers were stuck with ageing plant in a mature and cyclical market' (Unterweger, 1992).

There is, in fact, no doubt that wages in the supplier sector in Japan are lower than in the assemblers. Werner Sengenberger of the ILO's International Institute for Labour Studies has produced comparative information which shows the wage gradient, top to bottom in the UK and Japan related to the size of firm. (See Table 4.1.)

Table 4.1 Wage Gradient: Japan v. UK

	JAPAN		*UK*	
Size of firm	*Wage gradient* %	*Share of employment*	*Wage gradient* %	*Share of employment*
1000+	100	40.6	100	68.5
500–999	86.2	12.6	79.6	8.8
200–499	76.6	11.8	79.5	8.6
100–199	68.2	8.5	74.7	4.9
1–99	56.4	26.5	78.3	9.2

SOURCE: Sengenberger, 1992.

In the UK, all companies have wages which are close to 80 per cent of the highest, whereas in Japan the gradient slopes steeply downwards. Further, 26.5 per cent of Japanese companies are of the size which pays 56.4 per cent. The 1988 Japanese White Paper, *Small and Medium Enterprises* showed that 39.5 million Japanese worked in small and medium enterprises against 9.5 million in larger enterprises (the figures are complicated by the fact that the definition of small and medium enterprises varies between sectors) and that salaries in the small enterprises were little more than half those in the large.

IG Metall, the German metal workers' union, is somewhat ambivalent about lean production as practised in Japan, but it is critical of the attempts to introduce it into Germany which has strong trade unions, a highly qualified and self-confident workforce, a tradition of excellent working conditions and a value system centred on people. Siegfried Roth, a member of IG Metall's Executive Board, contrasts Germany's earlier attempts at teamworking based on the creation of attractive jobs and the promotion of qualifications, competence and high motivation with the lean production type of teamworking which, he believes, sees expansion and enrichment of work activity only from the standpoint of productivity. Management sees teamworking 'Almost exclusively as rationalisation measures and the aspect of social integration and humanisation plays only a small, subordinate role. Despite a great deal of lip service, management is miles away from attaching equal importance to human and economic goals.' And again, 'Low manning levels result in permanent overtime and stress, older workers are edged out in favour of higher performance younger workers, after-work life is given a low priority' (Roth, 1993). Manfred Schock, a trade union member of BMW's supervisory board said to me in February 1993 that BMW's management looked only at the cash savings. 'Do we in Germany want the same conditions as Japan? Do we want to improve our environment or make it tougher?'

IG Metall approves of *kaizen* as practised in Japan, where it directs its attention to both process and results and has as its starting point, people. In particular in Japan, 'A reduction of jobs does not result from the rising productivity achieved through *kaizen*.' In Germany it is being adopted by the automobile producers, 'as part of their struggle to reduce production time and labour costs . . . and in the classical Western style are overloading it with a short term profit and savings outlook' (Roth, 1992).

The Japanese approach then, according to IG Metall, values human labour and to be successful in Germany, it is necessary to combine economic and social progress with the well-being of all.

> One mark of an intelligent and socially harmonious system of production would most definitely be the avoidance of waste, increase in efficiency and declining costs. This cannot be tied to the goal of achieving competitive advantage through speed up, lay offs and exploitation of productivity gain. . . . A clear rise in efficiency can only be achieved when the workforce can see that all this is bound up with
>
> — an actual improvement in working conditions

— fair distribution of gains in productivity
— stabilisation of employment.

> *It is an illusion to think that employees will readily work for improvements to which they themselves fall victim* [my emphasis]. A production system that requires high morale, qualified workers and a commitment to constant improvement cannot be pushed through against the will of the employees. (Roth, 1992).

This is the corollary of expectancy theory which states that effort will be expended if the individual feels that the benefits to be gained are worthwhile.

It is clear that, whatever their motives, German managements have not yet accepted the underlying philosophy. In discussion with numerous German managers, I have found that their direction is all about structures, both physical and organisational. They have as yet failed to grasp that the great change, which must first come at the top, is a recognition that all people at all levels in their organisations are able to contribute effectively in improving the way things are done. The German system is so bound up with its structure of Works Councils, where all dealings are with the representatives of employees rather than the employees themselves, that they fail to see the wood for the trees. Following a visit to a number of manufacturing plants in Britain, including Nissan, the leader of a German delegation commented on the quality and flexibility they had seen, 'The trust and delegation of responsibility needed are not common in Germany – Germany must become flatter, less hierarchical and there must be more teamwork with responsibility pushed downwards.'

The Canadian critics

The Canadian Autoworkers Union (CAW) was born in 1985 when it broke from the North America UAW in protest at the so-called concession bargaining of the late 1970s and early 1980s, which was an attempt to give the US auto industry a breathing space to fit it to compete with Japanese imports and the new transplants. The CAW still clearly distinguishes between the interests of capital and labour and remains part of that section of the labour movement which believes that capitalist organisations can only succeed by exploiting the workers. Its experiences of Japanese production methods are based on CAMI, a General Motors–Suzuki joint venture based in Ingersoll, a small town of 8500 people.

The value of the CAW arguments is not how accurate or otherwise they are, but that in taking an extreme position, they illustrate the dangers that abuse might lead to. But the CAW rejects even this. Its argument is that abuse is built into the system. The main advocate of the CAW line is David Robertson, and when I asked him in November 1992, 'What went wrong at CAMI?' his response was, 'Nothing, everything that management was supposed to do, it did. And the workforce reacted increasingly against it. That is the lesson!'

To the CAW the objectives of lean production are to:

- reduce the number of labour hours per vehicle
- intensify the work effort
- eliminate non-value adding functions
- increase managerial flexibility and control
- undermine the independence of trade unions

The critical issue for them is, '*Who controls the shop floor*' and which side do the work rules favour. They reject a, 'logic of production based on competition among workers from different plants. It is the workers who are on the same team, not managers and workers' (Robertson, 1992).

They see the move to JIT and the elimination of buffer stocks as being against the workers' interests. Such a system requires jobs to be standardised, with imbalances being eliminated. But, they argue, it is these imbalances which provide workers with flexibility and the opportunity to create personal time (doubling up, banking, and so on). No car manufacturer can in fact eliminate the need for buffers – there will always be problems – but lean production shifts the buffer from being stock in production to the workers' personal time. 'Our willingness to make up after hours the production lost during the shift [means] the buffers are less visible. . . . We are the buffers. . . . It is not that Japanese production methods have done away with unnecessary buffers; it has simply shifted the cost of these' (Robertson, 1992).

Said David Robertson at a conference of the Transport and General Workers Union in December 1992, 'Lean production is intent on taking labour out of production and time out of labour. At the end of the day there will be fewer of us in the plant, and the jobs of those who remain are going to be worse.'

The CAW has, with the acquiescence of CAMI, undertaken a longitudinal study – a series of six monthly surveys with unrestricted access to the shop floor – to examine specific workstations, interview managers and, on a random basis, interview 10 per cent of union members. Their stated aim was to find out how lean production and the associated concepts actually operates and how it affects workers. The comparison of the results between rounds one and four (two years apart) are shown in Table 4.2.

Table 4.2 CAMI Attitude Survey

		Round 1 (%)	*Round 4 (%)*
Do you work harder than in traditional auto plants?	Yes	Not asked	78
Do you belong to a quality circle?	Yes	56	38
Is CAMI special, designed to change the way people work?	Yes	43	12
Does single status make managers and workers more equal?	Yes	43	6
Is management interested in the welfare of the workers?	Very	28	3
	Mildly	53	48
	Not very	15	35
	Not	4	15

SOURCE: David Robertson, TGWU Conference, December 1992.

The results, with all the caveats that have to be applied when union members are answering a union survey, show an increasing dissatisfaction with their lot. But one interesting point highlighted by David Robertson, which corresponds with the IG Metall attitude (and with expectancy theory) is his comment that, 'Workers were more likely to express approval for particular features of Japanese production methods when they could see real possibility for advancing their own objectives or for adapting existing structures to realise specific goals. Thus workers tried to appropriate the *kaizen* process to make work less stressful.' In discussion with Robertson in November 1992 he said, 'Workers will accept *kaizen* if it benefits them – if it makes their job harder or doesn't make any change they don't want it.'

Very clearly the Canadian Autoworkers Union has a political viewpoint epitomised by its comment that the critical issue is, 'Who controls the shop floor?' But in some of their points they are right; in particular the elimination of buffer stocks does mean that on some occasions catchback is achieved by scheduling overtime at short notice, but, if properly managed, this presents no problems. However, it is a practice which, if abused by management, is justifiably criticised. Where the political view also comes out is in their argument that the *kaizen* process is 'appropriating workers' knowledge'. This is an issue which defies logic, except that David Robertson will say that it is the very logic of the system which leads to abuse. If you believe that the workers' interest is inherently opposed to the employers' you will hold that view. If you believe that by sharing knowledge then profitability and security will accrue to all, it is the right thing to do.

What David Robertson does bring out though, is the great difficulty in translating the vision into reality. He says that, 'Vision becomes illusion' and this is the very point that Womack *et al.* make when they suggest that it is very easy to revert to type and lean production can easily revert to mass production. There can be no doubt that, as in all things, turning the vision into reality is difficult.

The British critics

Until September 1994, when the Trades Union Congress (TUC) published *Human resource management – a trade union response*, there was virtually no original critical analysis of lean production coming from the British trade union movement and most academic criticism was little more than a political diatribe.

For example, John Fisher, academic adviser to the Transport and General Workers Union, said at a union conference in December 1992: 'What the new techniques say is that if you can confuse the workers on this issue you can get increased productivity out of them without having to treat them as human' (Fisher, 1992). He sees flexibility as meaning more freedom for managers to assign work, and teams as powerful instruments of peer pressure.

I have been privileged to have spoken at several seminars organised for TGWU union officials. They asked strong questions and were not convinced that management was not simply seeking to screw them into the ground and marginalise the trade union. However, *they were concerned above all that the elimination of waste meant that the easy jobs, to which older workers move when they cannot keep up with the manufacturing pace, were disappearing.* This is not because they are just being difficult or resisting change for the sake of it, but because of a genuine concern about looking after their ageing colleagues. But I did not experience hostility to the concept. Practical people understand the realities of life; they do not have the luxury of the academics' ability to criticise from the outside. They have to earn a living and know that they have to compete in the real world. In fact, TGWU officials now appear to be less hostile than German management, who often appear unable to move out of their highly structured environment and fear genuinely devolving responsibility to people at the lower levels of the hierarchy!

The TUC is critical of lean production: 'It is a widespread trade union experience that the introduction of lean production, continuous improvement and total quality management constitute a concerted attempt to intensify the work rate whilst at the same time reducing the quality of working life' (TUC, 1994, p. 31). However, its critical analysis is more concerned with the selective application of human resource management techniques by employers who give little consideration to the wider implications. It favourably quotes Professor Keith Sissons, Director of the Warwick University Industrial Relations Research Unit: 'Whatever might be contained in company mission statements, there [is] a significant gap between the business school rhetoric of HRM and what [is] really happening in the work place' (TUC, 1994, p. 8).

The TUC sees dangers, especially where the introduction of human resource management is accompanied by derecognition or marginalisation of the unions, and regards union involvement as essential if the interests of people at work are to be safeguarded in any process of workplace change.

Paradoxically, though, the TUC quotes research evidence by Dr Neil Millward that workers in unionised organisations are more likely to have multiple channels of communication, more likely to be able to influence their working lives, more likely to receive information from their employer and more likely to have financial participation (57 per cent in unionised workplaces against 54 per cent in non-unionised workplaces). They are less likely to be in authoritarian or hierarchical organisations and just as likely to enjoy single status (ibid, pp. 11–14).

The TUC is not opposed to human resource management; its members must, however, be protected against potential abuses! In this it substantially differs from some of the more extreme opponents.

The American critics

Shigeo Shingo believed that it would be difficult for Japanese companies to succeed overseas if they sought to behave in the new country as they did in Japan. But most Japanese companies sought to manage in the USA as they did in Japan and all, except Nissan, sent hundreds of Japanese workers to their new plants to ensure compliance. The problem is that while there is much to learn from the Japanese, to seek to import without change causes major difficulties. And when several hundred people of any nationality are together they can become immune to the local influences. In this the Japanese behave no differently from expatriates of any nationality who gather together in large numbers.

The American intellectual critics of lean production are Michael Parker and Jane Slaughter, who warn of what they see as the dangers of teamworking. Flexibility means for them that workers can be required or induced to perform several jobs, giving management increased ability to assign workers as it sees fit. They believe that the detailed definition of every step of a task increases management control over the way jobs are done and that by co-operating with such systems workers participate in increasing their own workload. Like David Robertson they are hostile to an ideology which stresses competition between plants with workers joining with management to win work from other plants. It is Parker and Slaughter who coined the phrase 'management by stress' to warn of the so-called dark side of teamworking (Parker and Slaughter, 1988).

The established American unions have been slow to respond to the changes. In fact the AFL–CIO had admitted this. It was not until February 1994 that it published its guidance, when it said in *The New American Workplace: a Labor Perspective*, 'We in the AFL–CIO have, regrettably been insufficiently attentive to the needs of trade union leaders who are on the firing line. Not enough has been done to provide them with useful information, instruction or assistance' (AFL–CIO, 1994).

The AFL–CIO is primarily critical of the Taylorist model which it sees as permeating most of American industry, from banks, insurance companies and government agencies to fast food restaurants where, 'Each outlet throughout the country produces standardised results by giving each worker a narrowly defined task to be repetitively performed in a manner decreed by management.'

The AFL–CIO cites the failure of the QWL programmes of the 1970s and goes on to criticise:

> 'Feel good programs' and these 'involvement' or 'empowerment' programs which emanate from management and which stop at the task level [which] cannot, by definition, provide workers with any real power over their working lives. Rather these systems subordinate workers to management in essentially the time tested ways that have proved wanting. At bottom, then, these programs are a mirage; they offer the appearance, but not the substance of genuine worker involvement.

However, the AFL–CIO does not criticise 'Japanese-style production methods'. Its objective is to, 'combine individual participation through restructured work processes and redesigned jobs, with collective representation through restructured decision-making processes from the shop floor to corporate headquarters.' Its thrust is not to damn, as have other critics, but to bewail its previous lack of influence. 'In most cases unions have been unable to displace management's authority to dictate the system of work organisation.' In such circumstances it is not surprising that hostile shop floor activists have been able to take the initiative. They have filled what seems to have been a self-admitted vacuum. The union establishment is, however, now seeking to determine the direction of the debate with this third of three reports on the evolution of work. As the second was published in 1985, with a nine-year gap before the third, one wonders about the degree of urgency!

The critics of Japanese production systems present some powerful arguments. But unfortunately whether you are pro- or anti-Japanese production systems seems to depend very much on political leanings. What is lacking so far is an analytical approach which is constructively critical. I hope this book provides such a contribution.

RESPONDING TO THE CHALLENGES

It is clear that even before the bursting of the financial bubble the Japanese saw the 1990s as the time of market saturation, with the first response being to produce only what is needed when it is needed and the second to reduce dramatically the range of options offered.

There is now a fundamental change taking place in Japanese society with a realisation that concentration on the well-being of the population, socially as well as economically, is needed. The Japanese government's ten-year plan for industrial and social development prepared by MITI has as its theme for the 1990s, 'Creating human values in the global age'. It proposes, 'Free time for Japan's citizens to achieve their full potential according to their own choice and individuality and the opportunity to choose what to purchase and the chance to decide what to pay . . . Japan must adopt human-oriented international trade and industrial policies.' This plan does not commit anyone to anything, but it is a significant change of direction from previous ten-year plans which concentrated almost solely on the development of specific industrial sectors such as chemicals and heavy industry.

A report from a special committee drafting a New Economic Plan said, 'We must make Japan a society in which people can attain a better quality of life, an equitable society, where every citizen can both appreciate a comfortable and leisurely lifestyle and have equal opportunities to develop an individual sense of values.' And Masamuchi Shimizu of the Japan Management Association said, 'There are many admirable managers in Japan but if the working environment continues in the present direction, what Westerners regard as Japanese management style may not be appropriate' (*Financial Times*, 24 September 1992).

These pressures are impacting on working time. Many Japanese companies now boast of 'all out by 6.00 pm' one or two evenings a week. Toyota has said it will cut working hours by almost 10 per cent in the next two years and by 18 per cent in the longer term. The government approved a five-day week for national government employees from 1 May 1992 in place of everyone working alternate Saturdays. At the same time they reduced the basic working week from 42 to 40 hours. It should not be supposed, however, that this will be an easy road, particularly with the current economic difficulties. A survey of more than 2100 corporate executives by Keidanren (the Japanese national employers' organisation) showed support for shorter working hours but tempered by a belief that Japan 'cannot afford' to reduce the working week and that the Japanese have an innate love of work – but, it said, 'this love was fading among younger workers'.

Within the car industry, both Nissan and Toyota are in the process of lengthening model life, although only Nissan is firmly committed. Accordingly, Nissan's three-year management plan, begun in April 1992, aims to boost prices, prolong the model change cycle from four to five years, reduce the number of lines and introduce far greater standardisation of parts aiming to reduce the variety by 50 per cent. Nissan's new Sunny, released in January 1994, had 46 per cent fewer variations than the previous model. Profitability rather than sales growth is becoming the main concern. Toyota is, however, more circumspect. Chairman Toyoda has said, 'Because of the two factors – the wishes of the customers and the hopes of society, our technicians are unable to relax. There is a feeling that we are too exhausted and wouldn't it be nice to lengthen the model cycle, but it is difficult because not all of us agree on this.' Perhaps most importantly, MITI has said that customers are no longer fooled by gimmicks and has warned manufacturers that frequent model changes are an unnecessary waste of resource and labour time.

Within the manufacturing process, attempts are being made to ensure that technology serves rather than dominates. Said Mikio Kitamo, Toyota's Director of Production Engineering, 'The real intention is how to make work easy for people. We have not been successful replacing people with machines . . . if we do not make the work easy, we will lose people. If we make work more comfortable for people, people will stay at the plant' (*Financial Times*, 21 December 1992). Tadaaki Jagawa, Toyota's Director who supervised the design of a new plant said, 'If we don't attract workers, we don't even get to the point of worrying about waste. . . Maybe we made a mistake in designing such gloomy factories. I wish we had used more of our profit to improve working conditions' (*Financial Times*, 30 December 1990).

Technologically, change is under way – with most Japanese manufacturers experimenting with some movement from the conveyor type, final assembly line. In the early 1980s Honda introduced automated guided vehicles (AGVs) into its Suzuka plant. These allow the vehicle to be raised or lowered to the most suitable assembly position, can stop to allow the robot installation of components and vary their speed to catch up the gaps. Nissan in Kyushu, Mazda in Hofu and Honda in Suzuka have moved in this direction and all have considerably increased the automation of final assembly, which is extremely difficult compared with body construction. Automation levels of 30 per cent have been achieved and greater flexibility is now possible . Within these new systems painted body shells 'glide' through the final assembly process on self-propelled motor-driven carriers which replace the traditional assembly line. Their movements can be individually controlled at a specific pace and each can be stopped at any desired location, depending on the model carried and the components to be fitted. An automatic power lift system adjusts the height of each carrier at each station, minimising bending and stretching on the part of the operators. But it is not to be supposed that this means a move towards Volvo. For the new systems remain much more like conveyor assembly than Volvo's now abandoned dock assembly. However, they have also emphasised improvements to the working environment with, variously, air conditioning, quieter working areas, employee lounges, flowers, shrubs and picture windows, even spa-type baths.

The biggest manufacturing challenge of the 21st century will not be finding ways to replace people with machines – that will be easy – it will be to find means of combining people and machines in ways which remove the drudgery but allow people to contribute effectively to achieving high quality and improving continuously the product and the process.

The quintessential Japanese JIT system is beginning to be modified, although rarely has it operated in a pure sense. With suppliers beginning to locate at greater distances from the customer's plant, because of the difficulty in recruiting labour in the immediate vicinity, the small Japanese roads are becoming increasingly congested and manufacturers are experiencing delays in deliveries with consequential production problems. The most popular vehicles for delivering components in Japan are small trucks with payloads of 0.5 tonnes or 1.5 tonnes, whereas in the UK the largest articulated trucks can carry 24 tonnes. Peter Nieuwenhuis has calculated that taking into account the total size of the vehicle, delivery by small vans takes up 78 times the road space for an equivalent pay load and can cost eight times as much. Says Nieuwenhuis, 'As long as labour was plentiful the frequent journeys with light vans did not matter too much. As long as there was little traffic in urban Japan all those journeys with lots of small vehicles did not matter either' (*Engineer* 28 November 1992). Now, with suppliers locating further away, these journeys simply compound the traffic congestion problem.

It can also be costly and in Japan there is the beginning of a reaction against the system. In the good times the cost of multiple deliveries a day was acceptable, but in the petro-chemicals industry, where prices have fallen year on year throughout the 1990s, the trade association decided in 1994 that JIT deliveries of acrylic sheet would be stopped. They decreed that the three deliveries per day would be reduced to just one, unless the customer was prepared to pay extra for higher frequency. This was possible because of the size and power of the industry and though it is unlikely to spread to the small family firms, it is another straw in the wind.

JIT systems can also put considerable pressure on suppliers. It is not surprising then that many suppliers, who have less than total confidence in the system, keep stock up their sleeves 'just in case'. Even in the final manufacturing processes the retention of stock 'just in case' is not unknown. In the big campaign to improve productivity following the rapid appreciation of the yen in 1987, Nissan found millions of yen of stock secreted away by foremen, particularly of critical items!

Japan's 'sacred treasures' are changing. Soichiro Honda died in August 1991 and with him went the concept eulogised in *The Honda Book of Management* (Mito, 1990) whereby the directors sat together is an open plan office theoretically making decisions on a basis of consensus and teamwork. Yet it ended up with no one taking responsibility for decisions and a growing number of layers of middle management, with decision-making being passed up the tree. Honda's Soichiro Irimajiri said, 'We find that we have become very slow.' As with many elements of Japanese management practices, they worked very well in times of rapid growth and assured profits but when the market demands a rapid response they are less effective.

It is not only in the major corporate decisions that the change is needed. Having worked with Japanese people for ten years, it is evident to me that they do not really understand the Western ability and need to make rapid decisions with clear assigned responsibility. The arguments for consensus used to be that as everyone was involved there was commitment to the decision. While the decision might not be ideal and had taken a long time to reach, the *nemawashi* process meant that it would be implemented rapidly and fully once it had been put on paper and formally signed off through the *ringi* process. There were always two problems with this. First, as was once said to me, consensus means, 'A method of reverential enquiry to determine that your plan is in line with what your boss desires.' Most commentators fail to realise that Japan remains highly authoritarian and utilises top-down decision-making, *kono*. Ian Gow, one of the few Japanologists who really understands Japan, emphasised to me the critical difference between consensus *producing* a decision and consensus *around* a decision. The critical point for the Japanese is to have consensus before action. Second, once agreed and action is taken, it is very difficult to change. Mostly, the consensus method means that things do not go wrong and there is no *need* to change, but this breeds complacency and an inability to react quickly. When things do go wrong, so many people have been involved who subsequently have to be consulted, that the reaction is slow and often indecisive. Consensus is often an excuse for inaction.

Lifetime employment (LTE) is also threatened. LTE has never been contractual; 'lifetime' lasting for most people until the age 55 (now up to 60), and it only ever benefited about 20 per cent of the working population: the adult males working full time for a large blue chip company. However, the facts now suggest that change is under way. A survey on Japanese youth conducted by the Nikkei Research Institute (1990) found that 37 per cent of the Japanese workforce under 30 years of age had changed jobs at least once, 50 per cent of 29-year olds had changed jobs and the second highest figure, 42 per cent, was among the 22-year olds, suggesting that many young people switch employers in their first year after graduating from university. Of those who had changed jobs, 48 per cent had done so once, 24 per cent twice and 28 per cent three or more times. Further, six out of ten said they would like to change jobs; the other 40 per cent said that wanted to 'work for their present companies for as long as possible'. A record 2.77 million Japanese changed jobs in 1991.

From April 1994 Toyota began employing product designers on temporary contracts, the first time it has ever transferred its well-established policy from the shop floor to the design studio. While the intention is that the one-year contracts can be extended for as much as five years it saw the arrangement as the first step in establishing non-traditional ideas, especially as salary increases will be based on merit rather than seniority. In March 1994, Honda decreed that managers who are unable to win promotion will be classified as 'special staff' with a salary cut of 10 to 30 per cent. For those who cannot accept the loss of face there will be incentives to take early retirement or go to work elsewhere.

In April 1993 Japanese Airlines (JAL), faced with a massive decline in international air travel, extended its early retirement programme to employees aged 35–44 and offered one year's leave of absence to managers aged over 50 to encourage them to consider a second career, but with no obligation to leave the company. However, said a JAL representative, 'We have no intention of changing our basic policy of lifetime employment' (*Financial Times*, 28 April 1993). As long as lifetime ends at the age of 44!

The problem for Japanese companies is that the combination of lifetime employment and seniority progression has led to hopelessly inefficient administration. Scientific management never reached the offices. Although in the good times it was possible for the efficient manufacturers to carry the inefficient administration, this is no longer the case. One has only to walk through a Japanese office to appreciate the overstaffing. They have not yet gone through the administration revolution. Matsushita has realised its problems and is aiming to reduce its 20 000 administrators by 6000 by the end of 1996. Others are taking similar action.

Be that as it may, LTE has a lot of life left. In a major depression, Japanese blue chip companies go to great lengths to protect their staff from redundancies. Activities include the elimination of overtime, reduction in bonuses (up to 30 per cent of total earnings), bringing sub-contract work in-house and subsequently removing sub-contract labour. Temporary, seasonal and day labourers are not re-hired, regular employees are retrained and often are sent out to sell the product, many are sent to subsidiaries or sub-contractors, lay-offs and increased holidays are implemented and finally dismissal. What none of this says, however, is that many who are kept on with little to do, choose subsequently to resign voluntarily(!) and that those who move to sub-contractors or subsidiaries find that LTE does not apply and being the shortest service staff, when the next turn of the screw comes round, they are the people to go. The blue chip company has maintained its policy of no redundancy but a year or so later the transferred person is just as redundant!

Closely linked to LTE is the seniority progression system whereby salarymen (the university graduates), expecting to stay with one company throughout their working lives, could progress upwards at regular intervals, almost irrespective of ability. Both are now severely threatened. A 1993 survey conducted by Nihon Keizai Shinbun on 450 major listed companies found that 80 per cent of top managers wanted to see the seniority system abolished and one-quarter wanted to do away with LTE (*Nikkei Weekly*, 24 May 1993). Takuma Yamamoto, chairman of Fujitsu, suggested that the seniority promotion system had been losing ground for several years, giving way to performance-based systems. Sony and Honda have replaced their seniority-based pay with merit awards and are encouraging their staff to compete for promotion.

Akio Morita, founder of Sony, said:

> Japan must change. We are doing business all over the world, society is becoming borderless. The social costs of Japanese companies might be less than those US and European companies pay. It may be that difference which makes it difficult for them to compete. So in the long run we have to harmonise social conditions. (*Financial Times*, 27 May 1992)

Morita believes that wealth, which so far has accrued to business, should pass to workers and consumers in the form of better holidays, better pay, a shorter working life, a better environment and quality of life – particularly in improved housing. Nobuhiko Kawamoto, Honda's President, recognises that Japanese business must change:

> The traditional Japanese system is now in direct conflict with the competitiveness system of the Western world. Therefore we have to survive through this period of harsh competition and yet maintain the good features of the Japanese tradition. We want to give the next generation something to hope for! (*Financial Times*, 19 July 1994)

But the next generation is impatient. Japan is seeing the emergence of the *shinjinrui*, the new young breed, who have never known hard times and now want to share the benefits. Akio Morita is probably more in touch with these aspirations and wants change for the right reasons, not as is the case with most of his peers, simply as a result of economic pressures.

Perhaps the greatest indication of change is that until very recently few had heard a Japanese equivalent of the Western idiom, 'Thank God it's Friday' or POETS – 'Push off early, tomorrow's Saturday'. In late 1993 a Japanese colleague told me there was now a Japanese equivalent, '*Hana no kinyobi* – Friday's the greatest.' Maybe there *is* hope for the West!

THE SWEDISH EXPERIENCE

While they are frequently critical of Japanese production systems, at least the Swedes have tried a different approach and it is for this reason that I cite their experience in this chapter. In 1991, when visiting Volvo's new assembly plant at Uddevalla, some 80 km north of Gothenberg, I was told 'If we can't build cars this way in Sweden, we can't build cars in Sweden.' Two years later, both Uddevalla and Kalmar, Volvo's previous 'new way' assembly plant, were closed! Earlier, in 1991, SAAB closed Malmö, hailed as the 'auto factory of the future' and among the most worker-friendly in the industry.

Driven by the difficulties of getting Swedes to work in line paced assembly plants and inspired by Pehr Gyllenhammer's vision of a better way, Kalmar opened in 1974. Many still believe that it employed groups of people to undertake the final assembly of the whole car – the 'dock assembly' process. That system lasted but a few years: the increasing number of model variants made material supply difficult and failures to complete the tasks on time caused problems with the production flow. The plant did not achieve exceptional levels of efficiency and the amount of rectification work needed was no better than the traditional plant at Törslanda. When, in 1977, Volvo was faced with a production downturn, they responded by strengthening the management of Kalmar, and set each foreman specific goals including eliminating waste, improving material usage, improving quality and reducing the number of hours per car. In 1980 they introduced a performance based pay scheme related to hours per car, scrap and rectification, materials used, inventory levels and a quality index. By 1984 assembly time was 25 per cent better than Törslanda, buffer stocks had been removed and work intensity had greatly increased. The last dock assembly bay was removed in 1984. The official report on Kalmar stated:

> The workers say they do not regret the disappearance of the dock assembly, which was sometimes experienced as stressful . . . there was always some uncertainty as to exactly where they were in the work cycle at any particular moment and how much time remained for the allotted tasks. (Development Council of Sweden, 1984)

But Volvo learned from Kalmar. They found that its strength came not so much from the actual, physical process but from the genuine building of teams; what they called 'the little factory within the factory', perhaps no more than a two-person team working together along the line on a variety of tasks. They also learned that one of the key problems in Kalmar was getting the right material to the right place at the right time. With the growing complexity of automobile specifications and the varying and long job cycles, this had to be solved if the experiment was to be repeated. And at Uddevalla they did solve it, by establishing a large material centre where the major components were sub-assembled and then conveyed in the right sequence on automated guided vehicles (AGVs) to the assembly areas. This major breakthrough was essential to the main objective – doing away with the assembly line, At the Uddevalla opening ceremony, car division President Roger Holtback said 'I hope that one day somebody will be able to stand here and say Henry Ford invented the assembly line but Volvo did away with it.'

The Uddevalla project began in late 1985 when the ruling Social Democrats, Volvo and the Unions agreed a SKr 1.2 billion package to take over 2.1 million square metres previously occupied by the uneconomic, state-owned shipyard. From the beginning the management and unions regarded it as a joint venture, establishing a joint Working Commitment Group with the objective of achieving high quality and productivity in,'a pleasant working environment where people are happy to work and can continue to develop throughout their working lives.'

The unions' objectives for Uddevalla were:

- assembly of stationery vehicles
- job cycles of at least twenty minutes
- no machine pacing
- all direct workers also to perform indirect jobs

The basic production principles of Uddevalla were developed in experimental and training workshops before being tried for real. The concepts went through many changes amid much disagreement and, indeed, a number of the project team members left because they were unable to adapt to the new ways of thinking. Nevertheless a robust methodology was established.

In simple terms, the Uddevalla assembly method gathered together teams of eight to ten car builders. They received complete, painted bodies which had been transported from Törslanda and, working on up to four bodies at any one time, the teams undertook the complete final assembly of the car. Sets of components were delivered on AGVs in the correct sequence at intervals determined by the team. The assembly areas had a very low degree of automation but a high level of ergonomically designed tools. The car bodies were fixed on platforms which allowed for height adjustment, turning, and tilting through 90 degrees so that for much of the time operators were able to work in the upright position. Within limits the assembly teams were able to select the next vehicle they would build by reference to computerised information and their own rate of assembly.

Within the team there was no specific leader. The teams chose a co-ordinator or spokesperson with the position rotating around the group. The role of this person was to assign work to the team members, plan and report, lead team discussions, be both a peacemaker and a pacemaker and guide the team to achieve its goals. The teams reported to workshop managers who reported to the plant managing director – just three layers. Each team was required to build four complete cars a day and was responsible for its own quality. If problems were found during the final inspection, the car was sent back to the team if it was thought possible to rectify the faults in the team's area.

The training programme for the assemblers took 16 months – an initial 16 week period after which an individual would be expected to know two-sevenths of the build, and then a further twelve months during which the remaining elements would be learned. But this training covered not only the assembly skills: car builders were also taught teamworking, how to teach others, the spokesperson role and special skills – for example, recruiting, maintenance, quality, planning, information systems and problem-solving. Pay increased accordingly and a bonus system came into operation. This bonus system was based on quality (50 per cent), productivity (30 per cent) and accuracy of delivery (20 per cent).

All of this sounds wonderful and very much in line with the thinking of the behavioural scientists, but when I visited the plant it was experiencing 40 per cent labour turnover and 23 per cent absenteeism. The aim was to reduce these figures to less than 10 per cent. *The Machine that Changed the World* said, 'Simply bolting and screwing together a large number of parts in a long cycle rather than a small number in a short cycle is a very limited vision of job enrichment' (Womack *et al.*, p. 102). Said Shigeo Shingo, 'While the Volvo system rejects the *inherent inhumanity of the division of labour* [my emphasis] it also negates the beneficial effects. It is only natural that productivity should fall' (Shingo, 1988, p. xix).

There were other practical difficulties. First, eight people with two-hour job cycles building four cars a day meant a final assembly time of 16 hours per car. Nissan's Sunderland Plant is achieving body construction, paint application *and* final assembly in 9.5 hours. Similarly, SAAB found that Malmo took twice the European average time to build a car. Second, the extensive training needed to teach a two-hour job cycle meant that with continuing high labour turnover and absenteeism each operator was at a different stage of the learning curve, and with high interdependence this led to frustration; and third, the long job cycle and freedom to determine the build sequence resulted in a loss of control over the process. Long-term high quality demands both motivation of the workforce *and* control of the process. Without both, 'right first time' will suffer and high post-build rectification will be needed.

What Volvo sought to do was to relieve the tedium of the final assembly process by lengthening the job cycle. They failed to realise that if you have performed a two-hour job cycle several hundred times it becomes virtually as boring as a two-minute job cycle, and that when people of so many different levels of capability are having to work together this, in itself, builds frustration for both the more and the less capable. The objective was laudable but in seeking to build a volume product in a craft way they went down the wrong road to achieve greater employee satisfaction and commitment. They attempted to achieve job satisfaction in the work itself. In volume car assembly, where the process is inherently boring, such an approach is unlikely to succeed and, in any case, a final assembly time of sixteen hours cannot be profitable in today's competitive environment.

Volvo's Törslanda plant had a capacity of 900 cars a day but for most of 1992 output was about 400 cars. Announcing the closure of Kalmar and Uddevalla, Lennart Jensson, President of Volvo Car Corporation, said:

> The decision weighs heavily and was a sad one to make, especially since the employees have done such a good job in making the plants competitive. The fact remains, however, that we cannot produce more cars than we can sell. This measure is vital if we are to safeguard Volvo Car Corporation's future survival.

It was Uddevalla and Kalmar that closed, not Törslanda.

The closure of Uddevalla and Kalmar was a tragedy not only for the people involved, but also because we will not now know if such a process can be both socially and financially successful in the long term. For Christian Berggren, the great advocate of the approach, the key contributions were:

1. The integration of sub-divided and monotonous mass production work to more dignified and holistic tasks – they are technically feasible, compatible with varied market demands and socially highly desirable.
2. The broad development of the physical work environment, especially the ergonomic aspects of manual workplaces with the purpose of combatting repetitive strain injuries.
3. The efforts to make work systems less rigidly coupled and more adaptable to meeting diverse human needs. Sweden has no unemployment and therefore could not target an élite male workforce and had to acknowledge external obligations.
4. The high degree of involvement of unions in decisionmaking and planning processes as independent partners with legitimate interests of their own – unlike Japan where, despite the more assertive JAW stance, the enterprise unions don't follow. (Berggren, 1993, pp. 253–4)

The fact of the closures must in one sense mean that they have failed, but the lessons live on, and as technology advances it may become possible to combine moves away from the paced final assembly line with the lessons learned from Uddevalla. Change in the human-technical interface will come about not simply through change in the behaviour of people but through technological change.

5 Conclusions – and Beginnings

If a man will begin with certainties he shall end in doubts, but if he will be content to begin with doubts, he shall end in certainties.

(Francis Bacon [1561–1626], *Advancement of Learning*)

CONCLUSIONS – SO FAR

A number of conclusions begin to emerge.

1. Western industrial society is subject to a number of long-term fundamental changes – global competition, accelerating technological change, the shift from the collective to the individual, restructuring, downsizing, refocusing and a changing employment structure – all of which are having a major impact on the behaviour of organisations. Competitive advantage based on products or technology is rarely sustainable and high quality is now taken for granted. Established industrialised economies cannot compete with the emerging economies simply on the basis of cost and price, and manufacturers will increasingly produce where costs are lowest, and close to their markets. Success for the established economies will depend on quality, service and unit price and on the ability both to innovate and respond rapidly to the market place.

   Those who are content to do things in the same old way, who do not wish to innovate, will – in the main – lose out. This does not mean that those few organisations which have always offered traditional high quality and service have to change that element of their approach, but even Rolls Royce cars and the small, independent craft workers are changing many aspects of their businesses.

2. There is no absolute 'right' size for an organisation. There are only well and badly managed organisations, whether they be large or small. Large organisations which retain the baggage of growth by

acquisition or diversification and which seek to manage everything from a central headquarters will find that the costs and diseconomies far outweigh the benefits. The successful large organisations will ensure that power and responsibility lie in the correct place, whether it be at the centre or periphery, and will determine the appropriate level of co-ordination and if and where common services can be applied.

Successful small organisations will maintain the enthusiasm and commitment of the founder and/or managers but will acquire the controls which allow a professional approach to product development, manufacturing, quality, sales, cash flow and profitability.

3. Employment is more volatile. Full-time, 'nine to five' permanent employment is now a minority activity.

   The growth areas of the established industrialised economies are in the service sectors, although part of this is due simply to the redefinition of activities as work is contracted out. The balance of employment is changing rapidly in favour of part-time female workers employed in comparatively low-paid service sector jobs. The growth of small businesses is accelerating as large companies divest themselves both of non-core activities and of people who, if they are unable to attain new employment, increasingly establish their own new business. The balance between managerial/professional and unskilled jobs is changing in favour of the managerial/professional, although, with large companies reducing their middle management ranks, these new positions are likely to be in the more volatile smaller companies. Those who lack the necessary skills to be employable or self-employed will join the growing ranks of the non-employable. The emerging consensus is that the ability to create employment in the established industrialised economies will depend on a balance between high quality education and training, a dynamic labour market and ease of job creation.

4. Some elements of Taylorism are not dead, for we still have division of labour, standard operations and the 'one best method'; in short, control of the process. Taylor emphasised the elimination of waste, so did Shingo and Ohno. Taylor advocated, 'The deliberate gathering in of all the great mass of traditional knowledge', and so does *kaizen*. But Taylor failed to recognise that his division of labour, the separation of thinking and doing, the removal of discretion, and distinctions between functions, can lead to alienation and institutio-

nalised conflict. In such an environment people are expected to use their hands, not their brains, and as a result seek to produce at a quality and productivity *they* believe is right. The workplace can become a battleground with many adversarial groups, none of whom work together for the common good.

5. The Japanese emphasis on the definition of and adherence to the standard operation is critical to their success. It is the current best known best method of performing a task so as to achieve the required quality, cost and delivery in a safe manner and it forms the basis for training, control, consistency and improvement.

6. Companies have both to innovate and continuously improve, to always be evolutionary and periodically, revolutionary. Fundamental questions have to be asked about the organisation structure, systems, processes and products but once changes are made they must be continuously developed – if not there will be decline.

7. The elimination of waste is central to the Japanese way. But it is waste in every aspect of the business from inventory to walking time, from buffer stocks to unnecessary inspection. Waste is the great enemy.

8. 'Control of the processes', has to go beyond the physical process and reach into the business processes. Whether the business processes are about the recruitment of staff, the sequence of developing and introducing product changes, the arrangements for the supply and delivery of components or the method of assessing the performance of suppliers, they must be under control. However it is not unthinking control. The individual must be able to influence the way the job is done. Different people have different ways and the trick is to achieve the right balance, as we shall shortly see when distinguishing between prescribed and discretionary work.

9. Ford's insistence on a rigorous specification was a major contribution to achieving high levels of repeatability and was the starting point for later moves to achieve high-quality mass production.

10. The moving assembly line is still with us and for mass production no one has yet found an alternative which, economically, can achieve both the same quality and productivity. Even the Volvo system was

less than successful in achieving high levels of employee satisfaction and profitability, and with the closure of Kalmar and Uddevalla must, in one sense, be said to have failed. It did however teach us that it is possible to build complex products in a different way and that the objective of putting people first is not totally incompatible with a manufacturing process, even if the people do not always appreciate the new alternative.

11. Technological advances are, however, allowing moves away from line paced assembly work, except for the most intensive mass-produced products. Flexible manufacturing cells can expand the range of responsibilities and are allowing individual workers to have more control over their work. Flexible manufacturing processes are allowing customised production at almost the same cost as mass production. 'One of a kind' production is with us now and will increasingly become the norm. When these developments are combined with other activities designed to allow individuals more influence, it is possible to see the beginnings of a synthesis between high levels of commitment and high control of the processes.

12. The work of the behavioural scientists demonstrates that people are not motivated by bread alone. Once a person has a job then actual pay levels are not the prime motivators. Being able to contribute, exercise discretion and influence (both in influencing the task and in face-to-face contacts) and have those contributions recognised become important and people respond positively to such recognition. The corollary is that people who are not trusted will behave accordingly. Different people have different goals and react in different ways. Many now wish to move beyond 'self-actualisation' and give of themselves to the wider community. The link between the social and technical factors in the workplace and their relation to their external environment is profound. If people are not positively led and stimulated, it is easy for them to regress and adopt norms of behaviour which are not conducive to the mutual success of the individual and the enterprise. Imposed change is invariably resisted.

13. The Japanese concept (in the blue chip companies) that labour is a fixed cost and that operators have a brain as well as hands, adds a new dimension to the routine task. Teamworking, problem-solving, continuous improvement and quality built in at source, allow us to move from the alienated worker and create more fulfilling,

meaningful jobs. Involving people beyond the routine provides an essential stimulus to high levels of co-operation.

14. However, the basic task for many is unchanged, and while there may be significant modifications to the way work is structured and the involvement of employees greatly expanded, the fact of the routine, repetitive job has not gone away. We are moving into an era of **lean, volume production**. I use the word 'volume' deliberately because new technology allows us to produce numerous varieties from a common base.

15. Automation of complex or troublesome manual processes as the solution for the problems may lead to expensive failures. Simplification before automation may eliminate the need to automate, but if the need remains then at least the automated process stands a greater chance of success. Use the most appropriate technology, not necessarily the most advanced. Low-cost automation can work wonders. Always have regard to the interface between the people and the technology so that the people are able to influence what goes on. Consider also that great benefits can come from restructuring the processes before automation is even considered.

16. The introduction of new technology can mean the elimination of much difficult and tedious physical work but can also de-skill, creating another type of routine task. On the other hand, it can create an environment in which the operator is able, if allowed, to contribute way beyond the routine and in so doing develop and utilise new levels of knowledge and capabilities. Our lean, volume production can develop into **lean, people-centred, volume production**.

    Far too often technology is introduced without thinking of the people who will use it or without providing proper training. As a result fear sets in and it is resisted. When introduced properly, new technology becomes just another tool. The biggest manufacturing challenge of the 21st century will not be finding ways to replace people with machines, it will be to find means of combining people and machines in ways which remove the drudgery but allow people to contribute effectively to achieving high quality and to improving continuously the product, the process and the quality of their life.

17. Japanese production systems have over the last thirty years or so achieved higher quality and productivity levels than those of the West

but in many respects the West has now learned from the best of Japanese practices and is catching up. It is imperative that we do not regard Japan as an industrial Lourdes where a few days worshipping at the shrine will bring about the miracle cure. The constructive critic can add more value than a dozen sycophants. The West, when seeking uncritically to emulate Japan, aims at a target which in many respects is moving towards it.

The Japanese, however, have not yet learned from the West's specific expertise, particularly financial control, the clear definition of responsibility, the importance of product planning and marketing and the ability to make rapid decisions when necessary.

18. The elimination of waste does stretch the system and, if undertaken in isolation and taken to extremes, can create unacceptable pressures. This is true whether the waste is excessive people, activities, space, time or stock (whether inventory, work in progress, buffer stocks or finished goods). Just in time systems are sensitive and fragile, and susceptible to delays and interruptions when small problems can have a disproportionate effect on the whole operation. The elimination of waste, in removing the easy jobs, can create problems for the future as operators become less capable of handling those jobs which remain. There is, increasingly, no place to hide.

19. Much of Japanese success is due to factors such as their long working hours, the pressure to conform, the previously undervalued yen and a tied supplier base which does not offer the benefits of the blue chip companies but provides a cushion in the hard times. However, in design for manufacture, employee involvement, workforce experience and continuous improvement they are well ahead of the West. In many areas, particularly in the service sector and administration, Japan's efficiency and effectiveness are way behind the West. There are high levels of disguised unemployment.

20. The Japanese approach works in the interests of both the company and employees because there is a genuine sense of reciprocal obligations with, in particular, employees having security of employment. This approach has not been common in the West.

21. Japan's manufacturing is subject to new financial, cultural and social pressures and is undergoing significant changes. The sacred treasures of lifetime employment, seniority progression systems, enterprise

trade unions and consensus are under strain and, while they will remain for a long time to come, the beginning of the end is clearly evident. At the same time Japanese workers, particularly the young, are seeking the fruits of their labours, but are doing so at a time when corporate Japan is least able to satisfy them.

22. Trade union and academic critics are right when they highlight the problems if management attends solely to the short-term productivity and financial goals of what is a holistic system. However, those who denigrate the total system appear to do so from a political point of view which wishes to see capitalism collapse. Further, when they argue that these techniques are simply attempts to undermine trade unions, they fail to realise that their loss of influence is not due to anti-unionism on the part of management but their own failure to adjust to the new environment.

23. In some respects trade union influence will be strong in the short term when they seek to criticise but, as employees come to recognise that their success and security are integrated with that of the company, the role of the unions needs to change. Long-term influence can best be achieved if they recognise that the prosperity and security of the company and employees are bound together and that they should work within the system, seeking to minimise the potential excesses and ensuring that the benefits are properly shared. They are more likely to participate constructively if they are brought into the change process than if they are left outside.

24. Most managers are ill equipped to cope with these changes. They fear to devolve responsibility because they believe that if they do, their own responsibility will diminish. Those who have been brought up to control find if difficult to motivate. Therefore, they frequently seek to suppress initiative. If they are to facilitate the change process they must learn that devolving responsibility may alter their role but not necessarily diminish it. It becomes a top management responsibility to equip middle managers to handle the change process and this can best be achieved if they are intimately involved.

25. There will always be mavericks: organisations and people who break all the rules. Many fail and a few succeed, but those who do succeed, often do so spectacularly. They are the small groups given their head within a large organisation, or it may be the whole organisation. Cray

Computers, Virgin Atlantic, Body Shop, Microsoft and 3M are organisations which in their various ways have done things differently and succeeded. Peoples' Express and Laker Airways failed, not necessarily through their own fault.

These conclusions are, at this stage, simplifications and the detail will emerge as we progress through subsequent chapters. However, it is these conclusions, together with the long-term changes taking place in Western industrial society which led me to the simple model of the ascendant organisation described in Chapter 1. There is one further element.

PRESCRIBED AND DISCRETIONARY WORK

In 1961 Elliott Jacques used the terms 'prescribed' and 'discretionary' when developing his concept of 'time span of discretion' to establish the value of different jobs. While his job evaluation system never caught on as an analytical tool I use his terminology as the basis for a different concept.

All work can be divided into these two elements, the prescribed and the discretionary. Prescribed elements are those which have to be done in a specific way at a specific place, often in a specified time. Discretionary elements are those which are not time or task critical and over which the individual can have some flexibility and choice in whether, when and how they are done: for example, preventive maintenance activities, *kaizen*, problem-solving, housekeeping or training.

The balance between discretionary and prescribed work for the senior executive, shop floor operators and some other positions can be illustrated as follows :

Position	*Prescribed* (%)	*Discretionary* (%)
Senior executive	5	95
Line paced assembly operator	95	5
Shop sales assistant	75	25
Dentist	50	50
Lawyer	10	90
Maintenance worker	50	50

These examples are for illustration only – they have no analytical basis – but for *every* job there are prescribed and discretionary elements. What is essential is to make the small amount of discretionary work as meaningful as possible for those who have only a small amount. The line paced assembly operator may be trained to perform the prescribed tasks well, and may get satisfaction from a job well done, but it is the opportunity to influence the way the job is done that really motivates and that opportunity lies in the 5 per cent of discretion. If the senior executive loses 5 per cent, the discretionary proportion drops to 90 per cent. If the operator loses the 5 per cent, *all* opportunity to influence has gone, and true motivation, which comes from within, will be almost impossible to achieve. The result will be alienation.

But the great thing is that change can take place. The operator who varies the process according to his or her own best way or introduces a new lay-out; the hotel porter who instead of standing around is able to use initiative and make decisions to help the patrons; airline staff who genuinely believe in customer service; retail assistants who are given responsibility for display, promotions or re-ordering; administrative staff who are fully involved in improvement activities; these are all examples of expanding the discretionary at the expense of the prescribed.

THE NINE ALPHA ORGANISATION MAP

In Chapter 1, I presented the simple model which led to the ascendant organisation. However, life is not simple. In the simple model there is no room for the maverick organisation, nor for the autocratic, the country club, the authoritative or the dozens of other organisation types. The second 'Eureka' moment came when my friend and colleague, Barry Venter, Managing Director of Organisation Development International (a consultancy specialising in helping companies in very practical ways through the change processes) suggested that the model needed four axes, not two. During the course of an intensive week in April 1994, Barry and I, together with other members of ODI staff, developed what we came to call the 'Wickens/Venter Nine Alpha Organisation Map' (Figure 5.1).

Because I had started with four As in the simple model, we sought to continue the alliteration and with just a little licence believe we succeeded. Others may judge differently, but as Humpty Dumpty said to Alice in Lewis Carroll's, *Through the Looking Glass*, 'When *I* use a word it means just what I choose it to mean – neither more nor less.'

The positions on the map are, necessarily, simplifications. They are not absolutes, do not sit precisely on the axes, will overlap, and each will have both strong and weak versions. The shapes will not be precisely as shown.

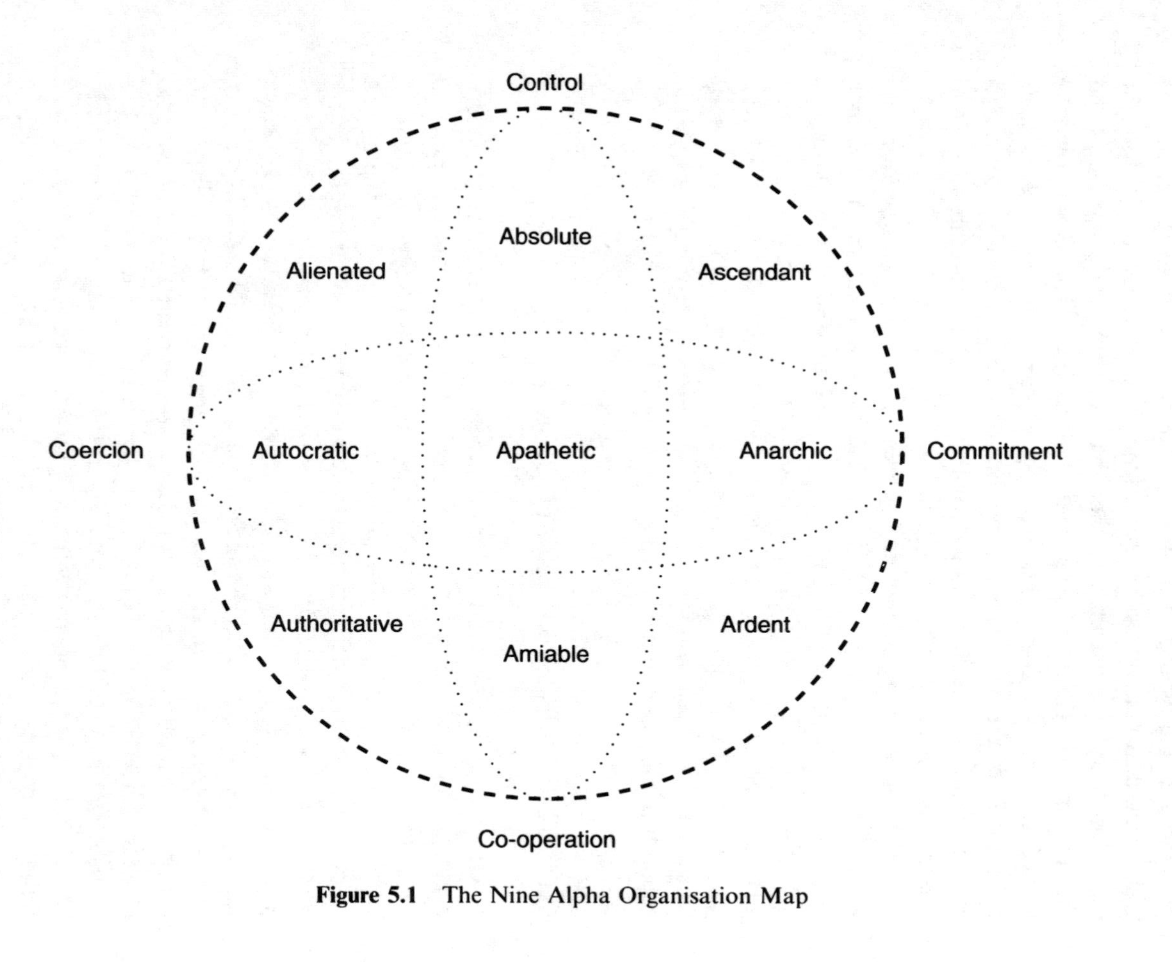

Figure 5.1 The Nine Alpha Organisation Map

'Apathetic', for example, is most likely to be an irregular oval, off-centred to the upper left. Readers may wish to draw their own axes and, preferably in a group, develop their own map. They will find it a stimulating and illuminating exercise.

Just as there are no straight lines in nature so there are few direct links between the organisation types. It is not necessary to pass through an adjacent type to reach your destination. The map suffers from the deficiencies of all two-dimensional representations when a more realistic representation would be a globe with routes both around the surface and through it. It does however assist in defining where you are and where you wish to be. At all times, seek to avoid 'apathy', but you may already be there!

THE AXES

Turning to the map, the first elementss to note are the four axes : control, coercion, co-operation and commitment. The first two are imposed and the latter two come from internal motivation. The central point is 'low' and the intensity increases as the organisation progresses to the outer limits. The definitions of the axes are:

Control Top-down imposition of standards, rules and processes. Command and direction are the normal methods of determining behaviour and achieving results.

Coercion Exercise of authority, and pressure to conform with the demands of those in 'superior' positions. Compels obedience often with the threat of sanctions.

Commitment Internalised individual belief in the values and objectives of the organisation and/or self. Highly motivated to work to achieve these objectives.

Co-operation Working together to achieve shared goals which will normally be those of the organisation.

There are, of course, an infinite number of degrees between the axes.

The axes are in part a reflection of the work of the behavioural scientists. I have noted McGregor's use of 'control' and 'coercion' and in his studies at the Hawthorne Plant Elton Mayo contrasted the previous coercion with the co-operation of the operators who, 'Became a team and the team gave itself wholeheartedly and spontaneously to co-operation in the experiment.' McGregor's Theory Y assumed commitment to objectives and contrasted it with control. 'If [commitment] is large, many conventional external controls will be relatively superfluous and to some extent self-defeating.'

THE ORGANISATION TYPES

The thesis is that organisation types are determined by the balance between the axes. Definitions become clearer the further out to the extremes the balance lies, but in the following descriptions I attempt to illustrate both the strong and weak versions and indicate where there might be overlaps.

Apathetic

There is virtually no commitment or co-operation. There may be some attempt at control and, perhaps, a little coercion by someone who seeks unsuccessfully to be strong. But because of the arbitrary nature of such attempts and the lack of commitment, the organisation is switched off. There is no central respected authority. Although the 'outline' of the apathetic organisation will be around the centre point it will be weighted to the upper left, that is towards the control/coercion axes. Such organisations may include large 'paper pushing' public sector organisations, comfortable private sector companies sure of their market and profits and any organisation which lacks leadership, clear goals and a sense of direction. Neither the management nor the workforce greatly cares, either about the organisation or each other.

Absolute

This requires a high level of control by the rules and procedures, with little room for flexibility: for example, an organisation in which there is a high risk potential – a nuclear power station; or externally imposed standards – an audit practice, or a requirement for consistent standards – microchip manufacture. High levels of technical training to clearly defined standards are evident and employment is often long term. Such an organisation can extend out to alienation if it combines with high levels of coercion and zero discretion, or can move to ascendant if individual contributions are allowed and valued.

Alienated

The alienated organisation combines high levels of coercion and control. It utilises a top-down imposition of rules and procedures with no attempt to involve the people or get their co-operation except by edict. Its management style overlaps with the autocratic but those in charge do not have the individual power of the true autocrat. It often leads to staff indulging in activities aimed at restricting individual performance or undermining the organisation. Examples may include line paced assembly work where individual contributions are ignored, a low-wage mass production textile factory based on piece work, time-driven project groups and organisations in which low-calibre managers care only about results and little about people. Labour turnover is high and skills development low.

Autocratic

This results from a high level of coercion with some rules and procedures and little commitment. Enforcement depends on bullying and the whim of those in charge. In its milder versions it may move towards apathy via arrogance or, if there is an attempt to restrict the excesses by having the bullies operate within rules, to authoritarianism. Autocratic organisations may include those with an owner–manager or a strong chief executive who seek to ignore formal structures or change them to suit their preferences. They retain the 'right' to hire and fire. Most car manufacturers have in the past been autocratic and some still are. Large organisations with corporate bureaucracies now temper the excesses of potentially extreme chief executives and in the mid-1990s such an organisation is more likely to be small or medium-sized but can exist in any sector.

Authoritative

Good level of co-operation based on legitimate authority resulting from an acceptance of the wisdom and knowledge of the leaders. May include a legitimate elected government. This legitimacy may, however, lead to an element of coercion and, perhaps, some autocratic or arbitrary behaviour. May include small organisations dependent on the knowledge and capability of the founder/leader, for example a consultancy, or larger organisations respected for their expertise. Generally, they recognise the need to develop and retain high-calibre people. An authoritative government can easily drift into becoming autocratic, especially if it has a dominant leader, or into apathy if it has been in power too long.

Amiable

The amiable organisation has a high level of co-operation, and is more likely to tend to commitment than to coercion, although in some such organisations the pressures of a few might result in a small amount of 'acceptable' coercion. It may include the voluntary, caring organisation or club led by enthusiasts, where participants' dedication is more to the activity and colleagues than to the bureaucracy. At one extreme there may be few rules, in which case it is easy to drift to anarchy; at the other the rules may be absolute, for example, the golf club. In the business world the amiable organisation may include the small, relaxed company content with its position in the market place. Such businesses can easily drift into apathy.

Ardent

This has high levels of individual commitment with a high degree of acceptance of the corporate goals. Such organisations are eager, zealous and fervent and like to see themselves as highly flexible and unrestricted by traditional controls and rules. Employment may be on short-term contracts with rapid movement between companies. Many organisations, encouraged by the advocacy of popular writers, would like to see themselves in this category, but few succeed for long. It is easy to drift into anarchy and, as such organisation grow they find they need controls to prevent this happening. The big question is whether they become ascendant or autocratic. If they fail they can also fall into apathy. Such organisations may include the creative boutiques, niche companies and the inspirational businesses dependent on keeping ahead of the game.

Anarchic

The anarchic organisation has high levels of individual commitment but virtually no control or co-operation. Such an organisation lies fairly flat along the commitment axis. People do what they, individually, think is right for the organisation or themselves without much concern for any corporate objectives (which in any case probably do not exist) or for others. They often indulge in 'fad surfing', riding the waves of whatever initiative seems attractive until it is beached. It is also easy for anarchic organisations to become apathetic as it is realised that no one really cares, or to crash into autocracy as someone determines that the organisation needs to be shaken up and sorted out as a prelude to moving to ascendancy. Such organisations may include sales companies operating on the edge of the legally acceptable, brokerages working on commission, creative businesses in which it is everyone for themselves or any organisation in which management has lost control.

Ascendant

The ascendant organisation combines high control of the processes and a high degree of commitment of the people. People accept the control because they 'own' the processes and are responsible for maintaining and improving them. Ascendant organisations are positively led by people who care about all the stakeholders and who seek to align the objectives of the organisation. They have an understood, shared culture which permeates all behaviour and ensures equity of treatment throughout. Ascendant organisations aspire to providing security of employment for their core workers and high levels of training and development for all. Responsibility is genuinely devolved allowing individuals, within the accepted framework, to be creative and make their own inputs. The organisation is able to respond flexibly to changing pressures. Such organisations combine the best of all cultures and can appear almost anywhere. There is little overlap between the anarchic and apathetic organisations and the ascendant, but absolute, authoritative and ardent can move 'through the globe' to the ascendant.

It is not to be supposed that becoming an ascendant organisation is the only desirable state. Apart from alienation and apathy there is something to be said in favour of all other organisation types and in some sectors, the ardent, authoritative and amiable organisations are highly desirable. At other times, absolute and autocratic may work well or be necessary transitional steps. Neither do I wish to imply that organisations cannot be successful for considerable periods of time unless they are ascendant. There will always be examples of the autocratic company, the amiable caring organisation or the ardent innovator which are extremely successful.

Similarly an organisation may comprise units of different organisational types. Whether this is good or bad depends on the overall objectives. For example, if marketing and product development are 'ardent', production is 'autocratic' and personnel 'authoritative', is the organisation as a whole 'anarchic' or 'ascendant'? When discussing leadership in Chapters 7 I shall show that a key responsibility of a leader is to align the organisation. Whether this is achieved by consistent or diverse behaviour patterns is a decision each organisation has to make for itself. The important point is that it must be a conscious decision and not just happen accidentally.

However, I do believe that all organisations which succeed and grow move towards the ascendant. Remember the definition of ascendant – 'rising towards the zenith.' It is about progression towards a condition, not an absolute. The most successful initially ardent organisations, for example, Body Shop, Virgin Atlantic and Microsoft, stay in business because they manage to introduce controls without losing the commitment of their people. The most successful initially absolute organisations, for example, British Nuclear Fuels, Toyota and Coopers and Lybrand, stay in business because they manage to generate commitment without losing their controls.

The task of Part II, 'Know-how' will be to show how organisations can move to becoming ascendant by ensuring that they maintain the balance between control of the processes and commitment of the people.

PART II

‘Know-How’

6 Culture, Vision, Mission – Whatever You Call It

When there is no vision the people perish.

(Franklin Delano Roosevelt, Inaugural Speech, 4 March 1933)

When Captain Cook asked the Chiefs of Tahiti why they ate apart from women, they looked at him in wonder and disbelief at such a foolish question. They thought and thought, and finally one offered the only explanation they had: 'Because it is right.'

(Anon.)

CULTURE

In July 1993 Lou Gerstner, the new chairman of IBM, when announcing that the company was taking an $8.9 billion charge to cover 60 000 job cuts and office and factory closures said, 'The last thing IBM needs right now is a vision. What IBM needs now is a series of very tough minded, market driven, highly effective strategies that deliver performance in the market place and shareholder value.' Gerstner's statement was in fact a contradiction in terms. Even though in IBM's 1994 annual report he felt the need to explain that he had not been accurately quoted (most had left out the 'right now') he was not in fact abandoning the need for a vision; he was seeking to replace one type of vision with another. He was seeking to change both the culture and the vision of the company and in so doing spent much of his first year halving the size of the board of directors, restructuring at the top and attending meetings with tens of thousands of employees all over the world.

Every organisation has a culture – even those which have never heard the word; even those seemingly few which have not prepared a culture statement. The difference in recent years is that organisations have consciously decided to attempt to define their culture, and write it down. Often, when written down it is called 'Our Vision' or 'Our Mission'.

There is a great confusion of terms! Such statements almost by definition take on a missionary zeal, they form the tablets of stone which come down from on high – with the result that there are only believers and non-believers, and if you are a non-believer, 'You are not one of us.' Top executives fail to realise that, just as declaring that the company is one big family does not create a family atmosphere, neither does a mission statement create a sense of mission. When such statements begin, as they invariably do, with words such as, 'We are committed to . . .', what right does the chief executive have to speak on behalf of the shop floor operator? *Commitment has to be earned, it does not come from words on a piece of paper.*

One of the great problems is that an organisation's culture and its professed mission may get in each other's way. The definition of culture may be complex, 'The pattern of all those arrangements, material or behavioural which have been adopted by a society (corporation, group, team) as the traditional ways of solving the problems of its members; culture includes all the institutionalised ways and the implicit cultural beliefs, norms, values and premises which underlie and govern behaviour' (Payne, 1991) or it may be simple: 'The way we do things round here.' And there are numerous permutations between the two.

In most organisations the culture is instinctive, whether we are speaking of the chiefs of Tahiti or Wall Street financiers. It is not overtly taught, it is absorbed. A strong culture is constantly reinforced, even when we think we are doing nothing. By behaving in broadly the same way as our colleagues, we are reinforcing our culture. Very rarely can a culture be imposed. Sometimes in a new organisation the founders can attempt to set the tone, but if that tone is not right for the people, the organisation and the time it will not survive – other forces will take over. In other instances a transformational leader who emerges at the time of crisis may seek to change totally the culture of the organisation. Some succeed, others fail.

Many factors affect the culture of an organisation. A local government department serving the community will have a very different culture from a private company competing vigorously in the open market. All may work hard and long but the values differ and so, therefore, will behaviour, not only in treatment of the customer or client but between people within the organisation. Large organisations, whether private or public, are more likely to behave in a similar way than are large private companies and small private companies. And national cultures impact on organisations. Nissan in the USA behaves differently from Nissan in the UK. The American love of invigorating messages, coffee and donuts and the glitter of in-house celebrations would not go down well in the UK where understatement is the order of the day.

Very rarely is 'Our Culture' written down as such, although 'Our Mission' increasingly is. The best culture statement I have seen is that of Sunrise Medical Inc., a California-based health care products company. Sunrise refers to its seven enduring values.

1. **Product Superiority**
   We are a product driven company: we are only as good as the products we make. We are committed as a corporation to offering products with genuine superiority in quality, innovation and value, but the most important of these is quality. We believe that product superiority derives from paying strict attention to the details. Precision is required throughout the design and manufacturing process so that our products will operate reliably for their intended lives. Our goal is to provide defect-free products and services to our customers.
2. **Service to Customers**
   In our company, the customer is king. Our goal is to achieve *perfection* in customer service: to leave every customer satisfied with our service every time. It is essential that we live up to whatever commitments we make. We must also outperform our competitors in demonstrating sensitivity and responsiveness to our customers' individual needs.
3. **Individualism**
   We believe in the dignity and worth of every individual. We will treat our Associates with fairness and respect, while encouraging them to think independently. Every job is important and must be performed well if we are to succeed. A career with our company must permit our Associates to achieve personal satisfaction while leading balanced lives.
4. **Teamwork**
   All of us together are stronger and wiser than any of us is individually. We will foster an attitude of teamwork and a spirit of enthusiasm within our company. Success within our company will come to people who are dedicated and resourceful, to people who assume responsibility, to people who care.
5. **Productivity and Performance**
   We must earn an attractive return for our shareholders, which in turn ensures our corporate future and permits us to reinvest in growth. The key to corporate performance is achieving steady improvement

in the productivity of all Associates. To do this we must harness our collective creativity and operate with the latest methods and technologies.

6. **Citizenship**
   Through our commitment to corporate excellence we will improve the welfare of those who use our products and advance the progress of society. We will also be good citizens of every community and every country in which we operate, thereby contributing to global prosperity and harmony.
7. **Corporate Character**
   We believe that great corporations, like great individuals, always act with integrity and character. When faced with moral choices, they do the right thing. They also bring a level of professionalism to everything they do. Above all, we are dedicated to being a company with character.

Although written from a 'We' viewpoint, this statement, by referring to the way Associates will be treated, does not make the mistake of assuming that it is initially owned by everyone. It fosters a positive approach to teamworking rather than stating, 'We are a team'. It is clearly a corporate statement to which, the Executive Board hopes, people will adhere. They recognise that the commitment has to be earned but by clearly stating the culture they set the tone by which behaviour will be judged.

I have met with the Sunrise executives and have given presentations at their seminars. In thanks they gave an advanced wheelchair to be donated to a local disabled person. From my experience Sunrise executives seek to *live* their culture, not just talk about it, and in so doing stand a far greater chance of having it permeate successfully throughout the company.

Another example of an expression of culture is that of Honda Motor Company's Management Policy, written in a blend of Japanese and English:

Proceed always with ambition and youthfulness
Respect sound theory, develop fresh ideas and make the most effective use of time
Enjoy your work, and always brighten your working atmosphere
Strive constantly for a harmonious flow of work
Be ever mindful of the value of research and endeavour.

The important point about Sunrise and Honda is that these statements are about the 'how' as well as about the 'what'. They are concerned with the behaviour of and attitudes to people. For the individual that is what matters – how he or she is treated and how they are expected to behave towards others, both within and outside the organisation. Writing it down does not, of course, achieve anything. A chain is as strong as its weakest link and as soon as one person in the chain does not behave in the way the written statement suggests then no one below that person will believe that the organisation really means what it says. A culture statement which is not followed is the worst of all worlds.

We must not suppose, though, that having a written corporate culture is a recipe for success, however much latter-day evangelists may seek to persuade gullible executives that it will bring about the desired miracle cure. John Kotter and James Heskett in their study of over 200 leading US companies found a weak relationship between strong cultures and long-term business performance. Companies which had done well in the past (Citicorp, Procter and Gamble, Sears and J. C. Penney), 'had become characterised by arrogance, complacency, inward lookingness, bureaucracy and politicking' (Kotter and Heskett, 1992). Strong cultures can actually contribute to decline because that very strength makes if difficult to change direction when needed.

Kotter and Heskett found that *only cultures which encourage flexibility and adaptive behaviour can achieve long-term success.* Such cultures placed a high value on leadership at the top and on meeting the needs and expectations of all stakeholders – shareholders, customers, suppliers and staff. They found 22 companies which scored highly on these criteria. Over an eleven-year period those companies with the highest rating increased turnover by 682 per cent against 166 per cent for the lowest, and profits by 756 per cent compared with one per cent for the lowest.

MISSION

An organisation's culture is deep within it. It cannot be changed overnight, as we shall see when we look at the culture change process. In this it is unlike a mission. (It is possible to distinguish between mission, vision, goals, challenges, and so on, but for simplicity I will stick to this one word, except when using an individual company's terminology.) A mission can be – and often is – changed overnight, although the way that change is achieved will be affected by the culture.

Sunrise Medical's corporate mission is:

> To build a leadership health care company, worldwide in scope, with a commitment to high quality products which use innovative engineering

solutions to improve peoples' lives. Our products increase patient mobility and independence, speed rehabilitation and recovery, and promote fitness and health. They focus on the needs of three special groups: the geriatric, the disabled and the health conscious consumer. It is also our goal to provide for our Associates a positive, rewarding work environment which stimulates personal growth and fulfilment.

Even in its mission statement, Sunrise is concerned with the people in its business, but unfortunately the quality of this statement does not equal that of its statement of values. It is too long and confuses the mission, description of its products and its values. The first sentence is all that is needed.

Compare Federal Express's:

Absolutely, Positively, Overnight

While this is as much of an advertising slogan as a mission statement, provided the management of the company demonstrates the continuing inspiration and control, people will sweat blood for that! It is the business equivalent of 'We will overcome!' or 'Liberty, Equality, Fraternity!'. In three words it defines the business, emphasises its competitive edge, provides the basis for all decisions, focuses on the task, establishes the measure of success, and, most important of all, IT INSPIRES. Whoever thought of it had a flash of genius. It is so much better than the original version, 'We will deliver the package by 10.30 the next morning.'

After that everything else seems tame. The mission of Citibank is :

To be recognised by customers worldwide as a team of professionals who create and deliver financial solutions

1. Create a customer-keeping vision
2. Saturate your company with the voice of the customer
3. Go to school on the winners
4. Liberate your customer champions
5. Smash the barriers to customer winning performance
6. Measure, measure, measure
7. Walk the talk

All good stuff, but one can imagine a group of executives sitting around a room with flip charts on the wall aided by a consultant with all the latest management books, and ending up with a handful of the latest managerial fads. Who on earth is going to be inspired by 'Liberate your customer champions'?

The first of Mars' five principles is:

> The consumer is our boss, quality is our work and value for money is our goal.

Digital Equipment Company's (DEC) aim is:

> To be recognised as the best provider of quality, integrated information systems, networks and services to support customers worldwide.

3M's UK group mission is:

> To provide and deliver on time products and services that conform to agreed specifications in line with customer requirements. In line with the corporate quality policy these products and services must be useful, safe, reliable, environmentally acceptable and be truthfully represented in their packaging. All operations will be managed with the total quality emphasis philosophy focusing on optimised operations principles, unit cost control and the maintenance of a safe working environment.
>
> All employees will be responsible for the quality of their own work and will be encouraged to exercise their initiative in search of continuous improvement.

Most of these are so boring that it is difficult to imagine anyone being inspired, and when you look at dozens the quality that is lacking is – imagination!

HOW TO ESTABLISH A CULTURE 'STATEMENT'

What all of this demonstrates, apart from lack of imagination, is that there is no single pattern, and all any company can do is what is right for it in its circumstances. The best (almost by definition) are inspirational, but make it too trite and it easily turns into a short-lived advertising slogan. Make it too long and it becomes a great turn off. Not every organisation can find three words which achieve all the objectives but, for the ascendant organisation, it is possible to develop an effective culture statement provided it *is* recognised that the statement by itself changes very little, although the process of getting there can be helpful.

The process begins by recognising that no organisation has a *right* to expect its staff to share its values or cultures and the executive group should not presume to speak about 'We' unless there is a genuine basis for it. A 1991 survey by Ingersoll Engineers of 150 companies found that 80 per cent had mission statements but in 89 per cent of cases they were written either by the chief executive personally or by senior management (Ingersoll, 1991). An organisation is not a family. 'We are all one family here' is one of the most hypocritical of business slogans. No children choose their family but, in the vast majority of cases, know that they will stick together and support each other in both the good times and the bad. An individual *chooses* to join an organisation and the organisation *selects* the individual. Breaking up is not hard to do.

The actual written statement, if there is to be one, can best be shaped if a wide range of people are able to participate in the process. There is no magic formula for this. Usually someone has to prepare an initial draft which should then be shared with a small group. The structure of that group will vary. It may comprise people at the top, representatives from all business units or functions, a diagonal slice, the trade unions, or any combination. If you have 'non-core' staff, bring them into the process, for they will certainly have a different focus. The important point is that many heads are better than one and by sharing, the ownership process begins. Some organisations may wish to take the sharing process even further and include a wider and deeper representative sample. Depending on size some may be able to involve the whole organisation. The incredible thing is that the senior executives, who probably thought they could do a good job by themselves, will find that the eventual document is better than anything they could have produced in isolation and they will also find that the broad principles they hold dear are shared by the vast majority of people. The ownership process will have taken a further step.

But during this process do not aim for a lowest common denominator statement on which everyone can readily agree, because it does not really require anything of them. A mission is not 'motherhood and apple pie'. It must inspire, challenge and motivate. It must require effort to achieve successfully so that people know something is demanded of them and it is worth striving for. Keep it short. It is easy to write long statements in which people subsequently get lost. It is incredibly difficult to be short, concise, meaningful and inspirational but the effort is worth it. But writing it down achieves very little, especially if it is imposed from the top.

True success comes with ownership by all. The ascendant culture cannot be imposed, unlike the culture of the autocrat. A culture in which, 'Everyone is committed to the success of the enterprise and which recognises and values the contribution of all' is not achieved by decree. To some, such a culture can only result from indoctrination and is seen pejoratively. To others it is the highest objective than can possibly be attained, but in either case ownership comes slowly as a result of the actions and behaviour of people, especially those in senior positions.

Six months after saying 'The last thing IBM needs right now is a vision' Lou Gerstner published his eight IBM Principles:

1. The market place is the driving force behind everything we do.
2. At our core we are a technology company with an overriding commitment to quality.
3. Our primary measures of success are customer satisfaction and shareholder value.
4. We operate as an entrepreneurial organisation with a minimum of bureaucracy and a never-ending focus on productivity.
5. We never lose sight of our strategic vision.
6. We think and act with a sense of urgency.
7. Outstanding, dedicated people make it all happen, particularly when they work together as a team.
8. We are sensitive to the needs of all employees and to the communities in which we operate.

These principles bear all the hallmarks of everything that is wrong. They were developed at the centre and handed down. They are written in the present tense as though they are already achieved. The chairman is speaking on behalf of all the company. Everything is written in terms of 'We', except that in no. 7, '*they* work together as a team' [my emphasis]. Perhaps the chairman is the only person who is not outstanding, dedicated and a member of the team! When IBM staff saw, 'We operate . . . with a minimum of bureaucracy' more than one commented that this brought a wry smile to a few faces. In a company that has gone through the traumas experienced by IBM the phraseology does not suggest it has learned a great deal about motivating people in the tough times! However, in addressing meetings of employees Lou Gerstner put the message more succinctly and much better, 'We don't move fast enough in this company. This is an industry in which success goes to the swift, more than to the smart. We've got to become more nimble, entrepreneurial, focused, customer driven. We must become a principle-based company, rather than a procedural-based company' (*Financial Times*, 28 March 1994). Lou Gerstner was demonstrating leadership of a style which does not need a lot of speeches. 'My choice in everything is to say nothing and go do it.' And he got closer to reflecting a real culture than in any written document. By the end of the first quarter of 1994 IBM, primarily through cost cutting, was making an operating profit.

To a great extent the culture of an organisation depends on its leadership and management. To this we now turn and later in Chapter 15 will consider the whole culture change process.

7 Leading the Ascendant Organisation

A leader is best when people barely know that he exists.
Not so good when people obey and acclaim him,
Worst when they despise him.
'Fail to honour people,
They fail to honour you.'

But of a good leader, who talks little,
When his work is done, his aim fulfilled,
They will all say,
'We did this ourselves.'

(Lao-Tzu, 6th century BC)

We need to distinguish between leadership and management, between being a leader and being a boss, between leadership at the top and leadership throughout the organisation, and between authority and authoritarianism.

LEADERSHIP AT THE TOP

Around 1990, Anglia Television produced a series on Leadership, using examples from the armed forces, the church, politics and business. They questioned me on the role of the supervisor and at the end of a lengthy interview threw the unexpected ball, 'What do you think is the difference between leadership and management?' My top of the head response was something like, 'Management is about the organisation and development of resources, whereas leadership is about getting people to do what you want them to do because they want to do it for you.' At the time I felt this was a reasonably good response.

Most writing on business leadership concentrates on the inspirers and transformers. Books are written by or about Lee Iacocca, Jack Welch, Ricardo Semler, Anita Roddick and John Harvey-Jones and often seem to suggest that leadership exists only at the very top and that it is only colourful personalities who make good copy. Or that it is only transformational leadership that counts. Although the top leader is critical to the success of the organisation, can set its tone and sometimes transform its values, such leaders, working alone, achieve nothing. *Leaders achieve results by working with and through people and exist at all levels of the organisation.* Many executives, managers, supervisors and operators are highly effective leaders of their own part of the organisation but may not have the capability of taking the step that transforms them into general managers. But that does not make them any less effective in the job they do. The greatest risk for an effective leader is to be surrounded by mediocrity and the greatest responsibility is to appoint good people.

In my own experience the most common traits exhibited by leaders who are considered successful in a traditional organisation are deep personal ambition, an ability to think ahead and a drive to ensure that their ambitions, both personal and business, are realised. Is this what is needed in the ascendant organisation? The answer is partly yes and partly no.

Most current definitions of leadership are about creating the vision or setting the direction. Murray Steele and Ann Brown have succinctly said, 'Leadership is about creating the conditions where people can perform to their potential in a fashion with which both they and their organisation are comfortable. It is about creating a vision of the organisation then articulating it so that others believe in the vision and successfully implement it' (Steele and Brown, 1990, p. 12).

This suggests a constructive, forward-thinking approach, but consider an alternative. Sir Neville Bowman-Shaw, chairman and joint owner with his brother of Lancer Boss, a fork lift truck manufacturer, tells the story of his 1987 meeting with the workers of a recently purchased Spanish company in the grip of the unions and losing money. Addressing the 400 employees he said, 'If you're going to bugger around I'll close the f– – – – – – g factory! Follow me, and we'll be able to take the company out of the trouble. Screw it up, and we'll close it down. Make up your bloody minds' (*Works Management*, January 1992). The Bowman-Shaws were autocratic leaders and did not disguise their them-and-us management style. In their British factory, works managers changed about once every six months because they were not allowed to run the job, and labour turnover reached 30 per cent in 1989 (*Works Management*, September 1994). As one manager said, 'There was so much fear in the place. Everyone had a plan but not necessarily the same plan!' In 1993 the German banks withdrew financial support; in April 1994 Jungheinrich of Germany acquired the British company. Six months later every possible performance indicator had improved dramatically, including labour turnover down to 8 per cent and absenteeism down to 3 per cent.

In Spain, Sir Neville was seen to act both as an autocratic and a transformational leader, and often in such situations it is a question of 'change or die'. There have been numerous such examples and in a certain way it makes life easier. At least the alternatives are clear. But such a confrontation style can only last for a short time. Sir Michael Edwardes at British Leyland from 1977 to 1982 was able to confront the extremists and win, and in so doing cleared the ground on which others were subsequently able to lay the foundation. Now, in the 1990s, his successors have constructed a successful company, The Rover Group. In 1974 I was put into the Ford Dagenham Metal Stamping and Body plant with the clear brief, 'Get back management control!' These simple messages focus one's activities and can be great fun, but in the long term it is no way to run a company!

Bill Hewlett, founder of Hewlett–Packard, had a better approach and would I am sure echo Lao-Tzu, 'What is the Hewlett–Packard way? I feel that in general terms it is the policies and actions that flow from the belief that men and women want to do a good job, a creative job, and that if they are provided with the proper environment, they will do so.'

An important responsibility of a leader, which is often alluded to but not specifically stated, is the requirement to *align the organisation, to ensure that all its components are pointing in the same direction.* The effective team leader begins with the individual and seeks to ensure that all are working together to achieve the same objectives. The leader of the whole organisation not only has to pull together his or her immediate team but also, by working through others and by direct intervention when necessary, has to ensure that all the organisational units are working together to achieve the shared objectives.

No doubt we have all seen and been part of organisations in which the left hand does not know what the right hand is doing or, if it does, either ignores it or seeks to go in a totally different direction. Often there is virtual warfare between different parts of an organisation. Organisations with multiple objectives allow individual units to concentrate on those aspects *they* consider important and if they achieve their priorities at the expense of others, so be it. It is not their fault that others have failed. That is why Federal Express's 'Absolutely, Positively, Overnight' is so good. It provides a focus with which all can identify. Many functions erect Chinese walls, barely speaking to each other. That is why the concepts of process re-engineering are valuable. They force the organisation to concentrate on the essential flows and break down the functional chimneys. Whatever the organisational structure or the sector in which it operates it is the responsibility of the leader to break down the divisions, share objectives, get everyone working together; in short, to align the organisation.

Speaking to a group of Nissan managers in August 1990, Jan Carlzon, President of Scandinavian Airlines said:

> The role of the leader will be that of a visionary, a strategic leader, who gives the objectives, who guides the way to reach those objectives. The formal organisation then educates and communicates and informs the people about what is the objective and what is the strategy so that people can take responsibility . . . the person who has total information cannot escape responsibility.

But the most difficult task for an executive is genuinely to devolve responsibility. The worst thing that can happen is for the boss to say something like, 'Right, this is now your ship, get on with it . . . . but could you just let me know on a weekly/monthly basis what you are up to; maybe we can have lunch together a couple of times a month.' That is sending out mixed messages. It confuses responsibility and authority and tells the subordinate that he or she is not really trusted. It is important to remember, however, that even if the leadership role changes from 'controller' to 'facilitator', the leader remains accountable for the performance of subordinates. The alternative is abdication of responsibility, and it is so easy for the lazy manager to drift from control to abdication.

The serious point is that it takes great confidence in one's own abilities and in the abilities of one's staff not to want to know what is going on all the time and not to feel threatened if your boss has to go to a subordinate to find the answer to a question. I like to think I am a genuine devolver. My philosophy is to appoint good people and let them get on and run their part of the organisation within the shared values. I do not require detailed reports on every aspect of their business, only on the key performance indicators, and rely on the judgement of the managers to let me know whatever else they consider important for me to know. But I am available for consultation when needed and will choose to become involved in any area which needs a prod. At the same time a golden rule is 'No nasty surprises'. If there is bad news coming, let me know early so that I can decide if I wish to become involved. I will talk to anyone without feeling that I have to go through the directors or managers, and am sure that no-one feels threatened by this.

Such an approach, which is compatible with the company's philosophy permeates the organisation – but it can lead to the occasional difficulty: 'You should have told me earlier' or, 'You should have known that'. However, the benefits of genuinely devolving responsibility – allowing people to develop and grow as individuals – far outweigh the occasional embarrassment. Such an approach allows the leader to concentrate on those aspects of the business he or she judges to be important. That, hopefully, is the difference between being a leader and being a boss.

There is no single pattern of leadership, although numerous researchers have sought to develop models and the fact that there are so many confirms that life is not simple. However, it is not unreasonable to seek to point to some behaviours and characteristics that can make for success in an ascendant organisation (recognising of course that someone will come along who will break all the rules and be totally successful). The following is based on observation and experience.

HOW TO LEAD THE ASCENDANT ORGANISATION

The leader who achieves long-term success in the ascendant organisation is likely to possess many characteristics which I divide into personal attributes, strategic perspective, communication and achievement.

Personal attributes

- Possesses a good level of general intelligence which can be applied in specific situations
- Possesses a good breadth of knowledge which can be applied in specific situations
- Has an empathy with people at all levels
- Focuses on those aspects of the business which are critical for success
- Analyses logically, thinks rationally
- Acts intuitively – and is right (most of the time)
- Has uncompromising, high levels of personal integrity, honesty and ethical standards and ensures that anything less is unacceptable throughout the organisation
- Has the wisdom to know when to do nothing
- Incorporates high energy, self-motivation, determination, courage and enthusiasm – in short, passion

All of these could be said to be innate and I do not wish to enter into the nature versus nurture debate. We all start with a certain level of capability and whereas I could never be an Olympic downhill ski champion, my own basic ability has, with practice and enthusiasm, helped me to conquer runs that I once believed impossible. Virtually all studies show that mental capabilities can similarly be developed, and with use comes confidence.

What matters is not simply having high levels of intelligence and knowledge but the ability to cut through the undergrowth and apply those talents to specific situations. *Applied* intelligence and knowledge are what matter. Equally if not more important is instinct – the gut feel to *know* what is right or to weigh up the odds, take a risk, and be right! Some may have this capability from an early age and they become the successful young entrepreneurs. Others take years to acquire it. Once when asked by a Japanese, Masaharu Futami, how I knew the appropriate response to a difficult situation, my reply was, '25 years of experience'. Intuition, for most of us, comes with experience and allows us to go from A to Z in almost one leap, automatically analysing the potential problems and alternative solutions found in steps B to Y.

Another Japanese, Hideaki Hirano, on ending his assignment in the UK, explained that a British trait he had learned to value was, 'Wait and see what happens.' Faced with a complex negotiation or problem, his upbringing had taught him to spend hours analysing numerous alternatives, preparing vast amounts of documentation. It was important to be seen to be doing something. 'But', he said, 'your approach of sometimes deliberately doing nothing, sitting back waiting, perhaps, for the problem to go away or for your opponent's move and then reacting instinctively is something we Japanese should learn.' We decided to call it *positive non-action*, and felt that it was better than negative non-action in which you do nothing simply because you cannot think of anything to do; and very much better than negative action in which you do something, whether right or wrong, simply because you need to be seen to be doing something!

Empathy with people at all levels is not usually on lists of leadership qualities but in the ascendant organisation it is critical. It means that leaders have a real understanding of the problems affecting others, how they feel and how they see the issues affecting them. Above all it means *caring*, not in a superficial, 'people are our greatest asset' way, nor in believing they can do no wrong, but just because it is right. Empathy results in leaders *understanding* the impact of their decisions on people and taking actions which support constructive relationships, whether it is the elimination of illogical differences in treatment or simply talking with people at the grass roots level in a way which reinforces their importance.

In May 1994 we experienced a classic example of empathy within Nissan. Our Executive Committee discussed a proposal for 1995 vacations. The Engineering Department planned a one-week shutdown in Easter 1995, necessary in their view to undertake major facility changes. Managing Director, Ian Gibson and I knew this would be unpopular with the staff who had co-operated fully in changed vacation dates in 1994 due to the recession. Ian made it clear that whereas staff did not like but understood why, in 1994, their vacation arrangements had been changed, in 1995 they would not like and would *not* understand. 'We had', he said, 'tremendous co-operation in 1994, and we cannot abuse that co-operation in 1995.' This was not a cynical, hard bitten view but a genuine belief that we had to do the right thing by the staff. The Engineering Department found a way.

Strategic perspective

- aligns the organisation
- develops a vision based on a strategic perspective rising above immediate problems
- has a concern for *all* stakeholders
- relates goals and actions to that vision and strategy
- instinctively feels for the impact of that vision on people
- constantly challenges the status quo
- has the determination to get there

The leader of an organisation has to be able to project several years ahead, to determine where it is going, how it will get there and the type of organisation it should be. At all times the short-term goals and actions need to be clearly related to the long term. But the vision is no good without the determination. In the tough times it will be the leader's responsibility to watch for the long-term goal and while there may be detours, and the goal may well have to be modified, the leader remains responsible.

Aligning the organisation is of critical importance. In simple terms this means that all parts of the organisation are working together to achieve the same objectives. But it does not happen by chance. First, the goals and objectives must be understood and shared and secondly, each part must ensure that its activities complement those of others and do not work in opposition. This does not mean that everyone behaves in exactly the same way but, as we have seen, in the ascendant organisation there are no Chinese walls and it is the leader's task to ensure that none arise.

In addition, the leader has continually to be challenging the organisation to improve. New ways to exploit technology, new approaches to the market and product development, new ways of motivating staff. Is the organisation right for tomorrow's environment? Few would go as far as Tom Peter's hyperbole, 'If you aren't reorganising pretty substantially once every six to twelve months, you're probably out of step with the times', but when he adds, 'The most efficient and effective route to bold change is the participation of everyone, every day, in incremental change' (Peters, 1988), I applaud him.

The leader of the ascendant organisation is also receptive to new ideas. However much I denigrate the 'instant experts', there is always value in going to the original source, whether it is a book or an organisation. Often they simply re-package things we are already doing (as might this book). Rarely is there anything which is totally new but a new perspective on an old concept can spark ideas which generate change. Hammer and Champy's *Reengineering the Corporation* presents little that is really new, based as it is on what many are already doing, but it causes people to think. It is not about new applications for information technology or 'downsizing' as the instant experts would have us believe, but about changing your mindset. Shortly I shall describe giving back to the first line supervisor many of the processes that over the years the functional specialists have taken to themselves. That requires a mindset change.

Communication

- inspires, enthuses and motivates others
- communicates the vision and strategy and creates the conditions which enable everyone to share it, primarily by asking them to contribute to it
- is a member of the team as well as leader of it
- recognises and responds to the needs and feelings of others
- relaxes and make others feel relaxed
- has respect for others, values their contribution and listens to and learns from them
- communicates in the appropriate way at all levels
- explicitly recognises the achievement of others, helps them through their shortcomings but takes decisive action when necessary

None of this is about the *techniques* of communication. Techniques are not difficult to learn. Real communication is about relating to people, respecting them for what they are and enabling them to develop into what they might become. The gift of feeling comfortable with people and making them feel at ease with you can be developed but some never achieve it. It is communication of this type, more than anything else, that results in true leadership in the ascendant organisation – people doing things for you and the organisation because they want to. People have to feel that their leader *cares*, not simply about the bottom line results but about them as individuals.

Being accepted as a member of the team is of vital importance. If people at all levels in the organisation do not feel that the leader is on the same side as them, that they are not *all* working to the same objectives, the critical trust and empathy will never develop. The transformational or inspirational leader may stand outside the team and may get things done but without making friends. Often such a person will get rid of those who do not agree. Margaret Thatcher was a transformational leader but no one ever suggested she was a member of the team. When she ran into difficulties, few were willing to forgive her excesses.

But it does not mean being soft: in fact it is often easier to take the hard line and get rid of problem people than to spend long periods seeking to correct and improve. However if there is no improvement then, after due process, the required action has to be taken. I once explained to a bishop, who was concerned about the performance of a parish priest, that he was doing no one any favours, least of all the parishioners, if he did not tackle the problem. Often, poor performers know they are failing and it comes as a relief when their boss finally communicates the concerns.

Achievement

- sets high performance and behavioural standards and objectives and leads by example
- is committed to growth
- is not satisfied with existing high standards, seeks improvements and better ways of doing things
- calculates risks and takes decisive action when required
- genuinely devolves responsibility, authority and accountability throughout the organisation
- assesses and measures achievement levels, sometimes objectively, sometimes intuitively
- is concerned with the 'how'

The leader of the ascendant organisation is results oriented and is never satisfied with today's standards. Personal effort is high and seen to be so, but these leaders recognise that it is only through others that sustainable achievement is developed. Teamworking is paramount.

The leader of the ascendant organisation must also be concerned with the processes, attitudes and relationships within the organisation – the 'how'. It is the easiest thing in the world for people at the lower levels, where the task is often paramount, to become so narrowly focused that they forget about the culture of the organisation. And it is the leader who has to pull them back. *It is easy for the tools of management to become the ends of management* but part of being an ascendant organisation is to *care* about the way you do things.

Perhaps the most important ability a leader can possess is:

> *Have the wisdom and judgement to employ good people and give them headroom.*

Richard Branson, Chairman of Virgin Atlantic Airways, recognises this. Speaking at the annual convention of the Institute of Directors in 1993, he said of his recipe for business success:

> The basic principles are that people matter and that small is beautiful . . . shape the enterprise around the people . . . plan and operate the enterprise so as to enable its key assets, its people, to work at their very best. This governs the priorities of the business, its size and style. Our priorities in managing the business do not appear in most management textbooks or most British companies. We give top priority to the interests of our staff; we give second priority to the interests of our customers; and third priority to the interests of our shareholders. Working backwards, the interests of our shareholders depend upon high levels of customer satisfaction, which enable us to attract and retain passengers in the face of intense competition. We know that the customer's satisfaction which generates all-important word-of-mouth recommendations and fosters repeat purchase, depends in particular upon high standards of service (and this) depends upon happy staff, who are proud of the company they work for. That is why the interests of our people must come first.

Many will disagree with the way Richard Branson puts his argument, and it is somewhat circular, but the essential point is that a good leader creates good followers. There are no bad soldiers, only bad generals. As we shall see in detail as we progress through Part II, the leader does not actually have to have a precise vision from the beginning. The leader's responsibility is to provide the spark which defines the broad direction and creates the environment in which all the people in the organisation can put flesh on to the bones, and often make fundamental contributions to the direction of the organisation and the detail of needed change.

In the ascendant organisation, leaders at all levels are *made*; in fact the very style of the organisation makes such development inevitable. There is not one of these characteristics that does not rub off on to everyone in the organisation and, apart from those few mavericks who succeed by being totally different, most of us learn from the behaviour and example of people we admire. When that behaviour devolves responsibility and authority, genuinely communicates, values the contribution of everyone and encourages continuous improvement, it becomes self-reinforcing and allows everyone the room and opportunity to grow. Douglas McGregor and Fred Herzberg would be proud!

Are these qualities displayed? A survey into the use of time conducted by Andy Garnett of The Industrial Society found that 135 directors and managers considered their top ten time wasters to be:

- telephone interruptions
- people dropping by
- poor information exchange between departments
- problems with computer 'techno-failure'
- changed priorities caused by colleagues
- lack of organisational planning
- poor listening skills of others
- inappropriate organisation structure
- moving goal posts
- putting things right that were not right first time

This list almost needs no comment: without exception they blame others for their failings. How can executives have the nerve to regard talking to people as the top two time-wasters while rating 'Poor listening skills of others' as seventh? It suggests an inability to appreciate the true role of leadership. It also suggests that many are a long way from the characteristics that make for success in the ascendant organisation.

They are not leaders, they are bosses. They are not *transformers*, they are *conformers*. They are people who resist rather than encourage change and are probably the most difficult group to weld into a team.

MANAGING

Recall my response to Anglia Television, 'Management is about the organisation and development of resources, whereas leadership is about getting people to do what you want them to do because they want to do it for you.' Separating – somewhat artificially – the management from the leadership roles, management is broadly about the formulation of policy, the organisation and co-ordination of work, the allocation of tasks, development of staff and determination of responsibility and ensuring that performance is in line with requirements. It is more about the present than the future and is inward-looking rather than outward-looking – doing things right rather than doing the right things. Henri Fayol described this as 'planning, organising, co-ordinating and controlling.'

Fayol, however, told us very little about what managers actually do and subsequent research by Henry Mintzberg led him to the conclusion that managers' activities are characterised by, 'Brevity, variety and discontinuity and that they are strongly oriented towards action and dislike reflective activities.' They prefer the verbal media, that is, telephone calls and meetings, to any other and much of their accumulated programs – to schedule time, process information, make decisions and so on – 'remains locked deep inside their brains' (Mintzberg, 1975).

There are dozens of models of management but the truth is that, to be successful, managers must both manage and lead. Leaders, also, must be able to manage, or at least be surrounded by people who can. A manager who cannot lead is a waste of space and money!

Managers and supervisors must be accountable for what they do and for what happens in their part of the organisation. Businesses are not democracies. While considerable responsibility and authority can be devolved, accountability must be clearly defined. The first line supervisor may assign an individual to be responsible for a manufacturing task and give considerable authority to that person to allow the job to be properly performed, but accountability cannot be devolved. If it goes wrong, it is the supervisor who is to blame, not the individual. The managerial role is therefore performed when an individual is held *accountable* for his or her own actions *and* for the actions of others. In seeking to determine if there are any managerial characteristics specific to the ascendant organisation the critical issue to consider is how far down the line accountability is passed. The ascendant organisation has positive leadership and devolved accountability at all levels.

The Japanese, while having much in common with the West, do have some different perspectives on the philosophy and practice of management. Many of these differences are illustrated throughout this book, but some others do sit most comfortably at this point.

A Japanese manager regards himself as a stage in a time continuum. When assigned to a new position he must finish what his predecessor left unfinished, take initiatives of his own and then lay the foundations for his successor. Yoshio Hatakeyama, President of the Japan Management Association, writing *for* Japanese managers, said of this middle stage:

> He must gather data and figures and learn the opinions of his staff and the desires of his superiors. He must weigh the entire situation of the organisation, decide what there is to be done, win the approval of all involved and strike while the iron is hot – that is, within his first three months in the new position. (Hatakeyama, 1985, p. 11)

On laying the groundwork for the successor he says:

> Laying strategic groundwork for one's successors entails spotting potential problems in their early stages and taking whatever action is necessary, either to begin solving them or to prepare for their eventual solution. In neither case will a manager see the results of these efforts during his own time on the job. Nevertheless it is the duty of every manager to effect a chronological division of labour – that is leave his successor an environment in which he can work efficiently. (p. 11)

All Western managers, whatever their organisation type, should take on board Mr Hatakeyama's precepts.

How many Western managers do we know who have built their career on the basis of, 'Get out before found out'? The Japanese, because they anticipate being with the company throughout their working life, know that they will almost certainly work with their successor again. They cannot be seen to have left the job in a poor condition. But they do wish to be seen to have made a contribution, so their objective is always to make at least one significant and lasting contribution in each position; a contribution that will be recognised by their peers as having added to the well-being of the organisation.

The leadership attributes described in this chapter permeate all levels in the ascendant organisation. Rather than describe minute differences at each level of the hierarchy, I shall now turn to the group who leads and manages at the sharp end of the business, the first line supervisors.

LEADERSHIP IN THE FRONT LINE

Whatever the attitudes of the top leadership, it is the people in the middle of the organisation, in particular the supervisors, who make things happen. Top managers can pontificate and inspire all they want but unless they get the supervisors on their side they will fail. *Supervisors, if carefully selected, well-trained, highly motivated and given the status and pay appropriate to being, 'the professional at managing the processes and the people' can make more difference to the long-term success of the organisation than any group other than top management. And even here it is the supervisor who delivers top management's policies in the workplace.* (*Note*: I use the term 'supervisor' to denote the first line of management. Often in traditional companies the 'foreman' is not even regarded as part of management. In other, delayered, companies this person may be called a team leader or manager and have anything from five to 100 direct reports. Where cell manufacturing has been introduced the title may be group leader or cell leader.)

Of all industrial nations, Germany has most developed the role and training of the first line supervisor. The *Meister* is an occupation which has its origins in the craft guilds of the middle ages (*Handwerkmeister*) but which has adapted to the requirements of modern industry (*Industriemeister*). The *Meister* in industry is responsible not only for supervising daily production but also for the training of apprentices; in fact, no firm can engage an apprentice without also employing a *Meister* with relevant qualifications to provide that training. *Meister* training takes up to 1000 hours of instruction spread over two to three years. It covers not only people management techniques but also technology, business management and law and instructional techniques, based on the not unreasonable assumption that the potential *Meister* has to be trained how to train! Other nations might do worse than heed this obvious point!

In the Anglo–Saxon world of Britain and the USA though, the role of the supervisor has always been uneasy. Located in the centre of an adversarial relationship, he or she has always been 'the pig in the middle'. Talk to any group of supervisors and you will hear a predictable tale of woe. 'I've never really been trained for the job. One day I was an operator, the next day a supervisor having to tell my mates what to do.' 'Nobody tells me anything, the unions know first.' 'I get kicked around by management, by the unions and if the lads are having an off day they take it out on me.' 'The management makes decisions without consulting me and I'm left to carry them out.' 'If I try to discipline someone, the personnel department doesn't support me.' 'Those 25-year olds from the

Finance Department keep coming down and make me justify every minor overrun against a budget which I had no say in fixing.' 'If I want to change something, the management doesn't listen because it costs too much and the lads don't listen because they won't change anyway.' This list could go on and on and, while making allowances for some degree of frustration, I have heard such a litany so often that I have no doubt that these views are commonplace and justified. As far as production supervisors are concerned, many companies are in a vicious downward spiral of low responsibility, low authority, low accountability and low pay. Good people avoid the job.

If that seems somewhat emotional, it is unfortunately a reflection of the truth.

F. W. Taylor had something to say about the supervisor. He saw the foreman's tasks as being divided between the planning department and the expert teachers (the functional foremen) . The planning department was responsible for the detailed written instructions on how best to do a job. The planning staff determined the tooling, the best and quickest motions and the timetable. It was the task of the functional foremen to see that the operators understood and carried out these instructions. But, said Taylor, 'Under functional management, the old fashioned single foreman is superseded by eight different men, acting as agents for the planning department.' (I only ever found seven!) The foremens' roles were divided as follows:

- *inspector*, who ensures the instructions are understood and teaches the operator to do work of the right quality
- *gangboss*, who teaches the operator how to set up the machine and do the job in the quickest way
- *speed boss*, who sees that the machine is run at the best speed and proper tools are used
- *repair boss*, who is responsible for the maintenance of the machine
- *time clerk*, who is responsible for pay, reports and returns
- *route clerk*, who makes sure that work is done in the correct order and is properly moved from one place to another
- *disciplinarian*, who handles the operator if he gets into trouble with his various bosses. (Taylor, 1911, pp. 123–5)

As is often the case, Taylor was only partially correct. His description of the different roles of functional foremen encapsulated the control elements of the task. But in separating the planning from the doing and then applying the concept of division of labour to what should be a unified task, he managed to destroy any possibility of effectively controlling the workplace. Further, he totally neglected the motivating role of the supervisor. No team can have seven leaders!

THE SUPERVISOR IN THE ASCENDANT ORGANISATION

Contrast this with best practice in the ascendant organisation *where appointment to the position of supervisor is seen as the beginning of a career, not the end of it.*

An unpublished paper prepared for the National Economic Development Office (NEDO, 1990) studied five companies considered to exhibit best practice in engineering organisations. These companies were Acco Cable Controls, British Aerospace, TG Brooks, X Ltd (an engine systems and components company) and Nissan. At British Aerospace, supervisors were appointed to replace four previous grades (senior supervisor, supervisor, senior foreman and foreman) and are expected to take on managerial responsibility for motivating employees to achieve the required standards of quality, timeliness and cost. The job description also involves them in the recruitment, development and training of staff, communications, leadership, resource management and requires of them the qualities of judgement, interpersonal skills, decisiveness, crisis management and critical awareness. Such a listing would more likely qualify someone for the chairman's role – if such attributes were a common requirement for such positions!

The NEDO study found that best practice companies sought to improve performance by combining advanced manufacturing technology with a desire to improve the competence and status of supervision. Within these companies they found that supervisors fulfilled a number of similar roles:

- technical leadership, quality and continuous improvement responsibilities
- work allocation, standard operations and supply/delivery of materials
- housekeeping, maintenance and health and safety
- recruiting, developing, appraising and training staff
- communication, motivating and team building
- personnel, disciplinary and industrial relations duties

In short, gaining the commitment of the workforce and control of the processes which is necessary to secure long-term success.

The Nissan supervisor's job is, perhaps, bigger than any similar job anywhere else in the world. The overall company objective is, 'To build profitably the highest quality car sold in Europe' and to achieve this the supervisor has to meet strict quality and production objectives. Everything else contributes to these ends. Responsibilities include:

- selecting the team
- training, skill measurement and staff development
- communication, visual management
- work allocation and line balancing
- establishment, control and improvement of the standard operation
- operator care
- productivity improvement
- material management
- cost control and improvement
- quality control and improvement
- housekeeping
- abnormality control, problem-solving
- total productive maintenance
- health and safety
- employee relations, discipline
- input into new models
- project work and studies

Much of this is discussed elsewhere, but some aspects are worthy of a expansion at this time.

Selecting the team

While the complex recruitment process is administered by the personnel department, the supervisor plays a vital and continuing role. Supervisors are present at every stage – the aptitude tests; the practical skill tests; they take the candidates into the working environment allowing them to assess the candidate in both the physical task and with the rest of the team (this also allows the candidate to assess the job and possible future team mates); they conduct the final interviews, make the final decision and, wherever possible, make the final job offer, face to face. While the personnel department follows up with the written job offer, what really counts is the personal, mutual commitment of the supervisor and the candidate. The supervisor can blame no one else for the selection decision and the candidate has a good feeling towards the person who made the job offer. That is not a bad start to the team-building process! Honda, incidentally, takes a different approach. Supervisors make the selection decision but they select for the company as a whole, not for the individual section. The critical points are *who* makes the decision and on what grounds. When the culture of the organisation is genuinely shared, the supervisors, and anyone else involved in recruitment, are able to select those who they feel will have an empathy with that culture. It then becomes self-reinforcing. This does not mean selecting clones but people who want to be treated as individuals and who are able to make individual contributions within a team environment. Everyone is different.

Being part of the team

The supervisor's desk is in the team meeting area (usually a clearly defined area about 8 × 4 metres). In this area there is a large blue table surrounded by benches, individual lockers, a sink, tea/coffee-making facilities and often a microwave cooker and refrigerator. Some have managed to acquire easy chairs, others are attractively decorated. These areas belong to the team; they have their morning meetings, tea breaks and, if they wish, their lunch breaks in them. All documents are kept in these areas. The supervisor eats and drinks with the team and they often socialise together. *While the supervisor is expected to lead the team, they cannot lead unless they are accepted as part of it.*

Communication

All communication goes through the supervisor. If something is worth telling, it is worth telling quickly and the only way to do that is every day face to face. Thus Nissan has established the five-minute meeting that takes place every day at the start of shift. At these meetings the supervisor talks with the team about matters of the moment affecting that group. If there is no business to discuss, they can talk about the local soccer team; it does not matter. The important thing is that the team is together, talking together.

It also means that if there is occasionally the great message from on high, the mechanism is in place to handle it and can be initiated within minutes if needed. The team becomes used to hearing things from the supervisor and the grapevine has less credence. I hold no truck with those who say everyone must get exactly the same message at exactly the same time. It really does not matter if different groups get slightly different versions of a message. But it does matter that they are told what is important to them in a way that is appropriate for them. While occasionally this may lead to inconsistencies, this is a minor problem which can easily be corrected, compared with the major problem of delaying communication because the written word has to be precisely correct!

Skill measurement and staff training

One of the most difficult questions ever asked, was Toshiaki Tsuchiya's question to John Cushnaghan, then Nissan's Production Director. 'How do you *know* the operators have the right skill level?' After several attempts to come up with an acceptable response John realised that while we trained and assumed we knew, we did not truly *know*. From small acorns grow great oaks!

The great oak was the skill matrix and what we came to call the ILU system. See Figure 7.1.

This matrix is visually displayed in the meeting room, everyone knows their own assessed capabilities and the capabilities of others. It is a simple

Task / Employee	1	2	3	4	5	6	7	8 – 20
Ian Smith	□		L	□			U	
Peter Brown	I	□						
Mike Jones						U	I	
Ron Watson	□		U	□	L	I	□	
Jill Roper		I			□			
Frank Giles		□	L					
Mary Wilson					U		□	
Kevin Cope			U			□		
↓ 20								

Code: Tasks can be performed

I To the right quality

L Quality and in the standard time

U Quality, standard time, train others

□ Quality, standard time, train others and trouble shoot/improve the operation

Figure 7.1 The Nissan Skill Matrix

but extremely powerful tool which the supervisor is responsible for maintaining. Every section will have its own optimum mix. Where jobs are all very different it may be 'Every job to have three people capable of doing it and every person to know three jobs' Where jobs are only slightly different the mix may be much richer; where training takes a long time and familiarity is needed to maintain capability the mix may be thin; where tasks are physically demanding and frequent rotation is necessary the mix may be rich.

The optimum mix for a section can only be determined by that section. The supervisor is responsible and accountable for determining that mix and for ensuring that the team as a whole achieves the required level. The supervisor will also undertake much of the instruction, although on the job training is the responsibility of everyone.

Line balancing

Line balancing is one of the most intellectually demanding tasks and in most organisations is the responsibility of industrial engineers. In simple terms it means ensuring that for a given volume, production rate and staffing level the work of everyone within the section is balanced, that is, the workload is evenly spread, build constraints are properly accounted for and everything is done in the optimum order (while this may sound obvious, the practicalities are much more difficult). In order to achieve these objectives, work has to be moved between operators and sections and both shifts have to be in full agreement – otherwise the standard operation is not common. The responsibility requires a deep understanding both of the tasks and the psychology of work.

Cost control

Supervisors are fully involved in developing their budgets for controllable costs. This includes direct costs, for example, materials used in actually building the car; indirect costs, such as gloves, tools, disposable material and so on; scrap costs and control over time. They are responsible for achieving improvements in all areas of cost including productivity.

Quality

It is the responsibility of the supervisors to ensure the required quality is achieved and in the event of problems they need to understand the true cause, whether it be faulty parts, technical issues or operator or process error. Supervisors are expected to respond quickly to feedback from audit studies and implement an abnormality control process leading to countermeasures. It is their responsibility to decide whether or not to pull in other departments. They feed back concerns to the operators both as and when they arise and in relation to problems experienced on the other shift.

The supervisor is the 'professional at managing the production process' and as such is at exactly the same level in the hierarchy as the other professionals, the engineers, financial analysts, buyers, personnel officers and so on. What you cannot do is to emphasise the importance of the role and then pay them £5000 a year less than other professionals. To do so would send out all the wrong messages. It would also mean that the supervisor would earn only slightly more than the rest of the team and in many organisations, because of a loss of overtime pay, it is even possible for promotion to result in a pay reduction. In Nissan, in 1995 the difference in salaries between production operators and their supervisers exceeds £9000. While there is an intermediate step of Team Leader, the difference demonstrates the importance of the role, therefore the best people aim for it, they receive high responsibility, authority and accountability. You are then into a virtuous upward spiral of high calibre people, high pay, high responsibility. Our Production Director, Colin Dodge, still considers this one of the best decisions we ever made.

It must not be supposed that it is only large sophisticated companies that are able to go down this road: Tinsley Bridge Limited, a small manufacturer of truck springs, was born via a management buy out from British Steel Corporation. Following a visit to Nissan, TBL's Operations Director, David Roberts, was convinced they they needed to change their supervisors' roles if they were to survive.

They wanted to get their supervisors to become team leaders, leading and briefing their teams on each shift and taking responsibility for attendance and discipline, running each section as a business in its own right, ensuring that effective maintenance was performed and high quality standards achieved. But to get to this point TBL's supervisors needed to make a culture change. They needed to see the logic of the proposed working method and their place in it. Primarily, they had to recognise their own importance. TBL's managing director, Michael Webber, said, 'It was vital that the supervisors saw themselves as managers and what is more as the critical point of management that makes things happen.'

With this in mind, and knowing in general terms what they wanted, Webber and David Roberts involved me in seminars which followed the classic pattern of getting people to define everything that is wrong and then come up with their own solutions. It is imperative to give *ownership of change*. Said Michael Webber, 'If we'd just told them what we wanted, cold, it would not have worked. They had to own that definition themselves.' But as important was the conceptual change that was taking place. Webber summed it up: 'The idea of leadership had got lost along the way. They did not see their role as leading, helping, developing and defending their people. They saw it as doing what management told them to do. We had to do something about that. They are the cornerstone to all we're trying to achieve.'

TBL *has* succeeded – it is still alive and with the major recession in its industry that is no mean achievement. It is still trying to improve and while supervisor development is not the only answer, TBL is convinced that it has played a critical role.

There are now attempts to put a framework on this changing role of supervisors. In its final report on excellence in supervision the National Economic Development Office (1991) defined what it called the 'four pillars' of the supervisors' job:

1. **Technical leadership** – Sufficient technical competence to appreciate and deploy new technology.
2. **Processes and systems management** – The ability to apply modern manufacturing techniques to the workplace requires that the supervisor has an overview of the production processes and an understanding of how his/her section fits into that system.
3. **People management** – This involves the creation of a positive human resource environment through activities such as recruitment, motivation and maintaining discipline.
4. **Training and development** – The supervisor is ideally placed to identify and help the skills needs of business. This involves having instructional and counselling competences of a high order to help meet those initial and continuing skill needs.

Although the British government closed NEDO down in 1992, the Engineering Training Authority has since undertaken a detailed analysis and defined principle competences for each of these four pillars. While there is the danger of paralysis by analysis, at least a framework is in place, which, if used wisely, can provide the foundation for a step change in supervisor capability.

HOW TO CHANGE TO 'TEAMBUILDING SUPERVISORS'

How then do organisations move from having 'controlling' foremen to teambuilding supervisors? Before they are able to commence such a process they need first to effect a change in the managerial culture, but if they do then decide to attempt to change the supervisors' role they will find two major problems. First, the supervisors have been hired to behave in a totally different way and second, following from this, they may be the greatest resisters of change. As the existing supervisor group will be critical in delivering the change if *they* are not convinced, it will not happen. In talking to many companies I have generally found their estimates to be that 60–70 per cent of the existing staff will be capable of making the transition.

Therefore, in moving from the traditional role to that of supervisor in the ascendant organisation, I advocate the following process:

1. Top managers must establish their vision of where they wish to be in, say, five years time.
2. They must genuinely share this vision and, if it includes a changing role at first line level, this group in particular must be brought fully into the development process, as did Tinsley Bridge Ltd. If it is their idea they will 'own' it, and it will happen.
3. Give an absolute guarantee that no one will lose their employment with the company if they are not able to make the transition – even though they may need to change their job. If they subsequently wish to leave, make generous separation payments.
4. Allow all those who wish to be considered for the new role to have the opportunity.
5. Appoint some incumbents, promote from the shop floor and bring in people from outside. Make sure that they all are carefully selected using the same standards for all. Do not appoint second best simply because you need the numbers.
6. Provide comprehensive training to ensure they are fully equipped to handle the job in the new way and provide subsequent opportunities for continuous development.
7. Provide continuing management support. Behave in the way you talk. If you want your supervisors to involve their people make sure *you* involve *them*.
8. Genuinely treat your supervisors as 'professionals'. Continue to expect high capability and high performance and pay them as you do other professionals.

I conclude this chapter with what I have found to be one of the most powerful theoretical concepts. Arnold S. Tannenbaum wrote in 1966 that, 'Paradoxically, through participation, management increases its control by giving up some of its authority.' His great contribution was to argue that influence is not a zero sum game. Indeed, lower-level workers can have greater control over what they do without detracting from the control exercised by their boss – the 'influence pie' can be expanded. The traditional authoritarian supervisor–subordinate relationship relies on the exercise of control and results in resistance, and the supervisors believe that if they give more authority to subordinates their own responsibilities will reduce – the zero sum. However, if supervisors allow subordinates to exercise judgement, make improvements and problem solve, the subordinates' responsibilities increase, and at the same time so do the supervisors'.

When seeking to understand why supervisors resist giving more responsibility to their subordinates, one needs therefore to appreciate that the traditional supervisor believes in the zero sum concept. Meeting with a group of resisisters to change, drawing the 'influence pie' on a flip chart and showing how it can grow as the roles change achieves more in five minutes than hours of formal presentations or awareness exercises!

All of this leads to changes in behaviour and to this I now turn.

8 Ascendant Behaviour

If you have 11 workmen you will never win. If you have 11 artists, you will never win. It is important that the team complements each other and we have that.

(Eric Cantona, Soccer International,
Manchester United Football Club, 1993)

In modern industry the co-operation needed involves the spirit in which subordinates exercise their judgement. Beyond what commands can effect and supervision can control, beyond what incentives can induce and penalties prevent, there exists an exercise of discretion important even in relatively menial jobs, which managers of economic enterprises seek to enlist for the achievement of managerial ends.

(R. Bendix, *Work and Authority in Industry*, 1956)

The concepts and practices of single status, teamworking, flexibility, employee involvement and communication are inseparable. Take away one element and the whole thing falls down. However, for clarity, this chapter attempts the impossible and separates them.

'EVERYONE A FIRST CLASS CITIZEN'

For several years, when giving presentations, I used the phrase, 'You don't get a first class response from people who are treated as second class citizens.' In 1989, in South Africa, I addressed some 200 top executives and was very much aware that at that time in that country (prior to the release from prison of Nelson Mandela) it would have a political as well as an industrial meaning. I thought the worst that could happen would be that I would be told to leave and decided to use it. One of the most exhilarating moments of my life was when I was spontaneously applauded. It convinced me that at least among top business executives there was a mood for change.

In the ascendant organisation there is no place for second class citizens. This does not mean that everyone has the same status. Status is a state of mind, it is your perception of your position in relation to others. The chief executive has a different status in the organisation from a manager or a shop floor operator. Nothing is going to change that but it is possible to eliminate the illogical differences in the way people are treated. In the ascendant organisation there are no reserved car parking spaces, no separate dining rooms for executives and no separate entrances (unlike Japan, where all three exist). The ascendant organisation provides common terms and conditions of employment.

Once you start down the common conditions route there is no logical stopping place. There is no case for one group of people having longer vacations than others – even if there are additional days related to length of service, the same formula should apply to all. Sickness benefits, medical insurance, pension plans, retirement age should be the same for everyone. If managers do not 'clock-in' no one should. This can even extend to the reward system. While salaries will be different, the actual structure has to be transparent. This does not mean that the structure has to be exactly the same throughout the organisation but it does require that any differences be based on logic and not unduly benefit one particular group. Exotic bonus systems based on short-term financial indicators which reward top executives generously but give nothing to anyone outside the management group have no place in the ascendant organisation. The reward system must motivate *all* staff, not just a few.

One of the early decisions we made in Nissan was that everyone would have the same workwear. Many organisations provide free protective clothing on the shop floor but few extend this to office-based employees. Our reasoning was not that we wanted to impose uniformity but that we did not want to create artificial divisions – the 'suits' in the office separate from and 'superior' to the people on the shop floor. It was another message that we were seeking to be different. The British preoccupation with stiff collars, ties and suits is a remnant of past traditions. Continental Europeans are much more likely to wear casual attire and Americans in manufacturing frequently do not bother with ties. In Nissan in the UK, many who work in the offices do not wear ties, others do. It is up to them. The message, however, is, do not perpetuate internal distinctions through dress. How that is achieved is up to individual companies.

A similar dilemma arises with working hours. Does everyone have to be at work for exactly the same period every day? Should the organisation allow flexitime? If it believes in common terms and conditions of employment *and* flexibility, which takes precedence? What is indefensible is that office workers should have shorter working hours than manual workers and I know of no one who has been able to maintain a rational defence of such a practice. There is an argument however that office workers should be able to operate a flexitime arrangement, even if to do so on the shop floor would be more difficult. I come down on the side which says everyone should be treated the same. In a manufacturing environment, if it is imperative that shop floor workers all have to be in at 8.00 a.m it is galling for them to see the office workers arriving when they choose. Even with the best of intentions, the lot of the manual worker is usually worse than that of people in the office and to allow one group the choice and the other no choice can only increase the 'them and us' syndrome. If, technically, it is possible to apply flexitime to everyone there are other arguments which will determine its value, but harmony is better than division. In an organisation which is totally office-based, offering flexitime to everyone may be the right thing to do.

When discussing this issue of common conditions the area that often generates most heat is payment for absence, whether it be for sickness or lateness. Traditionally, white collar salaried staff have been paid when they are sick or late; blue collar hourly-paid staff have not – they are not to be trusted. 'If we pay them when they're sick our absence rates will go up.' There is no greater 'them and us' division.

It is true that blue collar absenteeism is generally higher than white collar, but when we note that those who are least likely to be paid when sick are most likely to be absent the correlation is negative, not positive. The truth is that attendance is much more determined by commitment than it is by health. The reason why many people come to work when they do not feel 100 per cent is because they have interesting jobs, they feel their contribution counts and they do not want to let down their team. The reason why others do not attend in similar circumstances is because they do not have interesting jobs, their contribution does not count and they have no team to let down. The attitude develops that, 'If I am away for a day I lose a day's pay, the company loses a day's work and that's a fair trade.'

The alternative, paying for absence, generates a totally different approach. It creates commitment, a sense of responsibility and an attitude of not wanting to let down the team. It also allows control. It gives the supervisor the right to chase up people who have not telephoned in with their reasons, to follow up with questions and to pick up patterns of absence. If people abuse the trust they can be subject to disciplinary action – perhaps loss of pay or eventually dismissal.

The ascendant organisation creates the total atmosphere in which attendance on time is regarded as the norm. It generates commitment combined with control, but it is commitment and control where it counts – at the interface between two people, not between an individual and some remote human resources department. In Nissan our absence rate has mostly been below 2 per cent!

Of course, if all you do is suddenly start paying for sickness, and do nothing else, absence rates will rise. Such changes need to be part of a total concept, but if anyone argues that, 'We can't afford to make this step', they have not fully thought through the consequences of 'second class citizenship.'

There are few organisations that go to the extremes and I would certainly not argue that anything less than total harmonisation prevents such organisations from being ascendant. Some will argue that improving benefits as you rise through the hierarchy is itself a motivator and this may well be true. The key test is one of perceived fairness. There is *no* case that a shop floor worker should have a worse sickness benefit scheme than a senior executive. Indeed, if there were a logical argument it would more likely be the other way round. However, if people perceive that they are being treated unfairly they will react adversely. You do not get a first class response from people who perceive they are treated as second class citizens.

But this also means that some of the perks that come the way of top executives have to be denied to them. I have lost count of the number of invitations I have received to participate in golf matches and have listened to all the usual 'reasons' about doing business on golf courses and cementing relationships. *Basically, they are no more than an excuse to have a pleasant day out of the office.* There is nothing that cannot be done on a golf course that cannot be achieved elsewhere and if your relationship with a supplier or customer is such that you enjoy each other's company then do so at weekends or take a day's vacation. The shop floor operators would be delighted to be given the opportunity, but rarely do such chances come their way. When we are looking at perceived fairness, there is no justification for such differences of treatment.

Common terms and conditions are necessary but not sufficient to achieve that first class response. They are the initial step which has to be taken by management as a symbol of the confidence in the new way. But if that is all management does, it will get all the costs and none of the potential benefits. The way people are treated in organisations is critical to their behaviour. Karl Albrecht put it best, 'The way employees feel is ultimately the way your customers feel, . . . Many organisations turn their employees into quality terrorists by the way they treat them' (Albrecht, 1992, p. 145). To ensure that there are no quality terrorists we need to delve further into behaviour.

TEAMWORKING

There is possibly more misunderstanding about the concept of teamworking than about almost any other aspect of the ascendant organisation. The word 'team' has a nice cosy feel about it, and in the senior executive's lexicon has replaced 'family' as the desirable glue of corporate relationships.

One of the great problems is to define the team. Much analysis is concerned with task teams, that is, a group with a relatively stable and long-term relationship, with each member providing specific skills, for example the operations management group running major installations. Other studies analyse project teams and task forces pulled together to undertake a specific task, perhaps with membership changing as the project progresses through its cycle. *Ad hoc* teams are pulled together for short periods to solve specific problems and many will cut across all other activities. *The real gains, however, come from the permanent group working together to build a product or provide a service.* If such groups can develop into real teams, the benefits continuously accrue to both the individuals and the organisation and preclude the need for special action when other teams are established for specific tasks.

The other great mistake is to confuse teamworking with work groups. *Teamworking is a culture; work groups are about structures.* The former does not automatically flow from the latter. Just because we call a group of people a team does not mean that they are a team. In 1987, John Stewart, Ford of Europe's Director of HRD, said to the European Metalworkers Federation, 'Ford's Mission Statement makes it clear we are a team.' So it must be true! Moving from a sequential manufacturing process to cell manufacturing does not in itself create a team, putting people together in a quality circle or problem-solving group does not in itself create a team, autonomous work groups with high levels of responsibility are not automatically a team. Teamworking is not about interlocking circles nor about mixing 'ideal' personality types.

If any manager followed the advice of the theorists and sought to build a team based on the ideal mix of roles, sanity would quickly go out of the window. All most of us can do is to select people who combine the right skills and aptitudes with an empathy with our way of doing things. We then generally find over a period of time that particular strengths emerge and, if we have a series of project teams which form, break up and reform in different patterns, and if we have the luxury of choosing membership on the basis of personality as well as required skills, it may just become possible to choose some of the team members with reference to the optimum mix. In practice, such analysis rarely goes beyond, 'Joe's a good note taker' or, 'Janet will sort them out.'

Soccer star Eric Cantona, quoted at the head of this chapter, got something else right. He spoke of his love to win and added, 'For Manchester, it is the same. We have the same vision of football and victory.' Teamworking is not an end in itself, and it is so easy for a team to focus on its own internal dynamics rather than on its objectives. The sports team that is too involved in its internal relationships will lose sight of the key objective – scoring the goal, the touchdown or the try. The business team that does not keep its eye on the objective will similarly fail.

A team begins with individuals whose individual contributions are recognised and valued and who are motivated to work together to achieve clear, understood and stretching goals for which they hold themselves accountable and which are bigger than they could achieve by working separately. The good team has positive leadership, it has participated in developing the goals, and shares commitment. It knows it has a long-term reciprocal commitment with the organisation of which it is a part. It may have its stars – but they recognise that if the team is to achieve more than the sum of the parts, their task is to contribute to the greater good rather than solely work for individual glory. The other members are in this way able to achieve far more but, equally, recognise the contribution of the stars and do not begrudge them their place in the limelight.

In the business environment a key factor is that the team must be working together to assist in achieving the organisation's goals. When in the mid-1970s I was put into the Ford Dagenham Metal Stamping and Body Plant the most effective team was the group of militant shop stewards. They could run rings around most of the management. They were a cohesive group, positively led by Danny Connor, the Communist convener. They had clear objectives which were to ensure that any change was solely in the interest of the workers, to defend to the end any worker subjected to the disciplinary procedure and in so doing tie up the management in lengthy procedural debates, to denigrate the authority of the first line supervisor and manufacturing management, to create an atmosphere of continuous tension so that management was always uncertain as to what would happen next, and last but by no means least to make sure that they as individuals did as little physical work as possible. For many years they succeeded. Whilst not agreeing with their objectives, management had long feared their effectiveness. Those who recall the activities of Elton Mayo's group in the Bank Wiring Room will not be surprised that teamworking can sometimes be more effective when focused *against* the company than it can when the objectives are shared.

In the ascendant organisation the team is everyone working together for the success of the enterprise.

Once we are able to break out of the constraint of confusing structures with teamworking, the number of people involved does not matter greatly. There may be a limit to the size of a *micro* team, that is the small group in which everyone knows everyone else fairly well, but providing the concept starts from the bottom and works up there need be no limit to the size of the *macro* team. It is equally nonsense to say that once a production site or company reaches 500 people that it must be divided. Individuals primarily identify with and feel close to their immediate colleagues. Their immediate leader has also to be a member of the team. But the leader has a peer group – for example, other supervisors with whom he or she will also form a team – and a boss; and so on up and across the hierarchy with interlocking teams until the top team is reached, of which more later.

Successful organisations comprise multi-stranded, cross-linked chains of teams with every link strong. It then becomes possible for the individual in the micro team to identify with the macro team; not because they know intimately everyone in the organisation, but because they feel that everyone at all levels and in all functions or units are working together for the shared objectives and not for individual success at the expense of others. In a large organisation we can hope that the individual will at least develop the attitude that, 'I'll do anything for my group and they'll do anything for me' and, 'I trust the people at the top. I know what's going on and they're not just looking after themselves.' Maybe some will even be able to create the environment in which individuals are genuinely committed to the aims of the enterprise and see the whole organisation as a team. With this approach to teamworking it is possible for large sites with several thousand people to operate effectively. The actual structure becomes less important.

Some companies have physically restructured the manufacturing facility around the team. Nissan South Africa's Chief Executive, John Newbury, first visited Sunderland in 1988 and became inspired by the supervisors' team meeting areas. John determined that he would introduce such a concept in his South African plant where, to put it mildly, there was so much lineside stock that any casual observer would think it impossible to find the space. But John was determined and it was a classic example of strong leadership. The stock control system had to be changed, in fact stock had to be controlled. Major changes to the layout took place, space was freed and the floor of the meeting areas painted green. The 'green areas' were born; for the first time white supervisors mixed and spoke *with* the black workforce and that was the beginning of the change process – a practical demonstration that management wished to do something different. The 'green areas' concept has become celebrated in South Africa and many South African executives I meet know of this experience.

The irony is that we developed the concept from the meeting areas we saw in Rothman at Spennymoor, some 20 miles from Sunderland. Rothman abandoned the traditional layout of long production lines in favour of a production area coiled around the team meeting area. Rothman is a South African company!

It is, however, just as easy, if not easier, to structure the office environment around the team. To do this we need to move away from individual offices, partitioned sections and neat rows. Modern office equipment design allows desks and terminals. to be so configured that half a dozen team members can sit together in 'islands' facing each other. Everyone can be in touch with everyone else – privacy goes and there need to be separate meeting rooms – but the great advantages are in shared knowledge, enhanced communication and the sharing of tasks and responsibilities.

Probably the greatest indication to me that in Nissan we had genuinely managed to develop the team culture and genuinely devolve responsibility and involvement was when the supervisors in the manufacturing areas began a programme of taking their teams away for team building days. Because of major staff movements in early 1994 many people shifted to different groups and in the first two months of the year over 2000 people participated in more than fifty events. Their programme covered a wide range of activities aimed at developing teamworking, motivation, communication, problem-solving and relationships. With the training department they had developed exercises suitable for them plus a strong injection of beer drinking and a late night. The important point here is not how good the exercises were but that manufacturing believed in them and felt able to initiate them, and it was the team doing something together.

Building real teamworking is not just about techniques. It is also about having fun together. The Americans are far better at this than any other nation – the relaxed way of life, the love of the outdoors, the greeting,

'Where do you come from?' which immediately starts a conversation, all help to create an atmosphere of community. Americans work hard but have you ever stood at the factory gate or office door at the end of work on a Friday? I do not advise your getting in the way! I have seen and been involved in the American community spirit which the best companies are able to capture in a way I have never seen in Europe or Japan. It seems totally natural for a senior manager in the USA to sit down with a group of people from the shop floor and just chew the fat over coffee and donuts. In Britain, except for a few individuals to whom such relationships come spontaneously, it rarely works. The worst thing is to pretend to enjoy it. You will be found out.

Nissan in the USA gives its managers a budget to spend on the teams in their area. They do all sorts of things, but nearly always involve the family. Sometimes they come to the splendid sports facilities, other times it is a day out, but the important point is that the family can become part of the team. Such activities emerge naturally in the ascendant organisation; they are not forced. If relationships are bad then no amount of social activity will bring about an improvement; they will just be viewed as a cynical exercise. But if relationships are good they will add another turn to the already virtuous spiral.

HOW TO INTRODUCE TEAMWORKING

How then do we develop teamworking? There is no single prescriptive answer, but it must begin with the realisation that in organisations as they have developed, teamworking is not the natural order of the day. People have reached positions of authority generally by virtue of their success in the Western values of individualism, aggression and often because they have taken credit for success and avoided blame for failure.

The top group in an organisation is often the most difficult to weld into a team and the person at the very top, though perhaps the prime advocate of teamworking, may well be the prime example of, 'Do as I say, not do as I do!' The irony is that if often requires a strong individual who has reached the top in the traditional way to take the lead in changing the culture of the organisation, and such individuals, converted to the concept of teamworking, are the least able to behave as both a member and leader of a genuine team. We have seen Lou Gerstner's, 'when they work together as a team.' When an executive says something like, 'I'm telling you we're going to become a team' the immediate, sometimes unsaid, response is, 'Don't I get a vote.' *If we wish to develop a culture in which teamworking and involvement become the order of the day, the prospective team members must be involved in developing the culture that they wish to be a team.*

The behaviour of the leader is the key to the development of teamworking. In developing a one-off team of people who have never before been involved, the process can be as follows:

1. Select the members of the group based on their technical competences and/or aptitudes balanced with their broad empathy with this way of working. Try to select people whom you believe can work together, but often the best you can do is to avoid the obvious misfit (remembering also that the superficial misfit may turn out to be the grit which makes the oyster produce a pearl). There is no such thing as the ideal mix. People will grow with the experience.

2. It is not possible to *teach* teamworking but it is possible to put people into situations in which they come to *learn* of its benefits. Some form of team development activity may help and it does not really matter what form it takes, provided it has relevance to the task in hand. Physical activities may be of value as part of generally developing people, if they provide learning opportunities, but will be of little value when they are seen as a test of physical endurance and some sort of survival course. Relevance and immediacy are of far more importance for a group established to tackle a particular situation. A few days as a group, learning how to solve problems using the most relevant of the available techniques adapted to the project, is as valuable as anything. Truly successful exercises occur when participants are able to review their performance and realise, for example, that all gain by assisting each other, by bringing out strengths, by analysing mistakes and learning from them, by understanding that the process is important and by learning to plan before taking action.

3. It is during these days that the task must be fully explored. The most effective teams are given the broad goal, but participate fully in defining the precise targets and methodology. The Parkinson principle, 'Work expands to fill the time allowed to achieve it', operates at all levels and tough but just achievable time scales will place the right level of pressure on the team. What really counts is ownership of the goal and you achieve ownership by letting the team share in its precise definition and the means by which it will be attained. The contribution of the leader is critical. A dogmatic,

domineering approach at this stage will turn everyone off but abdication can lead to anarchy. The positive leader, however, is not afraid of the group making its own decisions, as long as they remain pointing in the required, broad direction or can genuinely persuade the leader that the broad direction needs changing. Team leaders not only get people 'to do what you want them to do because they want to do it for you' but are responsive to the needs of the team.

4. From then on the team must develop its own way of working. What matters is not that the rules or plan are the 'best' but that they are understood, shared and owned. The team can agree on confidentiality or openness, deputies allowed or not allowed, on-site or off-site meetings, regular meetings with joint activities or infrequent meetings with individual activities, roles assigned from the start or roles allowed to emerge; the initial leader remains throughout, another is appointed or the leadership changes as the project progresses. The permutations are endless and those that initially seem the most conducive to success may end up being of little significance. Ownership leads to self-accountability which in turn makes for success.

5. Establish intermediate goals and measure progress. The goals can be time-based using a master schedule to determine the dates by which key stages of the programme have to be achieved or they may be qualitative or quantitative. 'What gets measured properly gets done properly.' It is a measurable task based on fact not opinion, that makes the group function as a team, not some abstract call to work together. However, the team has to decide if those objectives which are really important are measurable and if those objectives which are measurable are really important. To distinguish one from the other is crucial and if not properly done will diminish the chances of success. Do not underestimate the power of positive feedback. Whatever the tangible results might show, a word from the team leader, 'You did a great job getting the programme back on time' is worth a hundred symbols on a master schedule.

A most vital lesson is, do not spend vast amounts of time learning the theory of teams or participating in team building techniques introduced by expensive consultants. *Just get on and do it.* If you have the will, a good leavening of common sense and have spent a few minutes reading the preceding five points you will be amazed at what you will achieve.

Make mistakes. Do not worry about getting everything right before you begin, because you cannot and will not . Next time you will do better!

But this is about teams that form, do their job and end. In the 1965 terminology of B. W. Tuckman, 'Forming, storming, norming, performing and adjourning.' In the ascendant organisation, most teams will be continuous – they will comprise people working together every day in their normal task. They will develop over a long period of time as trust builds up between the members. In such an organisation it may barely be necessary to go through the team development process that is needed when *ad hoc* work groups or task forces are established. The continuous team has positive leadership and shared goals. As we saw when discussing front line leadership, the leader has responsibility for selecting the members of the team. As a result he or she feels a commitment to the chosen people and the individual has a good feeling towards the person who has offered the job, and that is not a bad start for a relationship. Real teamworking, however, results from the total behaviour of the group – starting with communication.

COMMUNICATION

There is barely an analysis of problems within an organisation that does not conclude that, 'We need to improve our communications.' Most such analyses fail to distinguish between information and communication, and fail to take account of the fact that communication is taking place all the time, whether we like it or not.

Information is a one-way process, usually from the top-down. It relies on the corporate newspaper, the six-monthly video (often used as an ego trip for the chief executive), the notice board or, in very advanced companies, the formal brief, which is based on the mistaken concept that everyone should get the same message at the same time. Such methods take days or weeks to put together and usually if something is worth communicating the grapevine beats the management to it. The confusion between information and communication is well illustrated by a quotation from the Wall Street Journal (I found it in a 1994 diary). 'What do you mean we don't communicate? Just yesterday I faxed you a reply to the recorded message you left on your answering machine.'

Jack Welch gave an admirable definition of *communication* in 1987:

> We've learned a bit about what communication is *not*. It's not a speech like this, or a videotape. It's not a plant newspaper. Real communica-

> tion is an attitude, an environment. It's the most interactive of all processes. It requires countless hours of eyeball to eyeball back and forth. It involves more listening than talking. It is a constant, interactive process aimed at [creating] consensus. (Tichy and Sherman, 1993, p. 62)

One of the first lessons I learned from the Japanese is that if something is worth telling it is worth telling quickly and the only way to do that is face-to-face. Most people are interested primarily in what is happening in their immediate environment, and their interest decreases the more remote is the subject of the information. The focus must be a group of people with their immediate supervisor talking with each other on a daily basis on matters which affect them, in a way which is appropriate for them. In 99 per cent of cases it simply does not matter if one supervisor gives a slightly different version of the same story or chooses to highlight different aspects of a common message. What is important is that the team together communicates in a way that is right for them and that the team looks for information to its leader, who is able to respond quickly. If this is not a genuine two-way process, and if there is no subsequent feedback on any comments raised, then employees will regard the exercise as what it is, a cynical exercise in deception.

But it does not just happen. People cannot give their hearts and minds unless they know what is required of them and what they have achieved. Unless there is a systematic method of communication, Jack Welch's attitude and environment will achieve nothing.

Sometimes there will be the great message from on high that needs to be communicated in a specific way. One such instance in Nissan was in November 1993 when a formal staff briefing was issued about the plans that had been worked out by the Company Council to deal with the 1994 recession in the European car market. In order to avoid press leaks (another crime is for employees to read media versions before they hear from their own management) preparation of the document was kept within a very tight circle. It was then briefed formally down the management chain with the clear objective that the supervisor should be the person to give the message at the operating level. When it has become natural that the supervisor is the person who communicates about small matters it is also natural that this is the route for the big issues. Similarly, during formal negotiations it is the supervisor who informs staff about the progress of discussions. It then becomes the representatives' role to seek the individual and collective views of their constituents and report these back to management. Of course, management will also use the supervisory network to get a feeling of their teams' attitudes. Usually, if supervisors are fully in touch with their teams, the subsequent reports from representatives and the initial reports from supervisors will not be a million miles apart.

Much communication is non-verbal. Whether or not the organisation has a separate executive floor is sending out messages, as is whether or not the organisation has genuinely open plan offices with no one having a separate office. 'My door is always open' is another of those hypocritical business statements. It is open if you go through a procedure and get past the secretary! Far better to have a 'no door' practice in which people can just wander up to chat, and everybody can see what is going on. While occasionally irritating if you are in the middle of a conversation, it is very rarely abused and *if the person thinks it important to interrupt, then it is important*. In a way it is gratifying if people you have never met feel comfortable in wandering up to your desk to discuss a point that is important for them.

However, people should not feel that they can get something done by by-passing their own management and going directly to the top. Whether it is IBM's 'Speak Up' programme or Body Shop's (literally) red letters (whereby employees can write directly to the top), or an approach to my desk, the end result could be that the individual loses confidence in the supervisor's ability to solve the problem. It is a delicate balance. I know of one company which has a policy of rotating people every two to three hours. If this is not done, the individual can 'take it to the top' by phoning a 'hot line' in the personnel director's office. Office people become involved, questions are asked and whatever the reason or result, the supervisor's authority is undermined. This is clearly unacceptable and it is the responsibility of the management of an organisation to equip the supervisor to handle virtually all questions that arise. There will of course be the large corporate issues that need answering from the top, but in the ascendant organisation these will be few and far between. Much better that issues be handled at local level.

We all communicate all the time. As we walk through the door everyone immediately knows our mood. The manager who says a cheery and genuine 'Good morning' is constantly reinforcing the message. The manager who ignores most people most of the time is perceived as only going through the motions when he or she does attempt to communicate formally.

Managers being seen to be on the shop floor, not to ask stupid questions about an employee's background but to be genuinely involved in the process is vital; showing respect at all levels is fundamental, not by talking down to junior staff but by listening and talking at the correct level. The phrase 'Management by walking around' has achieved considerable popularity but like all such phrases it simplifies a complex situation. Top executives cannot manage an organisation by walking around it. They can 'walk around' their own immediate reporting staff by being in frequent contact with them and can get a feel of the company by being frequently at the 'coal face', provided the intermediate managers do not create a sanitised version of the real thing. Many top executives actually feel uncomfortable on the shop floor. They lack empathy. They are unable to bridge the perceived gap and, if they cannot,the shop floor worker will also feel uncomfortable, the contact will be artificial and they will end up doing more harm than good. Much better in these circumstances, after a few efforts, to retire to what they do well – which is certainly not managing an ascendant organisation! However if executives are able to get out of their offices, to get close to the people through honest and open communication they will begin to earn the trust that is essential to attain long-term success.

This does not mean that top executives should not communicate directly throughout the organisation. One of the most effective processes if handled well and one of the most self-defeating if handled badly, is the chief executive meeting face to face with all staff to talk about those issues that need that level of authority. I have been involved with both the good and the bad. The bad are impersonal and highly structured, with beautiful slides but with information pitched at the wrong level. They inhibit questions but if someone does raise a hand the question is invariably something like, 'That's all very well but we've been trying to get the washroom cleaned up for weeks. What are you going to do about that?' Or the trade union activist seeks to score debating points. Good presentations are as relaxed as it is possible to be, they may still use beautiful slides but they are pitched at the right level and the questions are related to the subject – because the 'washroom' issues will have been sorted at the point at which they occur. That is the job of the immediate management.

Communications must be truthful. Communicate in the bad times as well as the good. The worst thing that can happen is for employees not to appreciate that a company is in difficulty. They will know it anyway, but being told the truth by people they trust is what really counts. And that trust does not build up overnight. If the first time you genuinely communicate with people is in the bad times, you have lost before you have begun. A good leader spends more time communicating than almost anything else, but we know that leadership exists not only at the very top.

The good and the bad messages are most effectively conveyed by the immediate leader with the occasional direct injection from the very top. The ascendant organisation creates the atmosphere in which, within the team, communication is natural, spontaneous and genuinely two-way. The immediate leader is always walking around and is not by-passed. The chief executive communicates the vision and sets an example but not by usurping the responsibilities of the immediate leader.

INVOLVING PEOPLE

One of the problems when discussing involving people in the business is determining what the term means. We need to distinguish between Employee Involvement and involving employees. The first, with initial capital letters, is about formal structures, often negotiated with trade unions and involves the representatives of employees. The second is about genuinely involving all people in the organisation in those areas they can directly affect and ensuring they are fully informed about those areas they cannot directly affect. The definition becomes even more complex when we see that an Employment Department survey of employee involvement in Britain between 1988 and 1991 included publications, noticeboards, training and TU and staff association channels as forms of employee involvement (Hibbert, 1991) thus confusing information, communication and involvement.

General Motors is closely associated with the structuralist approach to Employee Involvement. In 1973 GM and the UAW created a National Quality of Working Life Committee, 'To improve the quality of work life thereby advantaging the worker by making work a more satisfying experience, advantaging the corporation by leading to a reduction in employee absenteeism and turnover and advantaging the consumer through improvement in the quality of products manufactured.'

GM saw itself as having a double goal, the humanisation of work life and improvements in productivity, but according to R. Timothy Epps, Vice President, Human Resources, Europe they recognised that these goals could, 'only be achieved by a new organisational structure and a new improved organisational climate of trust, participation, involvement and commitment.' In this GM was no doubt right, but to achieve it they pulled in one hundred outsiders to serve as consultants to their plants to aid the planning and design of their QWL programmes. In 1987 Epps was able to say that schemes, 'dreamed up by someone else and imposed on a group of people don't work. People must discover for themselves what these new ideas are and then feel free and be encouraged to design their own changes' (Epps, 1987).

General Motors' latest iteration of its employee involvement strategy is its worldwide Quality Network Programme. At corporate level a Quality Council has been established, chaired jointly by the company's President and the Vice-President of the UAW's GM division. At local level they have Plant Quality Councils composed of the UAW shop chairman, plant manager and other local union and management representatives who oversee and assist in the implementation of the Quality Network process. In Europe the programme was cascaded through the organisation with top executives joining together in Frankfurt for two and a half days of presentations by the top team.

It is difficult in some countries to separate employee involvement from the formal structure of representation and the involvement of trade unions. The Germans have taken the structure of involvement as far as anyone. Their Works Constitution Act provides for the establishment of Works Councils in workplaces with more than five workers. The legislation requires that, 'The employer and the works council shall work together in a spirit of mutual trust' and provides a clear statement of the issues which are the subject of co-determination. There has to be agreement on, for example, daily hours of work, temporary changes to the working hours, holiday entitlement and the development of a social plan to deal with the effects of redundancy or restructuring. Failing internal agreement, proposed changes may be referred to an arbitration committee comprising equal numbers of representatives from both sides and an independent chairman.

Works Councils have the right to be consulted on dismissals, reassignments and transfers and vocational training measures. But on some issues the Works Council has the right only to information, including job design and work organisation, the introduction of new technology, plans to alter the size and organisation of the workforce and information about the financial affairs of the organisation.

Although this system is credited with the harmonious relations of German industry, I have been told by many German industrialists that they see it as a weight around their neck. Heinrich Weiss, President of the Federation of German Industries, speaking to the Royal Society of Arts in November 1992, said that the process led to good industrial relations but slow decision-making. 'The process of seemingly endless discussions is becoming an increasingly great disadvantage in our industrial system' (Weiss, 1992), particularly when companies have to change rapidly for market reasons. Increasingly, German industrialists are trying to find a way round the system and a study by Industrial Democracy in Europe found that although the formal and actual *rights* of German workers representatives are among the highest in Europe, formal and actual management *control* is also among the highest (cited by Lane, 1989, p. 232). Perhaps this is why the resist *real* involvement.

The GM and German systems represent the structuralist approach to employee involvement. My descriptions are by no means complete but they illustrate the approach which is *primarily about involving the representatives of employees*, not about involving employees. As soon as an Employee Involvement package, with initial capital letters, is formally negotiated with a trade union it ceases to be about involving *employees*.

The Confederation of British Industry (CBI) recognises this:

> Nobody can compel enthusiasm. It tends to develop where jobs are satisfying; where opportunities exist for employees to contribute to workplace decision-making; where managers are readily accessible; where respect for the individual is shown; where information is shared and where everybody has a clear idea of their own and their company's objectives. This is employee involvement.

The full CBI statement of principles on employee involvement presents such a clear statement of what it really means that it is given in full in Figure 8.1. As a member of the team who drew it up I must admit to a certain amount of prejudice in its favour!

Central to success in involving people is not the structure but the range of subjects and the style, but at its simplest, and perhaps most profound, involving employees is no more than seeking the views of employees on how best to do something or how to resolve a problem. This can be at many levels but generally it is most successful when it relates to a subject over which the individual can have some influence, usually his or her job. This is the essence of *kaizen* which recognises that the person doing a job knows more about that job than anyone else and that people have brains as well as hands.

The impact is well illustrated by the comments of Janet Jeffries, a Section Team Leader and Senior Shop Steward at car component supplier Marley near Bristol. After working with Nissan's Supplier Development Team she said:

> For years it was taken for granted that shop floor workers left their brains with their clock cards. . . Supplier development training has changed all that and brought us out of the dark ages and into the 20th

The CBI believes that employee involvement:

— is a range of processes designed to engage the support, understanding and optimum contribution of all employees in an organisation and their commitment to its objectives;
— assists an organisation to give the best possible service to customers and clients in the most cost effective way;
— entails providing employees with the opportunity to influence and, where appropriate take part in, decision making on matters which affect them;
— is an intrinsic part of good management practice and is therefore not confined to relationships with employee representatives;
— can only be developed voluntarily and in ways suited to the activities, structure and history of an organisation.

Employee involvement promotes business success by:

— fostering trust and a shared commitment to an organisation's objectives;
— demonstrating respect for individual employees and drawing on the full range of their abilities;
— enabling employees to derive the maximum possible job satisfaction.

It is the responsibility of management to generate effective employee involvement through the systems and techniques at their disposal. These may include:

— systematic two-way communication on all company matters (within the limits of commercial confidence);
— regular consultation;
— problem-solving groups;
— decision-making at the lowest practicable level of authority;
— financial participation;
— harmonisation of terms and conditions of employment;
— seeking individual contributions aimed at achieving continuous improvement in the organisation.

Ultimately, success depends not on the number of processes introduced but on their effectiveness in securing genuine involvement.

SOURCE: CBI, 1988.

Figure 8.1 CBI Statement of Principles on Employee Involvement

> century . . . I was probably the most sceptical member of the first SDT team. I thought, 'Here we go, another way to increase production – but giving nothing in return'! How wrong can you be? From being a sceptic I soon became totally committed. I have now been part of three SDT teams and have watched the massive changes taking place. Cycle times, methods and layouts are studied by these teams and with the involvement of all the team, lots of changes are made. The environment is cleaner and brighter and layout changes have cut down on walking. Easy working has resulted in increased production without the need to work harder.

This is all about individual contributions, whether it is through ideas submitted or direct involvement. *The whole concept is based upon involving people in contributing to improvement as a normal part of everyday life.* Many companies will point to the enormous benefits they have gained from suggestions schemes, especially new style schemes in which the old bureaucracy is eliminated and the implementation and award decisions are made by the immediate supervisor. The Rover scheme, restructured on these lines, is certainly a vast improvement on the old scheme in which a suggestion disappeared, literally, into a black box, was reviewed at several levels, a financial saving calculated and it emerged maybe six months later with or without an award, depending on whether or not it was judged to have been within the individual's normal area of responsibility. The old scheme had, in 1981, a participation rate of 3 per cent with a yearly saving of £300 000. The new scheme in 1992 had a participation rate of 10 per cent with savings of £10 million. Managers have the authority to pay awards directly for ideas affecting their own area.

This is a great improvement, although having administered suggestion schemes I know most of the fiddles (on both sides) but, more seriously, they reinforce the view that 'thinking' is not part of the normal job; that quality improvements are distinct from the normal day-to-day task and manual workers in particular have to be paid extra to think.

In Nissan we estimate that about 90 per cent of the changes made to current production come from the people doing the job. In 1993, Neil Mackenzie of the QA Vehicle Test team proposed the deletion of a 'redundant' pulley on Micras built without air-conditioning. This was accepted and saved the company £1.5 million. It was the largest identifiable saving and he received a plaque and the team a refrigerator for the meeting room. There was also a report in the internal company newspaper. This was picked up by the local and national media and

Nissan was castigated for its meanness, with comparisons being made with other 'more generous' companies. They entirely missed the point. Everybody contributes to product improvement. Neil Mackenzie considered it a normal part of his job and said so in subsequent media interviews. *When you are motivated to work for the success of the enterprise, are given responsibility, are trusted and your contribution is valued and recognised, the extraordinary becomes the norm.*

It is at this point that we come close to resolving the problem of how to achieve the right balance between commitment of the people and control of the processes. As we have seen, one comes from within an individual and has to be earned whereas the other is an external imposition of procedures and standards.

All people in the ascendant organisation are involved in the *kaizen* processes and, therefore, continuously improve the existing standard operation. In most organisations the standard operation is the property of the engineering department, they write it, issue it and with varying degrees of enthusiasm police it. Consequently it is adhered to with varying degrees of enthusiasm. *In the ascendant organisation the standard operation in the property of the people doing the job.* They write it and adhere to it because it is theirs, and through their total involvement they continuously seek to improve it. When an individual gets an idea, he or she shares it with the supervisor who, if happy with it, gives the go-ahead. The individual liaises with the people on the opposite shift, ensures that making life easier in one section does not cause problems in another, and if everything is OK the individual physically makes the change, if he or she has the technical capability. Of course, there are a few rules. Nothing can prejudice the safety of the product in use, reduce quality or safety but within these rules it is the decision of the responsible production people as to whether or not to proceed.

Once the change is implemented, the standard operation is re-written and the revised method then becomes the 'one best way' which must be followed until the next change comes along.

In many organisations it may be that 100 per cent adherence to the 'one best way' is not critical; even repetitive tasks can have areas of discretion. The essential point is that such decisions must be deliberately made, not just happen.

In effect what happens is that control *of* the process is given to those who are normally regarded as being controlled *by* the process, and it is this as much as anything, when combined with all other concepts and practices, that marries together control of the processes and commitment of the people leading to the ascendant organisation.

The ascendant organisation does not negotiate technological change but has far more genuine involvement of employees in the change process than traditional organisations. If you genuinely believe that employees know more about the job than anyone else it makes sense to seek their views on whether and how changes are needed, but the process goes a lot further.

Involvement is not just about improvement. It is concerned with emphasising the discretionary as well as the prescribed tasks, ensuring that responsibility is devolved to the point where it can be most effective. It is about the exercise of judgement in circumstances where 'standard operations' cannot exist or where it is possible only to introduce a framework within which people can operate. Particularly in situations where people meet people, judgements can be made all the time, but there is nothing more irritating than hearing, 'Sorry, can't do that. It's against the rules. More than my job's worth. . .!'

In 1993 it was clear that the automobile industry was in a recession and in Nissan we took all possible action to protect the core workforce. Temporary workers' contracts were not renewed as they came to an end; some work previously contracted out was brought in-house; employees were found temporary assignments elsewhere in Nissan in Europe; overtime was cut; hiring was stopped and towards the end of the year we cut out the night shift. While stopping payment of the night shift premium, everyone continued on 100 per cent of basic pay, even though they were working 50 per cent of the time.

But by October it was obvious that the European car industry recession would be continuing for at least the next year and possibly beyond that. As a result we had an imbalance between our projected volumes and the number of employees, a not uncommon experience in the car industry. Most manufacturers, particularly in Germany, the land of co-determination, announced redundancies and lay offs. Instead, we involved all employees in the decision-making process. Operations Director, John Cushnaghan and I met with the Company Council, fully explained the position and set in train a company-wide consultation as to how we might handle the imbalance.

The ten elected representatives, and virtually everyone else in the company, doubted if we were genuine: there must be a hidden agenda but there was not. We genuinely wanted to involve everyone in the company in what for us was the biggest downside decision we had had to make and which would be the true test of whether our philosophy worked in the bad times as well as the good. The elected members of the Company

Council accepted this task and said that we should not be surprised if they came up with a different solution from anything we had thought of. In turn I told them that they were taking on a tough job – and they were.

They spent two weeks talking in small groups with virtually every employee in the company. Often these groups were sceptical that the company really wished to listen to their views. No one had ever been involved in anything like this and could not conceive that they would be genuinely consulted on such a matter. Many had come from traditional industries and had experienced redundancies, often simply by being called together and told that they were going. And when they reported back they amazed us.

They said that there was a clear recognition in the company that there were too many people for 1994 volumes; however they wished to avoid short-time working and get back to full work patterns as quickly as possible. They recognised that to achieve this we would need to accelerate our natural wastage rate and to do this there would have to be some sort of encouragement payment. If this was to be done it should be done quickly, it should be generous and there should be no compulsion. They also recognised that the company might have to refuse some requests in order to maintain its operational integrity. The thing that amazed us (or, perhaps, we should not have been amazed), was that, given the full business information, the workforce came up with the optimum business solution. They had got there in one go, and had presented a solution that management would not have put on the table but might over the course of several meetings have worked towards.

The other very important element was that they were fully in tune with Nissan's philosophy of treating people equally and said that while there was not an immediate workload problem in the indirect areas everyone should be treated the same; that if a separation package was introduced it should be offered to everyone. They did not wish it to be seen that any group was being treated more or less favourably than any other.

We subsequently agreed a package – separation by agreement – which provided that within a specified period (10 December 1993 to 28 February 1994) anyone could apply to leave and, if agreed (the company retained the right to refuse, to protect its operational effectiveness) a payment of six months' salary would be made. There would be no compulsion and no target numbers. We agreed that we would adjust the shift patterns, line speeds and work done in-house or externally to meet the available workforce.

The Company's response was greeted enthusiastically by the work-force. It was felt that the Company Council had done an excellent job. It proved that sensible people, treated as mature adults, given full information and asked for their views can come up with sensible answers. We had involved *all* the people in the company in the big issue, not just in the small ones – but the fact that they were used to being involved in the small issues in the good times, meant that they were quite capable of being involved in the big issues when times were not so good. There is a fundamental lesson lying in there. *Do not start the involvement process when times are tough – you will be found out. Begin in the good times and build up the credibility which will hold you in good stead when you really need it.*

Genuine employee involvement can pose difficulties for managers. The traditional power structure is hierarchical – the higher up the organisation tree you are, the more power you have and it is easy to become irritated when people at the lower levels want a say. John Edmonds, General Secretary of the GMB Union recognised this in July 1990 when he said to me, 'Proper systems of employee participation do not exist unless the employees have the right to say "No" and have their disagreement taken seriously.' He also pointed out that while the received wisdom is that a participative style of management delivers the best results, the power structure of businesses contradicts that kind of objective. 'It is a hierarchy, with all the power concentrated at the top, and permanent tension.'

But if the ascendant organisation has trade union representation it will not wish to exclude them. In fact nothing could be more counter productive. I shall fully discuss the changing role of trade unions in Chapter 14, but suffice it to say at this stage that a constructive relationship with trade unions, when they are committed to the success of the enterprise, can be of great benefit to both the employer and employees. Trade unions have the right to be informed and consulted about matters affecting employees and the Germans have, as we have seen, precisely determined those rights. There are areas which are clearly in the negotiation arena but involvement is a separate case. Few have sought to involve trade unions in the large macro decisions. It is not a matter for co-determination as to when a product shall be replaced and few trade unionists would argue to the contrary. However, expansion, contraction and relocation decisions have a profound effect on employees and trade unions should not be presented with a *fait accompli*, except in a crisis situation.

Probably the most constructive programme for involving a trade union in the fundamental decisions was General Motors' experience when establishing its Saturn project in Spring Hill, Tennessee. The project was launched in 1985 with the goal of designing and building a small car capable of beating Japanese products. The involvement process began in February 1984 when Don Ephlin, Vice-President of the UAW's GM department and Al Warren, Vice-President of GM's industrial relations group, pulled together six people with the aim of finding better ways for the union and management to work together in the new plant. This led to the formation of 'The group of 99', almost evenly split between union and management nominees, who travelled to 49 GM plants and visited 60 other companies around the world looking for success stories. They concluded, not surprisingly, that the key to success was people and how they identified with the company, whether they felt the company was involved with them or that it really cared? It was this group which prepared what came to be Saturn's Mission Statement, Philosophy and Values.

'The group of 99' produced two basic conditions; they needed a process of resolving conflict based on consensus and a recognition that the enterprise would be more competitive if technology and people were properly and fully integrated, meaning that the people using the tooling and equipment should be fully involved in its layout and design. That vision permeated Saturn so that in 1993 Richard LeFauve, Saturn's President said that the emphasis of Saturn was:

> The integration of people and technology and business systems so that there is a good balance. I think it came from a lot of UAW involvement as well as those of us who've been through the automation phase and have learned that machines don't contribute ideas for improvement. People are pretty special. You don't eliminate people, you give them the tools to get their job done in a productive fashion . . . If you go in with the objective of improving the productivity of your people they'll make it work. (International Motor Business, 1993)

Saturn seeks to involve the union comprehensively in the involvement process, which means to Richard LeFauve:

> When you go out and ask people what they think and when you take that data as the basis, in a sense their thoughts become the decision. . . . You're constantly responding to what I call 'noise' – the level of concern around a particular issue. I think we're very responsive to the idea that with a partnership with the UAW they start picking up what the issues are pretty fast, and with their input we tend to be very responsive. (Ibid., 1993)

Decisions in Saturn are based on consensus through Decision Rings and Action Councils, all of which have union representatives, with at the centre the Strategic Action Council jointly championed by the presidents of Saturn and the Union Local (branch). But surrounding the SAC and overlapping with it and each other are other Councils including Manufacturing, Technical Development, Customer Action and Product Action Development. The Decision Rings work at the business unit and 'module' (teams interrelated by geography, product or technology) levels.

A constructive trade union in an ascendant organisation will be able to make a constructive contribution to the debate – but it must be able to represent its members who collectively may have a different view about the company's plans. A trade union is not the mouthpiece of management and management must not use it as such. The Germans speak of the social partners and in the years of struggle and success this was possible to maintain, at a cost which the German economy in the mid-1990s is finding difficult to afford.

In 1992, International Survey Research (ISR) measured the gap in attitudes towards their companies of employees working in successful companies and in those that were less successful. The top five out of many factors were:

1. Job stability – the degree to which long-term staff are valued and feel secure
2. Safety and working conditions
3. Employee involvement – how much employees' views are solicited and management responsiveness to suggestions for change
4. Management style – how much they believe what management says and whether managerial decision are thought to be fair
5. Employee development – how far the company shows an interest in developing people and how well it promotes competent people. (ISR, 1992)

Not only was employee involvement rated third overall, but ISR found that the gap between the successful and unsuccessful was widening.

KAIZEN IN PRACTICE

I described the broad principles of *kaizen* in Chapter 4 and also referred to *kaizen* when discussing involvement – the elements are inextricably linked. *Kaizen* changes, by definition, are rarely big. The vast majority of people are not mavericks coming up with crazy ideas but when their mental juices are stimulated they will frequently come up with simple, low-cost solutions, often missed by the professionals who usually find the complex and expensive solution. Wolfgang Strinz, then the Chief Executive of Opel's Bochum plant in Germany, commented on a device he saw in Nissan for lifting petrol tanks to the underside of the car:

'Who developed that?' he asked a supervisor.
'The operators – it took them about three months'
'Did it work first time?'
'No, but they kept at it until they got it right. It may not look a masterpiece of engineering but it does the job and saves a lot of time and effort.'
Responded Strinz, 'We've been trying to do something like that for three years but every time the engineers come up with a new solution the operators don't like it, they can't work with it – and it's cost thousands of Deutschmarks.'

That is the difference between *kaizen* and innovation, between involvement and imposition and between ownership and external control.

Many of the *kaizen* activities relate to material delivery. Tremendous effort goes into reducing line side stock and ensuring that it is delivered to the operator in the correct mode. For example, the large rear axles were delivered line side in pallets which needed the operator to lift them out by bending, increasingly acutely as the pallet was emptied. After considerable experimentation, including assistance from engineers, the operators developed a gravity fed roller system which delivered the axles lineside at the right height on small platforms ready for placing into position. The platforms when cleared, dropped down and were gravity fed back to the aisleway to restart the cycle.

My favourite *kaizen* of all time is . . . drainpipes! In any form of manufacturing one of the most difficult material supply tasks is the delivery of small parts – nuts, bolts, grommets, and so on. They usually arrive in cardboard boxes and end up either in an untidy mess or, in decanting the parts half of them finish on the floor. The brilliant solution was to use small lengths of drainpipe attached to the pallets and angled down towards the operator. The two ends were half cut away so that the parts could be poured in from the rear and then drop down to the operator (with of course the front end stopped, to prevent them falling on the floor!) So successful has this been that banks of a dozen can now be seen. Such an idea could only come from the person doing the job. The professionals would come up with the £5000 solution; the operator's idea cost a few pence!

The history of *kaizen* within Nissan illustrates a number of points about both the company's culture and how *kaizen* can develop. After a considerable debate, and not having got the culture firmly embedded, we decided to try what we called *kaizen* teams and planned an extensive training programme throughout 1987. From January to May the steering committee was trained, then the appointed leaders; the first teams were formed and trained and *Kaizen* (with a big K) was formally launched in May 1987. The aim was that everyone at all levels should be involved, with directors providing a supporting and encouraging environment. Managers were expected to support, encourage, provide facilities and participate in or lead teams; engineers and other professional staff would provide technical support as well as leading or participating.

The teams were expected to work by having people share ideas, skills, problems and activities. They were trained in problem-solving techniques and other procedures to help them attain a better understanding of their environment, to appreciate that all employees have a valued contribution to make and to emphasise that the team building process is more important than the result. The first groups were from Body Construction and Personnel – the 'Diamonds' and the 'Pioneers'. The 'Diamonds' looked at the use of safety equipment in the Body Shop and how higher levels of production could be achieved at lower cost, and the 'Pioneers' at the recruitment management system. We went through all the usual paraphernalia including the big presentation to a wide spectrum of people within the Company.

The results were, in themselves, good but the process was uniformly criticised, including by those who had been advocates of what we had come to call 'Big K', compared with 'little k' which was the informal bottom-up approach. At a formal review in December 1987 the comments were:

- 'Big K' is too formal and structured – too much paperwork causes a reluctance to become involved
- groups do not like making presentations to large meetings.
- 'little k' is more important than 'Big K'
- the steering committee is too remote. The commitment has to be felt at the personal day-to-day interface
- results are too dependent on a good leader
- the problem-solving and team building training should combine

As a result 'Big K' was dropped.

We concluded that *kaizen* does not have to be carried out in formal teams meeting out of hours and that often an individual or small informal group can think of a better way in a very short time. *Kaizen* means thinking about what you do, how you do it and then finding a better way. It does not have to be big to be impressive. The essential points must be that:

- the search for improvement is continuous
- no improvement is too small
- once implemented, improvements must be maintained to ensure a steady progress
- any aspect of work performance and the working environment can be improved
- everyone can participate, not just experts

However, over time *kaizen* has become more systematic. We have introduced *kaizen* workshops, in which a small permanent staff can work on some of the more complex improvement tasks. At all times the safety of the workplace is paramount and what we were finding was that individuals, with the best will in the world, did not always have the capability of fabricating the devices that they conceived, or that they could not always think of the effect of such devices on adjacent sections of the workplace. Using welding torches, for example, is potentially dangerous and if the integrity of the weld is not right the device can be dangerous in use. Thus we have had to introduce some formality into who is able to do what, and while 90 per cent of the changes made to the day-to-day practices still originate from the production staff, more frequently the ideas are being separately developed. *The commitment of the people is now balanced with control of the processes.*

It is probable that this is inevitable in any organisation which develops the concept to a great extent. Peoples' enthusiasm may exceed their capability and while much remains with the originator, a responsible management must ensure a safe working place. The great thing, however, is that while one would expect this to dampen enthusiasm, the general reaction is that when people see their original concept being developed and made to look and perform better than they had originally conceived, it fires enthusiasm rather than dampens it. Many of us were worried about the potential for losing the spark. We need not have been.

Kaizen virtually institutionalises improvement – it builds it into the fabric of the organisation. And when it is in the fabric it results not just in small improvements but in the large innovations. A company which is constantly seeking to do things better will quickly get round to asking if it needs to do certain things at all and will find that often it does not. It will also breed a culture which welcomes the big change when it comes. Innovate and then improve.

3M is the classic example of a company which is constantly seeking to improve and innovate. Its target used to be that at least 25 per cent of its annual sales should come from products which had been on the market less than five years. In 1992 it raised the targets to 30 per cent and four years. This is from a company with some 60 000 products. Not all can be major innovations, but when you have a spirit which is dedicated to improvement in all things, then somehow the big ones emerge. And you do not hit these targets by sending small groups away to work in isolation – you hit them by sharing and by creating the environment in which all can contribute.

HOW TO INVOLVE PEOPLE

A pre-condition for effective involvement is that basic relationships need to be good. Openness requires trust, and trust takes a long time to build and is easily lost. Involvement, like teamworking, is not an abstract concept. *You do not achieve involvement by saying, 'We believe in involving people'. You achieve it by doing it.* And it does not have to start at the top of the organisation – although that might help. Everyone has a part of the organisation he or she is able to influence, irrespective of what is happening elsewhere, and involving people can begin anywhere.

The best way to begin is to define a very specific practical issue that needs to be tackled; it really does not matter very much what it is, except that it should be within the capability of the individual or the group to make considerable progress towards success. It does not matter what you call that group. Having given an individual or group the responsibility for a task, then let them get on with it. They will quickly find out that they need assistance in one form or other – training in problem-solving techniques, assistance from someone outside the group, and so on – and be ready and prepared to give it.

Once the problem is solved, do not necessarily seek the big presentation to senior management. There is nothing worse than seeing a group spending more time preparing a presentation on what they have achieved than they spent on the achievement itself. This does not mean that management does not take an interest in what is achieved but if involving people is to be the norm then you cannot have a continuous series of presentations which makes it abnormal. The acknowledgement and expressions of appreciation must come from the immediate manager, and if it is felt that something is particularly worthwhile a mention by top managers on their normal walkabouts, an expression of interest and a word of thanks is worth a hundred formal presentations and awards. *Genuine employee involvement has to become part of normal everyday life* not something special that is done on the second Thursday of every month! We are discussing the fact that responsibility is lying where it should be – not 'empowerment'. The presentation to senior management under 'empowerment' is rather like saying, 'Look boss, haven't we done a good job' and then getting a pat on the head!

This does not totally preclude the presentation. Many organisations swear by them, find that people enjoy making them and, indeed, speaking in front of an audience can bring out hidden talents in some and develop confidence in others. They may be a necessary stage but if responsibility really lies where it should and involving people is the norm there will be so many activities going on that formal presentations on everything could be self-defeating. When involvement means the exercise of discretion, particularly on a face-to-face basis, it is simply not possible to have presentations made on an individual's daily achievements, but it *is* possible for a good leader when on 'walkabouts' to take an interest in what they have been up to.

Perhaps we can even get to the stage where people at the 'centre' make presentations to the front liners to explain what the 'centre' is doing to help the 'front line.'

The award mentality is well illustrated by IBM. Between 1980 and 1985 IBM at Havant, Hampshire introduced quality circles, statistical process control, customer measures, departmental purpose analysis, zero defects, inventory times and workforce involvement. The awards included the Plant Director's Silver Salver, The Most Innovative Function of the Year, twelve Innovators of the Year for people with good ideas, twelve Quality Managers of the Year for managers whose efforts to encourage their staff shine out, four Departments of the Year for departments achieving major advances. For many companies such programmes will work. As we have seen, American companies, in particular, place great value on them and many people respond well. The hotel industry has a great penchant for Employee of the Month awards. If it works for you, great, but be aware that all such programmes have a limited life. Once it becomes 'Buggins turn', you will have lost it. Once people complain about the effort they have to put into preparing the presentation, you may as well give it up. Once it is seen as a paternalistic management handing out the goodies, you have gone back 100 years.

The real reward comes not when people receive awards but when they have real responsibility and know that their contribution counts, and is actually worth something to their organisation, their colleagues, and to themselves. The more they contribute, the more they are respected and trusted. Creating such an atmosphere is difficult because it does not come from awards or promotions. It comes from people caring about each other – not just the boss for the subordinate but also the subordinate for the boss. If the relationship is one of mutual trust it could become a natural outcome of a job well done. I can think of nothing more satisfying than to be told by a colleague that I did a particular job well. Recognition that is unexpected and unrequired is the best recognition of all.

What you find is that genuine involvement in real issues resulting in real achievement is communicated around the organisation like a house on fire. 'Why has nobody ever asked me? I could have told them years ago' is a not uncommon cry. It then results in a demand for more information about what is happening, 'Why is material faulty when it reaches me?' 'Why do we have to fill out so many forms?' 'Why can't I be trained to do this job myself rather than having to wait for someone else to come along?' And a million more questions!

Genuinely involving people can open Pandora's box. Management will have to give up some of its perceived control without necessarily knowing what the outcome will be. It may have to change its support structures – the job of the finance department may have to become one of providing information to help the direct departments do their job better rather than continuously asking those who add value why they have overspent their budget or exhorting them to reduce their costs even further. The payment system may have to change from rewarding service to rewarding initiative. The permutations are endless, but the important point is that such changes must follow and not precede. In the ascendant organisation the indirect departments provide a service to the direct. They do not control. We have seen what the behavioural scientists said. People respond positively to their own good experiences not to exhortations to improve, nor to punishment if they fail.

We should not pretend however that everything in the involvement garden is lovely. As with all practices, if there is lack of continuity of management support then it will fail, particularly if supervisors perceive that their traditional authority has been eroded. A two-year survey of employee involvement activities such as team briefing found they had little effect on the commitment of employees or their understanding of management decisions. 77 per cent of the 700 employees in 18 organisations thought briefing left their commitment to the organisation unchanged and 4 per cent thought it decreased their commitment. 66 per cent thought it resulted in no change in their understanding of management decisions and 5 per cent thought it reduced their understanding! (Employment Department, 1992).

To be truly successful, involving people must then be an integral part of every-day life, not something special. It must be integrated with the overall business objectives and strategy. The key to success is not the structure but the process, not the results but the trust which is built, not participation by representatives but the involvement of everybody, not a formal determination of prerogatives but an expansion of contributions, not only involving people in the good times but also valuing their contribution in the bad.

The simple way of involving people is just

DO IT!

We all have part of our organisation we can influence. Tomorrow, ask your subordinate or colleague what he or she thinks or if they can come up with a better way. That's all there is to it!

FLEXIBILITY

When we speak of single status, teamworking, involvement and communication in the ascendant organisation, we have in the same breath to include flexibility.

The origins of inflexibility in modern manufacturing can be traced back to the old craft guilds jealous of their prerogatives, status and skills; and to Taylorism and Fordism where division of labour broke jobs down into finite elements. Standardisation was the order of the day. The long-term fundamental changes which are taking place in Western industrial society demand that inflexible methods of working be removed. Flexible technology without flexible working practices is doomed to fail.

Flexibility comes in many guises and with an increasingly diffuse terminology. We distinguish, for example, between functional flexibility, numerical flexibility, organisational flexibility, financial flexibility, structural flexibility. We talk of organisations turned upside down, shamrock organisation, boundaryless organisations, the inside-out doughnut and time-based organisations, and seek to move from functional structures to business units to the re-organisation of our business processes. We decentralise or centralise and break our structures into core and periphery. Along comes another book based on what has happened in a comparatively small number of businesses and our magazines become full of articles and our mail boxes full of literature advertising the conferences and services of the scores of plagiarists who have latched on to the latest managerial fad, and who claim massive experience in a six-months-old panacea. We then think that we are flexible. We are not. We are just blown around by whichever fashionable wind happens to be strongest. We are the 'fad surfers'!

What we forget is that it is people who comprise organisations and people resist change. We do not achieve a change in hearts and minds by changing organisation structures or by firing large numbers of our staff. If we employ good people, the actual organisation structure matters very little, except that, negatively, it can become a straitjacket that inhibits rapid response to changing circumstances. Like governments, they have great potential for doing harm and little potential for good! Good people will make anything work, they are oblivious of the structure. It is when we employ second-raters that the organisation structure becomes a crutch and we look for the panaceas to provide the recipe which will take us from failure to success. As we shall similarly see when we look at the reward structures, *the organisation structure must be an outcome of good management not a substitute for it*.

In the ascendant organisation, the organisation chart *may* still exist but it will be dynamic, changing rapidly *after* the real world has changed. It will never determine what should be done and no personnel officer will ever say, 'You can't do that because it doesn't tie in with the rest of the company.'

One of the most important tasks in the ascendant organisation is therefore to appoint good people and let the organisation develop around them. The thought that you establish the structure and then fit the people to it is anathema to such a business. Simply do what feels right. If a business unit structure is right for you, then go in that direction; if a functional structure feels better, then go for it. If you find that it is better to concentrate on your core business and contract out non-core services, that is fine: but if you wish to retain all non-core activities in-house, and it is right for you, then stay as you are.

In any case, what is core and periphery? Frank Nicholson, Managing Director of Vaux Breweries in Sunderland, told me of their architects' department, some dozen people responsible for the structure and design of their pubs and other premises. Vaux saw this as peripheral to their core business and against the initial wishes of the architects decided to 'divest' itself of the department. The architects were helped in setting up their own business, were awarded work for the brewery but also sought other contracts. They now have a thriving business and no longer are someone else's periphery, they are their own core.

The ascendant organisation is a learning organisation – but it also forgets! It does not stand still and it does not create walls. If it is functionally based, the good people within it will freely move between functions, forming project teams, achieving results and concluding their work, and perhaps more important, will talk with each other and act together each day as the normal way of doing business. If it is based on business units or business processes, good people will move across and between the units or processes and will fully utilise those functional strengths which remain. It is the task of top management to create the environment which facilitates, not inhibits, flexible behaviour, and it contributes to this by not making a sacred cow of a particular form of organisation type or occupational structures, nor by retaining that which should be discarded.

The basic concept of the ascendant organisation is that it must facilitate change, not inhibit it. One of the most inhibiting of organisation structures is the matrix organisation. It is not difficult in a multi-national organisation to have a variety of bosses – in the national company, the functional or the product group. Who is the leader? What is the team? Where is the direction? How rapidly can you change? How many organisation charts have to be modified when an individual moves or a position is changed?

In this area, the role of the human resource function (if there is such a thing) is to help the units or functions develop their people, not control their structure. This is where trust and devolution of responsibility is tested. If you have good managers who can be trusted to make the right decisions in the interest of the organisation, they must have the responsibility to deploy their staff in the way they see fit. The watchwords must be *flexibility within a consistent framework*. That framework must be simple and understood and while we must never allow our businesses to calcify, neither must we allow such mercurial change that no one ever knows where they are.

Another organisational problem relates to rules and procedures. Ricardo Semler, author of *Maverick* and CEO of his own manufacturing company in Brazil, hates them. Rules and regulations, he says:

1. Divert attention from a company's objectives
2. Provide a false sense of security for executives

3. Create work for bean counters
4. Teach men to stone dinosaurs and start fires with sticks.

> Rules freeze a company within a glacier: innovation lets them ride sleighs over it. (Semler, 1993, p. 78)

All my working life I have guarded against detailed rules. 'Do what is right and be prepared to defend your position.' Therefore I can understand Semler's view – but he says nothing in his book about his company's manufacturing process, quality control or product change procedures and to achieve consistent high quality you must have clearly defined procedures. To pay people properly there has to be a procedure to ensure, for example, that overtime hours are accurately translated into premium pay. The examples are endless and to give the impression that procedures 'freeze a company within a glacier' is doing less than justice to those who have to run the company on a day-to-day basis and deliver high quality products on time at minimum cost. As we shall see in Chapter 13, adherence to clearly defined procedures is critical to achieving consistent high quality.

Many of the lessons of *Maverick* are of great value, and are of general relevance, but let us not be taken in by its hyperbole. Equally, let us not manage, literally, by the rule book. Look at your office bookshelves, count the procedure manuals, ask when you last looked at them and assess if you have them because they help the business, because they have just grown over the years, or if legislation requires it. If the latter, you may have no choice but if you do have a choice, exercise it wisely but exercise it!

Even the freewheeling Virgin Atlantic of Richard Branson found that commitment was not enough. Branson hired Syd Pennington from Marks and Spencer as Managing Director and he quickly found there was minimal control over practices and procedures. The trick for Pennington was to retain the commitment while establishing controls. All 3500 staff still have Richard Branson's home telephone number and can call him direct, but customer service is not just about smiling. Every eight weeks cabin staff are given refresher training and on every flight the supervisor writes assessments of three or four crew members, and standards and development officers fly every four weeks to report on specific aspects of service and specific crew members' performance. Commitment *and* control.

One of the real causes of inflexibility within organisations is the job evaluation system. For some twenty years I have argued against job evaluation, job descriptions and their associated paraphernalia. *Job evaluation is the managerial equivalent of the trade union restrictive practice.* In two companies, Continental Can Company and Nissan, I have, however, been able to develop organisations which had none of these and the process was fully described in *The Road to Nissan*. In summary, however, if you aim for total flexibility, a flat organisation, teamworking, devolved responsibility and continuous improvement with change being the only constant, then any process which analyses in detail what people do at any point in time, writes it up in immense detail, assigns a grade and a specific job title, allows grading grievances and so on, ends up by restricting rather than expanding what people do. I once prepared a 35 mm slide which shows a cartoon of a tombstone. Written on the tombstone were the words:

Job evaluation
Rest in peace
Dearly beloved by
Personnel Managers

Job evaluation creates vast amounts of work for people in personnel departments and a good living for those purporting to provide objective measures of relative job values. *And what added value does it bring to the enterprise? None.* All it does is add cost and inhibit flexibility.

I know why organisations have job evaluation – as an attempt to achieve an objective measure of comparative worth and a defence against the comparability arguments put forward by trade unions; but the ascendant organisation does not require precisely analysed jobs, described in minute detail and fixed at a point in time. I know that no organisation can simply abandon its system overnight, but in many organisations the tail is wagging the dog. The tail of maintaining the purity of the internal relativities and job descriptions is wagging the dog of flexibility, teamworking, continuous improvement and rapid response to changing circumstances.

Further, any job-evaluated structure only works if the results are perceived as being fair, so when raw scores fail to give the 'right' relativities the weightings of the factors are balanced so as to achieve an acceptable result. Of course, there will always be disagreements at the margins, but in any organisation a small group of people who know the organisation well can, within a day, come up with a broad ranking order of jobs, fully integrating the manual and non-manual. While it may be argued that this in itself is a form of non-analytical job evaluation (and I would concede the point) it is so far removed from the vast majority of analytical systems as to be something genuinely different. Job evaluation should be laid to rest. *R.I.P.*

The objective in the ascendant organisation is to minimise the job titles and the number of levels. For example, in Nissan we established a fully integrated occupational classification which includes the generic job titles Engineer and Senior Engineer. We deliberately avoided the '57 varieties' of engineer common in most large manufacturing companies. The only job description, and this is not written down, is that, 'An engineer will do everything an engineer is required to do.' The Senior Engineer is in charge of a group of half a dozen Engineers, but at any point in time may be doing work that is less, as, or more complex than an Engineer. Engineering, or any other work, does not come in discrete levels of complexity nor is it precisely divided into electrical, electronics, mechanical, pneumatic, layout, process, facility and so on. An engineer is restricted only by capability, not by narrow job descriptions. This does not mean that everybody does everything. Were that to be the case we would spend all our time training and no time working, but there are no artificial constraints on what people do.

The blurring of the differences between manual and non-manual roles and employment practices has led to an increase in the number of companies seeking to achieve totally integrated occupational structures. An excellent example of a long-established company which has created flexibility out of inflexibility is Tate and Lyle Sugars, the cane sugar refiner. Its grade structure covering some 750 production workers comprised 25 grades and 177 discrete jobs; differentials were small. The very structure discouraged flexibility and there was little interest in learning new skills. Faced with a mature market and soon to be subject to price deregulation, the company decided that it had to make substantial improvements in its productivity, primarily through radical changes to jobs and working practices.

As a result of negotiations with the trade union the company was able, from August 1993, to reduce the number of grades to three and the jobs to 31. For example, the new job of warehouse operator covers nine previous narrow jobs including, checker/warehouseman, deckdriver/stretchwrap operator, export marker/trailer train driver, crane driver and bargehand. In addition to undertaking a wider range of process tasks it was agreed that employees would undertake cleaning, routine maintenance, quality control, testing, problem-solving and administrative duties. Instead of detailed job descriptions they opted for generic descriptions outlining their broad purpose and key areas of accountability.

The formal agreement states that, 'Work will be carried out in a co-operative and restriction free environment' and there will be, 'the removal of all restrictive practices, including overtime guarantees, minimum manning agreements, output constraints and demarcation lines between jobs, grades and departments.' Employees are now involved with the testing and introduction of new work methods and technology. Work was reorganised into teams based on particular areas of the production process and tasks are rotated within the team. Employees are trained to work flexibly both within and across teams in which skills are interchangeable.

As a result of all this Tate and Lyle expects its output per employee to rise from 640 tonnes of sugar in 1992 to nearly 800 tonnes in 1994. The great thing, though, is that along with these dramatic changes Tate and Lyle was able to make significant moves to harmonise conditions of employment, particularly on sick pay, non-deduction of pay for lateness and enhanced holiday pay. This is on top of pay increases averaging 5 or 6 per cent. The company in one leap has not only dramatically increased its flexibility, but has also removed many of the structural impediments preventing it from becoming an ascendant organisation. This, of course, only takes the company a short distance down the road and unless attitudinal changes accompany the structural changes very little will happen. But the atmosphere in which the discussions took place bodes well for the future.

Real flexibility of working practices does not need to be spelled out in detail. The Nissan agreement with the AEEU says:

> To ensure the fullest use of plant, equipment and staff . . . there will be complete flexibility and mobility of employees.
> It is agreed that changes in technology, processes and practices will be introduced and that such changes will affect both productivity and manning levels. To ensure such flexibility and change, employees will undertake and/or undertake training for all work as required by the Company. All employees will train other employees as required.

Very similar words have since been used in many companies including Coca Cola, Rover, Venture Pressings and the General Motors/Isuzu joint venture, IBC Vehicles. But then you must use this flexibility. People easily revert to type. If a company establishes a multi-skilled maintenance technician position which provides that an individual can be trained to work in electronics, mechanics, hydraulics, pneumatics or electrics and then does not use the new flexibility, it has only itself to blame.

One of *the* sterile debates is between those who seek to distinguish between multi-skilling and multi-tasking. Critics argue that for most workers the move to flexibility means no more than their being required to undertake additional boring, repetitive jobs, and that multi-tasking is solely on management's terms. If that is all there is to it, the critics are right. If you have a two-minute repetitive task and are trained to perform three such tasks of a similar nature, no one in their right mind would suggest this is multi-skilling. It is simply more of the same and the operators are just as bored after four weeks performing three similar repetitive tasks as they would be if they had only one to repeat continuously. Indeed, if the cycle is two hours and they repeat it frequently, they will still become bored.

Multi-skilling in the ascendant organisation is not just about expanding the range of physical tasks for which a person is responsible. New technology means that the amalgamation of traditional work practices is only the beginning. Operators learning to programme CNC machinery or robots is a classic example of technology-driven flexibility. But true flexibility is concerned with expanding the role and responsibilities of every individual. It encompasses teamworking, small group activities, continuous improvement; taking on responsibility for quality and housekeeping, working with suppliers and internal and external customers; training others and becoming involved in multi-disciplinary teams. It means accepting responsibilities that once belonged to more senior, or more junior, people. Thousands of organisations can now point to a reduction in their number of job titles. Few have fully understood the implications of true flexibility.

The quotation at the head of this chapter referred to a spirit in which subordinates exercise their judgement. Such a spirit cannot be negotiated or demanded. Managements earn it over a long period and when they have it, it is precious and fragile, rarely robust.

COMMITMENT IN AN 'INSECURE' ENVIRONMENT

Involving people, either through the *kaizen* process or by seeking their views on the major decisions, can create the environment in which such involvement and commitment is earned. We have seen in Japan and elsewhere that commitment also develops when people feel secure in the job, when they do not feel threatened that improvements in productivity will result in a loss of employment. But we have also seen that full-time, long-term employment is now a minority activity and the question must be raised as to whether commitment can be achieved in such an environment.

The answer is not a simple 'Yes' but more a 'Yes, if . . .'. Security and commitment are not cause and effect. Some of the most 'secure' organisations fall into the 'apathetic' or 'amiable' categories with little commitment to the organisation as such. Alternatively, security is often at its lowest in the 'ardent' organisation but while people are there, their involvement and commitment are total.

Traditionally, construction workers have been employed for just as long as it takes them to complete their part of a contract and were paid on a time basis. As a result it was in their interest to stretch out the work, especially if there was no more on the horizon. Overruns of major projects, both of time and costs, would be a joke if they were not so serious. Quality problems are notorious. Such projects lack both commitment and control, but the fault lies not in the lack of security but in ineffective management. Projects were costed on a time basis and the contract was awarded to the lowest bidder, who then saw every difficulty, every 'unavoidable' delay as a means of screwing more money out of the customer.

When Akira Shimanuki arrived in Britain in 1984 to manage Nissan's Sunderland project, he knew nothing of this system. He had this strange idea that the customer should know what was wanted and understood how it could be achieved, the contractor should be able to assess the potential difficulties and quote accordingly and when agreement on price and time was reached it should be adhered to. He saw no need for penalty clauses if it was late, because it would not be late; and no need for bonuses if it was early because he did not want it early. During the foundation stone ceremony in November 1984 he told me that the first production car would roll off the line on 8 July 1986. It did. Since that time, the main contractor Sir Robert McAlpine, and quantity surveyors Turner and Townsend have managed some £150 million of construction investment over a ten-year period. Every stage has been on time at cost, the contract has become legendary and their total organisations have benefited from the experience.

The difference was in the management. It was difficult at first. The site managers did not appreciate that they had a client and project manager who understood the construction business and who insisted that if something came up which they had not anticipated, it could not just be passed on in extra cost. Gradually, however, they learned, became much better at planning and costing – and passed these requirements on to their sub-contractors. A pride developed in getting the job done on time at cost. In this instance, control came before commitment.

In a notoriously insecure business, effective management involved everyone, they became more flexible than they had conceived possible and commitment touched everyone working on the project.

Robbie Gilbert, Employee Affairs Director of the Confederation of British Industry told a conference at the University of Warwick in May 1994:

> The dilemma for employers is that whilst they want loyalty, certainly from their core employees, they are often seen to be less than loyal to those who work for them. Employers want to be able to face those who work for them with new challenges but sometimes to close the door, with them on the outside.

Commitment, though, does not come from the length or style of a contract. It comes from ensuring that irrespective of their employment status, everyone is treated with respect, no one is a second class citizen, the contribution of everyone is both valued and seen to be valued and the employer helps employees develop their talents and skills.

Security is, in fact, a hygiene factor. Having it does not give commitment, but not having it can lead to lack of commitment. But security does not have to mean a long-term relationship with a single employer. If it is a six-month contract, or if you know you can be called on as and when necessary, or if you develop transferable skills which allow you to move between employers, then that is security.

This latter arrangement has long been common among blue collar workers, especially qualified craftworkers. The term *journeyman* originates from the fourteenth century. The difference today and, perhaps why it is causing concern, is that it is becoming evident in white collar, professional and managerial groups. However, the issues are no different. Much depends on peoples' roles and tasks and the way they are expected to perform them.

The next chapter is concerned with these practicalities, with control of the processes.

9 The Processes and Practicalities

The continuing increases in purchasing power and leisure time that have made many Americans the envy of working people everywhere have not come from working ever harder – but from working ever smarter.

(William C. Freund)

One trouble with Americans is that we're fixers rather than preventers.

(General James Doolittle)

For years the aim of many manufacturers was to achieve full automation with centralised planning and control of the production process. The unmanned factory was the ultimate goal, achieving high levels of quality and efficiency at low-cost. However, automation as an end in itself failed to take into account the fact that the contribution of the people doing the job could be a major source of improvement in quality and productivity. But technology can begin to provide at least some of the answers. This chapter looks at what people actually do in this new environment which seeks to pull together control of the processes and commitment of the people. (Two key elements, the elimination of waste and the standard operation have already been discussed in Chapter 4 and readers may wish to refer back to the appropriate sections.)

CELL MANUFACTURING

There is considerable overlap between the concepts of teamworking, cell manufacturing and autonomous work groups. As we have seen, teamworking is not about physical structures but about people working together to achieve a shared objective. One does not automatically follow from the other although, in the right circumstances, the physical structure can help. Autonomous work groups (AWG) were defined by the Dutch employers' organisation, AVW, in 1990 as, 'Groups which take full responsibility for a discrete part of the process, forming part or all of a specific operation or transaction.' AWGs may be cells and cells may be AWGs, but not necessarily so.

When they were first introduced some twenty years ago manufacturing cells were concerned more with processes based on group technology to produce families of similar parts. Now, however, the trend is to develop focused cells equipped with all the machines, controls, people and support needed to make a finished product, sub-assembly or component. Manufacturing cells can be highly sophisticated, using CNC machine tools and flexible manufacturing systems, or simple assembly processes entailing little more than a reorganisation of existing equipment. Final assembly cells may even be fed by their own sub-assembly cells, their own sole supplier of components.

The actual work organisation within a cell can vary considerably, depending on how much authority the management wishes to devolve, but usually the operators will take on broader responsibilities. At a minimum, responsibility for quality and material movement are added to the production tasks but responsibilities can extend to routine preventive maintenance activities, problem-solving, improvement, material ordering, scheduling, and so on. Some may even become virtually self-contained business units responsible for their own cost and performance monitoring, relationship with suppliers, and the selection and training of their team members.

Ingersoll Engineers describes the trend to manufacturing cells as 'the quiet revolution' and has plotted its growth for several years. In 1990, 51 per cent of UK manufacturers employed cell manufacturing techniques and by 1993 this had risen to 73 per cent. By 1993 nearly a third of those with cells already had fully cellular operations and half were planning additional cells (Ingersoll Engineers, 1990 and 1993).

One of the most successful users of manufacturing cells is Rearsby Automotive, a long-established mechanical components manufacturer based in Leicester. Rearsby's Chairman, Ivor Vaughan, led a management buy out and set about trying to change both the culture of the company and its manufacturing processes. Rearsby was a typical metal basher with a complex process, top-down management by control, an order to delivery time measured in months, big stillages, high inventory, obsolete stock, too much scrap, high rework levels and no teamworking. Said Ivor Vaughan, 'We thought we were laid out well but we were totally higgledy-piggledy with vast storage areas and the manufacturing areas divided into specialities with no relationship to product flow.' In fact everything that could be wrong was wrong at Rearsby except that Ivor

Vaughan realised that, '*The only difference between us and the competition is us*' and was determined to do something about 'us.'

Rearsby recognised that traditional manufacturing loves stillages and fork lift trucks with maximum machine and process specialisation. In the words of Richard Schonberger:

> The clustered organisation is one that puts all the lathes and lathe operators together in one place, all the welders together in another, all the motor assemblers in another, all the engineers in another and so on. The clustering is bad for the obvious JIT/TQC reasons: extended product flow time, much handling and delay, losses of evidence of defect causes, bad co-ordination and high level of potential scrap and rework. (Schonberger, 1986, p. 103)

Ivor Vaughan also passionately believes in simplification, 'Look at a task, see if you can stop doing it, do less of it or let someone else do it.' Only when you have simplified it as much as you know how, put it in a cell with low-tech automation and then only use the cell when it is needed, otherwise leave it unused. Do not manufacture for stock but aim for such a quick response time that you do not need stock.

Simplification is Ivor Vaughan's vision, his stand. To him a stand is made by one person, not a group. It is saying, 'I declare . . . do it now . . . there is no evidence that it will work; if you wait for evidence it is not a stand. Our stand in Rearsby was simplification.'

Other factors are, however, essential for successful cell manufacturing. Prime among these is the need to train the supervisors and the operators and to involve the people who will be working in the new system in its planning, layout, systems and tooling. As always, achieving ownership and commitment is critical for success.

The key to success in Rearsby was that Ivor Vaughan realised he did not have a monopoly of wisdom. It was only through the people that he achieved success and, in particular, the operators were the greatest untapped source of knowledge. One operator took over the redesign of a section, she put different processes together, changed the method to group work, simplified everything as much as possible and took on additional work. She said, 'Under this system you're your own boss, its more varied, more interesting.'

The benefits were considerable; stock fell, lead times shortened and responsiveness rose, expertise became higher, productivity increased dramatically and above all, employee ownership became real. One dramatic example is that of a product which spent ten days travelling 2½ times the length of the plant, involving 21 people to undergo 99 seconds of processing time. At the cost of £2000 all the required equipment was brought into a cell, with the result that one person now controls the whole process and the cycle time has been reduced to 43 seconds!

Cell manufacturing is not the only key to manufacturing success. It is most suitable for batch operations where there are regular product changes. For other types of product the continuous flow process is more appropriate. However, modern manufacturing success depends on much more than just the physical processes.

AUTONOMOUS WORK GROUPS

We have seen the Dutch employers' definition of AWGs but perhaps the extreme description of autonomous work groups was given by Jan Gulowsen in 1971 (cited by Berggren, 1993a). His criteria for autonomy was whether the group could:

1. Influence its own qualitative goals (the choice of product).
2. Influence its quantitative goals (the number of units produced).
3. Choose if it will have a leader and if so, whom, (to handle the group's relations with its surroundings).
4. Determine which extra activities shall be undertaken.
5. Decide when it will work.
6. Select the method of production.
7. Determine its internal distribution of work.
8. Decide questions concerning recruitment.
9. Determine how particular work should be carried out.

Gulowsen's study did not include modern mass production. For him, self-management means that the group would participate in determining the framework under which it worked and would operate within negotiated contracts for specific periods.

However, you do not have to go as far as Gulowsen. There are varying levels of responsibility in autonomous work groups, ranging from the 'not very autonomous' when the team is responsible, perhaps, for housekeeping, training each other and maintenance and repair; through a middle range in which responsibility extends to relationships with suppliers and customers and choosing the team leader; right through to the highest level, which would be recognised by Gulowsen, but which might also include team appraisal, compensation decisions and internal discipline.

Each of these examples has its own hierarchy of involvement. Iain Kennedy, Plant Director of Northern Telecom in Northern Ireland, has listed what he sees as degrees of involvement:

Identification	Group is asked to identify problems in their work area. Any solutions that are developed or any action taken are solely the responsibility of management.
Recommendations	Group makes recommendations to management relating to problems they encounter in their work area.
Resolution	Team is directly responsible for identifying and implementing solutions to the problems encountered in their work area.
Ownership	Of all aspects including implementation of solutions. Team also addresses competitive, organisational and customer related issues.

While it is easy to quarrel with terminology, and some will argue that AWGs are *not* leaderless groups, the fact is that all groups have leaders. (Even Gulowsen's listing allows the group to choose whether or not it wishes to have a leader – I wonder who leads this decision-making process.) It is central to the ascendant organisation that responsibility is devolved and when many hierarchical layers have been eliminated there simply is no alternative; but organisations cannot succeed without both positive leadership at the very top *and* at the head of the group. Without such leadership the group will quickly become disoriented and lose momentum. One of the key tasks of top leaders is, then, to select and equip people at all levels to take on the leadership roles. The ascendant organisation needs a leader of leaders.

A company which has opted for teamworking, autonomous work groups and cell manufacturing is Seaward Electronics, a medium-sized manufacturer of high-quality specialist instrumentation based in the north-east of England. Seaward's acronym is SMART, Self Managed And Regulated Teams.

Seaward was structured on a traditional functional chimney basis with purchasing, quality, production, material control, and so on, but undertook its own business process analysis and reorganised into product groups with manufacturing teams under team leaders. It gave to the team leaders responsibility for production, quality, service and calibration, material scheduling, expediting, supplies, stock, performance statistics, and personnel assessment and training. The plant was reconfigured so that instead of the assembly process being based on division of labour, every operator was trained to produce the full product in self-contained units. In addition, they became responsible for their own quality, test and repair and, with the devolution of stores to the point of use, for their own stock picking. Mick Pattison, Manufacturing Manager, told me, 'It's far better for the operators to select what they need for an instrument. They know what they need. All the storeman used to do was look at a list of part numbers, and that led to mistakes.'

Seaward Electronics is not a large company, it employs around 150 people, but it demonstrates what can be achieved with a positive leadership which is willing to create the environment in which people are able to use their brains.

TOTAL PRODUCTIVE MAINTENANCE

In the traditional company, workers and management rarely have enough time to look after their equipment or undertake routine maintenance. They enter into a vicious spiral of running the equipment until it breaks down, calling for the maintenance staff who are not available because of all the other demands on their time, losing production so they have even less time to maintain the equipment . . . and down they spin, out of control.

At its simplest, involving production operators in routine maintenance is based on the concept, 'If you use it, you keep it from breaking', and this means, at the minimum, cleaning, lubricating, replacing consumable materials, and undertaking routine maintenance. But this is the minimum.

Total productive maintenance (TPM) means something different in virtually every company. For the Japanese it has to be part of *genba kanri*, workshop management. The Japanese Institute of Plant Maintenance says, 'TPM aims at maximising equipment effectiveness with a total system of preventive maintenance covering the entire life of the equipment. It involves everyone in all departments and at all levels; it motivates people for plant maintenance through small groups and voluntary activities.' It requires everyone to be developed to their full potential and requires a high degree of professionalism among the production workers.

The concept of the professional production worker is important in developing the ascendant organisation. Such people are not craft workers in the traditional sense; they do not engage in the complex maintenance work that requires a specialist, although they will undertake first line maintenance and will help the specialist as required. This entails not simply routine preventative maintenance work to prevent breakdowns, for breakdowns are the tip of the iceberg. TPM requires attention to be paid to set up times, minor stoppages, and problems with speed, defects and yield. Maintenance is everyone's responsibility. TPM recognises that if the equipment is not right then quality will suffer. Its traditional goals were zero breakdowns but modern analytical techniques seek to analyse the potential incidence, impact and cost of breakdowns to assess the cost-benefit relationship of *total* productive maintenance. In simple terms, TPM is costly in time and materials. In circumstances in which a non-critical machine is costly to maintain and quick and easy to repair then, provided performance does not deteriorate to the unacceptable, it may be better to extend the maintenance cycle or not maintain it at all. At the other extreme, critical equipment with high impact may need to be maintained more frequently. There are many examples of maintenance inducing problems, the cost-benefit decision is complex, and the decision process must involve the production people.

In practice, like *kaizen*, TPM recognises that the person doing a job knows more about the 'feel' of the equipment than anyone else and can often predict a problem before it occurs and will fix it. Where limited technical judgement is required, the operator will be trained to carry out all the planned maintenance, rectifying any faults that are found. The operator will also be trained to train the robots; that is, based on accumulated knowledge of the process, using remote control, will guide the robot through its actions and 'fix' each action in the optimum position.

These responsibilities give a high level of ownership. In a traditional environment reprogramming or retraining robots or CNC machines is the responsibility of the professional maintenance people or engineers. If it is not right, the operators disown it and wait for maintenance or engineering to repair it. If, however, the operators have themselves reprogrammed the machine and it is not right, *they* readily take remedial action.

The role of the professional maintenance staff changes dramatically. They become responsible for the complex planned maintenance programmes where specialised technical knowledge and judgement are required and attend to complex breakdowns which the operators are unable to fix. They are responsible for analysing problems and undertaking *kaizen* activities. They may undertake equipment performance analysis aimed at, for example, reducing maintenance frequency, improving maintenance instructions, adjusting spare part stock levels, improving quality or reducing scrap.

TPM, however, goes further – for the goal must be not just to keep equipment working but to improve its performance and ensure it is regularly upgraded. Very rarely is equipment delivered and installed in a perfect condition. Because of the partnership between operators and maintenance staff they can work together from the very beginning to improve its condition, often very significantly, particularly in reducing cycle time, increasing efficiency or in making it more ergonomically acceptable.

TPM is, perhaps, more accurately defined as *total partnership maintenance*.

CHANGEOVER TIMES

John Scott of the Strathclyde Institute has calculated that around 40 per cent of production time does not add value, even in the best organised plants. Half of that non-added value time is due to changing over and adjusting tools. The problem is that most improvement activities have focused on making the added value part of the operations more effective, not on reducing the non-added value activities. If we are also to concentrate on the latter we need to pay particular attention to reducing the time taken between completing one run and starting the next, so that we minimise the 'OK part to OK part' time. This can have a dramatic effect on the subsequent length of the production run.

For example, in the automobile industry we used to take four hours or more to change the dies in our giant body panel presses. Consequently, when they were running, we wanted to keep them producing for as long as possible. We would stamp two-week's supply of a single panel and live with the inventory costs, slow response, undetected quality problems, and obsolete stock. It made management lazy and the workforce careless. Today we can change the dies in four minutes. In machining operations highly skilled technicians used to take an hour to change the tools but now a combination of operators and automation can do the job in seconds.

Ohno and Shingo developed the concept of 'single minute exchange of dies' (SMED) in which they aimed to achieve die and tool changes in less than ten minutes. Under this system the aim is to maximise the amount of setting which is done *outside* the machine while it is still working, first by distinguishing internal from external work and then seeking to convert as much internal setting work to external. Having done this, the next step is to eliminate work that needs to be done while the tool is actually being fitted into the machine. Finally, the amount of external work is reduced. Once this is achieved, machines need not be run for hours, producing sufficient stock for several weeks. They can be run for minutes. Stock is reduced, less storage capacity is needed, quality problems are minimised and the operators are fully engaged virtually all the time. They can be trained in all tasks, setting, operating, quality checking, material delivery and removal. The old job of machine-minder disappears, so also does the tool setter who used to receive a four-year training programme, achieving a high status but in a very restricted area of skill.

What this means is that operating and technological advances allow us to manufacture in small batches while retaining the advantages of mass production. We can thus respond more rapidly to the changes in market place demand. Said Taiichi Ohno, 'Procure only what is needed when it is needed and in the amount needed' (Ohno, 1988b, p. 15). He did not believe in demand forecasting; it's better, 'going to the racetrack and betting on horses' (ibid, p. 126) and Shingo wrote that, 'The root of all evil is planning for demand on the basis of speculation' (Shingo, 1988, p. 49).

INVENTORY REDUCTION

While component inventory is only a part of the JIT system, it is an important part. Richard Schonberger says that it originated almost by accident in the Japanese steel industry in the late 1950s at a time when the steelmakers' over-expansion had led to very high stock levels. Consequently, the shipbuilders could get very fast delivery and because of this they dropped their safety stocks from one month to three days and received their new orders just in time (Schonberger, 1982, p. 17). Taiichi Ohno, on the other hand, visited the USA in 1951 and 1952 and, inspired by the 'customer pull' system he saw in American supermarkets (whereby the customer 'pulls' the product from the shelves and it is then replaced), developed the first *kanban* system in 1955 in Nagoya (now renamed Toyota City). The significance of Toyota City is that the supplier plants are mainly located within a very short distance of their only customer, Toyota, thus reducing the risk from traffic delays and making possible the low stock system.

JIT is very much a philosophy, not just a manufacturing practice. In Japan the emphasis of JIT is on the 'J' – just. Deliver *just* what is necessary, build *just* what is needed, use *just* the required amount of effort, have *just* the right amount of stock in the system. It is about the elimination of waste. In the West we have tended to concentrate on the 'IT' – in time, and build up our stocks to give us the protection we feel we need to enhance on time delivery, 'just in case' our suppliers run into difficulties or our machines break down or our workers go on strike! Concentrating on the 'in time' element actually achieves little and in fact can be positively harmful. It can give the impression of efficiency when all that has happened is that the inventory holding is passed from the customer to the supplier, or that a huge warehouse is built, space is rented by the supplier and the inventory holding is relocated.

JIT does not totally eliminate stock and to attempt to do so will result in disaster. No manufacturer can contemplate a system which is so fragile that a traffic accident can cause major disruption to the manufacturing process. But again, new technology is enabling manufacturers to get close to the ideal. First, the risks must be reduced and then the safety cover can be minimised. The risks can be reduced by suppliers locating close to the customer and by working towards mutual commitment. Synchronous supply can then become the step beyond just in time. Synchronous supply is the technique whereby electronic data interchange (EDI) allows the computer of the customer to 'talk' to the computer of the supplier. As the customer's computer schedules the product build sequence it links with the supplier's computer and says, 'Start building a component to this specification.' The supplier follows this instruction, places the components in pallets suitable for direct line side delivery, puts the pallets in a small truck, delivers to the customer's plant, hitches the pallets to a small tractor and delivers direct to lineside. The component has gone from production line to production line with no intermediate storage and arrives genuinely just in time. Some may arrive just a few minutes before needed and at the most there will be an hour's stock at the point of production. Production has truly pulled supply.

Such a system is highly efficient, very fragile and relies heavily on the skill and commitment of all people at every stage of the process. It places a responsibility on the supplier's staff, far greater than anything under the traditional systems, and depends on high levels of attendance. When staffing levels are reduced to eliminate waste it becomes critical that those people who are employed have high attendance rates. There is no fat to cover absenteeism. Many doubted if such commitment could be achieved in the West, where individualism and competitiveness are the order of the day. Some companies have succeeded surprisingly well. In Nissan, at the extreme, we are down to stock arriving at lineside ten minutes before it is needed. One hidden benefit – minimal stock makes stocktaking day so much easier!

MATERIAL SUPPLY

JIT is as much a philosophy as it is a practice but the hard edge of the process is control of the logistics. In fact, in a complex manufacturing process it is logistics management that makes the material supply element of JIT work. Materials managers are fond of saying, much to the annoyance of production people, that production is easy; the difficult part is getting the right components to the right place at the right time in the right quantity. If you can achieve that with virtually no stock in the system you have cracked the production problem. The aim is to minimise inventory without increasing risks.

Of course, they are wrong in underestimating the complexity of the production process – but when you consider the fact that a car can have about 3300 parts with ten or more colours and that there are around 7000 variants, the difficulty of achieving the logistics objectives 100 per cent of the time is immense. Very few succeed.

Richard Lamming, in an attempt to provide hard evidence of delivery performance, studied the actual experience of 47 companies receiving 4600 deliveries over a two-week period in 1993. He found that only 14.7 per cent of deliveries were made on time on the *day* or within the *week* specified. He also found that 62 per cent of items delivered for use in production have a specified delivery tolerance of a week or more. Only 6 per cent of customers specified a tolerance of plus or minus one hour and only 26 per cent a tolerance of within a specified day (Lamming, 1993). This means that the vast majority of deliveries have a tolerance level far greater than that acceptable for JIT processes and that, in any case, only a small proportion actually achieve even these slack tolerances. So however much companies may profess to be working towards JIT, the only hard evidence shows that the real world has barely scratched the surface.

Against this overall performance level of 14.7 per cent on time achievement within a one-week window, Nissan in the UK is achieving in

1994, 96 per cent on time deliveries within a two-hour window! In Japan the figure exceeds 99 per cent. If we are to talk of really moving towards JIT, that is the level that has to be attained!

To get there, two building blocks have to be in place: a materials resource planning system and sophisticated logistics control.

Basically, materials resource planning (MRP) is a number-crunching exercise. It allows the manufacturer to order materials based on its own forward orders, taking into account current inventory. The original version of MRP failed because it took no account of the supplier's capacity to build the required parts. MRP II corrects this by putting a master scheduling system at the front end, with the intention of identifying parts that are both critical for the build programme and subject to capacity constraints. Once the potential mismatch is identified, it then becomes possible to change the planned build sequence and reschedule the parts delivery.

MRP is demanding and is only really necessary for those companies whose products comprise a large number of constituent parts and a complicated bill of material. It requires from engineering, accurate and up-to-date bills of material; from purchasing, accurate lead times; from production, the disciplines to work to the schedule and from material handling, the capability of maintaining accurate inventory data. As a result a high level of user education is necessary to make it operate effectively and many systems fail because of the lack of commitment to train users properly. They also fail because the users are often not involved in designing the system – no ownership – and because they are introduced where the application is inappropriate for the product, that is, where there are few component parts and relatively simple structural layers within the bill of material. Thus, when managers find they are being required to use a complex programme when all they need is a simple tool, they lose interest. A final assembly operation with hundreds, if not thousands, of components needs MRP; a press shop does not. So, within an organisation, different material control systems can be used. 'Simplify before automating' applies here just as much as in manufacturing.

To reduce inventory significantly it is necessary to go further and examine the total logistics of the supply chain.The companies that really have the answer are the fast moving supermarket groups. Manufacturing needs such a supply system in which there is minimal stock in the store, virtually nothing at the supplier and the only stock on the road is in trucks which are moving, not standing in a lay-by waiting to be called in!

Nissan, after an extensive study of road hauliers, chose Ryder Distribution to develop its delivery network. Under the eventual arrangement Nissan, through electronic data interchange, advises the supplier what and when to build and Ryder, the precise time at which to collect. On a round robin basis the truck calls at about six suppliers on an optimised route plan picking up a part load from each. Each truck travels to a central cross docking facility where the mixed loads are transferred on to large final delivery trucks in the optimum sequence for delivery to the manufacturing plant. We have calculated that with about half (67) the UK suppliers on this system, if each individual supplier were to deliver separately they would cover an additional 5 million miles per year and the plant would be so congested that it would grind to a halt. As it is, the system allows an average inventory holding of less than one day with no warehousing, no stock at the suppliers and the trucks are moving all the time. Components are presented in the optimum way for the end-user and the quick return of re-usable packaging to the supplier is assured. It sounds complicated and technologically took a huge amount of development. But it works. Stock turns exceed 200 per year!

This again returns us to commitment and control. JIT provides the commitment but MRP and logistics provide the control.

LEVEL SCHEDULING AND DISTRIBUTION

The JIT system and the elimination of waste require a high degree of predictability, almost a contradiction in terms. If a manufacturer of complex consumer durable products relies on confirmed end-customer orders before commencing the build of the product, the orders will be irregular, production staff will be standing around much of the time and the customer will have to wait for delivery. But most customers, when we have made up our minds to purchase a new dishwasher or motor car, do not want to wait. We want it now, not in two months' time when the order has creaked through the system with only a few hours spent actually building it. The problem is that manufacturers like low inventories of components, but low inventories of components depend upon predictable volumes and predictable volumes result in building for stock. Demand pull exists to the point of manufacture. Thereafter it changes to supply push.

As a result customers often either have to wait or settle for an alternative specification. Only 25 per cent of British customers get the exact specification of car they originally wanted, 55 per cent accept different specifications and 20 per cent do not buy (Harbour, 1993, p. 12).

There is a loss of profit from lost sales, wrong stock in the system and substantial carrying costs. Dealers often have to offer heavy discounts to dispose of wrong stock, particularly when there is a market slump or when new models are about to be introduced.

The objective of a distribution system must be to get the right product to the right place just in time, with the minimum of stock in the system and at the lowest cost. But if such a system creates major inefficiencies for the manufacturer and therefore adds to costs, there must be a balance. Achieving that balance has in the past been an art. Fortunately, technology is beginning to turn it into a science – but there is a long way to go.

Technologically, a customer could go into a showroom, virtually design a car on a terminal, adding or deleting options to the price limit, and finally press a button which instructs the manufacturing plant to build the car of the customer's choice. From just in time to real time! The problem is not the ordering. It is having to stock the components necessary to meet all possible options. To make such a system fully operational there will need to be a dramatic commonisation of non-visual and performance parts plus a range of customised options. But to avoid high inventories of the customised options the JIT systems will have to link electronically with key suppliers who will be directly instructed to produce and deliver the components. The logical conclusion is a production run of one; the end customer pulls final production! Anything else produces waste.

By going down this route we are on our way to defining the key business processes: customer ordering, communication to the manufacturer and component supplier, manufacturing the components, assembling the final product, distribution to the customer. It is only these stages that are both essential and/or add value. Anything else, including any middle stages of order processing or product storage, adds cost and the organisation should work hard at eliminating it.

Unfortunately such an approach, because of the irregular nature of customer demand, will lead to major manufacturing inefficiencies. The compromise solution comes from the fast moving consumer goods industries and begins with accurate sales forecasting. Short of economic catastrophe, most manufacturers of consumer durables maintain rolling monthly forecasts twelve to eighteen months ahead and become more precise as production dates get closer. Often this final schedule is frozen two weeks to a month before actual production, allowing ample time for most suppliers to deliver. In practice most organisations can predict that 80 per cent of orders will come from about 20 per cent of the range and this allows the development of regional or national distribution centres from which the 80 per cent of predictable orders can be distributed without requiring dealer swaps. Such centres allow for a lower stock base, reduced carrying costs and quicker service.

With such systems it should not be impossible for a customer to receive a car within a week of ordering it from stock and within three weeks if it is a special build.

THE FIVE 'S's

To achieve such efficiency requires, however, much more than a highly skilled group of operators. It requires high levels of housekeeping, a task which is much maligned because of inadequate understanding of its value. Western managements pay lip service to housekeeping. While visiting a medium-size enterprise in Japan I noticed sets of small scales at various points.

'What are they for?'
'Twice a shift we sweep the floor and weigh the amount of waste we collect, usually a few grammes per operator!'

The largest weight used on these scales was 100 grammes!

To the Japanese, housekeeping is much more than sweeping up. They have introduced the 5 'S's:

Seiri (consolidation)	Separate the necessary from the unnecessary and dispose of the latter (for example, tools, machinery, defective products, documents)
Seiton (orderliness)	Put the necessary objects in a safe place, convenient for use. Arrange in rows 'A place for everything, everything in its place'
Seiso (clean up)	Maintain a clean and safe condition and while cleaning, check for deterioration and change
Seiketsu (cleanliness)	Routinely maintain cleanliness and order to prevent deterioration
Shitsuke (discipline)	Train everyone to systemise the discipline. Follow the procedures (standard operation, safety procedures, start and finish times, keeping appointments, and so on).

While the 5 'S's go significantly further than simple 'housekeeping', they achieve nothing if they are not implemented and assessed. Not just by a walk about but in a systematic way – that which is properly measured is properly done! Nissan has consolidated the 5 'S's into 3 'S's for practical day-to-day purposes – *seiri*, *seiton* and *seiso* and the senior supervisors regularly *measure* achievement. For example, under *seiso* one of the questions asked is, 'Are things scattered (parts, dust or debris). Is there dirt or leakages?' and the area is assessed on a scale shown in Figure 9.1.

Points are awarded and when the points from all other elements are added, an overall rating is achieved. Depending on that score is the timing of the next inspection. The worse the score, the sooner the next visit!

The responsibility for achieving the required level lies with the operators. There is not an army of cleaners to do this work for them. Involving the people doing the job means that they find the true cause of any problems that exist and can then deal with the problem at source.

Floors	— no scattered objects – fewer than five scattered – more than five
Parts and containers	— None dirty – fewer than five dirty – more than five
Racks and chutes	— None dirty – less than 20 per cent dirty – more than 20 per cent
Machinery and workbenches	— No dirty machines – one or more dirty
Tools, instruments and gauges	— None dirty – one or more dirty

Figure 9.1 The 3 'S' Rating System

VISIBLE MANAGEMENT

The Japanese practised 'management by walking around' long before it became fashionable in the West.

The success of their approach was brought home to me by seeing Toshiaki Tsuchiya, Nissan's first UK Managing Director, in action. Although his English was not good, he was totally at home on the shop floor, in the manufacturing environment. He was able to communicate effectively because he *understood* what the manufacturing process was about. Because he understood and because the people understood that he understood, he gained respect and was able to set ever increasing standards. He was not 'a suit' from the office putting in a symbolic appearance asking stupid questions about how long someone had worked for the company and what job they did before joining! And because he understood, his presence was never feared or resented by the supervisors.

Visible management, however, goes further than managers being visible. To the Japanese it is a pictorial display of the performance of the section but it is used also to highlight potential problems. Using diagrams and graphs, performance achievements against quality, cost, volume and people (QCVP) are displayed on boards adjacent to the workplace; they are maintained by the team and require the performance to be readily known to everyone, the team, the managers and casual visitors. But, as with most things Japanese, there is a philosophy behind it. A visiting Japanese, Hideo Kakimoto, said:

> To use visual management to our advantage we must have the courage to make the problem clear to all of the people by means of words and graphics. . . To help you learn and achieve your targets you must have a person who has a strong character who can find potential concerns before they happen and graphically display the potential fault. . . *Solutions are easy to find, anticipating the concern is much more difficult.*

Performance measures which are displayed can include:

- the zone objectives and achievements to date, including productivity and quality improvements
- current volume and quality achievement
- energy costs
- use of direct and indirect material
- scrap costs
- staff training/skill level
- attendance
- safety record
- facility utilisation rates, and so on

The format is standard but the measures may vary and a high degree of individuality in the presentation develops. Some are so artistically produced they are a delight to study; others are very basic. They visibly indicate to the individual the way his or her efforts contribute to improved performance; they can give a broader understanding of the business and provide a simple and accessible format for introducing people to basic graphical and statistical concepts. While some of the information may originate from outside the group – for example, the actual cost of non-production material – most originates from within and often an individual operator will be responsible for completing and maintaining a specific chart as part of the 'discretionary' work. They bring home to people those elements which are controllable. 'Scrap', for example, will be shown as 'The cost per car of the scrap created in this section' and similarly with energy costs and the use of material. Individuals cannot always appreciate that they can have an impact on the company's total costs but they can see it as a meaningful objective to reduce the use of indirect materials in their section from 11 pence per car to 9. This is cost control where it really matters!

Whereas such an approach is easier in manufacturing areas where results are easily measured, it should not be supposed that it cannot be as effective in an office environment. For example, in Nissan all indirect departments have their own visible management boards. Performance indicators in purchasing include localised parts reject ratios, warranty claims, design initiated cost reductions, annual settlement levels, training, travel and overtime. In the training section performance indicators include training days delivered, non-attendance on scheduled programmes, progress on developing new programmes, external qualifications achieved, flexible learning centre usage; all measured against previously determined targets. Many organisations measure performance. How many display it for all to see?

OPERATOR CARE

As we have seen, *The Machine that Changed the World* barely mentioned the impact of lean production on the people in the organisation, and people like David Robertson have stepped into the breach maintaining that it is the logic of the system that leads inevitably to such problems. The constructive critic, however, seeks to avoid such situations arising.

Often, manufacturing processes *are* demanding, both physically and mentally, and building motor cars is more demanding than most. It is a managerial responsibility to minimise the impact of these demands on the people and to plan production so that staffing levels are always right for the product mix, not fixed at the lowest level. Ever since we introduced the concept of continuous improvement one of the improvement objectives has been to make the jobs easier.

One of the areas of great neglect in the design and engineering disciplines of manufacturing industry is the long-term failure to apply ergonomic principles to the build of the product. The academic education of undergraduate engineers barely recognises the requirement and most manufacturers have done little more than pay lip service to the concept.

Within Nissan we have developed a specific company policy that, 'The ergonomics of building a car will be a fundamental factor in the original design, engineering and specification of the product, facility, tooling and processes. Such factors will also be included in all changes, improvements and *kaizen* activities.'

As a result the input into new model programmes specifically requires supervisors and engineers to study difficult jobs on the current model with a view to eliminating them at source on future products. The capital budget approval process has a specific 'Operator Care' section as one of the justifications for capital expenditure. Ease of working requirements are included in facility specifications and standards.

The only long-term solution is to design out the problems, to design for manufacturability; but in the short term it is the supervisors who have the responsibility of solving current difficulties. After a stuttering start, using external ergonomic consultants who proposed analytical techniques which could only be used by professional consultants, we gave the task to a group of supervisors. The results were fantastic.

Their objective was, 'To investigate, trial and implement a common method of assignment assessment acceptable throughout the company.' The starting point was the wealth of experience they had acquired from implementing practical solutions to difficult problems, albeit without a great deal of structured analysis. The process was to understand the theory, examine various methods used across the company, determine the methodology most appropriate for general use, revise that methodology, run a trial in the various shops, evaluate the results, modify where necessary. Once their proposal was considered acceptable, they worked with people from the training and safety departments, who in any case had been involved from the start, to develop training programmes which were then implemented on a company wide basis.

The two points of this story are first, that the potential problems of lean production are being addressed to prevent them becoming real problems. Second, and yet again, in the ascendant organisation ownership is everything. The supervisors developed their own systematic method of assessing the difficulty of jobs – a way which is quick, accurate and allows rapid action. It does not have the complexity of a 'professional' process but it does utilise ergonomic analysis in a way which is easy to use and allows 200 people, not just one specialist, to study jobs and their impact on staff, and allows those 200 people to initiate remedial action, whether it be facility change, low-cost automation, process change, further training or revised job rotation. To return to a previous point, they were not 'empowered' to do this. It was simply the right place and when they needed corporate assistance they delegated upwards!

In industry, particularly in the USA, two-hour job rotations are not uncommon, but there can be no precise formula. Within a work group there will be a variety of tasks each making different demands. Some will be easy, others difficult; some will take a long time to learn, others a short time; some will use shoulder muscles, others the wrist. The optimum rotation pattern can only be determined within the group, advised at shop floor level by the experts. The responsibility of top management is to recognise that there is a potential issue and to provide the training, the resources and above all the commitment to resolve it. Genuinely devolving responsibility means that prevention or resolution takes place where the problems can occur.

There are literally hundreds of minor improvements that can be made once operators and their supervisors have real responsibility and the resources to implement change. Often, descriptions of such improvements are meaningless unless you can actively see the operation, but in March 1993, in order to promote these initiatives, the NMUK production department began to produce its own, very simple *Genba Kanri News*. Handwritten, photocopied and with simple line drawings, the publication served to illustrate small but significant achievements. The very first example in the very first issue showed this simplicity.

The objective was to alleviate bending and stretching over an assembly jig and prevent the potential for back and arm strain. The jig was at an angle of 45 degrees and fairly deep, and the operator – using power tools – had to bend over to reach the rear, resulting in considerable strain. To correct this, the jig height was raised, relaid in the horizontal plane and a central section cut away, thus allowing the operator to work closer to the component. Although very simple, this study resulted in four improvements:

- operator care – no bending or stretching
- improved quality – spot weld positions more accurate with no 'edgewelds' or burrs

- reduced cycle time by twenty seconds
- improved safety

Operator care does not just make the job easier!

10 Beyond TQM – Integrating Quality

If our factories through careful work, assure the quality of our products, it will be to the foreigners' interest to get supplies from us, and their money will flow into the kingdom.

(Jean-Baptiste Colbert, Finance Minister to Louis XIV, 1664)

THE CHANGING NATURE OF QUALITY

The quality revolution has long been with us. Despite Jean-Baptiste Colbert's seventeenth century recognition of its importance, it was not until the 1950s that the work of people like W. Edwards Deming, Joseph Duran and Armand Feigenbaum began to become influential, first in Japan, then in the USA, and later in other parts of Western industrial society.

Since the 1950s the attitude towards quality has rapidly changed. Though not absolutely precise, the progression has been something like:

1950s 'What's this about quality?'
1960s 'Nice to have good quality but we can sell all we produce so it's not critical.'
1970s 'Japanese quality is good and we need to match their levels but it will add to our costs to get there.'
1980s 'Crosby tell us that "Quality is free". If we get it right first time, that actually saves us money.'
1990s 'Achieving high levels of quality consistently, gives us a competitive edge.'

But, by the 21st century, consistent high quality will be the norm. It will give no competitive advantage. It will not win the race. It will be the entry price to get to the starting gate. If you do not have a high level of quality, and are not continuously improving it, you may as well not bother.

The simplest and to me the best description of TQM has been given by Professor John Oakland. He has written:

> Go to a company that sports posters instead of beliefs and the falseness is rapidly apparent. *TQM moves the focus of control from outside the individual to within*; the objective is to make everyone accountable for their own performance and to get them committed to attaining quality in a highly motivated fashion . . . Consistency can only be achieved if we ensure that for every product or each time a service is performed the same materials, the same equipment, the same methods or procedures are used in exactly the same way every time. The process will then be under control . . . Control by itself is not sufficient. TQM requires that the process should be improved continually by reducing its variability.

John Oakland is not a million miles from the synthesis between motivation and control.

Evidence of the success of formal TQM programmes is patchy and contradictory. A survey by Arthur D. Little of 500 US companies found that only one-third felt their programmes were having a significant effect and A T Kearney, management consultants, found that, 'About 80 per cent of all TQM initiatives fail to produce tangible results. A significant proportion flounder after the initial period of enthusiasm, training and team formation. Some lack the unrelenting sustained commitment of senior management; some stall in spite of the commitment'.

Two UK surveys, both published in 1993, presented conflicting views. Coming out of the University of Bradford, *Does TQM Impact on Bottom Line Results*? reported on a study of 29 companies over five years of audited results and showed that around 22 of the TQM companies outperformed their industry averages in profit margins, return on total assets, turnover per employee, profit per employee, total assets per employee, fixed asset trends and average remuneration.

Although not proving direct *causation*, the authors believe that the results point towards a strong *association* between the introduction of TQM and bottom-line results. 'TQM merely offers companies the opportunity to carry out improvements and focuses on getting closer to customers. It is only a licence to practice. Companies must still have the right strategies in place, the right products and services, the right commitment and the right investment strategies to be successful' (Zairi, Letza and Oakland, 1994).

On the other hand, a research report by the Institute of Management of 880 responding companies found only 8 per cent rated their quality initiatives as 'totally successful' with the majority claiming 'a moderate degree of success' or neutrality. Fewer than half of those surveyed said that the initiatives had led to an improvement in sales or profitability. One respondent said, 'The worst problem for those of us who believe in quality excellence is the tenuous link between our success in the commercial environment and the quality of service. Most of our customers buy on price as long as there is an acceptable level of service.' As I said, high quality is the entry price.

CUSTOMER FOCUS

What is quality? Armand Feigenbaum defined it as, 'The total composite product and service characteristics of marketing, engineering, manufacture and maintenance through which the product and service in use will meet the expectations of the customer' (Feigenbaum, 1983). This definition, though complex, brings in all key functions in working together to satisfy the customer. Definitions which speak of 'zero defects', 'right first time', 'fitness for purpose' are OK, but in a limited way. They seem to restrict quality to the manufacturing process. In one of his typically provocative statements Tom Peters said, 'Phil Crosby's "Get it right first time" is the single sickest statement I have ever seen' (Peters, 1992).

However, most *final* customers do not choose to use such definitions. They might ask questions relating to the product's reliability, features, durability, performance, safety, ease of use, ease of maintenance, environmental friendliness, after sales service, newness or uniqueness. They are concerned with point of sale service, resale values, price and value for money. For many products the issues may be of status, appearance, aesthetics and perception: the intangibles which may be the deciding factor. The customer's definition is often irrational, illogical and always changing. Rover's marketing director, Rod Ramsay, said of his company's marketing strategy, 'The bottom line principle is simple. We want people to think, "I'd look good in a car like that" – because in reality that's what people buy cars for these days.' *Perception is reality.*

Most writers on quality ascribe to the customer their *own* beliefs on what quality issues are important. However, Mintel, the market survey organisation, undertook a comprehensive survey of what the customers actually valued (Mintel, 1993). Under separate lists for products and services the top five attributes were:

Products	**Services**
Well made	Helpful staff
Safe to use	Efficient service
Value for money	Knowledgeable staff
Reliable	Clear pricing
Durable	Guarantees

Even here, the specific listing varied with social grouping and age but on examination we see that the product planning, marketing, design engineering, manufacturing, pricing, sales and service, legal, recruitment and training functions all have a part to play in ensuring that the customers' priorities are satisfied.

Following Mintel and accepting irrationality, quality must never be defined in terms of the provider of the product or service but in terms of the customers' needs. Therefore, in relation to the final customer, I offer the following definition:

The quality of a product or service is the customers' perception of it, taking into account their total experience of those features they consider important.

These features might include price, sales experience, specification, performance, reliability, durability, ease of use, after sales service, disposal and image. Not all customers will regard every element as important and most will have different priorities. Some may include elements I have omitted. 'Value for money' is often mentioned, but I would regard that as a conclusion arising from the sum total of the elements. One element may balance another.

In October 1993 I purchased a new briefcase from the Salisbury chain store at what I thought was a good price. The sales staff were helpful and knowledgeable. It had the right specification and looked good. However, I quickly found that the locks did not operate well and after two months one lock catch broke off. I had not kept the receipt, but the staff could not have been more considerate. They immediately changed the briefcase without question. Unfortunately, the lock catch of the second briefcase broke in exactly the same way. Again the staff were helpful and explained that they had received several complaints, the manager had tested the catches herself and found that it was a general problem with the batch received at her shop. She had sent all unsold stock back, had been assured that no other store had experienced problems and now had a new batch. But then I had the same problem with the third, and again with the fourth, until I asked for my money back. Would I shop there again? Yes, because on balance the understanding and assistance was good. Would I purchase the same make of briefcase again? No! Another customer, however, might be far less patient and regard the initial fault as condemning the product and the shop, however helpful the sales staff might have been. The permutations are endless.

The beginning of the road of integrating quality into the culture must be to get close to your customers to understand what really comprises added value for them, and move from simply meeting the customers' needs to working together to develop both their demands and your capability of meeting them. The most successful companies have the most demanding customers but it means developing the relationship so that it becomes one of partnership. This means, for example, ensuring that the technical staff meet with your customers to ensure that you have a precise understanding of their needs and the use of your product; that you obtain detailed feedback on your product's performance and reliability; that you know the quality of service provided by your representatives and how they *perceive* your product in relation to your competitors.

But staff can be wrong. Barrie Hopson and Mike Scally tell the story of British Airways, when in 1993 staff were asked what they thought their customers wanted. They responded with requirements such as safety, good timekeeping, baggage arriving safely, good food, friendly service. True, but this is what the customers *expect*. When it comes to gaining positive goodwill customers want to be made to feel special, to be welcomed, to see staff demonstrating care and concern for the more vulnerable passengers, to see mistakes and difficulties dealt with well, with sensitivity and concern. It is these things that make for a real high-quality service (Hopson and Scally, 1989, p. 21). But not for everyone. The regular business traveller may not want smiles and assistance but simply to be left alone to get through the journey with the minimum of hassle. The real trick is to recognise that different people have different needs and treat them appropriately.

This personal service can only be given by a motivated, dedicated front liner – in the 50 million moments of truth of Jan Carlzon's SAS staff, or when the check-out assistant thanks the customer, not when 'Thank you for your custom' is printed on the till receipt!

Awareness of customer care is not new but the crucial contribution of the front line employee to the achievement of genuine and sustainable improvements in meeting customer needs is less well integrated in corporate goals and strategies. For that you need employee ownership, which is not achieved by sending people on customer care courses.

Smiling is not enough: you must have the systems and procedures in place to support that smile, otherwise it is seen for what it is – superficial gloss. However well the customer is treated by Carlzon's front liners, if the planes do not run on time or are not clean, no amount of smiling will compensate for a poor service.

Many like to say, 'Our staff are our greatest asset', even though few executives actually behave in the way they talk. But when they make such statements they are unconsciously separating the staff from the organisation. The executives do not *possess* the staff. The staff *are* the organisation and if this is the case the greatest assets of the organisation are its customers and the whole organisation must be dedicated to that belief. If organisations fail their customers, that is when they go out of business.

The internal quality objective of a business must then be to ensure that it is managed so as to meet its external customers' definitions of quality. As John Oakland implied, you do not do this by sticking up posters around the building. Nor do you achieve success by the grand single programme. It is achieved by combining motivation and control, and we begin our examination at the beginning – designing for quality.

DESIGN FOR QUALITY

Depending on the product, some 70–85 per cent of its lifetime costs are determined at the design stage. Once it is accepted for production, a company will be lucky if, over the life of the product, it is able to reduce total costs by more than 10 per cent. Similarly with quality. The product which is difficult to build at its production launch is likely to remain difficult for years to come. Marginal improvements may be made to the product, facility and task, but rarely will the 'pig' ever become a 'pussycat' (with apologies to pigs).

This is not the book to go into immense detail about the practice of simultaneous engineering, but in pursuing the synthesis between commitment of the people and control of the processes we cannot neglect this concept which, if properly managed, can have a fundamental effect not only on the quality of life of the people but also on the quality of the product and subsequent customer satisfaction. The quality of the final product, however defined, is in great part dependent on the quality of the parts that go into making it and the quality of the final assembly process. I offer therefore what I hope is a reasonably non-technical explanation.

Before the era of simultaneous engineering, the product design process was something of an ivory tower activity paying little attention to the demands of the market place, and no attention to the needs of suppliers or production. Suppliers were given a detailed component specification and asked to quote a price – usually the cheapest got the business – which was then split between at least two suppliers who could be played off against each other at the next tendering round. As a result they had no incentive to undertake long-term investment in their own design capability or in facility investment or in the training and development of their staff. If they might not have the business next year, why bother? Manufacturing engineers who had to design the facility were able to see the product but, inevitably, late design changes and delays meant that their time was squeezed. Production management barely got a look in, and were unable to contribute suggestions, or request features that might assist the build of the product. The results were that the design and development process took a very long time as each stage had to be completed before the next began, and quality was a major casualty. No one really owned the product.

Simultaneous engineering seeks to integrate all stages of the process from market research and product planning through styling, design, engineering, prototype build and test, facility design, production, marketing and sales. It involves multi-disciplinary teams, including people from the component suppliers, who have to be involved at a very early stage of the project. Some of the key elements include:

- the product being defined in terms of the customers' needs
- design for ease of assembly (for example, right sequence, minimum number of parts, one way assembly, constant orientation, minimal handling, multi-functional parts especially small fasteners, and simplicity)
- simultaneous development of the product and process
- high level of component integration
- clear project leadership with a team empowered to make decisions
- strong support from non-involved functions
- early definition of much of the specification
- team members co-located in open areas
- few top management reviews

Simultaneous engineering requires not only considerable overlaps between the product development stages but also early involvement of suppliers. When suppliers were regarded almost as the enemy, to be screwed into the ground on price and beaten over the head on quality, this was clearly not possible – but with the development of partnership sourcing it becomes a practical reality. Under this concept the customer enters into a long-term relationship with a single source supplier. They are committed to work together in many areas but, in particular, suppliers are assisted in developing their design engineering capabilities. It is ridiculous, for example, that in the past suppliers have employed specialist external companies to produce prototype parts. They learn nothing by giving this responsibility to someone else. More can be achieved by high levels of pre-production quality assurance than by all the post-production fixes. It allows companies to aim for reject rates of parts per million instead of parts per thousand.

One result of simultaneous engineering is that design problems come to the fore much earlier in the process. These problems are registered as design changes and the later a change the more difficult and expensive it is to introduce. This process, however, not only shortens the total product development time, it also pulls forward design changes. The Japanese have been at this much longer than Western manufacturers and the typical number of design changes in the period prior to start of production is illustrated in Figure 10.1. The exact pattern will differ according to the product, but the principle is to maximise the number of changes *before* start of production and then after the immediate post-production hump reduce them as quickly as possible.

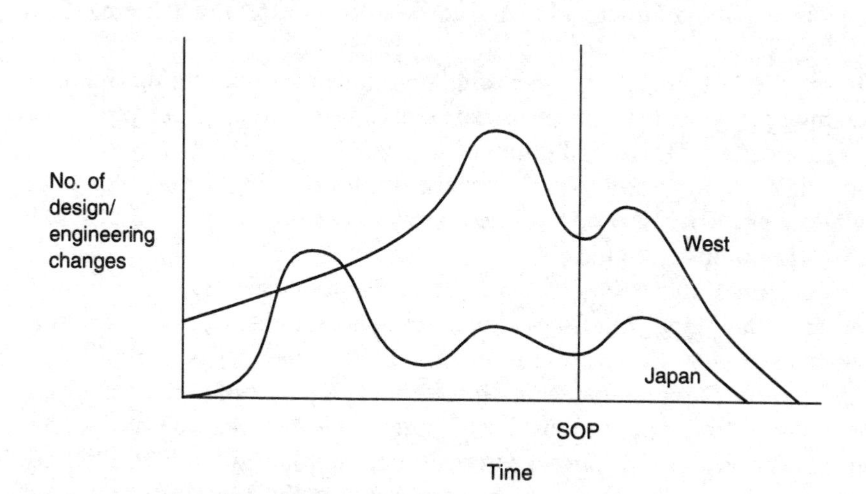

Figure 10.1 Design Changes over Time

The traditional pattern unintentionally leaves much of the product design to the customer – either the internal customer, that is the production people who have difficulty in building the product – or the external customer who finds that the product does not perform. But simultaneous engineering, in shortening the total process, allows the latest technology to be introduced and, for fashion-related features, allows the most up-to-date to be added. Customer needs can be determined and accommodated in the design stage. As new, lower-cost products are developed they can be introduced more quickly. Together, these elements can add up to a higher quality, more advanced but cheaper product hitting the market quicker. For some manufacturers it may even mean they can charge a higher price. Whatever the pricing strategy, at a time when product life cycles have dramatically shortened, six months earlier to market can make the difference between profit and loss.

Team Taurus was Ford's first attempt at developing a product through the multi- disciplinary approach. Led by Lew Veraldi, my old boss from Ford's European Product Development Centre, the team sought to bring in everybody, including the shop floor operators. Said Veraldi,

> Involving all groups in the process actually lowered costs . . . It was much easier to get people to talk about and come up with *constructive* changes when they couldn't pass off responsibility by saying 'that's really a manufacturing problem, not a design one'. There were no specific incentives set up for this project other than pride of workmanship . . . We motivated people by making sure they had an equity in the product and then listened to them carefully. (Quinn, 1988)

It is clear, then, that successful simultaneous engineering requires teamworking and involvement of the highest order throughout the organisation. The contribution of everyone is valued but they work together for a greater goal. It is not about so-called 'skunkworks' in which a group of mavericks are sent away to develop the product that will turn the company round.

Sometimes mavericks do succeed – *because* they are exceptional, because they break the rules rather than change them. The group may work as a very effective team but unless the remainder of the company feels part of the company team, then isolating a particular group can have a demoralising effect elsewhere. What is needed is a culture which involves *everyone*, so that all can deliver to high levels. Only in this way will a company be able to achieve consistent, high performance, and continually improve existing products. Ninety-nine per cent of people are not mavericks; they are normal in the best sense of the word. The task is to involve everyone, and, if there are exceptional performances, to ensure that the lessons are spread throughout the organisation.

BUILDING FOR QUALITY

In 1992 I was invited to give a presentation, *The people side of quality* to the directors of a major British company. In preparation for this they sent me copies of their documentation on Total Quality Management, beautifully produced, saying all the right things, quoting all the right people, setting up all the right systems with facilitators, co-ordinators and change agents and presenting all the right training programmes. But after several years 'at it' they still had problems. Although quality had improved, they felt that they had not made a major breakthrough; there was no real commitment throughout the organisation. Their problem was contained in their stated, 'at it'. They still thought of TQM as something slightly separate from the normal day-to-day business. It convinced me that when quality is properly integrated into an organisation it does not need glossy publications, facilitators or change agents. There need be no training courses specifically dedicated to quality and no TQM programme. We must achieve a company in which the commitment to quality is absolute at every level, permeates everything, is organic and although none of the training programmes is about quality, *all* of them are. While there are no change agents, everyone is an agent for change.

The ascendant organisation moves beyond seeing TQM as something separate needing capital letters (even if it is defined as embedding quality into the culture) to a state in which the achievement of existing high levels of quality and progression to ever higher levels is the normal way of life of everyone. Real success comes when there are no quality programmes as such, *but when quality is an integral part of the business.*

That is very easy to say and very difficult to achieve. First we must examine in a little more detail what it means and, as with all concepts, it depends very much on the right balance between control of the processes and commitment of the people.

The control of the processes begins with our old friend, the standard operation. By definition, any deviation from the standard operation will result in a worsening of quality. It establishes the standard to be achieved and the method of achieving it. It defines the material to be used and the equipment – every time in the same way. If there is no standard operation, quality will be determined by the experience of the operators and in a volume manufacturer or service organisation this will lead to an unstable process and unstable results. There will be no base from which change can be determined or improvements measured. In a craft based organisation such differences may, of course, be desirable.

The standard operation, applied properly, assigns responsibility for quality to the operator and the team. If responsibility is passed to an inspector, the attitude develops that, 'If I don't do it right it will be picked up.' To counteract this the Japanese developed the concept of the internal customer – meaning that you do not pass faulty goods to your neighbour or to the next section. But if you do not have time to complete a job or a fault occurs, you may either stop the process and seek assistance or flag up the fault so that it may be corrected. 'Neighbour checks' mean that within a zone each person is responsible for checking someone else's work. To do this effectively, operators need to learn at least the jobs before and after them. One of the myths about Japanese management practices is that they do not inspect. The ideal for bought-out components is that the confidence level in the supplier is such that there is no goods inward inspection but throughout the assembly process there is virtual 100 per cent checking, not by inspectors but by the operators themselves. The important point is *never criticise if someone admits a mistake*. As soon as you criticise, people stop admitting; more mistakes go through which have to be rectified later or creep through to the customer only to be found out when the product is in use.

In many processes, statistical process control (SPC) will help. SPC is a sampling and measurement technique aimed at reducing variability by setting tolerance limits and observing trends within these limits. Its advocates suggest that properly implemented it works by highlighting early any trends away from the standard or by quickly showing up random irregularities, suggesting that the process is out of control. Its detractors regard it as an 'after the event' check which tells that somewhere in the batch things started to go wrong, whereas we need to know *now* in order to detect problems immediately so as to prevent waste. In any case, it is argued, you can have a series of components which individually are within tolerance levels but cumulatively drift out of specification. Effective control requires 100 per cent checking and in many cases the only practicable way of achieving this is through automatic measuring devices, either by touch sensors or, with the latest technology, by laser scanning. As with all things, the objective is to achieve the right balance. In the 1970s and 1980s Ford went overboard on SPC, with the emphasis on the 'control'. Considerable improvements were achieved but because of the pressurised way it was introduced there were few heart and mind conversions.

POKA YOKE

Prevention is better than cure. The technique advocated by the Japanese is *poka yoke*, 'mistake avoidance', or autonomation – automation with a human face. It recognises that mistakes will occur particularly at the people–machine interface, and although with effective training they will be minimised, this is not enough. It also recognises that statistical methods of measuring quality are a mathematical compromise which attempt to achieve a balance between minimum inspection costs and maximum confidence. Sampling methods can never achieve 100 per cent assurance, although they do give useful information on the ability of a process to operate within tolerance limits. Such methods do, however, mean that some errors will be undetected, that the mistake can be repeated and rectification work will need to be done. *Poka yoke* aims to design the process to prevent mistakes or to detect them immediately and avoid repetition.

Poka yoke is neither new nor particularly Japanese but whereas in the West prevention devices are used mainly when the consequences of failure are serious, in Japan they are commonplace. *Poka yoke* devices, for example guide pins, contact plates, limit switches, error detectors and alarms, counters and check lists, are applied at four strategic points in the process:

Cannot start — A device detects an error in the system and prevents the process from beginning.

Cannot continue — A device detects a fault during the process and sounds an alarm and/or stops the process.

Cannot release — A device prevents the product from leaving the process if the operation has been incorrectly/incompletely performed.

Cannot pass — Following completion, the *poka yoke* device undertakes a 100 per cent check and prevents defective parts being passed downstream. The closer the device to the process the fewer defective parts are produced.

Poka yoke devices may be active or passive. Active devices make something happen – shut down the system, do not release clamps or eject rejects. A passive system provides a warning signal; at which point the operator has to take action. But whatever method is used, at the most one defect occurs before the problem is spotted and because the system is automatic, it spots them all (provided of course that it is properly maintained!) This enables the operator to attempt to define the cause and initiate remedial action.

Poka yoke is about control, but control without commitment will not achieve sustainable success!

COMMITMENT TO QUALITY

All the techniques in the world will not, however, give that true commitment to quality without which it cannot become an integral part of the business. We are not helped by the use of confusing terms like, 'The cost of quality' or, 'Quality is free'. Quality does not come free: it requires investment of time, money, training and facilities as well as moving control of the process and motivation of the workforce on to a different plane. There may be a pay off, you may stay in business and the investment may have a good payback – but it is not free. We should not speak of the cost of quality but rather of *the price of poor quality*, which may be to go out of business.

Quality is not a voluntary activity.

One of the great mistakes that many Western companies have made is to believe that quality circle activity in Japanese companies is voluntary. Although the Japanese love to give this impression and, theoretically, participation might be voluntary, the social sanctions on individuals who choose to opt out are such that either they quickly fall into line or they leave the organisation. Such circles are in fact an integral part of the group's activities, used as a means of making progress towards achieving the targeted improvement objectives which are displayed on the visible management boards and closely monitored. Because Western managers believe they are voluntary and because trade union pressure often reinforces that position, they are established as Quality Circles (again with initial capital letters) with voluntary participation. This sends out all the wrong signals. 'You can choose to participate in improving quality and if you do not or if you get bored and drop out there is not very much we can do about it' or, 'Quality improvement is the thing we do every other Tuesday. Join in if you want to!'

Yawata Iron and Steel, when it began its quality circle campaign, said:

> One of the most serious problems facing modern industry is how the prosperity of the company and human satisfaction of the workers can be made compatible. These seemingly contradictory requirements – higher efficiency and regained humanity – must be met simultaneously. The solution is to create a system that links together the hearts and minds of the workers as human beings and helps them to display their respective capacity and creativity. (Moto, 1982)

Yawata clearly had an understanding of the issues this book is seeking to address, even if its solution was simplistic.

Quality circles are a classic example of the Western belief in the miracle cure resulting from the five-day study tour to Japan with little knowledge or perception of the theory behind the concept. We see what is happening on the surface and believe it can be transferred. In most cases we fail. Those few companies that succeed in the long term understand that much else must also change. Japanese QCs are but one example of their small group activities which developed out of a concern that workers in large organisations felt alienated because their area of discretion was so small that they could not perceive their individual contribution was important nor have any feeling of accomplishment. These small group activities include the morning exercise period, a two or three-minute formal meeting before work begins, and drinks after work; but also productivity sessions, problem-solving teams, zero defects campaigns as well as quality circles. To the Japanese the important point is that it is the group doing something together; the means are often more important than the end and perhaps most important of all, *they take back to their workplace and to their normal job, the experience and knowledge they have gained in the small group activity.*

In the West we have said, 'Our quality is bad, Japanese quality is good. Japan has quality circles so if we introduce quality circles our quality will improve.' We then go through a process of establishing a steering committee, a facilitator, circle leaders, phased introduction programme, presentations to management, and so on. No wonder we fail. Responsibility for quality cannot under any circumstances be removed from line management. Whatever we call the process, the line manager must be responsible for getting the group started and support it as it develops its own dynamic. The line manager might assign it tasks or receive results from its own internally generated activities but the immediate supervisor, not a facilitator nor a steering committee, must have responsibility for motivating the group.

Such activities have to be about much more than quality; they should be a natural extension of the way the team normally operates, choosing to pull in other people who can contribute, and they must not result in a bureaucratic structure. They are not voluntary. If the supervisor asks, 'Will the three of you have a look at solving this problem?' or, 'Do you think you could find a better way of doing this?', that for a period *is* their job. What is important is that the supervisor creates the climate in which such an approach is natural and that those involved are properly trained in the best methods of achieving results.

INVOLVING ALL OF THE ORGANISATION

Quality is not just about the manufacturing process or the face-to-face provision of a service, although both are of critical importance. Ethicon Ltd, the Edinburgh based subsidiary of health care company, Johnson and Johnson, has recognised this more clearly than most. Writing in the company paper *Quality First* in July 1991, Operations Director, Gerry Fagan said:

> There is no area of our business which is less important than any other in making sure that quality happens and that the final product meets customer requirements to specification, on time and at the right price. No matter which department an employee works in they, as an individual and as part of a team, have a bearing on one or several of these three essential ingredients.

For example, an individual's first introduction to a company is usually the advertisement or casual application. How well is the advertisement worded? Does it tell the applicants what they need to know? If they telephone are they answered promptly and courteously by people who know to whom they should be referred? If they write, do they receive an immediate acknowledgement instead of either being ignored totally or having to wait weeks? If they phone to determine progress, are they answered quickly and correctly, or are they told something like, 'We've had hundreds of applications. Yours is somewhere in the pile and I'll get round to it eventually?'

CLUB MED

There are many well-told stories of quality success. Instead of repeating the usual Milliken or Xerox stories, I shall turn to Club Med and thank George Binney (1992) for this example.

Club Med, the French holiday company, was established in 1950 and quickly built an image of sun, sea, sand, sex and sangria. From that time it has expanded to become an organisation employing some 24 000 people in holiday villages and hotels around the world. In 1985 it began its own TQM programme – seeking first to define what quality meant to its *gentils membres* (GM-customers) and at the same time to understand the approach developed by companies regarded as quality leaders. It then established a group of six people to work on the project and each developed a network of fifteen others representing a cross section of staff. Together they prepared a Quality Charter containing ten dimensions of quality as perceived by the customer.

Club Med Quality Charter

- To arrive and live at the village without worry and risk
- An attractive location
- To be paid attention, receive generosity and imagination
- To be able to use the village's facilities easily
- Everything works and is clean
- Freedom of choice
- To eat and drink, what, when and as much as the GM wants
- To meet people easily
- To learn new skills
- For the contract to be honestly respected

The Chairman, Gilbert Trigano met with the group of six on a weekly basis.

The next step was to develop standards for each activity, using a three-part framework:

- What is the standard (expressed from the customer's viewpoint)?
- What task must the *gentil organisateur* (GO – nice organiser) undertake to deliver this standard?
- How is this task to be carried out?

The standards applied to tangible measures – cleanliness, appearance, availability and the intangible – problem-solving, quality of attention, and so on. Several hundred were developed and in the process many GOs were involved, so that while the company benefited from their input the ownership process had also begun.

The next step was to bring together the village managers at a week-long seminar presided over by Gilbert Trigano, to share with them the rationale and the way the standards should be used. Critically, the managers saw the standards not as a straitjacket but a formalisation of much of what they were already doing. They could be used to good purpose for training and benchmarking, and for achieving consistency. Especially, they would have flexibility in applying them to their own specific situation. The seminars were then cascaded throughout the organisation.

Having set the standards, Club Med wanted to learn about their impact. About 250 000 questionnaires are returned by GMs every year. A computer system analyses the results, allowing corrective action to be taken, trends analysed and team performance evaluated. Letters are separately analysed to follow up issues raised on a personal basis. The commercial director for each market also solicits information from Club Med's own distribution network, from travel agents and through GM focus groups. Even while on holiday, GMs views are formally solicited by the manager via a Round Table and, informally GOs pick up comments and are encouraged to act on them.

The Club Med experience demonstrates not only the importance of ownership but also of feedback from the customer. Van den Berghs, manufacturers of Flora margarine, include their company phone number on every pack. 'Phone the Flora Food Company 0800 446464. Questions, comments or suggestions about Flora. Call us FREE Monday to Friday 9.00 am to 5.00 pm.' About half the 500 calls a week are resolved immediately. In the USA 83 per cent of branded goods carry a telephone number. In France the figure is 30 per cent, in Germany 15 per cent and in the UK just 8 per cent (*Financial Times*, 13 January 1994). Burger King displays its phone number prominently in its restaurants and on take-away bags. Coca-Cola has been printing a careline number on its products since 1992, and in 1993 received about 145 000 calls. Steve Harris, head of Coca-Cola and Schweppes Beverages quality assurance in the UK, has seen the number of complaints rise but argues, 'We are making it easier for consumers to tell us if they are dissatisfied.' On the positive side, such calls can provide early warnings of quality problems and can be used to track customer satisfaction.

HOW *NOT* TO INTRODUCE AN INTEGRATED QUALITY CULTURE

Jonathan Smilansky, formally General Manager of VISA International and now an independent consultant, has shrewdly determined how *not* to introduce TQM. His recipe for failure is:

1. Get the senior management team to agree – with someone at the top being 'sold' TQM, consultants involved, top team workshop, and so on.
2. Tell everyone that 'we are doing it' with conferences, newsletters and briefings prophesying that all will become clear when they are trained.
3. Train, top to bottom, about customers and suppliers, and measurement and service level agreements and empowerment and the upside down organisation and cross functional teams and the basic tools and the gurus.
4. Start to improve everything. Tell everyone to go back and improve quality, one step at a time, maybe set up cross functional teams and talk about internal customers
5. Give out the hats. Recognise and reward with hats and pens and shirts and competitions and lunches with the boss and maybe even a 'trip to Disney'. (Smilansky, 1992)

What is wrong with that? As Smilansky says, 'TQM is not a religion, it's a tool.' Remember that a realistic definition of quality must be written in the terms of the customer. TQM is only an internal process aimed at achieving an objective. It is not an end in itself. If we are to integrate quality into the whole company, there are essentially three main elements: the strategic, the planning and the practical. All three must be firmly embedded. The trouble with most recipes is that they forget some of these ingredients or demand a precision that is not possible. The following is therefore presented as a guideline but, as will quickly be seen, it returns to a main theme of this book – control of the processes and commitment of the people.

HOW *TO* INTRODUCE AN INTEGRATED QUALITY CULTURE

I divide this into strategy, planning and the process.

Strategy

In seeking to integrate quality into the whole organisation, the task of top management is to determine that the quality of its products or service will be defined in the end-customers' terms and that standards will continuously improve. It is then its role to create the environment within the organisation to enable this objective to be achieved, recognising that it will not know the 'how' in detail. Top management must recognise that there will be a few surprises along the road and have the courage to accept that if the direction taken is broadly consistent with the long-term objective, it is better than one which is imposed. It is, therefore, critical that top management is both consistent and persistent, that it does not interfere nor keep seeking the quick bottom line result, and recognises that absolute integration will take many years – although specific practical success can come very quickly.

There is not one way of developing this strategy. There is usually an initial inspiration that comes, perhaps, from someone reading a book, attending a seminar or being beaten over the head by a market place failure. It may be the chief executive or someone else in the organisation. *It does not always have to start at the very top.* Much is written and said about gaining commitment from the very top, and if quality is to be fully integrated then at some stage the CEO will have to be convinced, but, as I have previously argued, leadership can exist at all levels. We all have part of our organisation that we can influence and in some instances examples of success lower down the organisation can become a catalyst both laterally and vertically. Indeed there may often be advantages in this route, for the worst thing that can happen is for an initiative to be seen as, 'Another bright idea thought up in the ivory tower and imposed on us.'

Planning

At whatever level the initiative begins, the first stage must be to *understand* what quality means for your customers, for it is only when proper understanding is achieved that the benchmark by which future results are to be assessed can be established. For many, this may be uncomfortable. It is much easier to jump in as an act of faith and subsequently applaud success based on some after-the-event criteria.

The great thing is that, when properly handled, the medium can easily become the message. Following top management's definition of the broad strategy, the first task must be to select a group of experienced people from the organisation to go through the steps necessary to understand what quality really means. Very specifically I do not mean an overseeing strategy group but people *who will actually do it*. It may comprise a mixture of line managers and service departments from all locations, a horizontal slice or a lateral slice; it may include trade union representatives. Only the organisation can determine the right mix, but there are three golden rules

- Each member must have high personal credibility within the organisation.
- Each member must be an innovator and achiever.
- Each member must retain his or her normal responsibilities.

The first two are obvious but the third is not. As soon as someone is moved from the normal day-to-day job, the group becomes a little more isolated, it becomes something special, resources disappear. The group will wish to call on others, and if they no longer have line responsibilities their ability to do so may be reduced. This does not mean that they will have double the work (although it may well mean having more). They may depute some of their normal work but *not* their assignment.

The corollary is, do not appoint as the facilitator or co-ordinator someone who can be 'spared' from their normal job. Quality is a responsibility of the management of the organisation and if they are not prepared to give the time and authority of people who have real responsibility then they should not start the process. Equally, do not give the *responsibility* to a consultant. There is little that cannot be done by a capable group of managers who understand the business, but the value of someone from outside is that he or she can ask the difficult questions, can challenge and prod in a way that even the most capable insider cannot, and the outsider can sometimes help by cutting through the organisation's politics – as long as the consultant does not bring a precise formula and is a servant of the process not the leader.

Within the overall strategy it is this group that will undertake the studies, calling on others when needed, and this will lead to them determining their own broad targets for the organisation. But they must remember at all times that, just as with them, commitment follows involvement. They must walk like they talk and not live in isolation from the rest of the organisation for several months and suddenly produce words of wisdom and precisely determined targets from on high. They may believe they have a monopoly of wisdom but they will be amazed at the contribution others can make. Again there is no prescription for how this is done – small departmental groups, multi-site, multi-functional, horizontal, vertical, lateral, customers, suppliers, trade unions, and so on. All can contribute, and being given the opportunity to do so is just as important as the value of that contribution.

The group itself may need some training or team-building activity but this should not be overstated. A group of people selected in line with the three criteria will probably know each other and will previously have proved their problem-solving capabilities. In any case, they will have the ability to determine their own strengths and weaknesses and know when to seek advice and assistance. But any development or training must be done just in time. There simply is no point in bringing in an outsider to train or build a team in advance. Again, it makes something special of a process which must become integral, but lower in the organisation it may become clear that such a need exists. If so, let it grow out of the process, not be a pre-condition.

The process

The steps in the process which leads to integrating quality are then as follows.

Step 1

Determine and then list the customers' perceived critical success factors. This can be achieved by a variety of means and may involve the use of outside agents. Most effective are the views and requirements of your own customers. Ask them what they want, how they judge you, assess past problems and future needs. Club Med did a superb job. Next, listen to the views of your own front line staff – the people who meet the customers, listen to their complaints, know why they receive or fail to receive repeat business, understand the problems caused by failure to deliver on time. But front line staff will not always tell of their own failings, perhaps their rudeness to a customer, their own inability to arrive on time, their lack of knowledge of their product or service or their ignoring the customers' real needs.

Step 2

Compare yourself with the opposition to understand where they are now and where they are likely to be in a few years time. Companies have always done this, whether it is 'tearing down' a rival company's new products, or the small local store checking out its rivals' prices.

The most sophisticated comparisons are now termed 'benchmarking', defined by Rank Xerox as, 'A continuous, systematic process of evaluating companies recognised as industry leaders, to determine business and work processes that represent best practices.' Benchmarking is about more than quality, and can be more than just making performance comparisons within your own industry. If you stay within your own industry you will be stuck with the standards of your industry.

ICL had a concern about its technical manuals. Customers had difficulty finding their way around them. It looked at its competitors' manuals and found it had little to learn. The breakthrough came when it examined railway timetables and cookery books. In particular, the benchmarking team found that Marks and Spencer's cookery books were masterpieces of clarity – with outstanding illustrations, precisely defined ingredients and clear instructions. If ICL's technical manuals now look like cookery books, it is no accident.

Looking at the very best, wherever it occurs, helps raise expectations of what it is possible to achieve. The highest standards of cleanliness and hygiene are in hospital operating theatres, the fastest changers of mechanical parts are Formula One Grand Prix pit crews, the best organised and efficient distribution systems are in the perishable goods sectors. Studying the very best generates ideas about different ways of doing things. So whether you undertake a sophisticated exercise, affordable by only a small proportion of organisations, or look at not only your immediate rival's shop but also the layouts of totally different types of store, no organisation seeking future success can ignore the need.

Step 3

Determine where you are now in relation to these success factors and the competition and where you want to be. You may not want to be the number one innovator or the most aggressively profitable – or even of the highest quality. It is no good aiming for high quality if your research and knowledge determines that quality, in the narrow sense of the word, is not a factor in your market place, and at least you will save yourself a lot of time, money and effort. There will be products and markets in which, provided the product does its job for a short period and is of low price, it is better for the customer than a long-lasting, higher priced item, whether it be cars or kettles. I saw in a London underground train an advertisement for the Kwik Save discount store, 'Remember when they used to pile it high and sell it cheap – we still do.' If that is what your customers want and that is the business you are in, there is absolutely no problem. You are meeting your customers' perception of quality.

Step 4

Prioritise your key measures of externally assessed quality success. Whatever part of the market you wish to be in, you must know what you wish to achieve and how you will measure progress and determine success or failure. It is easy to go for everything – but a mistake. It is far more difficult to focus on a small number of clearly definable targets: for example, percentage of on-time deliveries to rise from 75 per cent to 95 per cent in two years; returns to fall by ten per cent per annum for five years, invoices accurately completed to rise from 90 per cent to 100 per cent in six months. However, recognise that a universal standard may not be appropriate. Much will depend on the circumstances of different parts of the organisation. For a job placement service the number of people successfully appointed may be very different in an area of high unemployment from those appointed in one of low unemployment, and targets must recognise what is realistically achievable. If, however, they were to choose, 'Those still employed by the hiring organisation after one year' the league table of success might well be reversed. Some organisations may choose to use both measures or to assess the rate of improvement as being a better indicator than absolute achievement. Such decisions can only be made within the organisation after extensive analysis and discussion.

Step 5

Determine measures of internally assessed quality which, if achieved, will correlate with external success, but do not be too prescriptive. Allow the measures to be developed at the operational level. If everyone is to buy-in to the targets then, as far as possible, they must be *their* targets. In a multi-plant organisation, with some old and some new facilities, it does not, as with the external measures, make sense to impose an organisation-wide standard of rejects per million when rejects per thousand is the maximum that can be obtained without significant capital investment. If the job placement service has a run-down facility with a poor ambience, customer satisfaction indices of the way they are treated are starting with a major handicap, but if this is to be regarded as a key measure *adopted by the staff* nothing could do more to stimulate efforts to improve that ambience. If, however, it is imposed from above, nothing could do more to demotivate. 'We can never do well so it's not worth bothering' can easily become the pervading atmosphere.

Step 6

So far, no name has been given to this process, nor has there been any great announcement, but certainly it is no secret (secrecy is the kiss of death). It is just happening. The organisation itself must decide if it wishes to focus attention by giving it a name or if it just wants to get on and do it. There are benefits and dangers in both directions. Focusing can concentrate attention but lead to a 'flavour of the month' attitude. Getting on and doing it can cause some confusion as to what is happening but lead to a greater chance of it becoming integrated into the organisation. 'We're integrating quality' by itself tells us very little but something needs to be said at an early stage. Maybe, 'We're starting a process which we hope will involve everyone in the company in ensuring we all get much better at understanding and meeting our customers' needs,' will provide the starting point. Whether or not a name is needed will emerge. The danger is to develop an acronym too early, thereby fixing the concept and raising hopes which can easily be dashed. The whole organisation will be learning, and from learning comes change.

Step 7

There comes a point when progress and achievement are necessary. The broad targets need to be established and made known within the organisation. If people have contributed, they will not be surprised and if the job has been done properly, many will have been working to their own objectives long before any corporate targets are made known. If managers, supervisors or operators say, 'Let's not wait, let's just get on and do it' then, *provided they have not omitted their own analysis and planning*, that is great. Indeed, as it discusses the overall direction, the lead group may well wish to encourage such jumping the gun. Leadership exists where you find it and there is nothing like solid achievement to motivate and nothing like the odd failure to learn from, provided it is constructive. There is no need to wait for the major training programmes to be completed, for in large organisations they will take years and small organisations may not be able to afford them. Problem-solving techniques can be built into a normal part of supervisor and management training programmes and they can then teach those who report to them.

The projects or tasks do not even have to be about specific quality issues. If the job is made safer or the ambience more pleasant, quality will improve, and the next project may be about quality. The need for multi-functional teams will also emerge. The production group will realise that it cannot improve a process without involving the engineering, safety and finance departments. Those involved in recruitment cannot change selection methods without consulting everyone else – or they can, but only at the expense of heavy criticism. Multi-functional teams in such an organisation are constantly forming, achieving and disbanding. They are the way of life.

Step 8

Some organisations will find that such an approach will totally change their recognition system. They may find that they no longer need a bureaucratic suggestions scheme built up from the time when operators were not paid to think and which resulted in an idea being dropped into a box, perhaps to emerge six months later with a decision to pay ten per cent of the first year's savings, all precisely calculated. If a financial reward scheme is to be retained or introduced, the decision process must be close to the operator, with the immediate boss having the ability to make decisions. Alternatively, the company may believe that such integration means that everyone is paid to think and contribute and that recognition means the boss taking out the team for an after hours drink. Others may opt for the formal presentation and lunch with the chief executive, although I would suggest that such an event could be another kiss of death if the chief executive or individual is uncomfortable with it.

Even deeper, it may turn out that the whole payment structure built up over the years will need to be revised. Individual piece rates or bonus payments are often incompatible with such an approach, as we shall see in Chapter 13, but do not rush it. The need for change, if need there be, will emerge. No one can know in advance.

Deeper still, the need for a total restructuring of the organisation may be an outcome. Organisation structures that have developed over the years without being fundamentally challenged may be seen as an impediment to achieving the new goals. I have criticised those who present new concepts as instant general solutions. It is rather like going to a doctor who, immediately you walk in the door, says, 'I've got just the thing to cure you, here it is. Now, what's your problem?' If any reader believes the analogy represents an unfair criticism of the approach of the instant experts, I suggest you sit through one or two presentations!

There is no doubt, though, that a clear definition of the key business processes can for many organisations help define where attention should be concentrated. Determine which processes genuinely add value and which add cost. Analyse the core processes and the support functions and ask questions as to whether large headquarters departments and functions are really necessary or can best be devolved to the operating units. Every part of the organisation has a role to play in improving quality. If a target is to achieve an improvement from, say, 20 per cent of the invoices you receive to be paid on time to 80 per cent, ask what prevents it happening right now. You will find that much of the problem is due to incorrectly completed invoices, no record of orders placed, and no record of receipts. Your invoice processing people will be spending hours tracking one invoice through the system but the *real* answer may lie deep within your own mindset.

Why do you need individual orders and invoices anyway? Electronic requisitioning and payment systems now allow a customer, when distributing its final schedule to suppliers, to generate automatically an instruction to build and ship the components. It is possible for the components to be delivered direct to the point of assembly with no logging in, with completion of the final product being, in effect, acknowledgement of receipt. This in turn generates payment instructions which are accumulated on a monthly basis and then paid by direct bank to bank transfer of funds. This is an extreme position. It is dependent on high levels of trust, accurate bills of material, no or low stock and clearly defined and up-to-date pricing, and particularly important for small suppliers of services, low-cost technology is not yet available. But it is the way to go and it is not all or nothing. Nissan's spend is approaching £1 billion per annum. There are eleven people working in 'accounts payable'!

Read people like Hammer and Champy, but whatever your current situation, the eventually determined changes will emerge from the analytical process and may not be about cutting headcount or substituting computers for people. They may not even result in the removal of functional chimneys. They will, however, provide an answer based on a proper understanding of your organisation's needs and, provided you are prepared to slaughter your sacred cows if necessary, will enable the whole organisation to move to a state in which a commitment to high quality is fully integrated.

Step 9

It is critical that everyone should know how they are performing against the targets and it is here that the visual management systems and daily communications processes come into their own. It may be necessary to make a 'song and dance' about it for a while, but unless your company's normal style is to celebrate achievement, aim to accept high quality as a fact of life as quickly as possible. If quality is to become the norm it is simply not possible to make a big noise about it all the time.

Step 10

The final stage comes when quality is fully integrated into your normal way of life and permeates every level in the organisation. None of your training programmes are specifically about quality but all of them are. The commitment encompasses everything you do from the recruitment process, employee involvement and control of the processes to termination procedures, relationships with trade unions and new product development. Measurement of quality will be the norm and all employees will seek continuously to improve on their previous achievements. All elements of the business will be aligned.

However, even if you reach this happy state, you will not be able to relax. Without continuing top management interest and attention, standards can easily decline. A company can systematise all it wants but people always know where the emphasis lies.

Top management attention has to be maintained for ever!

Finally

Finally, and optionally, you may decide to go for accreditation under ISO 9000, the international standard which assesses whether your procedures and practices enable you consistently to achieve your desired quality level. I end with ISO 9000, not begin with it, for it is a bureaucratic process and unless there is already a deep commitment to high quality it could be a great turn-off.

ISO 9000 does not define your quality level. That remains the responsibility of the organisation. But the disciplines are important and the ISO 9000 requirements will expose weaknesses in your systems. The continuing audits will ensure that you are kept on your toes.

ISO 9000 will add more control to your commitment, but if you do not already have commitment it will be putting the cart before the horse.

11 Partnership Sourcing

When capacity permits, manufacturers are better off with single source suppliers. A carefully selected and managed supplier offers the greatest guarantee of consistently high quality, namely commitment to the product.

(David N. Burt, *Harvard Business Review*, 1989)

There is a Japanese word, 'karanage' which means simply asking your suppliers to cut prices without doing anything on our part. This does not work any more.

(Yoshifumi Tsuji, President, Nissan Motor Company, 1993)

ADVERSARIAL RELATIONSHIPS

Central to the quality of a finished product is the quality of its components and materials. Whereas most organisations profess concern about the quality of their bought-out parts, the ascendant organisation is also concerned about the quality of the actual relationship with its suppliers. Traditionally, customers have sought to keep their suppliers at arms length, some even preferring tension or an adversarial relationship. In the automobile industry, the major assemblers each had several thousand suppliers, most with short-term contracts, usually based on price. At the end of the product development process, which had been undertaken primarily by the customer, a number of suppliers were called in, given the detailed specification, and asked to submit competitive bids – often with little information about customer's expectations, cost and quality targets and with unrealistic volume information. The buyers enjoyed playing one off against the other, usually selected at least two suppliers for every component 'just in case', with the decision being primarily based on price. The customer had little or no interest in what happened inside the suppliers' plants and discouraged suppliers from visiting its own assembly operations. The relationship was often restricted to those directly involved in buying and selling and, in particular with new products, the customer had little idea on the quality level until the product arrived in the warehouse.

Suppliers, because they had no guarantee of a long-term business relationship, did not seek to achieve a true understanding of their customers' needs. Knowing that they were going to be screwed on price, they kept their costs secret. They had little incentive to invest in design and development capability because, usually, it was not required of them, and they were not brought into the picture until very late in the development process. What secrets they had, they were not prepared to share. Consequently they learned little and were able to contribute nothing to ongoing improvements except to complain that their manufacturing task was difficult. Often they were not even able to accommodate their customers' requirements because of their facilities' limitations. With no certainty of a future relationship, investment in the facility to meet specific demands was a low priority.

The result was a relationship in which neither party had much understanding of the others' business. The customer designed and engineered the component, built the prototype or had it produced by a specialist company, tested it and produced the final specification. As a result the supplier had little knowledge and experience and often produced components which were not up to the job, resulting in a need for considerable debugging. The supplier had often acquired the business on the basis of artificially low prices and constantly sought price increases for every subsequent modification. The customer was prepared to tolerate high reject levels as the price to be paid for this relationship but screamed all the time at the suppliers for their inadequate performance and threatened them continuously that they would lose the business. The financial equation was (is) based on 'cost plus':

COST + PROFIT = PRICE

This meant that a pre-determined profit margin was added to the cost so that if costs rose, profits followed. There was no incentive to reduce costs and the relationship became one of adversarial price control.

JAPANESE SUPPLIERS

In Japan, the assembly companies typically have not thousands but around 300 first-tier suppliers, many of which they partially own. Each supplier is the single source for its components and often has only the single customer. The supplier is regarded as the expert in its components and has experienced design and engineering teams who will be deeply involved with the customer throughout the product development cycle. Often the customer will give only the broadest specification and the supplier will take on the responsibility of developing the system.

The end result has been that Japanese component manufacturers performed better than their Western counterparts on virtually every criteria. In 1993, Anderson Consulting (in conjunction with Cardiff Business School) published the results of an investigation into the productivity and quality performance of 18 matched automotive components companies, nine in Japan and nine in the UK. The key comparators are shown in Table 11.1

Table 11.1 Automotive Suppliers' Performance

Factor	*World-class plants*	*Other plants*
Units per hour (100 = best)	95	54
Throughput time (100 = best)	59	32
Quality (% defects)	0.025	2.5
Rework/rectification (% labour time)	1.5	4.1
Stock turnover ratio (p.a.)	94	32
Stock of finished goods (hours)	6	23
Inventory (hours)	11	75
Frequency of delivery to customers (hours)	3	18
Number of live parts	188	161
Parts introduced in last 12 months (%)	44	17

SOURCE: Anderson Consulting, 1993.

The study found that the, 'high productivity and high quality' plants were all Japanese and that not one British plant ranked 'high' on both scales (Professor Dan Jones to author, December 1992). Not all the world-class plants were Japanese and not all Japanese plants were world-class.

These figures show that the world-class plants had an almost 2:1 productivity differential and a superiority in quality of 100:1, and that this superiority was achieved despite a higher number of live parts and a significantly higher rate of new product introduction. The world class plants had one-seventh the inventory and delivered to customers six times more frequently.

In looking for explanations the survey found that, statistically, automation counted for only 10 per cent of the difference, training effort was not greatly different and, to their surprise, the levels of responsibility devolved to the work teams did not differ greatly. *The major difference was the contribution of 'team leaders' to a number of key areas* including inspection, rectification, routine maintenance and quality improvements, 'which was double that of team leaders in non-world-class plants. In most activities the team leaders played a pivotal role in world-class plants. . . These findings suggest that the role of the 'empowered' operator in world class manufacturing may have been overstated and that the crucial difference lies at team leader rather than operator level.' They also found that 80 per cent of the workforce in the world-class plants were involved in problem-solving groups against 54 per cent for the rest and they met more frequently. All the world-class plants used salary and individual merit schemes which included shop floor operators and used company-wide performance appraisal schemes.

There are, however, fundamental differences between Western and Japanese relationships, primarily stemming from the fact that in the West the partnership will usually be between wholly independent companies, with the supplier not being wholly dependent on a single customer. As Yoshifumi Tsuji's quote at the head of this chapter suggests, Japanese customers have been prone to dictate prices to their dependent suppliers and, because of their existing high level of capability, the customer rarely seeks to be involved in *how* the supplier achieves the requirements. It is a partnership in only a limited sense of the word.

PARTNERSHIP SOURCING

The application of partnership sourcing in the West was neatly described by the Confederation of British Industry in 1991:

> Partnership sourcing is where customer and supplier develop such a close and long-term relationship that the two work together as partners. It isn't philanthropy: the aim is to secure the best possible commercial advantage. The principle is that teamwork is better than combat. If the end customer is to be best served, then both parties to a deal must win. Partnership sourcing works because both parties have an interest in each others' success. . . It means rejecting the 'master–servant' syndrome where the supplier is merely told what to supply and the customer told the price. Instead the partners agree on common goals and build the commitment, trust and mutual support necessary to achieve them.

The key principle of partnership sourcing is that it is a whole company philosophy. It does not apply solely to the buyer/seller relationship but permeates the whole of both organisations from the chief executives downwards. It involves all functions, but particularly quality assurance, product development, production control, manufacturing, finance, and training as well as purchasing. It requires that both partners work together for mutual success, are open with each other and recognise that, as with the definition of quality – the ultimate beneficiary has to be the end-user of the product or service.

Central to partnership sourcing is the establishment of a long-term relationship so that the environment is created in which the supplier has the confidence to invest in its design and development capability, its facilities, and in particular in its people. Without good, well-trained and highly motivated people able to communicate directly with each other, no company is able to achieve anything. It is not, in fact, necessary to have a long-term contract to achieve this relationship – once there is confidence between the partners, the only formal negotiations need be about price, although there will be continuous involvement in discussions on quality, new product development, delivery and management capabilities. The customer is simply not going to turn off the supplier nor will it seek annual tenders from competitors. The suppliers are stakeholders in the business of the customer and must be treated as such. They become mutually interdependent; the relationship is one of trust, with both partners winning. If it is seen as a win-lose relationship, there is no partnership.

As a result, the supplier is able to participate fully in the development of new products and has far earlier sight of, and involvement in the process. The supplier has to understand fully its customers' standards and targets and be able to respond to change requests; it needs to possess technical knowledge of the manufacturing processes and be able to input into cost reduction and design change activities; it needs to be able to test its products to standards required by the customer and deliver trial parts from production tools; it needs to have state-of-the-art knowledge of its business and be able to generate improvements on existing products. All of this leads to a comprehensive interchange of information, often with the supplier being required to develop knowledge of relating components even though they may not be its direct business. It also leads to more 'black box' technology, with the supplier taking responsibility for whole systems rather than components. This in turn results in the elimination of sub-assembly operations in the customers' facility.

In order to achieve these standards the customer needs to have a comparatively small supplier base. In 1985 Peugeot of France had 2500 European suppliers of manufacturing materials; in 1992 this was down to 950 and Peugeot's objective for 1995 is 650. Chrysler in the USA had 2100 suppliers in 1988 and by 1994 had reduced to 1250. Its objective is to remove a further 400 by 1997 and buy-in more than 70 per cent of its components. IBM reduced its UK suppliers from more than 5000 in 1988 to 2740 in 1991. On a totally different scale, Apollo Fire Detectors of Hampshire with an annual spend of £8 million, found that it had 800 suppliers providing 4000 different components. As part of its move to partnership sourcing it reduced its suppliers to 54, with 95 per cent of its spend going to 25 of them. Nissan has never exceeded 200 first-tier European suppliers and most sophisticated manufacturers are going along the same path. It is simply not possible to enter into partnership sourcing relationships with thousands of suppliers, so customers are looking for suppliers of systems rather than components – and who are able to offer high levels of service in broad product ranges.

Under these arrangements the pricing equation fundamentally changes. The customer, with knowledge of the internationally competitive prices, aims to know the final selling price of the product and works backwards from there. Toyota buyers, for example, are networked throughout the world so that at any time they can check what other plants are paying for specific components or systems. Through value engineering the supplier develops the component to achieve the price the customer is prepared to pay. The price equation becomes:

PRICE – COST = PROFIT

The customer requires detailed knowledge of the suppliers' costs – open book costing – so that they can work together to reduce these costs.

During the life of a product the customer will expect the supplier to offset inflationary increases by becoming more efficient, although customer required product changes will be paid for. The customer will seek price reductions due to cost savings arising from improvements in areas such as productivity, scheduling, design changes and quality, resulting in the following movements in the financial equation:

↑ (PROFIT)

PRICE – COST = PROFIT

↓ (COST)

The customer will work with the supplier to help reduce its cost, and will then expect to share in that increased profit, and the following year will, therefore, seek a price reduction:

PRICE – COST = PROFIT
↓

But the supplier will continue to work to reduce costs so as to maintain an acceptable profit level. The cycle continues with the benefits shared.

John Gillett, IBM's Procurement Manager, has summarised what he sees as the benefits of partnership sourcing:

For the purchaser

- joint development of the design, with early vendor involvement
- reduced design lead times and fast introduction
- product designed for value added manufacture following early involvement of supplier
- product availability when the market place is ready
- assured source of defect free supplies on time
- eliminates need for 'just in case' planning
- 100 per cent value added
- working together gets cost out
- lower paper processing costs

For the supplier

- continuity of customer relationship
- an assured market
- co-operation in the development of all overheads and skills necessary to achieve customers' demands
- better planning leading to more economic use of resources
- lower selling costs leading to other customer opportunities

It has to be accepted, however, that there is a potential downside. In some circumstances single sourcing may be a slightly more risky strategy and in the years of a high incidence of industrial disputes could not have been contemplated. Although there is a risk that such times will return, the concepts of the ascendant organisation – including the interdependence arising from partnership sourcing – make it less likely. There remains, of course, the disaster scenario and although in many businesses there will be alternatives, in those in which the safety of the product is paramount it will not be easy to secure rapidly alternative sources of supply at the precise specification. On the other side of the coin is the possibility of complacency, and many find it difficult to understand how such long-term commitments cannot lead to the relationship becoming too cosy. Such attitudes fundamentally misunderstand the nature of the relationship which by definition entails a search for continuous improvement and cost reductions. In any case most companies single source – internally. The managing director of a small engineering company which has done it says people are needlessly nervous. 'I ask them, "How many paint shops do you have? How many computer systems"? They're single sourcing internally, but don't realise it.'

But how do you avoid complacency? The answer is to measure performance.

Nissan's measurements system is based on five factors – quality, cost, delivery, design and development, and management. Each factor is broken down into numerous elements, targets are established and achievement measured on a quarterly basis. For example, delivery is broken down into production delivery, service delivery, load presentation and project management and each of these into a further four or five measures. Overall delivery of production parts on time rose from an average of 84 per cent in 1992 to 96 per cent by 1994. Every supplier knows his performance on a monthly basis. Inventory reduced from an average of 1.66 days in 1992 to 0.97 days at the end of 1993. Every supplier knows his own figures. Twenty-seven per cent of suppliers are responsible for 80 per cent of Nissan's expediting effort. They all know who they are. They all knew in 1993 that in 1994 their delivery window would reduce from three to two hours and that greater emphasis would be placed on load presentation problems, for example, mislabelling and mixed stock concerns. Partnership sourcing does not result in complacency!

IBM has rightly said that partnerships will work when:

- the risk is optimised
- benefits are measurable and mutual
- the strategy has been totally researched
- the business demands it
- there are few/no surprises
- there is regular effective communications at all levels

In short, where there is trust.

SUPPLIER DEVELOPMENT

One of the key elements of partnership sourcing is the willingness of the partners to work together for mutual improvement. Kodak has its quality improvement facilitators whose aim is to immerse both its own operations and suppliers in their quality culture. Glaxo has sought to bring together competing suppliers into one transparent team; ICL, which spends £800 million per annum with suppliers, launched its Vendor Accreditation Programme in 1991 and identified 200 key suppliers out of 6000 with which it aims to develop long-term strategic partnerships; Xerox has its supplier certification programme, Continuous Supplier Involvement, aimed at close operational linkages and has trained 30 000 employees of its suppliers in its 'leadership through quality' programmes.

Nissan's Supplier Development Team (SDT) concept began in late 1988 when, on a trial basis, the company commenced working with twelve suppliers, all of which had demonstrated a positive attitude to improvement activities and a willingness to seek the same level of performance as their Japanese equivalents. It is a long, never-ending process and works by recognising that change cannot be forced on anyone. It is about changing peoples' attitudes, gradually altering their traditional ways of working and thinking and securing their ownership of and commitment to their activities. It requires investment in people, resources and time by both the customer and the supplier in anticipation that there will be a considerable return. But it also recognises that however committed may be the chief executive, the real improvements take place when managers, supervisors and operators share that commitment. The real work is on the shop floor.

Once suppliers are identified, bring them into the discussion process, usually beginning at the top, but at least involving people known to have real influence within their organisation. As a result, develop an initial work programme with those suppliers with whom you feel comfortable both in terms of their attitude and the number you can manage. Nissan began with twelve, but for most companies this will be too many.

The SDT approach recognises that they must not usurp the suppliers' authority as the role is one of education and training in quality and improvement techniques so that the suppliers themselves may identify areas for improvement; then, for a period, supporting the suppliers' initiatives, assisting in the development of improvement plans and monitoring progress. Specific areas include quality, production processes, stock control, maintenance, housekeeping and safety. They look in particular at the leadership given by managers – do they have a philosophy compatible with the objectives and if so is it shared? What is the morale in the company?

Very specifically the teams may work on non-Nissan activities – for the whole idea is to develop the total capability of the supplier, not just those elements which relate to Nissan. Suppliers with multiple customers can often be confused by the different requirements of their various customers and though this cannot be totally removed, it is recognised that the knowledge will be shared anyway.

Reorganisation, both structural and physical, often follows. Some of the most frequent results are a desire to move to cellular manufacturing systems, a desire to establish their own *kaizen* programmes and a major enhancement of the role of the supervisor. Also with it comes a dissatisfaction with the performance of the supplier's suppliers and the programmes are now being extended to the second-tier suppliers. In 1994 the DTI decided, in conjunction with Nissan, Toyota and Honda, to organise a visit to Japan for a group of second-tier suppliers extending the concept throughout the supply chain.

The tributes to this process have been many. VDO is a German company which assembles instrument clusters. Peter Callow, Managing Director, said in 1991 that there were many MD type reasons for being enthusiastic:

> We use half the floor space, productivity increased by a conservative 50 per cent, work in progress reduced by thousands of per cent, end of line rejects decreased by 200–300 per cent and we measure throughput in minutes and hours rather than days, and all this has cost us next to nothing.

But there are other benefits:

> All of our manufacturing staff have been involved in the process of improvement; they have been consulted, asked to identify problems, and most importantly have their ideas incorporated into the new ways of working. The use of multi-disciplinary teams has empowered people to make changes in systems, manufacturing methods and layouts. Very often it has been the first time that individuals in our teams have experienced that kind of freedom . . . The ten day improvement activities have acted as vehicles for education, training and development of many of our staff. Our experiences have made me realise how important is the manufacturing system as a whole, in particular we have begun to focus our attention on the issue of material handling and

the role of *our* suppliers in improving our competitive position. The cynics, me included, have been silenced.

True to its word, VDO has extended SD activities to its own suppliers. Pressac, a Nottingham-based company, supplies flexible and rigid circuits to VDO for its instrument clusters. VDO introduced them to the quick changeover concept, which resulted in 80 per cent reduction in changeover times and, subsequently, to cell manufacturing and *kaizen* – resulting in 40 per cent labour saving, 40 per cent space, 85 per cent work in progress and 80 per cent reduction in lead times. The techniques have been introduced in other Pressac factories and are being incorporated into a new £2 million facility.

A 1991 study by the National Economic Development Council into the experience of Nissan's suppliers compared the difference in attitude between suppliers and potential suppliers towards a number of elements that go towards partnership sourcing. The percentages having a favourable attitude to a number of criteria are shown in Table 11.2.

Table 11.2 Suppliers' Attitude to Partnership

Criteria	*Nissan Suppliers (%)*	*Potential Suppliers (%)*
Zero defects	62	45
Prices based on Japanese standards	61	36
Team leading style supervision	76	36
Operators to be responsible for quality, inventory and expediting work	100	54
Provision of detailed costs	62	45
Establishment of customer specific teams	69	12
Reduce prices while increasing quality	62	45

SOURCE: NEDC, 1991.

The conclusions of the NEDC study on these suppliers is that dealing with Nissan impacts on virtually every aspect of their organisation:

- On the factory floor the emphasis is on flexibility and team work, which often means autonomous work cells and a team organisation.
- The quality emphasis is on pre-production quality assurance and defect prevention.

- Suppliers' management systems have changed to customer oriented teams, with the effort and resources . . . often being disproportionate to the level of business.
- Management style and culture are affected, with the emphasis on openness and communication.
- There is continuous pressure to improve, which often means reducing costs. Nissan focuses on the suppliers' manufacturing costs and works with the firm to reduce these costs, to enable it to reduce price. Nissan is active in helping the supplier to become more efficient, and, when economies are made, will expect the supplier to pass on most, if not all, of the savings.

This last statement is only partially true. Nissan expects its suppliers to remain profitable and when the cost reduction is solely due to the supplier's efforts, they receive the benefit.

The suppliers benefit. In mid-1993 Volkswagen, when announcing its intention to double the value of its components purchased in the UK, commented that UK component makers had become much more competitive as a result of their exposure to the latest quality, production, delivery and working practices in an area of increasing competition, and that made UK suppliers very attractive to Volkswagen. 'This is not just due to low labour costs and currency but also to product development capability, quality and just in time delivery with the Japanese transplants working on the supply base.' One of the prime causes of business success is to have very demanding customers who will work with you rather than regard you as an adversary.

HOW TO INTRODUCE PARTNERSHIP SOURCING

Because it is about relationships between different organisations, partnership sourcing is probably more difficult to establish than any other concept associated with becoming an ascendant organisation. However, if both parties are at least part of the way down the road, the basic understanding will already be there. More than anything else it demands trust and this does not come easily when antagonistic attitudes have developed over the years. The essential ingredients for a successful partnership include a genuine commitment at all levels of both organisations, with leadership from the top, coupled with open communications, information and genuine understanding of what is expected of each other. The true partnership means that the supplier also teaches the customer. This can only come about as a result of training, patience and the experience of working and learning together. Although the more advanced partner will normally take the lead, arrogance will cause failure.

The first big task is to determine within your own organisation that this is the route you wish to take. This decision will not always be easy. Much of the initial responsibility will lie with the purchasing team and they will need to be convinced that there are advantages in this new approach, recognising that their skills may need to change and that other people – engineers, designers, quality assurance, trainers, and so on, will have an increasingly important part to play in the relationship. The people directly concerned have to be fully involved in the decision-making process and they then have to be equipped to operate in the different way. Essentially, the buyer becomes a business manager responsible for the management of external resources. It is the buyer's job not simply to buy at the cheapest price but to be responsible for the whole of the relationship and its development, and this requires a very different level of capability. Certainly, if you are to use existing staff to develop new ways with your suppliers, you need to be confident that they have the right level of competence and experience before letting them loose on people who have not even reached the starting gate.

The next step is to acquire an understanding of what others are doing and assess what it is possible to achieve. This can go to extremes such as visiting appropriate companies in Japan, or be done by visiting local organisations which have made progress. The essence is to understand jointly what you wish to achieve and this can be done often by no more than sitting together and thrashing through some of the old difficulties and determining what you want to do about them.

Although many of the rewards of partnership sourcing are qualitative, the route to the qualitative is via the quantitative. Therefore, it becomes necessary to establish practical programmes, to have clearly understood responsibilities and to establish targets, certainly for the areas in which improvements need to be made. Initially these need only to be in very general terms, for usually the supplier will be surprised at what is achieved. Broad areas might include quality improvements, stock turns or shop floor layouts but the detail has to be left to the subsequent improvement teams. Nothing is more likely to cause failure than the feeling that 'Big Brother is watching us.' Ownership must be with the supplier, not the customer.

The techniques of improving shop floor management are not the be-all and end-all of partnership sourcing. Working together to improve the supplier's design and development capability is a much longer-term operation and depends very much on bringing the supplier into the design process at an early stage. The companies will have to determine their own right time for this, based on their developing experience.

Some suppliers think that it is partnership solely on the customer's terms and that when the going gets tough, the relationship will revert to its previous adversarial nature. If this is the case, it is a partnership in name only. True partnerships come with trust, and trust follows positive action benefiting both partners. It takes a long time but it is worth it. Ivor Vaughan of Rearsby said, 'There's a lot said about partnership, but Nissan *lives* it. I am always referred to as *the* supplier. Nissan makes the commitment and its actions support it.'

12 Every Worker a Knowledge Worker

The basic economic resource – 'the means of production' to use the economist's term – is no longer capital, nor natural resources (the economist's 'land') nor labour. It is and will be knowledge.

(Peter Drucker, *Post-Capitalist Society*, 1993)

Said Ford to Mazda, 'How do you justify your investment in training?' Said Mazda to Ford, 'We don't understand the question.'

(Stuart Hamer, Director of Education and Training, Ford of Europe, 1993)

THE FUNDAMENTALS

In the ascendant organisation every worker is a knowledge worker.

In Chapter 1 we briefly reviewed the fundamental long-term macro changes which have taken place in advanced industrialised societies. The globalisation of commerce and industry, the growth of technology and the need to react rapidly to the market place mean that advanced industrialised societies with high wage and social costs can only succeed by having a highly trained and motivated workforce able to contribute effectively, to be able to work in teams, to be flexible and to innovate. When responsibility, authority and accountability are genuinely devolved they have a fundamental impact on the knowledge and capability requirements of the workforce and their subsequent training and development.

In the USA, a 1991 report by the Secretary's Commission on Achieving Necessary Skills (the SCANS report) said, 'The message to us was universal: good jobs will increasingly depend on people who can put knowledge to work. What we found was disturbing: more than half our young people leave school without the knowledge or foundation required to find and hold a good job.' This condemnation was echoed in Britain in 1993 when a study of employers' satisfaction with the basic skill supply of applicants showed 28 per cent to be inadequate in numeracy skills, 28 per cent in writing skills, 25 per cent in oral communication skills and 18 per cent in reading skills. While this shows that the majority are rated, 'Fairly adequate' or, 'More than adequate' the study argued, 'That is only because the demand for skills is socially and economically sub-optimal . . . if you aim low, you are unlikely to be disappointed' (Atkinson and Spilsbury, 1993).

The SCANS report defines well what it sees as the foundation of skills and personal qualities that lie at the heart of job performance. Although it regards these as, 'Essential preparation for all students, both those going directly to work and those planning further education' they are so appropriate to the foundation skills needed for work in the ascendant organisation that I give them in full in Figure 12.1 'A three-part foundation'.

The SCANS report goes further, for in addition to the foundation skills it defines five competencies which it sees, 'at least as important as technical expertise' and which, '*are applicable from the shop floor to the executive suite*' (my emphasis – except, of course, that in the ascendant organisation there is no executive suite!). Competencies span occupations and hierarchal levels although of course the balance will vary. While one might quibble with the detail, again the listing is so relevant to the ascendant organisation that it is given in full in Figure 12.2, 'Five competencies'.

On the top of all this, there is the specific technical knowledge needed – for, however good the problem-solving skills or ability to keep records, unless the individual can actually do the job, whether it is engineering, nursing, accounting, deep sea diving or operating the machine, no amount of foundation skills or core competencies will achieve success.

The problem with the SCANS Report is that it is asking too much of the education system; it is applying the standards of the world of work to the world of education. When we have an education profession that in most countries barely understands what is actually happening in the world of work, and at the same time, after ten to twelve years of full-time education, is producing failure rates of the order indicated, one cannot expect change to occur at a sufficiently rapid pace to match the changing demands of the world of work. We cannot wholly blame the educationalists. Business executives have totally failed to communicate their changing needs, and the social mores in some countries are not conducive to supporting the teaching profession. *However, if basic literacy and numeracy are the engines which drive all subsequent performance it is not unreasonable to comment that if the engines which*

Basic Skills: Reads, writes, performs arithmetic and mathematical operations, listens and speaks

A. *Reading* – locates, understands and interprets written information in prose and in documents such as manuals, graphs, schedules
B. *Writing* – communicates thoughts, ideas, information, and messages in writing; and creates documents such as letters, directions, manuals, reports, graphs and flow charts
C. *Arithmetic/Mathematics* – performs basic computations and approaches practical problems by choosing appropriately from a variety of mathematical techniques
D. *Listening* – receives, attends to, interprets, and responds to verbal messages and other cues
E. *Speaking* – organises ideas and communicates orally

Thinking Skills: Thinks creatively, makes decisions, solves problems, visualises, knows how to learn, and reasons

A. *Creative Thinking* – generates new ideas
B. *Decision-Making* – specifies goals and constraints, generates alternatives, considers risks, and evaluates and chooses best alternative
C. *Problem-Solving* – recognises problems and devises and implements plan of action
D. *Seeing Things in the Mind's Eye* – organises and processes symbols, pictures, graphs, objects and other information
E. *Knowing How to Learn* – uses efficient learning techniques to acquire and apply new knowledge and skills
F. *Reasoning* – discovers a rule or principle underlying the relationship between two or more objects and applies it when solving a problem

Personal Qualities: Displays responsibility, self-esteem, sociability, self-management and integrity and honesty

A. *Responsibility* – exerts a high level of effort and perseveres towards goal attainment
B. *Self-Esteem* – believes in own self-worth and maintains a positive view of self
C. *Sociability* – demonstrates understanding, friendliness, adaptability, empathy and politeness in group settings
D. *Self-Management* – assesses self accurately, sets personal goals, monitors progress, and exhibits self-control
E. *Integrity/Honesty* – chooses ethical courses of action

Figure 12.1 The SCANS Report: A Three-Part Foundation

Resources: Identifies, organises, plans and allocates resources

A. *Time* – Selects goal–relevant activities, ranks them, allocates time, and prepares and follows schedules
B. *Money* – Uses or prepares budgets, makes forecasts, keeps records and makes adjustments to meet objectives
C. *Material and Facilities* – Acquires, stores, allocates and uses materials or space efficiently
D. *Human Resources* – Assesses skills and distributes work accordingly, evaluates performance and provides feedback

Interpersonal: Works with others

A. *Participates as Member of a Team* – contributes to group effort
B. *Teaches Others New Skills*
C. *Serves Clients/Customers* – works to satisfy customers' expectations
D. *Exercises Leadership* – communicates ideas to justify position, persuades and convinces others, responsibly challenges existing procedures and policies
E. *Negotiates* – works towards agreements involving exchange of resources, resolves divergent interests
F. *Works with Diversity* – works well with men and women from diverse backgrounds

Information: Acquires and uses information

A. *Acquires and Evaluates Information*
B. *Organises and Maintains Information*
C. *Interprets and Communicates Information*
D. *Uses Computers to Process Information*

Systems: Understands complex inter-relationships

A. *Understands Systems* – knows how social, organisational and technological systems work and operates effectively with them
B. *Monitors and Corrects Performance* – distinguishes trends, predicts impacts on system operations, diagnoses deviations in systems' performance and corrects malfunctions
C. *Improves or Designs Systems* – suggests modifications to existing systems and develops new or alternative systems to improve performance

Technology: Works with a variety of technologies

A. *Selects Technology* – chooses procedures, tools or equipment, including computers and related technologies
B. *Applies Technology to Task* – Understands overall intent and proper procedures for set up and operation of equipment
C. *Maintains and Troubleshoots Equipment* – Prevents, identifies, or solves problems with equipment, including computers and other technologies

Figure 12.2 The SCANS Report: Five Competencies

determine aeroplane or automobile performance failed at the same rate as those determining people performance a certain amount of passion would be generated and not a few executives, managers and operators would lose their jobs! The business world has long learned that high quality and right first time is far superior to after-the-event rectification. Nothing less should be required of the world of education.

Particularly as employment is likely to change more frequently, and the demands become those of dealing with people and processing information, the importance of the SCANS targets becomes evident. SCANS was an American report, and the great problem for the USA is the unevenness of its school system. At its best it provides numerous opportunities for young people to progress to higher education and numerous second-chance opportunities. At its worst, in the inner cities, many young people are deprived of the opportunity even to achieve basic literacy and numeracy.

If success at school was achieved, the sterile debate as to whether people are educated for life or educated for work would come to an end. The world of work is an important customer of the education system, and must be deeply interested in its output and quality, and entitled to make a contribution to influencing its shape and intent. The other major role which employers should recognise and value is the need to develop the whole life potential of the individual as a member of society. What is gratifying, however, is that with the way business is developing, the education system, properly focused, can achieve both objectives. The crime is education for education's sake; particularly in Britain where the cloistered academic has sought narrow specialisation from the age of 16–18 to fit the young person for a university in which the don chooses to teach the educational élite in great depth in a subject in which he or she happens to be interested. Or in Germany, where it is quite usual for formal education to continue well into a student's late twenties – even though vocational training for the early leaver is well developed.

A JOB WITH TRAINING – GERMANY

Vocational training systems vary greatly throughout the world but it is impossible not to mention the long-established German dual system which, even with its inflexibility, is often regarded as the model to which to aspire.

Briefly, in the old Federal Republic of Germany, 90 per cent of all school leavers received vocational education and training, and in excess of 70 per cent entered training through the dual system under which, as apprentices, they spend about three days a week on in-company training and up to two days a week in a specialised training school. (Up to 40 per cent of the off-the-job training is in general education, including mathematics and politics.) Training is available for around 380 classified occupations ranging from motor vehicle maintenance to florist. All firms which wish to employ an apprentice have to be approved by the local Chamber of Industry and Commerce (membership is compulsory) as a training company. The local Chamber is responsible for the assessment of final examinations and is the awarding body for vocational qualifications. The cost of on-the-job training is borne by employers but the apprentices' pay is initially 30–40 per cent of that of the skilled worker.

However, the majority of firms in the old FRG choose not to be training firms. Of the 2 300 000 companies, only about 500 000 provide training and only they are allowed to recruit young people. They often take on more than they can permanently employ, and at the end of their training about 60 per cent of all qualified apprentices leave the firm for employment elsewhere. This is regarded by the training firms as part of their social responsibility and by many of the non-trainers as a free ride. I have difficulty in seeing it working in this way in many other countries!

The system is criticised for its inflexibility. Herman Schmidt, President of the German Federal Institute for Vocational Training, has pointed to the increasing difficulty in meeting new demands as agreed curricula rapidly became out of date. The system produces narrow specialists. He sees the future as moving towards a broader vocational education producing flexible generalists rather than one based on specialist skills. In the engineering occupations, recognising that in twenty years' time there will be virtually no unskilled workers and that skilled workers will take on more responsibilities, they have introduced the criterion to, 'plan, execute and control all work tasks within their occupation' as a less prescriptive and more project-based general competency (Schmidt, 1992).

However, the advantages of universal commitment outweigh the disadvantages of inflexibility. The amount of training is important, just as is the quality, although for those who enter higher education a system which can delay entry to the labour market to the late twenties or early thirties does suggest that more is not always better, and some Germans look with envy at the ability of the Japanese, US and British systems to react rapidly to changing demands.

The key lesson from the German experience is not about structures, what is taught or how it is taught but that *no young person should begin work without there being a commitment on the part of the employer to provide training and on the individual to participate in that training.* In the ascendant organisation such training will not be restricted to the narrow occupational requirements but encompass the broad range of foundation skills and competencies envisaged by the SCANS report.

A JOB WITH TRAINING – JAPAN

The Japanese, however, do very well without formal vocational qualifications. Alun Jones, Personnel Director of Sony UK, has wisely commented on the great divide between the British and Japanese approach to training:

> The British are taught they have a responsibility to train people and tell them what is going on, otherwise they will not understand. The Japanese approach is from the opposite direction. They talk about an individual's responsibility to learn. It has a tremendous impact on what training means. While the British will lay on courses the Japanese see no need. They believe people will learn when they need to and if they are not motivated to find out then perhaps they should not be doing it anyway.

A 1979 study by the Tokyo Human Development Centre of the effectiveness of small group activities in Japan clearly illustrated employees' perceptions of the individual learning experience benefits of such activities. The greatest benefits were in the personal development of the individual, with small group activities impacting positively on:

	%
• improved skills	70
• job knowledge	84
• motivation	68
• enjoyment of job	64

The more tangible measures showed lower positive impacts:

• improved efficiency	70
• improved atmosphere	53
• improved safety	48
• improved quality	33

Although this survey is fifteen years old, it is still quoted favourably by Japanese sources as being indicative of what they see as beneficial outcomes.

Thus, for the Japanese, small group activities such as quality circles are not just aimed at achieving specific objectives; they are seen as part of the overall education and learning experiences of individuals in the workplace. The most accurate description is *near-the-job* training rather than on-the-job or off-the-job training. Near-the-job training involves study of what is going on, getting behind the obvious, using problem-solving techniques or the seven tools of quality control. Such small group activities for the Japanese serve to improve workers' confidence and their personal development and knowledge base. The very nature of the activity is such that it enhances skills and this in turn allows more devolution of responsibilities. Thus a virtuous upward spiral can be created, but it is a gradual process. If people are pushed too far, too fast and are expected to perform beyond their capabilities, they can easily become demoralised, switch off and turn the upward virtuous spiral into one which spirals downwards.

The Japanese, though, have the great advantage of slow burn development. When it takes fifteen years from university graduation to become a manager or eighteen years from high school graduation to become a foreman the need to develop people rapidly is greatly reduced. The university graduate is hired into a company, not an occupation, and during those fifteen years will be given a wide range of experiences in a variety of departments. They prefer not to allow specialisation to develop. They do not want narrow accountants, buyers or personnel officers. Their engineers will work in manufacturing engineering, production, quality assurance or purchasing, The aim is to develop people who have a broad understanding of the business acquired by on-the-job experience with instruction given by the immediate superior; by rotation of projects and assignments and often by considerable self-learning through correspondence courses. They look for interaction and interchange between individuals, particular those in the same year or from the same university. Because of the seniority progression system under which it has been rare for the 'junior' to overtake the 'senior', the latter is not worried about teaching the former. In fact, as part of his appraisal, his ability to bring on the younger man is a significant factor in the overall assessment. With the beginning of the decline of the seniority progression system in favour of a merit-based approach, it will be interesting to see if this responsibility is in future pursued with the same enthusiasm!

Some Japanese are, however, becoming dissatisfied with the traditional slow burn development and as lifetime employment begins to break down and as individuals increasingly choose to exercise their individuality, they will increasingly question a process which broadly provides for everyone to progress at the same slow pace irrespective of individual ability. In mid-1991 Daiken Trade and Industry (fibreboard manufacturers) announced its New Personnel System, which allows promising workers to rise through the ranks based on their expertise and merit as opposed to seniority. Said Personnel Chief Kazuhiro Izumi:

> We have to give people more training and more explanation about their training. People want to be told what their potential is and they want to know where their skills fit into the company's plans. Young people have lost loyalty because there are more jobs than people and so we want to give people more skill and make them feel useful. (*Financial Times*, 16 December 1991)

Izumi felt that Japan's on-the-job training was failing to keep pace with employees' expectations. In particular, Japanese companies are finding when they assign people to overseas locations that their specific expertise does not match that of the professionals in the host country.

CONTINUOUS DEVELOPMENT

What this leads to is the fact that the ascendant organisation will have a commitment to the *continuous development of all staff.* This becomes particularly important when we remember that most organisations have flattened their hierarchies. At one time most people who envisaged that they had a career were able to look forward to rapid progress up the hierarchy. 'If I'm not promoted every three years something is wrong!' But with flattened organisations, the elimination of jobs and more people competing, perceived promotion opportunities are no longer as apparent. It then becomes imperative to motivate staff in a different way, particularly as people can be an appreciating asset; the longer their service, provided they are continuously developed, the more valuable they become.

The Japanese have long recognised this increasing value and have introduced what they call a qualifications system based on ability, length of service and the individual's total contribution . Typically there are nine or ten levels. For example:

Qualifications

Counsellor
Vice-counsellor
Senior manager/engineer/.supervisor
Manager/engineer/supervisor
Sub-supervisor
Assistant senior manager/engineer/supervisor
Assistant manager/engineer/supervisor
Clerk/operator
Assistant clerk/operator

Since this ranking is separate from the chain of command, no special authority is given, although there is extra pay. For some levels (for example, Assistant and Assistant senior) written examinations have now been introduced, and for every appointment a thorough assessment of the candidate's suitability is made. Basically the system recognises the total contribution and experience of people for whom there may not be a formal slot in the chain of command but who are greatly valued. Japanese will often be more proud of their honorary title than their formal one. In March 1994 I explained this system to an ecumenical seminar of the most senior church leaders in the north of England and it generated great hilarity. I was somewhat puzzled until the Archbishop of York explained that the church had been appointing honorary canons for hundreds of years, for exactly the same reasons.

What then, is this concept of continuous development? I define it as:

> **'A continuum in which in a structured way all people learn, are challenged and motivated so that they can grow and develop as individuals throughout their lives'.**

It is a continuum on two axes: the vertical, as the individual progresses upward through the hierarchy; and the horizontal, as the individual progresses over time, even if he or she remains at the same level. It is conscious and structured rather than accidental and haphazard, although some of the best learning opportunities arise in an unplanned way. It applies to all staff, not just a selected few. It refers to learning rather than training, although much learning arises from training and development activities. It speaks of being challenged and motivated because personal growth comes not only from obvious learning experiences but also from assignments and projects. It refers to growth not just in the narrow sense of acquiring skills, but also in the development of the whole person.

Finally, it is for life in two senses: it never ends and it is for the whole of life, not just for that part spent at work. A tall order!

The thought processes that went into my developing this concept took a long time to mature. One strand was my increasing dissatisfaction with the traditional concept of management development. The real breakthrough came when I realised that 'management' is not a separate career, that management education should not start when someone is appointed a manager and that *the real strength of an organisation comes from the continuous development of all people and not just a selected few*. The focus has to move from teaching managers, to helping people at all levels to learn, grow and develop throughout their lives.

This comes about not simply through training programmes but by involving people throughout the organisation in the continuous improvement of the business processes and in the development of their own skills, competencies and contributions. As we have seen, involving people in developing the culture of the organisation is critical to gaining ownership – but it goes further. It has to be a continuous process in which objectives are mutually defined, not as top-down targets to be imposed and measured on a pass/fail basis but as shared definitions of what is to be achieved; not simply in terms of tangible targets, but also in behavioural competences. We need to create a partnership between managers and staff in managing their overall performance.

However, a word of warning. Life is not perfect, and while the continuous development process reaches all the way through the organisation and I argue that management development as such must not be extracted and treated as a separate subject, an organisation which ignores the specific development needs of its actual and potential managers does so at its peril. Identifying those who are likely to be able to progress through the managerial ranks and ensuring that they have the opportunities to develop and broaden their competencies and skills, is vital for all organisations.

This does not mean 'fast tracking'. Given the right opportunities and exposure, those with the ability will emerge and everyone, including their peers, will recognise who they are. I am not a great advocate of detailed succession planing. As an intellectual exercise it can use up many pleasant hours, but as a precise tool it is usually hopeless. People are rarely in the right place at the right time and it is amazing how often when forced to appoint unexpectedly that the initially 'less than ideal' person grows with the job. The critical task is to ensure that you have talent both in depth and breadth by appointing good people and giving them a range of experiences, assignments and training which fit them for the future development of the organisation. And take risks. There is nothing more challenging, more daunting and potentially more satisfying for the individual and beneficial for the organisation than placing a manager in a role in which he or she lacks detailed knowledge. Provided you have confidence in the individual's overall capabilities, the task-specific knowledge, within reason, is the easiest element to acquire.

In the ascendant organisation attempts have to be made to ensure that objectives are integrated with the business strategy and permeate throughout, not only top-down but upwards and laterally, and this can only be done by involving people at all levels. The very process is part of their development. Top management, as a team, needs to begin the process by determining the corporate objectives; but in cascading through the organisation the process has to be not one of top-down imposition, but of asking people what they can do to contribute, discussing it, assessing the impact on their colleagues and agreeing not only the objectives but also the means of achieving them and the measurements to be applied. At all stages discussions between those affected takes place. The Japanese use the term *hoshin kanri* (policy deployment) for this process and the discussion and debate over the objectives is termed 'catchball'. It is a superb process for determining what really are the key objectives and for ensuring that they are genuinely shared.

This in turn can lead to the process now fashionably described as performance management:

> A partnership between managers and the individuals who are members of their teams. This means that at every stage the aim is to obtain joint agreement on roles, accountabilities, tasks, objectives and competence requirements, as the means of measuring performance, on the assessment of results and the factors affecting them, and on development and performance plans. (Armstrong and Murlis, 1994, p. 216)

This can lead to a two-way assessment of performance, not by 'upward appraisal' which can end up with subordinates' views of their boss going to the boss's boss, but a genuine exchange of views, including an understanding of what the subordinate needs from the boss. Such a process in a non-threatening relationship can result in great mutual benefit, but if it is at all threatening will result in mistrust and bad feeling.

Many organisations have various elements of performance management in place: the definition of the strategy, policy deployment, objective setting, performance appraisal and performance related pay, the assessment of development needs, on-the-job and off-the-job training, and so on. However, performance management is concerned with the interrelation between these elements so that the whole becomes greater than the sum of the parts. In most organisations such concepts apply at the professional and managerial levels. In the ascendant organisation they must permeate throughout, but if they are to be consistently maintained there has to be control of the process. Commitment is not enough. This chapter is concerned with the continuous development of all people and it is simply not possible to apply an informal approach when hundreds or thousands are involved. The breakthrough for me came when I realised that starting at the top of the organisation was like beginning where you want to be, not where you are now.

BEGINNING AT THE BOTTOM

Start at the bottom of the organisation, not at the top.

This thought is so blindingly obvious that in retrospect I wonder why it took me five years to realise it! This does not mean that the development of people at lower levels has been neglected, but that invariably it is regarded as something separate from the development of those at the top. In the ascendant organisation, however, many of the attributes once regarded as being the prerogative of people called managers, now become important at all levels in the organisation. Concepts such as teamworking, flexibility, *kaizen*, staff selection, problem-solving, appraisal, JIT, training, total productive maintenance and scores of others become an essential part of the toolkit at all levels. The ascendant organisation cannot wait until people reach a management position before being introduced to such concepts. An appreciation has to begin in the very first days of a career in the organisation, irrespective of the level at which the person is hired.

At this early stage the depth of knowledge is necessarily limited, but as the individual progresses both in time and position, the initial appreciation progresses through awareness, knowledge, understanding and finally to full capability, as a result of which the individual can train others and modify the practice. As per the definition, it is a continuum.

The production operators in the ascendant organisation will, then, have a number of capabilities, so far removed from the tasks of F. W. Taylor's operators as to be unrecognisable. They need to be flexible, able to contribute to improvement activities, quality conscious, able to plan and deal with contingencies, to operate either alone or within teams, to work to and interpret instruction, to monitor and control progress and to practice care in all they do. They will use their brains as well as their hands. These capabilities will be the core. The technical tasks then become easy.

I now wish to put some meat on the bones, for continuous development is not just a concept, it is a practical reality. But it is also a *process* which, like all other processes, has to be controlled; it is so important that it cannot be left to chance.

HOW TO INTRODUCE CONTINUOUS DEVELOPMENT

Step one in the process is to ask the questions, 'What do people need to know to be able to do their jobs effectively?' and 'What competencies and capabilities should they possess?' You will not get the full answers by asking top managers, for they have but limited knowledge of what their staff need to know and do to achieve the results. I did this when I first initiated the process. Asking directors what their people actually did was a salutary experience. Between us we came up with some 250 skills, capabilities and competencies. When the training staff took over and started talking to the people actually doing the jobs, their initial listing exceeded 1250! Therefore, begin by painstakingly questioning the people actually doing the jobs. Start at the bottom of the organisation and gradually patterns will emerge. There will be some common skills, competencies, capabilities or knowledge that apply to most people at a given level in the organisation, irrespective of where they work. There will be others which are specific to people within a specific function or business unit.

Step two is the commonisation process. If the task is being conducted by a team, get them all together to share their knowledge. There will be much in common but some will have discovered areas that have been missed by others. At this stage, attempt the first rough tabulation – perhaps distinguishing as follows:

Core Skills	Attributes, knowledge, competencies, capabilities, which are common to all people in this position irrespective of where they work
Professional Skills	Attributes, knowledge, competencies, capabilities, which are specific to people in this position in this department/business unit/function etc.

Step three is to return to the departments and verify and/or amend the tabulation, seeking sign off – if appropriate – at manager level.

Step four is to add in what I prefer to call the 'magic powder' element. We all know people who have acquired all possible knowledge and skills but remain useless at their job. We equally know people who have little experience but are superb. The difference is the 'magic powder' – it is specific to an individual and, by definition, cannot be defined in advance. You only find out what is missing, if you ever do, by observation, experience, analysis and discussion, and it can sometimes be a difficult process. I once spent a long time with a manager trying to find out why he was not as effective as he might be. We concluded that it was his inability to see the wood for the trees. He was so involved with wanting to know the detail that he not only burdened himself with much unnecessary information, but also burdened his staff with putting it together. The result of our discussion was the development of a deliberate 'stand aside – give them headroom' plan, an art which often requires great self-confidence. The answer might have been different. No one knows until there is a totally open and honest joint assessment of needs.

On a formal basis, I translated 'magic powder' into 'personal effectiveness' and defined it as 'Development initiatives specifically tailored for the individual to enable each person to perform effectively at their existing level or above'. Such initiatives might include projects, assignments, transfers and external experiences. However, I still insist on using 'magic powder'. It is much more evocative of what is really meant, and is readily understood by everyone.

Step five is to determine the delivery process. Some deliveries may be through formal training programmes, but learning is not simply about attending formal courses: it is active as well as passive. The responsibility for continuous development lies within the line department, shared between the boss and the individual. *It is imperative that the individual examines and understands his/her own needs and objectives and agrees them with the boss.* The Japanese have long regarded the ability to develop subordinates as a key responsibility of a manager, and fundamental in the ascendant organisation is the delegation to line managers of the responsibility to assess training and development needs, and frequently for ensuring that these needs are met. Many of the professional skills can in fact only be delivered by the line department; they are too specialised to be delivered by anyone else. But this involvement also creates ownership – the feeling that their contribution makes a difference and that it gives a sense of reality to the learning process. One of the most important core skills is therefore 'Training/coaching/mentoring' for, if those who have responsibility for developing others have not been taught how to do so properly and effectively, they cannot be blamed if they fail. Working together, systematically explaining and practising skills is easy to do badly and very difficult to do well.

The Japanese also value self-learning and expect the salaryman to make considerable personal efforts to develop his skills and capabilities. In the West we are often passive, expecting teaching to come to us. How often do we hear complaints from employees such as, 'The company doesn't do enough to develop the staff?' Often such complaints are justified but the responsibility of individuals to help define and meet their own needs is also clear. The employer is not a spoonfeeder. Neither, however, must the employer neglect its responsibilities. As in all things there must be a balance.

It is clear that a well-trained, highly motivated workforce can be a sustainable, appreciating asset, but still many organisations are reluctant to train, primarily because they are afraid of losing people in whom they have invested time and money. Continuous development can make a contribution to alleviating this problem. While, in the West, little can be done to prevent the individual who is offered a massive salary increase leaving for a 'better' job, those companies who offer continuous development are more likely to retain staff than those who do not. Such companies are more likely to combine a wide range of attributes of the ascendant organisation. But if they do not, the risk of losing people remains. One of my favourite aphorisms is, 'If you continuously develop and still lose significant numbers of people, you have got your development right and most other things wrong!'

Some companies have taken the development of their employees beyond the job-related route. The most celebrated is the Ford Employee Development and Assistance Programme (EDAP), a joint initiative between management and the unions which initially provided up to £200 to each employee who chose to undertake training courses. The Company thought that, based on US experience, around 5 per cent of the workforce would take up the offer; the actual figure is 30 per cent.

In all, about one-third of Ford employees have taken programmes, with the most popular being bricklaying, computer literacy and languages.

This was very much an act of faith. It was established in 1987 after the then very difficult pay bargaining was over, almost as a means of trying to find something on which management and unions could agree and could work together to achieve. The end has justified the means. It has developed considerably from its early beginnings, and has inspired similar programmes, notably in Rover, where the Rover Employee Assisted Learning Scheme (which is part of its total Rover Learning Business concept) allows every employee £100 tuition fees every year for 'lateral' personal development in business areas not specifically related to current job skills. Asked in 1990 if the Ford programme had spin-offs in terms of improved industrial relations, John Hougham, one of its architects, found it difficult to quantify but said, 'If people are enjoying learning and this is associated with the company, the company must be better for it.' However, more immediately it encourages people back into education, particularly those who previously had considered themselves educational failures, and Ford's experience has been that many progress to more academic or job-related courses.

THE LEARNING ORGANISATION

Although another jargon term, the ascendant organisation *is* a learning organisation, which can be defined as, 'An organisation which facilitates the learning of all its members and continuously transforms itself' (Pedlar *et al.*, 1989) or, as others might argue, 'A learning organisation continuously transforms itself and in the process continuously develops all of its members.'

However, as I have previously argued, an organisation by itself achieves nothing. It does not have a life of its own, it is not able to achieve anything without the intervention of people. It is the people who are able to create the climate in which the organisation is able to be transformed. A more appropriate definition of a learning organisation is therefore,

> **'One in which the people create the climate that facilitates the continuous development of all members who as a result are able continually to develop the organisation.'**

I use the word 'develop' rather than transform. 'Develop' suggests a steady evolution and in most organisations, if this is happening, the more dramatic transformation will not be needed.

Almost everything in this book is about learning and development and though in the learning organisation there is not necessarily a large amount of formal training, unless the people have the capability and opportunity to develop themselves and their jobs they will not be able to develop the organisation.

Peter Bonfield, CEO of ICL, recognises this. He uses the term, 'the resilient company': 'The resilient company is a learning company, it has processes for transferring intelligence throughout the organisation; it makes frequent adjustments to the company's course and thus takes advantage of any and all opportunities. The resilient company is *not* on autopilot.' In 1983, having recognised that it had to change from being a technology driven to a market-driven company, ICL launched 'The ICL Way' with the message that it aimed not just at satisfying and delighting the customer but:

> The more we focused on the customer the more we realised that we had to become a fully open company . . . Because we are open, we are able to embrace new concepts swiftly and efficiently. By developing our people to think in an open way they are much more flexible and responsive to change. They embrace change willingly so that they can meet the challenges which come with openness. (Bonfield, 1993)

Bonfield believes that the key to ICL's resilience is the commitment and the professionalism of its people:

> Investing in people makes simple common sense in a business which changes as swiftly and radically as ours. To be resilient in adversity it is absolutely imperative that our people are able to respond and react in an innovative and entrepreneurial way. We have to recruit the best, nurture them and then let them create new opportunities for themselves and for ICL . . . We have developed a culture of mutual support across the company . . . we have people from different divisions working together, all pulling in the same direction. And we do that with minimal central control or interface.

I do not give a step-by-step programme for achieving this Utopian condition, for it is not possible to teach an organisation to learn. It must learn to learn and it can only do this by experience ('it', of course, being the people in the organisation); by the mobilisation of all the knowledge and skills of all the people working together for the common good; by recognising that past success does not determine future success, indeed too much success can lead to complacency. Managers in such organisations are happy to devolve responsibility and to allow all people to contribute and to challenge the established way of doing things. They create an atmosphere which removes blockages to experimentation. However, people are also trained; it is critical to understand the correct techniques before you can go about breaking the rules. While the occasional genius may do everything wrong from the start, most of us are not geniuses. Even Picasso, who broke all the rules, understood and worked to them before he broke free and, in management jargon, created a paradigm shift.

Should we always be seeking the paradigm shift? The answer depends on where we are. Few would argue that moving an autocratic organisation to ascendancy is anything other than a paradigm shift, and moving to anything from apathy certainly is. Moving from functional chimneys to re-engineered business processes may well be. At the micro level, changing an airline's philosophy from one of flying planes to moving people is dramatic enough to deserve the term. Regarding people as possessing brains as well as hands requires a major paradigm shift for many managers.

But (and it is a big 'but'), once you have become an ascendant organisation with all that entails, including the inherent capability to be able, 'continually to develop the people and the organisation', do you need any more paradigm shifts? As we have seen, continuous development of the small things creates the atmosphere in which major changes of the large can become the norm. I do not want to develop this into a circular argument, so therefore I conclude, rightly or wrongly, that the objective of an organisation which has reached this 'zenith' is to develop continuously so that it needs no more paradigm shifts! Except that once in a while . . .!

A 1991 report by the British Institute of Management on flat organisations examined among other things what it called underrated qualities. Included in this list was 'Commitment to learning'. While nearly three-quarters of respondents strongly agreed that, 'Human resource is a critical success factor', only 26 per cent rated, 'Commitment to ongoing learning', as a very important management quality and only 26 per cent rated, 'Individual learning and development' as a very important factor in a new philosophy of management! (Toulson and Coe, 1991).

As previously indicated, one of the most important characteristics of a learning organisation is that it must learn how to forget. We have a long way to go!

13 The Long and the Short of the Finances

The worst crime against working people is a company which fails to operate at a profit.

(Samuel Gompers, President, American Federation of Labor, early 20th century)

If top salaries are seen to reflect greed and the abuse of power an atmosphere can grow in which fiddling of expenses or other dishonest practices become commonplace.

(Philip Sadler, Vice-President, Ashridge Management College, 1993)

CORPORATE FINANCES

The debate over the so-called financial short-term view said to apply in the USA and Britain and the longer-term view said to apply in Germany and Japan has long been with us. In the 1980s it was easy to demonstrate that the German/Japanese model was superior. In the 1990s it can now be argued that the coziness of the German social partnership between the banks, managers and unions; and the *keiretsu* of Japan disguised many deep-seated ills, which the aggression of Britain and the USA exposed and resolved. But, it can also be argued that the *real* economies of Germany and Japan remain strong *because* of the roles of their banks and the workings of the *keiretsu* whereas in Britain and the USA competition and takeovers, promoted by those whom Lester Thurow has called, 'Financial Vikings who raided everything' (Thurow, 1993, p. 281), weakened the real economy. Although, says the counter-argument, those that remain are stronger for it.

This debate will not be resolved, least of all by pointing to the current leading organisations. However, the financial climate within which managers operate does affect their day-to-day behaviour. If there is a continuous, narrow concentration on short-term financial objectives – quarterly profits, return on net assets employed, earnings per share, and so on – it does make it more difficult for a manager to take the longer-term view. More difficult but not impossible.

The narrow concentration on short-term financial objectives, managing by the numbers, leads to an imbalance in the day-to-day operation of an organisation. In my days with Ford and Continental Can Company the job of the young graduate financial controller was to go on to the shop floor to get the supervisors to justify why they had exceeded, for example, their budgeted use of indirect materials or overtime levels, and pull them into line. Cost meetings were interrogations of the operational managers by the finance managers – accused and accuser. Whereas this may have satisfied the finance manager's ego, the end result was that the operational people were scared to make decisions, had little authority and consequently high-calibre people fought shy of these critical jobs. In a Japanese company, it is the task of the finance department to provide a service; to provide the cost information which will help the operational people do their job better. Although, again, the sceptics may point to the current difficulties of Japan, it is an undeniable fact that the Japanese approach enhances the status and responsibility of the line manager and makes the job attractive to high-calibre people. And it is high-calibre people in the front line who deliver real, long-term success for an organisation, even if financial manipulation can achieve particular short-term gains, or in some cases, losses.

This imbalance impacts not only at the operating level, but also at the top of a company. The debate even divides the financial establishment. Speaking at the conference of the Institute of Directors in February 1990 Lord Alexander of Weedon, Chairman of National Westminster Bank said, 'There has been too much tendency to concentrate on what is in the short-term interest of shareholders, for whatever reason. I believe there is too much need for the management to concentrate on the immediate danger of takeover, and that can affect research.' Decisions are taken, 'on the basis of the short-term interest of our shareholders, compared with those of our competitors in France and Germany who can take the long-term view.' To the short-term shareholder what the company itself does is largely irrelevant and its staff of little consequence. The company is a name on a spreadsheet and trading is done on the basis of the 'research' of those whom Nigel Lawson, when Chancellor of the Exchequer, described as 'teenage scribblers', bright, educated, and inexperienced, whose task is to create a market – buy at 190 and sell at 220! The impact of such an attitude on the management of a company is said to be that it forces it to maximise short-term profits in order to maintain the share price at a level which protects it from a hostile takeover bid.

The other side of the financial establishment argues to the contrary. Peter Stormouth Darling, Chairman of Mercury Asset Management, the investment division of merchant bankers S. G. Warburg, argues:

> Takeovers are a useful part of the market system. The threat of takeover acts as a spur to management to do its best for its shareholders and even an unsuccessful takeover bid is likely to have beneficial effects on the company which defended itself successfully. To remove the possibility of takeover would result in a gradual decline in competitiveness and efficiency in UK industry. (Darling, 1990)

The UK has a particularly active takeover market. In 1954 there were just over 2000 quoted manufacturing companies. 400 of these were acquired by 1960. In the period 1972–1982, 137 of the largest non-financial companies were taken over, but a 1990 study by the Department of Trade and Industry into the impact of takeovers on subsequent performance found that either takeovers failed to generate increased efficiency or that the evidence was inconclusive.

In Japan, groups of companies (*keiretsu*) join together through cross holding of shares, and though each member company may have less than 2 per cent of any other member firm, when every member has 2 per cent in every other member a large protective shareholding builds up. (The major blue chip companies hold significant proportions of the equity of many of their key suppliers.) Only 30 per cent of equity is listed and available for trading and management is insulated from takeover because changes in ownership have to be approved by the full board, all of whom are internal managers and executives. The Japanese board may have from thirty to fifty members but it plays only a ceremonial role. In the post-war period the firms were mainly financed by bank lending and today banks and insurance companies own around one-third of Japanese shares.

In the USA, individuals own some 50 per cent of shares by value, compared with less than 25 per cent in Britain, Japan and Germany. As a result the individual American share-owner holds only very small amounts of the equity of any company and plays virtually no role in monitoring the performance of its managers. However, regulators ensure that they received comprehensive financial information and that this information is equitably shared. Institutional ownership of American companies is now around 40 per cent, but because they came in late and have comparatively small stakes, they too have adopted a 'hands-off' policy. Because Federal law allows companies to be incorporated in whichever state they choose, they tend to go for those which have the friendliest laws. When I was with Continental Can Company many were choosing Connecticut, but New York, Delaware and Pennsylvania are also favourites. Banks and insurance companies have had only limited ability to own shares, leaving the way open for the hostile raiders and it is this threat which has ensured that managers are constantly on their toes to achieve performance, share price and dividend pay outs.

In Germany, about 5 per cent of the population are shareholders, compared with over 20 per cent in Britain and the USA. German law requires that managers put the interests of 'the company', which is difficult to define, ahead of the interest of other parties, including the shareholders. Only about 660 companies have a stock exchange listing and all but 50 of these are controlled by family shareholders, banks or insurance companies. Companies obtain their funds from self-investment and from the banks, not from the stock market, and a representative of the bank may sit on the supervisory board, the *Aufsichtsrat*, often chairing it. Their approach has been to maximise the wealth creating capacity of the enterprise.

The long-admired German two-tier board system is, however, being questioned – are the supervisory board members so close to the management that they cannot exercise proper supervision and, 'Who supervises the supervisors?' The near collapse of Metallgesellschaft (the German metals, mining and industrial group with nearly 260 subsidiaries, 58 000 employees and DM 27 billion turnover) in January 1994 following its ill-judged speculation in oil futures (which resulted in a £1.32 billion refinancing package), has brought to the surface long-held doubts. Does the relationship between the banks and the management and the freedom from the fear of hostile takeovers engender a complacent and non-enquiring frame of mind? When German banks hold 179 seats on the supervisory boards of the top 100 companies and they see their stake as a symbol of continuity, can we expect a vigorous analysis of the type presented by predatory Vikings?

Although it can be argued that the Metallgesellschaft supervisory board should have seen the problems coming, and despite subsequent protestations by the Chairman that it was deceived by deliberately falsified information, there can be no doubt that once the banks were aware of the situation they moved with alacrity to *help* the company. They provided more than DM 1.5 billion (£580 million) to enable it to meet its immediate commitments. Six out of eight members of the board of managing directors were replaced, the creditor banks agreed a massive equity for debt exchange and later a huge recapitalisation was agreed by the shareholders. John Craven, the only non-German on the board of managing directors of Deutsche Bank, said, 'I would submit that this is an extraordinary feat which would have been difficult, if not impossible, to achieve in the timescale involved under other systems, and one which is deserving of praise rather than criticism' (*Financial Times*, 18 February 1994).

The German *Aufsichtsrat* and the management board (*Vorstand*) have a duty to look after the interests of the company as a going concern and all the stakeholders. This includes the suppliers, customers, the workforce, the management and the community, as well as the creditor banks and shareholders. In Germany, as in Japan, the approach of the banking system in the difficult times is to do what it can to help pull the company through. It sees the company as a community to be preserved. Takeovers of weak companies are almost unknown. In the Anglo–American culture a sign of weakness is an immediate call to the predatory Vikings.

Daimler–Benz is the first German company to be quoted on the American stock exchange and as a result is having to adopt American accounting practices. In the past, as with most German companies, it sought to preserve the value of capital invested, protect the dividend and minimise its operating surplus which determined its tax charge. American shareholders require not only the preservation of capital but a return on it, and as a result D–B is engaged in a major review of the performance of newly established 'business units', Businesses which do not meet its 'return on capital' criteria are either being brought into line or sold off. In April 1994, D–B cut its dividend from DM13 to DM8 and, according to Michael Geiger, an analyst with NatWest Securities in London, its 1993 profit of DM 600 million under German accounting rules will turn into a loss of DM 1.7 billion under American rules (*The Economist*, 9 September 1994). Which system is better for the long-term health of the organisation?

This author does not know the answer, nor, I suspect, do the hundreds of others with vested interests who argue in favour of one system or the other. When I see Japanese companies within a few months switching totally from an argument that it is market share which counts to, 'We have to improve our short-term profitability dramatically', I am left in a state of some confusion. For the long-term benefit of the small enterprise, is it good or bad that British entrepreneurs have to put up their homes as collateral whereas their German equivalents do not, or that British companies pay two to three times as much in dividends as German? Is it better to have growth based on deal-making rather than on the organic development of the company? Will Hutton, Economics Editor of *The Guardian*, has written:

> What drives business strategies and internal organisations alike is not the needs of production markets but the capital markets. For example, internal accounting systems in continental and Japanese companies are designed to signal what the rewards are for building market share or growing a company. In Britain the systems are about cost minimisation, risk aversion and delivery of sound results for external shareholders. (Hutton, 1991)

Whatever the rights and wrongs of the debate, it must be clear that the financial climate does have an effect on managements' perceptions of how they should behave if they are to satisfy their shareholders. As we have seen in other areas, it is often perception that counts. Equally, the shareholders' perception is important. Donald Brydon, managing director of Barclays de Zoete Wedd Investment Management, argued in 1990 that he doubted that if less was paid out in dividends, more would be spent on research and development. 'Why is the result not just as likely to be expenditure on plant and machinery, pay, advertising, higher stocks and a whole host of other absorbers of cash?' (Brydon, 1990). Investors generally do not have a high opinion of managers!

Learning from the debate, some actions can be taken that are within the control of the management of the ascendant organisation if they are to be assisted in managing for the long term. The following list is primarily aimed at the Anglo–American tradition:

- The roles of chairman and chief executive should be split and, depending on the size of the company, there is a strong case for the chairman to be part-time and, perhaps, non-executive. A key responsibility of the chairman is to appoint the chief executive.
- Non-executive directors should be appointed by the whole board not just by the chairman and CEO. They should be genuinely independent of the management of the company, avoiding cross-membership and mutual back-scratching.
- Non-executive directors should be primarily responsible for the performance of the directors and management. They must have full access to all information and, as necessary, audit their performance. This has been the case in the USA since 1989. They must ensure that executive directors salaries do not get out of line with performance.

- Directors should be judged on the basis of the long-term performance of the company, including investment in product development, facilities and people development, as well as on the financial returns. Such assessment should be against specific pre-determined financial and non-financial objectives and should recognise the need to prepare for *future* performance.
- Directors' contracts should not be for a longer period than other employees. They should be subject to the same penalties for poor performance, that is, after due process, dismissal without compensation. We have to avoid the situation in which the way to get rich quick is to have a long-term rolling contract and then foul up.
- There should be full disclosure of directors' remuneration, including the value of share options, that is, exercise price and the value of those taken up.
- Directors must communicate effectively with the financial institutions to ensure that the institutional and other investors fully understand that the ascendant organisation is working for the long-term success of the enterprise, not just for short-term financial performance.
- Directors must ensure that the finance function has measures which relate to the long-term objectives and though applying financial vigour is seen as being supportive rather than inquisitorial.

Directors' pay structures will be discussed in detail later in this chapter.

NON-FINANCIAL INDICATORS

The bulk of this chapter will be taken up with compensation and benefits, but before moving to this subject it is necessary to look for a moment at non-financial indicators. The ascendant organisation recognises that long-term profitability will be optimised by attending to a wide range of performance measures, not just short-term profit targets. Current profitability is a result of past actions. Future profitability depends upon present actions and we have, therefore to be concerned with *the quality of inputs as well as the performance of outputs.*

Charles Handy has developed a 'scorecard for business', listing things that do not normally count or get communicated:

- the intellectual assets of the company (including brands, patents and skill base)
- expenditure on the enhancement of these assets (including R and D and training and development)

- the introduction of new products or services
- employee morale and productivity
- quality of goods and services
- customer satisfaction
- investment and expenditure on environmental control and improvement
- expenditure on community work
- investment in the community. (Handy, 1994, p. 226)

IBM measures its 'Baby Blues' on seven parameters; revenue growth, profit, return on assets, cash flow, customer satisfaction, quality and employee morale. Rank Xerox had, up to the mid-1980s, a bonus system for senior managers only, in which 30 per cent of their remuneration was tied to the return on net assets employed and percentage revenue growth year on year. From the mid-1980s it increasingly introduced quality of service as measured by customers' perceptions of its performance against competitors. Headquarters staff were included in 1990 with the opportunity to earn a maximum of 2.5 per cent annually for meeting the customer satisfaction targets.

In his book, *Out of the Crisis*, Deming produced a comprehensive listing of performance criteria for a hospital ranging from 'Incorrect dosage of drugs' to 'Complaints from patients'; from 'Mortality rate in emergency room' to 'Average length of stay in hospital' (Deming, 1982, pp. 203–5). Although he was writing of the American private hospital system he chose not to include financial measures. The point is that by concentrating on financial measures you are forced to look at short-term performance. By concentrating on the fundamentals of the business then, providing the pricing is right, the financial performance will look after itself.

Malcolm Smith (1990) has summarised some 65 possible non-financial indicators. Some of these are indicated in Figure 13.1 overleaf. Clearly there are many more and it is up to each organisation to determine those which are relevant for it. The facts of life are that staff come to regard those areas that are measured as being important and will pay attention to them. So, do not measure for the sake of it. If the unimportant is measured, time and effort will be wasted.

THE PRINCIPLES OF PAY

The reward structure must be an outcome of good management, not a substitute for it.

Focus of measurement	*Non-financial indicators*
Quality of purchased components	Defects ratio
Equipment failure	Downtime/total time
Maintenance effort	Production lost through maintenance
	% failures: planned/unplanned
Cost of downtime	Cost of production lost
Waste	% rework – scrap
Quantity of output	Actual v. target
Reliability	Warranty claims/cost
Quality	% conformance to quality standards
Market share	% increase in market share
Employees	Educational attainment
	Training costs v. payroll
	Absenteeism
	Labour hours per unit
Customer awareness	Complaints
	% repeat orders
	On time deliveries

SOURCE: Smith, 1990.

Figure 13.1 Non-Financial Indicators

There is no such thing as the perfect reward structure. Those which begin by being comparatively simple gradually become complex; those which initially motivate are quickly taken for granted; those which begin by being fair gradually take on the semblance of unfairness as adjustments are made in response to short-term pressures; payment by results systems become out of date as organisations move from a desire to maximise output to a need to achieve just the required output at a specified quality in a specified time.

New technology and working methods blur the distinction between white collar and blue collar work. Teamworking, continuous improvement, flexibility and the emphasis on quality, all of which encourage an operator to stop work and highlight a problem, correcting it if necessary, are death to a piecework system. Individual merit pay, without effective guidelines and an understanding of the need to operate within the budget, can easily get out of control as managers who 'like to be liked' over-rate their staff and accelerate their progression through the salary range, while staff in other sections, whose managers are 'harder', compare themselves unfavourably.

The long-term macro changes taking place in advanced industrial societies impact on remuneration systems. While materials and products are priced within a global economy, labour is still priced locally (even for top executives, despite the attempts of some to make comparisons with the salaries of their American counterparts). Customers demand high levels of service, high quality and rapid innovation and, as a result, reward structures have to facilitate quick responses. The decentralisation of organisations poses the dilemma of choosing between a centralised reward structure based on a unified set of values or a decentralised system which supports success in different ways in different units. Centralisation can unify, but can also result in unnecessarily high wage costs in some locations or business units. Decentralisation can divide and lead to leapfrogging, but also keep some costs down and motivate in the right way in the right place.

How do we find a way through this maze if we are to develop a reward system appropriate to the ascendant organisation? Are there any guidelines which might help?

The answer is 'Yes', and happily they lie within the very concept of such organisations. *Primarily, a reward structure must be integrated with and support the organisation's culture, business strategy and objectives*, recognising, in particular, that the ascendant organisation depends wholly on the capabilities and commitment of all the people to establish and achieve those objectives. It is, however, but one aspect of people management and must connect with all others – the way work is organised, how people and their work are valued, how performance is managed and how people are trained and developed.

The ascendant organisation works on the assumption that the required quality and volume levels are achieved and people should not be paid 'extra' for achieving what they are paid to achieve. *Production and quality levels are not voluntary*. If it has established a JIT system, eliminated waste and is setting improvement targets, it aims to hit the targets precisely. It does not want a payment structure which allows the staff to choose to achieve less than the required levels, nor to motivate the staff to hit or beat the target. If it achieves less, there will be waste in the system; if it achieves more, it will run out of stock. *It is management's job to motivate the staff, not the payment system's.* It follows that the basic wage should be 'right', that is accepted as 'liveable' and equitable, both internally and externally.

There needs to be room for pay progression, both as part of the performance management system (whereby corporate, business unit and individual objectives are developed, shared and assessed and individual development needs identified), and to encourage, recognise and reward both individual and group achievement. Some organisations may wish to recognise input as well as achievement, particularly at the operational levels. However, such recognition needs to take account of long-term overall performance, not just those elements which are tangibly measurable. The contribution to the team, a flexible attitude and innovation are not always tangibly measurable but may be far more important to the success of the enterprise than, say, an individual's attendance record.

The third 'firm' point is that the reward system must be transparent. This does not mean that everyone should know everyone else's pay, although if the system is equitable there is no great harm in this, but that the principles are known, are seen to be fair and just and that there are no hidden extras for a fortunate few. *The ascendant organisation wishes to secure the commitment of everyone, not just those at the top.* Again, this does not mean that, for example, a bonus formula should be exactly the same at every level; but it does mean that if some are able to share in the success of the enterprise, *all* should be able to share.

As a result of these 'firm' points, it is clear that direct 'payment by results' (PBR) systems have no place in the ascendant organisation. They need constant maintenance as variables change, allow individuals to choose the volume level they will achieve and prejudice the chances of participation in improvement activities. They fail to take account of the total contribution an individual could make. Standards are often slack, with 'beat the clock' being the name of the game, and those who play more craftily end up having the easier time, with a resulting feeling of unfairness and possible disruption. Management abdicates its responsibility to motivate the workforce and gives it to the payment system.

Even in the textile industry, noted for its adherence to piece rates, leading companies are experimenting with team or cell working, with group bonuses or even flat rate pay replacing individual PBR. Courtaulds Textiles, famous for its Jaeger and Aristoc brand names but faced with low-cost competition from Turkey and the Pacific Rim, regards the elimination of piecework as a long-term aim, as the culture in which a worker seeks to maximise earnings through developing skills on a single machine is seen as blocking both flexibility and speed of response.

Courtaulds has sought to introduce group based systems and teamworking with a fixed wage with, sometimes, a small bonus.

PERFORMANCE-RELATED PAY (PRP)

Derek Torrington, of the University of Manchester Institute of Science and Technology, has said of PRP systems 'They're like illicit love affairs . . . when you're not personally involved in one you feel you're missing out on something marvellous. When you are involved, you spend most of the time being miserable' (*Financial Times*, 15 January 1992).

Much of the problem is that organisations do not really understand what they want PRP to achieve and even less whether their system contributes in any way to enhancing performance. Are they seeking to assess the quality of input or the achievement of output? Is the reward to be related to an individual's or the team's performance. What is the team? Is the reward to be paid as merit and integrated into salary, or is it to be paid as a non-integrated lump sum? Or is it a combination of the two? If the organisation knows its long-term business goals, does the reward system support them? Is the system so complex that the individual can barely relate individual performance to reward? Is the same system appropriate for all people in the organisation? In a crisis situation, what will motivate people more – a large increase or a pay freeze? Derek Torrington was right. A badly-implemented PRP system can create more misery then motivation.

In January 1994 (BT) British Telecom, Britain's largest private sector company, adjusted its ten-month-old PRP system for 26 000 of its managers and professional staff because its pay levels were regarded by top management as being over-competitive and the cost would exceed its planned overall increase for managerial staff. Concerned that its salaries were in the upper quartile of the market range, David Scott, BT's Industrial Relations Manager, was not worried about the demoralising effect, '[We] have to lose managers in the next financial year anyway' (*Financial Times*, 2 February 1994). This in a year in which BT made around £2.7 billion profit!

Many argue that PRP just cannot work. Alfie Kohn wrote in the *Harvard Business Review*, 'Research suggests that, by and large, rewards succeed in securing one thing only: temporary compliance. When it comes to producing lasting change in attitude and behavior, however, rewards, like punishment, are strikingly ineffective. Once the rewards run out, people revert to their old behavior' (Kohn, 1993). Kohn supports the thesis that reward systems cannot be a substitute for good management. 'Treating workers well – providing useful feedback, social support, and the room for self-determination is the essence of good management. On the other hand, dangling a bonus in front of employees and waiting for the results requires much less effort.'

The Institute of Manpower Studies (IMS) has been researching the impact of PRP schemes for several years and according to Research Fellow Marc Thompson, 'Across all organisations studied, the effect of PRP was at best neutral and mostly negative' (Thompson, 1994). The problem is that most organisations do not know if their PRP scheme is working, because they do not monitor it on that basis. Contrary to the 'firm' point that reward structures in the ascendant organisation must relate to the business strategy, such questioning by IMS, 'usually drew blank expressions.' Further probing often revealed that PRP has not been thought through from that standpoint. It was seen as the 'thing to do'. It was an act of faith.

However, despite the 'non-provability' of the effects of PRP, most managers and staff believe that, like the work of the behavioural scientists, 'It feels right'. In the IMS study over two-thirds of employees were in favour of the principle. The problem is in the practice.

One of the most difficult decisions in applying PRP in the ascendant organisation is whether or not to bring teamworking into the equation. As with quality, production and service levels, people should not be paid extra for achieving what they are paid to achieve. Further, no team is totally self-sufficient; its success depends on the previous learning experiences of its members, the framework within which it operates and the support it receives from those less directly involved. Some team members make an outstanding contribution to a team that does not succeed; others may make a poor contribution to a successful team.

Helen Murlis, Director of Compensation and Benefits of Hay Management Consultants, told me that much exploratory work on team rewards ends up by deciding on cash bonuses (which may work for one-off teams but when teamworking is the norm will be less appropriate), or a realisation that an individual's general contribution to continuous teamworking can best be valued and recognised through a well-developed performance management process.

One company which has successfully incorporated 'teamworking' into its performance management process is Sun Life Assurance. It describes teamworking and gives negative and positive examples before asking for an overall rating:

Teamworking
Valuing teamwork and the desire to co-operate and take an active part within the team and to align own behaviour with the needs, priorities and goals of the team:

Negative examples
- Show reluctance to help others in the team
- Keep self to self, fail to participate
- Be insensitive to others in the team

Positive examples
- Build on the suggestions of others
- Show understanding of colleagues' difficulties
- Volunteer to help others with exceptional workloads

It is always possible to quibble with the detail of such descriptions, but Sun Life has shown that it *is* possible.

SKILL-BASED PAY

Another area of doubt for PRP in the ascendant organisation is skill-based pay, that is, paying for the acquisition of specific skills. Without doubt there are advantages in the systematic acquisition of skills based on modules, especially when designed to lead to a multi-skilled workforce able to undertake a wider range of tasks. This in turn can lead to a slimmer, more efficient organisation with those who remain able to look forward to further training and progression.

Pilkington Glass has a single status basic pay structure divided into four grades, each with four skill steps. Each step requires a number of competencies to be achieved. For example, an Administrator (Financial Services) Grade C has skill levels structured as follows:

Skill 1 Basic maths/English
Basic keyboard skills
Experience of office work

Skill 2 Competence in one of the task areas listed below
Operation of associated mainframe and PC systems

Skill 3 Competence in two task areas
Use of PC for spreadsheets and other applications

Skilled Competent in three task areas
Capable of developing own systems and procedures, for example, PC applications
Awareness of business

Task Areas 1. Credit control
2. Management accounting
3. Salary administration, cash.

In addition to demonstrating their skill level, Pilkington staff have to spend a minimum time at each level, and progression to the next step depends on a combination of performance and training as determined by a review board. Pilkington reckons it takes about two years to progress through the four steps and each step attracts an increment of around £400 to £500 a year. Those who can acquire more skills are allowed to do so, but without further payment, and those who cannot make it to the 'skilled' level remain at step three.

As we have seen in Chapter 12, the continuous development of all people is one of the fundamental concepts of the ascendant organisation and this development takes many forms, only parts of which are directly tangible. Therefore skill-based pay can lead to difficulties. Pirelli Cables built up its pay structure in the 1980s on the basis of a comparatively low base pay plus additional payments as people acquired measurable skills. In 1992 there were 30 modules each attracting an additional payment of £300. The problem was that Pirelli management did not want its employees to achieve skills in all 30 modules, the optimum number being six or seven. However, employees' expectations were raised, so that they wanted to chase modules in order to get the higher pay and became dissatisfied when management found they did not need such a high level of flexibility and prevented them from so doing. The system also inhibited cross functional flexibility. 'If I've not been trained and am not being paid then I can't do the job.'

There are, then, examples of successful and less successful modular training programmes. However, fundamental for the ascendant organisation are concerns about rigidities which can arise when pay is linked to modules which are precisely defined. As the organisation's needs change and the individual has to be retrained, does there need to be further payment? And, if those needs change faster than the retraining capability, what does the organisation do? Allow the individual not to change? Perhaps most seriously, the success of the ascendant organisation depends not only on the acquisition of tangible skills but on the continuous development of all staff, often in areas that are not measurable.

In simple terms, the ascendant organisation which emphasises the continuous development and flexibility of all staff must seriously question whether it should pay for the acquisition of skills except, perhaps, as a transitional step.

In this debate on PRP I leave the last words to Andrew Lebby of the Performance Group of Washington DC, who in responding to Alfie Kohn's *Harvard Business Review* article wrote, 'Just as it is easier for some parents to show love with gifts rather than with hugs, it is often easier for organisations and managers to show gratitude with money than with words' (*Harvard Business Review*, November–December 1993).

SALARY PROGRESSION

Salary progression is a system whereby an individual receives pay increases based on both contribution and achievement and which are consolidated into base pay.

There are numerous methods of facilitating salary progression, all with their advantages and disadvantages. Table 13.1 is developed from Helen Murlis's work and shows some of the more common systems. In the ascendant organisation the rigidity of option 1 (defined cash or percentage increments), the possible demotivating effects of option 3 (increments to a merit bar) and the perceived unfairness of option 4 (total

Table 13.1 Salary Progression Systems

Type	*Advantages*	*Drawbacks*
1. Defined cash or percentage increments	Simple, easy to administer	Rigid, no fine-tuning possible
2. Variable cash or percentage increments within guidelines	Can be flexed progressively or regressively	Control of costs. May need distribution guidelines. More difficult to understand
3. Increments to merit bar, then totally discretionary	Recognises high performers. Greater control of costs	Can demotivate those below bar. Can be abused
4. Total discretion within a budget or merit pot	Highly flexible, recognises mainly highest performers. Total cost control	Possible inconsistency and discrimination. Perceived unfairness. Requires high quality management which may not exist.

discretion within a budget) place them low on the order of acceptance. Option 2 is favoured. It provides for variable payments within clear guidelines and, within the rules, can be flexed. However, there need to be control processes to ensure that people are treated equitably and costs do not run out of control.

Some organisations now consider their salary progression schemes to be totally performance-related with no general cost of living increases. IBM has long held this view, and a new entrant in the 1980s, Mercury Communications, a subsidiary of Cable and Wireless, rejected both job evaluation and grading. Instead, it established individual contracts, the main element of which is performance-related individual pay. Under this system, pay is based on the market worth of the individual and his or her performance assessed during the annual appraisal or performance review. There is no automatic cost of living increase. Mercury undertakes extensive pay research to determine that its salaries are correctly positioned in the market place and it is here that, like all such claims of 'no cost of living increases', the argument falls apart. In simple terms, why is it that in the early 1980s such companies were giving merit increases of 15–20 per cent and in the mid 1990s they are less than 5 per cent? The answer, of course, is to keep in line with the market, and market salaries increase in line with general inflation. There is nothing wrong with eliminating general increases; indeed, provided the criteria of simplicity and fairness are maintained, there are positive advantages. However, let us not pretend that payments under such systems are wholly merit-based and unrelated to the going rate of salary increases.

If an element of pay is to be related to performance, logic demands that there be some method of assessing performance. What is surprising, therefore, is that the guru of quality, W. Edwards Deming was totally opposed to such evaluation. In fact he cites the evaluation of performance, merit-rating and annual reviews as one of his 'deadly diseases' (Deming, 1982, p. 101). Peter Scholtes, a disciple of Deming's teaching on this subject, writes that for Deming, 'Merit rating rewards people that do well in the system. It does not reward attempts to improve the system' (Scholtes, 1987). He believes that if you eliminate appraisals it frees massive resources for real work.

Deming and Scholtes stylise evaluation systems as being based on establishing measurements of standards against which performance is judged – units per day, calls per week, timely completion of a project, and so on. They relate it to past performance. But, they argue, an employee's work is tied to many systems and processes – individuals cannot be appraised apart from the systems in which they work, nor from their group. Says Scholtes, 'Performance evaluation encourages "lone rangers" . . . [It] will force workers to choose between individual reward and recognition of teamwork. Such a choice will seldom reinforce teamwork.' It encourages mediocrity and safe goals, it encourages employees to work around the systems, not improve them; it will, over time, become top heavy as ratings drift upwards, and will always create losers. Or so the argument goes.

If such a stylisation were right, Deming and his disciples would be right, but in their universal condemnation they are wrong. However, if a performance evaluation system is solely top-down and seen as an end in itself, they are right. But performance evaluation is not irredeemable if it is part of an overall performance management process and, among other elements, assesses the individual's contribution to teamworking, innovation and flexibility.

An effective performance evaluation system within this framework will support the culture of the organisation, valuing all the elements the organisation values, and will therefore assist in driving it in the direction it wishes to go. It will be as objective and consistent as it is possible to be and, in the process, will help reinforce the organisation's definition of good performance and whether and how it is being achieved. It will also provide the link between corporate and development needs and the performance-related pay element of remuneration. This is a lot to ask of any system. A 1990 survey by the Wyatt Company found that only 20 per cent of 600 personnel professionals described their performance management process as 'effective' and only 11 per cent said they had systems which delivered performance pay effectively (Wyatt, 1990). But success is possible.

However effective or ineffective the performance management system might be, there remains a need to assess performance. Theorists might advocate concepts such as performance contracts, which might work well at management and professional levels, but the vast majority of people in many organisations have not even reached the point of having their performance assessed in *any* way. To make the leap from zero to performance contracts is impossible, particularly when the majority spend most of their time working on 'prescribed' tasks.

Within the ascendant organisation the rules of transparency and common terms and conditions mean that if some are to have salary progression, *all* are to have salary progression. However, in view of the very different types of work and responsibility, it may not be possible to develop a single performance evaluation system that applies to everyone. The important points are that the system(s) should be fair, that a 'blue-eyed boy' syndrome is prevented from developing and costs should be controlled. There is no magic formula for this but I favour a forced choice approach in which the appraiser has to rate characteristics against specific statements. Examples of this are shown in Figure 13.2. Such a system should not be restricted to a top-down box ticking exercise. At all levels it must be part of a two way discussion of corporate and individual objectives and individual development needs.

The critical point in any performance evaluation system, but particularly for those which relate to salary progression, is the overall performance rating. Appraisers like to be liked and can easily over-rate their staff; the phenomenon of rating drift occurs; 'average' becomes unacceptable, 'above average' is the norm (and 'above average' then

Quality of Work
Consistent highest quality in all aspects
Good in most aspects
Of varying quality
Not acceptable

Teamworking
Always seeks to involve others
Works well as a team member
Makes a good effort
Dislikes teamworking
A total loner

Creativity/Initiative
Dislikes change
Does not initiate
Welcomes new initiatives
Regularly seeks improvements
Too ready to introduce change

Job Knowledge
Knows fully all aspects
Acceptable job knowledge
Below required level, but progressing well
Below required level, but not progressing well

Objectives
Does not achieve any objectives
Achieves some objectives
Achieves all objectives
Regularly exceeds all objectives

Flexibility
Rigid and inflexible
Acceptable flexibility
Welcomes new methods and tasks
Constantly seeking to increase personal flexibility

Figure 13.2 Performance Evaluation Factors

becomes the average!) and salary costs creep upwards. In an attempt to avoid this, the rating into which the majority of people will fall has to be defined in a way which will be regarded as acceptable. While a slight positive skew in the rating distribution curve is acceptable if by design, it is unacceptable if it happens by accident.

One way of overcoming this is by giving clear guidelines as to the proportion of the population which should fall into each rating level. Nissan's ratings, their description and guideline percentages of the population falling into each level are shown in Figure 13.3.

The real trick lies in controlling the distribution of ratings and the responsibility for achieving this lies with managers. Each year every manager, after consultation within the section, has to predict the distribution of ratings within his/her area of responsibility. This information is passed to the personnel manager who collates it, produces

Outstanding (2 per cent)
Leaves little to be desired. Consistently makes significant contributions both individually and to the team. Consistently exceeds objectives.

Highly commendable (25 per cent)
Normal tasks and assignments particularly well handled, and often makes further contributions. Regularly exceeds objectives.

Fully proficient (70 per cent)
Fully acceptable performance. Normal tasks, assignments and objectives properly handled.

Below expected performance (with **Unsatisfactory** – less than 3 per cent)
Normal tasks and assignments not properly handled. Not all objectives satisfactorily achieved. Above normal supervision required in some areas.

Unsatisfactory
Clearly below minimum requirements. Objectives not normally met nor work completed. Deficient in most major aspects.

Figure 13.3 Performance Ratings

pretty graphs showing the prediction against the guideline and, at a meeting of all managers, everyone sees everyone elses' predictions. If a manager significantly deviates from the guidelines, he/she has to justify to all the others why their section has, say, twice as many 'Outstandings' as everyone else. If they can succeed in convincing their peers, who usually will know the individuals concerned, they have probably got it right. There is no tougher jury! Because the system has gone through seven or eight cycles we are now able to track the trend through the year, and measure the year-end actuals against both the guidelines and the predictions.

This may seem mechanistic, and to a certain extent it is. It is a controlled process and while it may seem less avant-garde than those in the forefront of thinking would wish, it provides for consistency, equity and a high quality of assessment. It would be somewhat difficult to implement performance contracts for 2000 direct production staff! And if it is difficult, it will not be properly implemented and will then fall into disrepute. It is just one method, among many, but the important point is that it works in its environment, and when in 1993 around 4 per cent of the company at all levels and in all functions were involved in a root and branch review, nobody sought to make fundamental changes.

Having determined the method of evaluating performance, the actual methods of progression along the salary range are many and varied. We have seen that they can be discretionary or fixed, constant percentages or constant amounts, progressive or regressive, large or small. What really counts is that people perceive that they have been properly evaluated, their contribution has been recognised and that they have been fairly treated in relation to others. Increases in the range of 2 to 5 per cent, depending on performance, seem about right, remembering that in this system such increases are additional to general increases. Further, the ascendant organisation recognises personal achievement in many ways – the 'Thank you for a great job', the night out or the refrigerator for the team – and if this is done properly, salary progression is the cherry on the icing on the cake.

It has been argued that such a system requires a sophisticated workforce, that people like clarity, that they need increases of 10 to 15 per cent if they are to be 'meaningful'. The ascendant organisation *has* a sophisticated workforce; it is able to absorb and fully understand such an approach and it does not require 10 to 15 per cent pay increases to secure commitment!

PERFORMANCE BONUSES

Salary progression results in pay increases which are normally consolidated within base pay. Without any pretence of precision of language I use the term 'bonus' to describe discrete, non-consolidated payments based on defined elements of the organisation's performance. Unfortunately, there are more potential pitfalls here than in any other area of reward management. Rather than go through an endless analysis of the thousands of permutations, I shall nail my colours to the mast and state that if an ascendant organisation is to have a bonus system it is most likely to succeed in the long-term when it is based on *measured achievement against defined, mid-term performance goals which are integrated with both the business values and needs and when individuals are able to appreciate how their performance can make a contribution to that achievement*. The same principles must be applied throughout the organisation. Beyond this, the permutations flow.

I have argued that in the ascendant organisation people are paid to achieve the standards expected of them and that the merit pay element recognises the individual's contribution to both input and output on a micro basis. The individual's contribution to the team is incorporated at this level. *A bonus, if it is added, must be based on solid achievement, not inputs, and the achievement must be against clearly stated targets and be measurable*.

The bonus system must be integrated with the organisation's values and business needs. It is simply no good emphasising long-term growth while rewarding short-term profit, or preaching that 'our employees are our most valued asset' but utilise a formula which rewards senior executives with bonuses of 30 per cent of base pay and operators with 5 per cent. In the ascendant organisation the formula must be transparent. Some argue that, in order to achieve perceived fairness, it should be progressive: others that it should be regressive, (that is, the payment should increase or reduce as the base salary increases with, at the extreme, everyone receiving the same cash amount irrespective of base salary). I have yet to meet a senior executive who is motivated solely by money; the most common motivator is the need to make things happen. Although few will turn down a pay increase, we do seriously have to question whether the arguments in favour of the international market rate are anything more than mutual nest feathering. When European executives begin to make favourable salary comparisons with their Japanese as opposed to American counterparts, then they will deserve to have their comparability arguments taken seriously.

Perhaps the greatest practical difficulty is to devise a system in which the individual can appreciate how his or her contribution impacts on the corporate performance. Even in those areas where there is an apparent high correlation, for example, 'Sell more TVs – increase profit', life is not that simple. Discounts may be so high as to eliminate profit, it may be at the expense of quality or service and result in low repeat business or recommendations. Even when life *is* like that, the sales success is dependent on a wide range of product development, manufacturing, marketing and logistical support. As we have seen, an organisation may well make more money on support services that on direct sales. Who then is direct or indirect? My conclusion is – do not attempt to incorporate this type of link into the formula. To do so will result in so many permutations of such great complexity that the result will be total confusion. *The individual must be able to make the link, but that is the responsibility of day-to-day management, not the bonus system. If management has failed 364 days of the year, the bonus payment, though nice to have, will not succeed on the 365th.*

Bell and Hanson (1987) have compared the performance of 113 profit-sharing companies with that of 301 which did not share profits. Using their indicators of financial performance, the contrast is striking (as shown in Table 13.2). On all measures the profit-sharers had a better performance, ranging from differences of 6.1 per cent on dividends per share to 50 per cent on return on sales. It is not possible, though, to attribute cause and effect, and Bell and Hanson acknowledge that it is good management that brings about high performance. For them, good managers usually have clear and defined objectives and the ability to harness all the resources necessary to achieve them. They recognise that their most important resource is people (Bell and Hanson, 1987, p. 61). Evidence of improved performance *as a result* of such schemes is hard to come by. The often-used argument about gaining employee commitment may have some validity, but when bonuses are related to corporate financial performance it is difficult for an individual to see how his or her performance can make much difference to the pay out. In any case few companies leave their scheme unchecked if profits regularly rise – adjustments to the formulae are made and few companies over the long-term average much more than 5 or 6 per cent.

How should a bonus system be constructed? There is no 'right' way and it may even vary within a company, although the ascendant organisation with its desire for equity and transparency will aim for flexibility within a consistent framework rather than inconsistency, opaqueness and inequity. Whereas salary progression systems can be based partly on

Table 13.2 Financial Performance: Profit-Sharers v. Non-Profit-Sharers, 1977–85

Measure	*Profit-Sharers*	*Non-Profit-Sharers*	*Actual Difference*	*% Difference*
Return on equity (%)	25.1	19.9	5.2	26.1
Return on capital employed (%)	20.6	15.5	5.1	32.9
Earnings per share (pence)	16.3	12.8	3.5	27.3
Return on sales (%)	8.4	5.6	2.8	50.0
Annual growth in sales (%)	15.5	13.7	1.8	13.1
Annual growth in equity (%)	17.6	16.0	1.6	10.1
Annual growth in profit (%)	13.6	9.7	3.9	40.2
Divdends per share (pence)	5.2	4.9	0.3	6.1
Total annual returns (%)	24.8	18.0	6.8	37.8

SOURCE: Bell and Hanson, 1987.

inputs, bonus payments should be related to outputs which are determined in advance and are measurable – and this is a problem.

Target-setting is imperfect. It is extraordinarily difficult to determine the right measures and if they are correct at the beginning of the review period the chances are that the needs will have changed by the end. If the measure is based on profit, what is profit? Particularly in multi-national organisations, profits can be manipulated by transfer pricing arrangements which can be adjusted to changing tax régimes, or for strategic reasons to make the performance of a particular national company appear better than others. Even within a country, changes in transfer prices can have a dramatic effect on profitability. It may even be in the corporate interest that particular business units or national companies are seen to be making a loss. Corporate financial performance may depend on exchange rate fluctuations as much as, if not more than, on 'real' achievement. A company's share price may be affected more by overall market performance than by its own performance and the impact on measures such as earnings per share can be dramatic. Should the individual benefit or suffer?

The most popular methods of constructing performance bonuses are based on pre-tax profits and earnings per share, but return on capital and cash flow measures are also frequently used. However, the ascendant organisation may wish to take account of both financial and non-financial indicators. It is vital that long-term goals be established, based on real added performance – perhaps on growth in earnings per share over a specified period, achieving target profit or exceeding target pre-tax profit by specific amounts; or, in the non-financial areas, perhaps on specified increases in customer satisfaction ratings or growth in market share. There should be more than one target and it must be *sustained* performance that is rewarded. The targets may vary over time depending on the economic circumstances and the organisation's objectives. From 1994, IBM has linked bonuses to business units and determined that 5 to 10 per cent of employees' pay will be linked to the performance of the business unit in which an individual works. Measures will vary according to the objectives of the unit. Those for the research centres will, for example, be very different from those for the PC business. This is entirely right.

The review period may differ according to seniority. At the very top level I would advocate a discrete review period determined in advance, with the exact time depending on the business cycle – but less than three years is likely to be insufficient for people to be able to demonstrate a sustained contribution.

How large should they be? The advice given by consultants Buck Patterson is typical, 'Bonuses should be of a size that is right for your company and this will depend on its position in the market, where it is in the growth–maturity cycle and a host of other factors' (cited by *IDS Management Pay Review*, November 1993). Although the consultants were speaking of bonuses at the top level, the words ring true throughout the organisation.

However, the actual distribution of bonuses is shown by 1993 research from Monks Partnership. Eleven per cent of board directors received bonuses which exceeded 30 per cent of their salary, 22 per cent had bonuses of 20–30 per cent and 25 per cent received less than 15 per cent. Compared with these figures, senior managers were less generously rewarded – 5 per cent went over 30 per cent and 42 per cent received bonuses worth less than 15 per cent of salary (Monks, 1993).

1993 research by Hay Management Consultants found that 74 per cent of directors had bonus schemes, 68 per cent of senior managers were similarly favoured, but only 20 per cent of other managers had schemes. No figures were given for other staff.

Not only, then, are senior staff more likely to receive bonuses, but the more senior they are, the bigger will be the bonus as a proportion of salary. Arguably, this might be correct if it could be demonstrated that company performance correlated with senior executives' pay. I shall return to this point shortly.

PAY AT THE TOP

In addition to cash bonuses, the ownership of shares in the company for which you work is often regarded as one of the most successful means of motivating people. In Britain the position is complicated by the government's encouragement of employee share schemes (which provide tax incentives for employees to buy shares using the proceeds of 'Save as You Earn' savings plans) and discretionary share option schemes in which a company may grant options to selected employees to buy shares. There is little evidence to suggest that companies that operate such schemes perform any better over the long term.

Experience in the USA is similar. According to the National Center for Share Ownership, about 9500 American companies, accounting for almost 10 per cent of the workforce, have employee share ownership plans, but in almost all cases workers own only a very small percentage of the total equity. According to Joseph Blasi of Rutgers University, most studies of such organisations agree that employee ownership confers very little competitive advantage (*The Economist*, 11 June 1994).

Frequently in the USA employee buy-outs are used as part of a concession package designed to get the company out of a tight spot, not as part of a cultural change. In 1993 TWA exchanged 45 per cent of its equity for $660 million of concessions from its employees. Ten years earlier, Eastern Airlines swapped 25 per cent of equity for $100 million of concessions, but when the airline management subsequently sought further concessions the result was confrontation. Eastern Airlines was subsequently sold to Texas Air and went broke in 1991.

Often such plans are put into place to make employees 'feel part of the company' but they will fail in this objective if their ability to share in success is limited to a 'Save as you Earn' scheme at junior levels or is a result of concession bargaining, while senior executives have share option which enable them to make capital gains of many thousands of pounds. Such schemes in Britain allow executives to purchase shares between three and ten years in the future at the exercise price, (that is, the price prevailing at the time the options were granted). In the ten years since such schemes were first established (1984), the stock market rise is resulting in very large payouts.

The size of executive share options can be seen from an analysis of exercised share options in the third quarter of 1993. Of 145 share options monitored by *IDS Management Pay Review* (February 1994) the average profit was £102 221 (139 per cent). Typically, the option was exercised after five years. The question has to be, why are such benefits denied to the majority of employed people?

In February 1994 John Cahill resigned as chairman of British Aerospace after only two years of a five-year contract. The formal announcement said little more than, 'This is an appropriate moment for him to relinquish the chairmanship.' But Cahill held options on 908 000 shares at an exercise price of 260 pence. At the time of the announcement the share price was 543 pence and Cahill stood to make £3.21 million. Although he waived salary payment for the remaining three years of his contract, the question also has to be asked – is it right that senior executives should have long fixed term contracts, especially rolling contracts, when usually their only practical impact is to generate large payouts if the incumbent leaves early, for whatever reason? The answer is that it cannot be right. When everyone else in the organisation is on, say, three months' or one week's notice and rarely receives any other payment when they leave, there can be no justification for three-year rolling contracts with generous payouts applying solely to people at the top. In June 1994, Postel, a pensions investment institution managing £25 billion, said it would vote against the re-election of directors who had rolling contracts exceeding two years.

Peter Drucker has long argued that a chief executive's pay should be limited to 20 times the average pay in the company. In American manufacturing companies the 1992 average was $40 000 after tax and, said Drucker, 'You can live on $800 000.' Lester Thurow reported that in 1990 American CEOs were making 119 times as much as the average worker, compared with a Japanese factor of 18 times (Thurow, 1993, p. 138).

Despite the headline-grabbing multi-million dollar salaries paid to a few ('Disney chairman Eisner cashes in stock options for £91 million' or, 'Toys Я Us CEO gains $6.7 million bonus on top of $314 000 salary') a Towers Perrin study of more than 350 companies showed that in 1990/91 the average salary of an American chief executive was $1.4 million, inclusive of all cash and options. Clearly there are vast differences within these average figures, but when chief executives are paid $10 000 000 and more, even if the profit-related pay formula produces this result, we have to question whether the formula was properly set and whether the compensation committee was indulging in little more than mutual back scratching. In the UK, is it really possible to justify EMI's head of its music business, Jim Fifield, receiving a basic salary of £2.1 million plus a £5.0 million performance-related bonus and, for changes in his terms of contract, shares worth £6.4 million?

Successful chief executives are a rare breed and the company depends – for good or ill – very much upon its CEO, but research into the pay of the directors of 77 of the *Financial Times* Top 100 companies concluded that there is no discernible relationship between their pay and their companies' performances (*IDS Top Pay Unit Review*, August 1991).

Alfie Kohn cited research by Rich and Larson, who in 1982 examined compensation programmes and returns to shareholders in 90 USA companies to determine if top executive incentive plans made a difference. They were unable to find any difference. In a rising stock market most executives stand to gain, irrespective of their own company's performance. A 1994 study by the National Institute of Economic and Social Research found that between 1985 and 1990 top executive pay increased in real terms by 77 per cent against 17 per cent real earnings growth. (NIESR, 1994)

Philip Sadler, Vice-President of Ashridge Management College, has written:

> Where the differential between the top person's pay and that of the rank and file is perceived as unjustifiably large the consequences can be serious. Not only can it breed divisive class conflict and make wage restraint virtually impossible to achieve it can also lead to a deterioration in the moral climate. If top salaries are seen to reflect greed and the abuse of power, an atmosphere can grow up in which fiddling of expenses or other dishonest practices become commonplace. (*Director*, September 1992)

The truth is, of course, that real commitment comes from being genuinely involved in the business and if the 'rank and file' perceive that they are not part of the same team as the top executives, the chances of success are greatly reduced.

TOP PAY IN THE ASCENDANT ORGANISATION

How then, in the ascendant organisation, should the top executives' salaries be set? Again, there is no magic formula, but there are some principles which are not a million miles away from the principles applied throughout the organisation. First, the salary package must allow the organisation to attract, motivate and retain the right people. We live in the real world and have, therefore, to compete with other organisations which might not see internal fairness as an objective and may wish to apply 'creative' reward structures to their top people. However the ascendant organisation *does* see internal fairness as a factor and will not apply such reward structures, which might motivate those at the top but cause resentment everywhere else. Secondly, just as at the bottom of the organisation, the basic salary must be recognised as the payment for doing the job the person is paid to do. If the key task is to improve market share by 10 per cent over the next three years and improve net profits by 5 per cent, that is the job the CEO is paid to do. There can be no doubt that the CEO would in any case have had a hand in setting those targets!

And, it can be argued, they need no more than the right base salary to do what is required. If we accept that the base salary is the payment for doing the job and that we should not rely on the payment system to motivate, why should different criteria apply to the top executives? More than anyone else, they are motivated by the ability to make things happen. Provided the money is right, they do not *need* more to make them do their best for the shareholders and if they are motivated by money (greed), their thinking is more likely to be short term (especially if the expected time in the job is short) rather than in the long-term interests of the organisation. Throughout my career, I and all other executives with whom I have worked, have done our best for our companies. A bonus for achieving or exceeding our targets is nice, and not refused, but it is not that which motivates us. Do not the teachings of McGregor *et al.* apply at the top as well as at the bottom?

Having said that, many will wish to establish performance-related pay for the senior team members, and much more difficult therefore is the reward for individual contribution, which is likely to form a higher percentage of their total pay than at other levels. *The chief executive should be both leader and member of the team, and is probably more dependent on that team than anyone else in the organisation.*

Unlike most other members of the team (the organisation), who have a salary progression system based partly on inputs, there is an argument that the CEO and other top executives should be rewarded *only on outputs*, and on outputs which are specifically determined in advance and are measurable. Here the same problems arise as at other levels: profits can be manipulated and performance affected by factors beyond the executives' control. If, after all these difficulties, it is still decided to go ahead then the targets should not only be measurable, they should be adhered to. No allowance should be made for the unexpected. It is the top team's job to expect the unexpected! Otherwise the criteria should be as for other staff.

But what is the right money? Drucker's factor of 20 , the Japanese 18, the British 35 or Thurow's quoted American figure of 119? There is no absolute answer and in the end we are left with what *feels* right to all the stakeholders. There is no point in trying to create a formula. Pay is emotional and the best any organisation can do is to create a system at the top of which it is not ashamed, which it does not need to hide and which serves to motivate all the people and not just a few.

If the same rules apply to every organisation, the argument that, 'We need to pay big money to get the right people', flies out the window. There is nothing wrong with stock options and *everyone* sharing in the success of the organisation. Indeed, it is to be encouraged. What is wrong is that a favoured few should benefit disproportionately, and when companies seek to disguise such benefits it does not actually suggest that they are proud of them!

Rosabeth Moss Kanter speaks of post-entrepreneurial pay systems, arguing that many organisations are gradually changing the basis for determining pay 'from *position* to *performance*, from *status* to *contribution*.' She is undoubtably right that this is the way to go and she criticises merit pay for offering increases which are too small to be meaningful. Her solution is, 'bucks for behaviour', and she advocates as many as five variables in determining pay:

- a guaranteed small amount based on level and position
- an individual merit component
- a group or division gain-sharing component
- an overall company profit-sharing component
- short-term bonuses and awards for exemplary team and individual contributions. (Kanter, 1989, pp. 229–66)

It would seem that Kanter has not had to administer a large payroll. Please protect us from Greeks bearing gifts.

14 Trade Unions in the Ascendant Organisation

It used to be easy to hate managers, really easy, because they were so awful. It's a bit more difficult these days because they have become a bit cleverer. The company [Ford] seems to have realised that you can catch more flies with honey than vinegar.

(Jimmy Airlie, National Officer, Amalgamated Engineering and Electrical Union, November 1987)

THE DECLINE OF TRADE UNIONS

The structural reasons for the decline in trade union membership are well known; the changing structure of industry, increased unemployment and the ending of full employment as a strategic goal, the expansion of the service sector, the increased employment of women, expansion of part-time employment, government hostility, and so on. All of these factors impact on both the absolute numbers and the percentage of workers in trade unions. Despite their very different histories and structures, there is scarcely a trade union movement throughout the established, industrialised world that is not experiencing a significant decline in membership.

According to the International Labour Office's 1993 World Labour Report, union density in the UK has declined steadily since reaching its peak in 1979, and in 1993 was 35 per cent; in Spain membership is down from 18 per cent in 1980 to 11 per cent; Italy has seen a fall from 44 per cent in 1980 to 34 per cent; Japanese density rates dropped from 30 per cent in 1982 to 24 per cent in 1993; in the USA, where trade unions once covered about 30 per cent of workers, the figure is now down to 16 per cent. In Germany the figure is 34 per cent, although some 90 per cent of workers are covered by union agreements. In Canada, according to the ILO, trade union membership has continued to grow, primarily because of the growth of the public sector membership; 'a growth which has been sustained by the efforts which the Canadian labour movement has made to appeal to the changing needs of the workforce as well as to promote a broader acceptance of its policies among the Canadian public' (ILO, 1993, p. 38).

In almost all countries, trade union membership levels are now higher in the public sector than in the private, often by 20 to 30 percentage points. The 'typical' trade unionist is now more likely to be working in a government office or teaching than to be working at a lathe in a privately-owned engineering firm.

Trade union structures may be based on industries (as in Germany, although the metalworking agreement covers thirteen different industries); the company (Japan); political or religious tendencies (France); industry sector (USA); or have just grown (UK). They may be centralised as in Germany and Sweden or fragmented as in Japan, where there are thousands of individual company unions. The basic drives may differ. To stereotype these drives, American unions are basically economically motivated and Japanese unions are essentially collaborative, seeking to work with management for the success of the enterprise. German unions have a strong social agenda, with the concept of social partnership being the core of relationships (but, it is argued, this agenda has led to social benefits packages far beyond the capability of Germany companies to sustain for long periods and which, in the 1990s, are now beginning to be cut back). French unions have a strong political agenda but exercise this in the large state enterprises and have little real influence elsewhere. British unions combine economic objectives with class-based politics, but have been partially marginalised by their inability to attract members in the new industries and by government hostility since the early 1980s.

Negotiations may be centralised but take place at different times of the year, as in Germany; or decentralised but take place at the same time, as in Japan (the *shunto* – the spring offensive – which is an offensive in name only); they may vacillate between centralisation and decentralisation, as in Sweden (currently decentralised); there may be pattern bargaining, as in the USA; or a mixture of everything, as in Britain. Legal frameworks differ, the range of services varies widely and the level of professionalism differs greatly.

However, despite these differences, since the 1950s virtually all have experienced a decline in membership and most in influence – first in France in the 1950s, followed by the USA in the 1960s, and the UK in the 1980s. It simply is no good pointing at the structures of trade unionism in the industrialised world, suggesting that one country has got it right and that if only the others would emulate it they, also, would be rejuvenated.

The ILO in 1991 brought together analyses from 11 trade union federations in eight industrialised countries, and in its 1993 World

Labour Report highlighted a number of key challenges for trade unions in the 1990s:

- focus on the service sector, for example banking
- do more to attract workers in the private sector, particularly in privatised public enterprises
- for white collar workers, offer services based not just on group solidarity but also on individual needs
- give higher priority to womens' needs
- seek to extend legislation to protect part-time and peripheral workers
- develop strategies to attract young people
- become involved in the introduction and consequences of new technology
- increase the range of benefits exclusive to members (excluding 'free riders')
- increase international co-operation

All of this is good stuff, but *the* critical issue for trade unions lies not in seeking to attribute cause to any particular accident of history, geography or structure, nor in trying to find a response to what are essentially structural issues. *The critical issue for trade unions is to determine their role in organisations which have responded to the long-term, fundamental changes in industrialised societies by totally changing the way they manage the employment relationships.* In short, what is the role of trade unions in the ascendant organisation?

For the greater part of the twentieth century large scale enterprises were highly centralised, with rigid hierarchies and power based on a 'control' philosophy. Because of the multiple layers, discretion was minimal and rapidly reduced down the hierarchy. So-called scientific management rigidly defined jobs, breaking them down into simple tasks and reducing the skill and discretion levels, labour was hired and fired according to demand; and large indirect departments removed authority from the front line managers and supervisors. The paradox was that while trade unions abhorred many of these practices, it was these very conditions that led to their growth and success, often built on the view that there was an inherent conflict of interests between employers and employees and their unions. A further paradox is that during their period of greatest power, trade unions reinforced many of the central tenets of scientific management. By insisting on narrow job definitions, protecting skills and restricting flexibility, by insisting that, 'an operator is an operator is an operator' and by rejecting management attempts to use the brain as well as the hands, they gave scientific management a further turn of the screw, resulting in the contribution of all operators being far less than their inherent capability.

THE NEW AGENDA

The Irish Congress of Trade Unions (ICTU) has carefully studied what it calls work organisation initiatives (teamworking, multi-skilling, JIT, internal customer, self-directed work groups, and so on) and summarises the choices for trade unions as being opposition, pragmatic scepticism or shaping the agenda (ICTU, 1993). The Congress has produced an excellent summary of the risks and benefits for trade unions of a variety of responses. This is given in full in Table 14.1.

As far as the ascendant organisation is concerned, if unions are to play a constructive role, they have either to adopt the positive approach or actively promote their own agenda.

The key issue for trade unions as we approach the 21st century must then be, 'In this new environment can we define and then provide a service which members, actual and potential, want?' And 'members' can be just as much 'non-core' as 'core' staff. In this sense members play a vital role. They *are* the union but also see themselves as its customer. Customer requirements change, often rapidly and erratically. The customer pays a price, the subscription, for a service. Many regard it as an insurance premium to provide protection in time of need. If the price is too high in relation to the service, the customer, if he or she has a choice (and increasingly the trade union's customer does have a choice) will no longer wish to pay. The individual member is primarily interested in, 'What will the union do for me and my colleagues in my company?' And when the basic pay and other benefits are right and when the employee feels valued as an individual the answer is often, 'Not much'! It is what the member, not management, wants that counts.

The British Trades Union Congress, in its 1994 publication *Human resource management – a trade union response*, finally got round to offering guidance to its members. It argues, 'If the employer is genuinely concerned to improve the performance of the enterprise, is committed to involving workers in the running of the company and is seeking to develop a real partnership with recognised trade unions then HRM and collective bargaining can work in harmony' (TUC, 1994, p. 6). This requires a 'serious commitment to employment security', well-paid, rewarding jobs with opportunities to progress, investment in training, an

Table 14.1 Summary of Benefits and Risks Associated with Options for Trade Union Response

Option	*Benefits*	*Risks*
Opposition	• Maintains traditional adversarial approach • No need for union to adapt or change	• Unions by-passed by management • Members questioning relevance and value of union membership • Miss opportunity to be involved in QWL • Damage to Ireland's perception
Local response only	• Allows issues to be addressed without having a formal policy • Maintains adversarial position nationally while representing a 'positive' response locally • No blurring of traditional IR agenda • No need for unions to change or adapt	• Wide variety of local practices • No support or guidance from trade unions • Reacting rather than influencing management proposals • QWL initiative remains with management
Minimalist approach	• Provides clear policy and guidelines • Provides framework for local officials and members • Maintains uniformity of approach	• Takes no account of local practices — existing relationships — reasons for and scope of initiatives • Limits scope of local officials to develop optimum solution • Could be perceived as negative, if conditional upon achieving 'up-front' agreement
Positive approach	• Allows for a tailor made approach • Allows unions to optimise their level of input • Opportunity for greater involvement of members • Builds members' identification with union • More involved in shaping final outcomes	• Could blur traditional 'us and them' relationships • Blurring of traditional bargaining agenda • Undermining of union solidarity • Variety of local outcomes
Actively promote with own agenda	• More involved in setting the agenda • Seen to address wide member needs • Closely involved in ongoing membership	• Could be perceived as 'doing management's job' • Undermining of union solidarity

SOURCE: ICTU, 1993.

end to short-termism and a social partnership. The TUC is particularly concerned with ensuring fairness of treatment in recruitment and selection practices, performance appraisal, salary progression and in ensuring that teamworking does not lead to undue peer pressure to achieve targets! I would not disagree with this listing but the problem is not convincing me; it is convincing potential members!

The new approach of some trade unions is contained in *A New Agenda – Bargaining for Prosperity in the 1990s* prepared jointly by two British trade unions, the GMB (a general union covering a wide range of occupations in many industries) and the Union of Communication Workers (UCW). They state, 'Trade unions should wish to work together with employers and government to create a successful industry, a strong economy and a caring society in the 1990s.' In discussing what they refer to as the revolution of rising expectations, they say:

> Performance levels must reach record heights if Britain is to enjoy economic success in the 1990s. Achieving them requires more than cost cutting. The pressures to improve the competence and the commitment of employees is increasing. Customers are demanding ever better goods and services. This means scrapping penny pinching attitudes to investment in training. *Britain's workers want greater opportunities to develop their talents* . . . They wish to escape the drudgery of dead end jobs and take pride in work that is both worth doing and done well.

And later:

> Technical innovation is causing rigid production methods to give way to flexible manufacturing systems offering reliability and variety at low unit costs . . . In future even greater weight needs to be attached to team work, motivation and commitment. Success and security, profitability and prosperity require that management and labour work together to make the best use of the talent available in each enterprise. (GMB/UCW, 1992)

In discussing the fresh approach, the GMB and UCW coin the beautiful phrase, '*The New Agenda would make the quality of output rather than the price of inputs the centrepiece of talks between trades unions and employers* . . . work organisation, training and quality should form the focus . . . Discussions should concentrate upon productivity and ways of bringing the ingenuity of employees to bear on questions of quality.' From another direction, Bill Jordan, President of the Amalgamated Engineering and

Electrical Union tells the story of one of the best AEEU officials who addressed the new employees of Toyota in Leicester. He gave a peroration on the benefits of trade unionism and what the union might do for them, and then asked for questions. One man put up his hand, 'What's your union's attitude to quality?', he asked. The official thought for a moment or two and then said something rather inconsequential, which served only to demonstrate that the union did not have a view. In the process he learnt a lesson about the attitude of workers in the new environment of the mid-1990s. Bill Jordan is one of the more advanced thinkers and tells the story to make the point that even the best officials have some way to go.

The objective of union officials like Bill Jordan and John Edmonds is to create, 'A successful industry, a strong economy and a caring, sharing country in the 1990s.' This is right. There is no merit in unions seeking to alienate employees from their employers, particularly when we note that every listing of employees' desires is headed by a wish for 'job security', but as we have seen, 'security' is not now achieved simply through full-time permanent employment. Previous generations of trade unionists created a climate which fought against change, whether it was of technology, manning levels or work practices. They sought constantly to increase wages, often irrespective of ability to pay. They believed that security of employment came from increasing the period of notice or negotiating generous redundancy payments. American unions have based their security objectives on a rigid adherence to the concept of seniority, particularly when it comes to shielding jobs. General Motors' agreement provides that workers cannot be laid off for more than 36 weeks, during which time they receive 95 per cent of their average pay. After this they must be recalled, and if no job is available they will be assigned to a 'bank' or 'pool' and receive full pay for training or special duties until a job is found. They only face loss of income if GM's $4 billion income guarantee fund expires. The aim is to discipline employers not to lay off workers due to the prohibitive cost. Does it work? GM is in the process of closing 21 plants!

Trade unions, in their negotiating role, must be wise enough and professional enough to balance the two aims of ensuring the success of the enterprise and achieving the equitable distribution of the gains. Their agenda needs to broaden even further: IG Metall in its 1991 paper, *Tariff Reform 2000*, anticipates that bargaining will move beyond the bread and butter issues to focus on matters such as pay and grading structures, training, working conditions, health and safety, environment, workplace democracy and the abolition of the blue collar–white collar divide. It wishes to give high priority to the humanisation of work. 'Work organisation should be designed in a manner which enables work to be performed for the duration of a working life up to the age of 65, without detriment to physical, mental or spiritual health.'

Employees are now realising that their only real security comes from working for a successful enterprise. The power of the trade union or their period of notice is meaningless if the organisation cannot provide a service or product which will be purchased. An example of enhanced security is Rover's 'New Deal' which ended white collar–blue collar distinctions, ended demarcations, introduced a new disputes procedure, guaranteed job security and introduced teamworking. In launching this in 1992 George Simpson, Chief Executive, wrote to all employees, saying: 'Necessary reductions in manpower will be achieved in future with the co-operation of all employees through retraining and redeployment, natural wastage, voluntary severance and early retirement programmes.' This assurance greatly contributed to the major changes that have since taken place in Rover. Rover was, perhaps unknowingly, combining the need for security and flexibility.

As part of the move towards an emphasis on individualism and teamworking, companies are seeking an increasing amount of creative input from their workforce and often the key relationship is becoming the direct relationship between the individual and his or her immediate boss. Good internal relationships in such organisations do not primarily depend on the relationship between the company and the unions as organisations, but on the face-to-face relationship between individuals. It is based on a belief that if staff are not treated properly, with respect and trust, they cannot be expected to behave similarly towards their customers, either internal or external. It involves a belief in the goals of the organisation and is totally removed from the imposed compliance on which traditional trade unionism thrived.

There remain some in the trade union movement who have failed to perceive that long-term fundamental changes are taking place. We have seen the reaction of the Canadian Autoworkers Union (Chapter 4). The left-wing Centre for Alternative Industrial and Technical Systems, in attacking both Ford and Nissan, has described teamworking as, 'Yet another strategy for increasing control of workers and attacking the legitimate operations of unions' (CAITS, 1988). Many local trade union officials see teamworking as a mechanism for by-passing them, with the new-style supervisor being able to speak directly with employees. Under the old arrangements the trade union official used to by-pass the supervisor by going direct to the manager. Even the sophisticated

European Metalworkers' Federation, in referring to decentralised structures, states, 'Management sees these forms of work organisation as a means of weakening the trade unions . . . it is extremely dangerous for both workers and their trade unions if management is allowed to proceed without control.' They are mistaken. There are in the USA managers who are pleased to see the power of unions reduced (often using sophisticated union avoidance consultants) but few elsewhere have set out with this as their objective. Managers' objectives have been to ensure that their company responds positively to the changing environment. This response has created new structures and the basis of new relationships. The danger to trade unions lies not in managers going on the offensive against them but in their failure to recognise and respond to these changes.

Some are responding. Sigi Roth of IG Metall is thinking about the role of teamworking in Germany. He aims for a high degree of decentralisation and self-organisation, with tasks shared to a much greater extent than at present. This means workers not just moving around within the manufacturing operations, but rotating through areas such as material supply, quality control and maintenance. He seeks an environment with high-quality working conditions and human-oriented values in which goals are agreed and manning levels co-determined, particularly with reference to the integration of older and disabled workers and the training of unskilled and semi-skilled workers. He looks for group discussions to be held during working hours involving a self-confident, critical and highly qualified workforce, and for spokespersons to be democratically elected and then have involvement at all levels of decision-making within the company. I have shared a platform with Sigi Roth. He is convinced that Europe needs a solution which conforms to the European social and trade union tradition of binding together economic and social progress for the well being of all and in the interests of social equality and justice (Roth, 1991).

The European Metalworkers' Federation is thinking constructively about the future role of trade unions, and in 1992 produced a document, *Mechanical Engineering in Europe in the year 2000*, which outlined its views. It recognised that the move to employee involvement impacts on the relationship between management and the workforce, dissolving the old blue collar–white collar demarcation and rejoins the Taylorist separation of planning from execution. But it also recognises that reorganisations can lead to employment instability, especially when markets are saturated and there is no economic growth. In such circumstances, 'Since this aspect of productivity is completely neglected by management, the task of maintaining a balance between the two dimensions lies with the unions.' For them, this must lead to more free time for workers for training/reskilling and for improving working conditions, with at least 5 per cent of annual hours being allocated to these tasks.

The EMF is also concerned to achieve, 'A more integrated firm, characterised by a more horizontal hierarchy and above all by the dynamic involvement of all the workforce in decisions concerning the present and future operation of the company.' To achieve this, workers and unions must play an active role in work and company organisation concepts, personnel development, technical and production process concepts and even in the actual production conception. In particular, they aim for the humanisation of work, 'To eliminate pressure and stress, to provide the necessary staff and rest periods, to carry out a reasonable volume of work and allow for necessary breaks.'

Some remain much more negative, believing that managers have a hidden agenda which aims to shift power from the union representative to the first line manager. John Fisher, briefing delegates at a Transport and General Workers Union conference, wrote:

> Even if a company is keen to involve the unions in this [TQM] process it is often at a 'higher' level where the union becomes *identified* with the system. Meanwhile the *direct* role of the union in representing people at the *lowest* level is reduced or eliminated. So, although it is important to respond to the usual invitation to be involved in change, it is also essential always to keep an eye on the unions' influence at the lowest level, where the work is done and the problems arise. Involvement on working parties and steering groups is fine, but every employee needs to know who their steward is and where they are, otherwise the union will wither from the base. (Fisher, 1993)

However enlightened a company might be, the traditional role of trade unions does not go away. In organisations which are devolving responsibility to local management, it becomes increasingly important that local trade union representatives have sufficient skills and understanding to allow them to respond in an informed way to local initiatives.

Trade unions must continue to represent effectively those employees who have a grievance or who are subject to the company's disciplinary procedure. Even in the most enlightened company, there will still be individuals who do daft things and in such circumstances it is recognised that the individual's and employer's interests will diverge and that high-quality, third-party representation is needed. The British Trades Union Congress, in its October 1993 evidence to the House of Commons Employment Select Committee, quoted a survey which showed that 93 per cent of respondents chose, 'To protect me if problems came up' as a 'very' or 'fairly' important reason for joining a trade union. But this protection is not only needed in times of relationship difficulties. The TUC states that in 1992, trade unions took up over 150 000 personal injury legal cases and won more than £250 000 000 in compensation for their members! (TUC, 1993).

Many trade unions throughout the world are rapidly extending their range of financial services, providing benefits for members only. This is particularly prevalent in the USA. These benefits extend to savings plans, insurance, assistance with loans for house purchase, credit cards, road rescue services, discount travel, welfare assistance, convalescence and support services and private medical insurance. In 1985 the American AFL–CIO recommended a Union Privilege Benefits Program designed for former members whose branch was dissolved because of plant closures. Designed to provide ongoing benefits for laid-off workers the programme attracted four million associate members.

In 1994, however, the AFL–CIO produced, rather belatedly, a significant review of the future role of trade unions. I referred in Chapter 4 to its criticisms of the 'dominant American model of work organisation' (AFL–CIO, 1994), but it also seeks to define a new model which incorporates five principles:

- a rejection of the traditional dichotomy between thinking and doing, conception and execution
- the redesign of jobs to include greater variety of skills and tasks and greater responsibility for the ultimate output of the organisation
- a flatter management structure
- an insistence that workers, through their unions, are entitled to a decision-making role at all levels of the enterprise
- the rewards realised from transforming the work organisation to be distributed on equitable terms agreed upon through negotiations between labor and management

The first three of these principles are common with those of the ascendant organisation. The fourth, however, seeks to extend significantly the influence of the 'workers', through their union, on the strategic decisions of the organisation. For example, on the acquisition of new technologies, changes in products or services, how much work will be done, where and by whom? Their argument is that, 'Because workers have long-term ties to their jobs, they bring a long-term perspective and can be counted on to promote policies designed to ensure that businesses have long-term futures and can provide long-term employment at decent wages.'

Unfortunately, the history of the trade union movement, particularly in the USA, has been one of resistance to change, insistence on the seniority principle, the protection of jobs through costly lay-off agreements and, in the good times, the maximisation of wages almost irrespective of the impact on the employer. In seeking to establish a model in which strategic decisions are made jointly between management and workers, the AFL–CIO pre-supposes a responsibility which, in the majority of cases, has yet to be demonstrated. This is reinforced when their comments on the fifth principle state that, 'This means, in the first instance, a negotiated agreement to protect income and employment security to the maximum extent possible.' They still fail to realise that such negotiated agreements can give but short-lived security.

Real security comes from working in an organisation which is able to anticipate and respond rapidly to customer demands. As we shall see shortly, trade unions *can* have a partnership based on mutual recognition and respect and *can* make valuable contributions to the strategic direction of the enterprise. Even when such partnerships exist, there will be different objectives and trade unions have the right to express their views. In the end, however, the management of an organisation is paid to make decisions affecting its long-term future and that responsibility cannot be shared. The established American unions, in coming to the opposite conclusion, are leading their members down a blind alley.

TRADE UNIONS IN THE ASCENDANT ORGANISATION

To use the GMB/UCW terminology, there *can* be a new agenda for trade unions in the ascendant organisation. What should this be? First, the trade unions *can* have a role. In general terms the organisation and the union can establish a partnership in which they jointly commit themselves to the success of the enterprise; the company recognises the right of its employees to join the union and for the union to represent its members; and the union recognises that management must exercise its right to take action in the interests of the organisation. The precise regulation of such relationships will depend very much on the history and legal framework within which they operate but the principles are sound and universal.

Even such seemingly innocuous proposals are controversial. Nissan in the USA made the conscious decision to set up in Tennessee, a Southern 'right to work' State and successfully fought off a long campaign by the UAW to secure negotiating rights. In the UK, however, we established a single union deal with the Engineering Union from the very start, although it would have been possible to have tried the non-union route. *Provided the union is committed to the success of the enterprise* no one need fear it and, in preventing some of the excesses that free market management may get up to, the union can play a role that in the long term is beneficial not only to its members but also to the management.

Unlike most who write on trade unions, I have faced them at their most hostile. In five years at the Ford Dagenham Metal Stamping and Body Plant, I personally handled hundreds of strikes, have been involved in numerous physical confrontations, have had my office smashed up around me, have been in the middle of several demonstrations and once handled a riot. I was at the front line of the revolution where, to some of the extremists, those trade unionists who supported the Communist Party were regarded as right-wing class collaborators. I can therefore say with some authority and not a little understatement, that if the unions are not prepared to work with management for the success of the enterprise and look only to defend their members, restrict flexibility, cause disruption, create tension and secure the greatest gain for the least effort, they are to be resisted.

I have time and time again emphasised that if employees are to contribute continuously to improving productivity which might eliminate their particular job, they must have, within the definition that applies in the flexible environment, security of employment. And I do distinguish between employment security and job security. As we have seen, Nissan's October 1993 consultation with employees on how best to handle the anticipated 1994 car market decline, led above all to a call for job security, with a clear recognition that this would mean some voluntary job losses and retraining. Trade unions are coming to recognise the distinction between employment security and job security, between employment and employability. In these rapidly changing times the successful organisations will be those who offer the former but gain acceptance that job flexibility can make a significant contribution to that end. And job flexibility requires a commitment to training and retraining. This is the beginning of a constructive partnership.

Nissan's Managing Director, Ian Gibson, and I have stood up in front of all the workforce and committed the company to aim to achieve security of employment. Although many may consider that a rash statement, *we believe in it for our company*. It is not contractual, but it is written with our blood; by saying so publicly we were deliberately forcing ourselves into a commitment we would have to live up to when the going got tough – and it did. When top executives are prepared to put themselves on the line and then deliver, it is of such things that trust is built!

However, to suggest that all organisations offer this commitment would be crazy. We were able to do so, as was Rover, because our staffing levels were 'about right'. We had already achieved a high degree of leanness, our core processes were clearly defined and much of the peripheral work had been contracted out. If necessary, some could be called back in. But many organisations are not yet in this position. Many still have excess staff numbering tens of thousands. No organisation with that type of surplus can offer security of employment. When, however, it has gone through the reduction process, it should then be able to offer security for those who remain. Once at this 'base' level, all organisations should seek to accommodate marginal fluctuations. The costs are small and the potential benefits great.

Within the increased emphasis on individualism and teamworking companies are seeking an increasing amount of creative input from their workforce. With the proviso that trade unions must also be working for the long-term success of the enterprise and its employees, it is clearly possible to envisage a scenario in which they welcome this trend as an important step on the road to genuine employee involvement. They must not interpret it as an attempt by management to divorce employees from their union (for it is not) but an opportunity to achieve what they have claimed to be seeking for years. I have previously referred to the paradox of production processes versus individualism, but management-inspired teamworking provides the unions with the chance to gain real influence in areas that are fundamental to success – organisation structures, work methods and patterns, facility layouts, the environment, training, product changes, new technology and so on, not with a view to resist such change but to facilitate it in a manner beneficial to both employees and the company.

However, some trade unions are able to make constructive contributions in this area and genuinely inform their members of the potential problems if lean production and control of the processes are pushed too far. Much of manufacturing work is tough and, as shown in Chapter 9, one of the neglected areas of management is ergonomics, the physical interface between people and process. This is one of the areas in which trade unions will be able to make a significant impact – but not simply by being difficult. 'Easy working' improves the working environment, product quality and productivity. Most managements and trade unions have barely begun to address these issues in a constructive way. The unions of the future must, and if they do they will find that they can have a real impact where it matters to most employees – in their place of work.

Another factor is that, with declining membership, unions, though recognised as the bargaining agent, no longer represent much of the workforce. The Germans have long lived with this situation and get over it because the theoretically non-union works councils represent employees, not union members. Many unions have, however, refused to represent non-members, even though they have accepted that the pay deals they negotiate will cover union and non-union members alike. This stance is now being challenged as trade unions are no longer the sole representatives of employees

Nissan's Company Council was very much influenced by the German model. While recognising the Engineering Union as having sole representational rights for *all* employees below managerial level (including engineers, shop floor workers, indirect workers, supervisors, and so on) we thought it was more likely that manual workers would join the union than white collar workers. The Company Council was structured so that all employees, union or non-union, would have representation. Our belief was that about 70 per cent of our total population would join the union, with a higher proportion among shop floor staff. It has transpired that over the years membership has been around 45 per cent (compared with a UK private sector figure in 1993 of 23 per cent). We also thought that, as in Germany, active trade union members would be elected to the Company Council. This has not happened.

This creates a problem for trade unions in such companies, for anecdotal evidence from similar organisations suggests that this experience is not unique. The message for trade unions must be that in such organisations they have to make extraordinary efforts to demonstrate their relevance. The national officers of the Engineering Union originally believed that simply signing a single union deal with Nissan would result in employees flocking to join. It did not. They have to earn membership. Nissan must be the only company which has, in 1988, invited the President and General Secretary of a Union to address all employees in an effort to increase membership and in which the Personnel Director wrote to all employees extolling the virtues of trade union membership, emphasising that success had to be three ways – the company, the employees and the union!

Bill Jordan, President of the AEEU subsequently wrote:

> One thing took me completely by surprise. We had difficulty recruiting members into the union at Nissan. We asked for the opportunity to talk to the workforce and I was surprised to be given that opportunity on the day that the managing director was to address the whole workforce. Having talked about what had happened in the previous year, he then to my utter astonishment, personally introduced me as a leader of a union with whom the company had nothing but the very best of relationships, and suggested that it was in the interests of everyone in the company to be part of the Union. How many MDs would take time out to promote that sort of harmony? (Jordan, 1991)

The problem for most unions in such organisations is that it is not management opposition but a co-operative management style that contributes to low membership. Old-style union officials were brought up on the assumption that there was an inherent conflict of interest between capital and labour and that a worker's first loyalty was to the union. Adapting is difficult.

It is about time that trade unions realised and acted on the fact that what unites people because they are all employees of the same company should be stronger than what divides them because some are skilled and others semi-skilled, some are supervisors and others supervised, some are blue collar and others are white collar. When you have teamworking, flexibility of working practices and are harmonising the terms and conditions of employment, there is no case for having separate bargaining units within the enterprise. There is no reason why a supervisor cannot sit on the same side of the bargaining table as the people who work for him or her nor why, on that same side, there cannot be engineers, finance staff and other white collar employees. Those who argue that this cannot work have not seen it in operation.

The trend towards performance appraisal and merit pay provides opportunities for trade unions to play a new and constructive role. For so long, their attitude has solely been one of saying that irrespective of ability all should be paid the same and then protecting the inefficient. This must be modified to include encouraging and rewarding the efficient but in such a way as to ensure that it is done fairly, that equal opportunities apply to all, that the appraisal and merit system is equitably applied and is relevant to all elements of performance (not just the tangibly measurable), and that all are given the opportunity to progress. Further, there is now no logical case why the terms and conditions of employment should differ between white collar and blue collar workers. Instead of some unions seeking to perpetuate differences of treatment, all trade unions should seek to establish timetables within their negotiating groups for complete harmonisation, with the only difference being pay and closely-related elements.

Along with this goes flexibility. Unions should be seeking to eliminate all management and trade union restrictive practices which inhibit what people do. The GMB–UCW New Agenda says, 'Unions must escape from a self-defeating fixation with tightly specified job descriptions and embrace the adaptability that comes from broader job definition.' Managements are also backward, in retaining their love of job evaluation and job descriptions which are their equivalent of the trade union restrictive practice. The unions and managements that will succeed in the future will seek jointly to break out of this straitjacket.

Trade unions, when recognised, are critical to the change process. John Monks, General Secretary of the TUC, said in August 1993 of the British Government, 'It's not encouraging the change through partnership, change through security model. I would like to see that become a national style and if Marks and Spencer and Nissan can do it then so can other High Street shops and final assemblers.' Change is now the only constant. Trade unions must encourage and support change. We are past the time when every change of technology, working practice or staffing level can be the subject of negotiation. Instead, when decisions affecting these issues are being pushed way down into the organisation, the unions have a real opportunity not to resist changes but to facilitate them in a manner beneficial to both employees and the company. To do this they must first demonstrate that their approach is constructive and directed towards success and growth; and secondly they must make a real effort to train their representatives in understanding these issues.

Unions have barely penetrated the growing band of non-core workers, and when such people are often less well treated than their permanent full-time colleagues, they have a glorious opportunity to make a difference. But it requires effort, and such attempts as there have been were short-lived and resulted in high cost per new member. John Monks has great concerns in this area, particularly with regard to the training of the non-core, peripheral workers. He said to me in March 1994, after visiting Nissan, that, to say the least, he found a certain incompatibility between the desire of many organisations to reach world-class standards and the increasing use of peripheral workers with low levels of training. John was clearly highlighting a potential problem and he uses this in his campaigning rhetoric, but at the grass roots, the British trade unions have only rarely reached the starting gate.

There really is no need to be frightened of trade unions. Managements, broadly, get the unions they deserve and if managers abuse their authority, they deserve to be checked. Remembering that the *real* relationship is that between individuals in the place of work, constructive unions can, as John Monks hopes, be genuine agents of change. To do battle with trade unions simply because they are trade unions is short-sighted. I have both literally and metaphorically battled with the extremes of trade unionism and know that many executives who claim not to be 'anti-union' but 'pro-worker' speak with forked tongues. There is nothing wrong with wanting an easy life, wanting to treat people well and finding it more comfortable not having to negotiate with trade unions, *but what counts is what employees want*. If they feel the need to have a trade union represent them, management has created that situation and unless that same management can correct it, who are they to deny recognition?

In the past trade unions have opposed change, but they can have a constructive role in the ascendant organisation, provided they are prepared to change their approach. If they wish to oppose, management must recognise that such opposition, if supported by the workforce, will make it more difficult to progress towards becoming an ascendant organisation. Management must then determine its strategy accordingly and resist.

Some may have the luxury of being able to indulge in confrontation, as did those of us in the British car industry in the late 1970s. Others may seek to de-recognise the union, as a few British companies have done in the 1990s or as has long been the case in the USA. However, it has to be recognised that it is difficult to be confrontational and constructive at the same time, and, if the objective is to move towards a constructive relationship with a trade union rather than obliterate it, management must often take the first step. Militant trade unions are only one of many potential resisters of change and management strategy in seeking a culture change has to take all such resisters into account. The culture change process is long and difficult. To this, I now turn.

15 Becoming Ascendant

There is nothing permanent except change.

(Heraclitus, 501 BC)

We trained hard and it seemed every time we were beginning to form into teams we would be reorganised. I was to learn later in my life that we tend to meet every new situation by reorganisation. And a wonderful method it can be for creating the illusion of progress while producing confusion, inefficiency and demoralisation.

(Gaius Petronius, 1st Century AD)

There is nothing more difficult to handle, more doubtful of success and more dangerous to carry through than initiating change in a state's constitution. The innovator makes enemies of all those who prospered under the old order, and only lukewarm support is forthcoming from those who would prosper under the new.

(Niccolò Machiavelli, *The Prince*, 1514)

We all resist change – unless it is our own idea. Then we want everyone to accept it!

Virtually the whole of Part II has been about 'becoming ascendant', but having the ingredients and making the cake are very different things. With the same ingredients one cook can create a disaster and another a masterpiece. In Chapter 6 we saw how to establish a culture statement but a written statement by itself achieves very little even if the learning process is highly beneficial. This final chapter before the 'postscript' and summary is concerned with the total change process. The great cooks vary the ingredients and introduce their own special something, so, as always, it is indicative rather then prescriptive.

HOW NOT TO CHANGE

Mick Crews, an old friend who has moved from the business world to the voluntary sector, tells the delightful story of the Change Agent, who, after a long period seeking to implement change in a variety of businesses, had just been appointed to the position of Group Stability Agent in a large organisation. His task was to ensure that the Chief Executive's policy of 'No change whatsoever' was implemented to the letter. On meeting a former colleague, he was asked:

'That must be difficult for you after all those years as a Change Agent. Don't you need to develop a vast amount of new material and programmes?'

'Not at all', was the reply, 'I just use the same programmes I developed when I was a Change Agent. Nothing really changed then, so I don't see why anything will change now!'

Christopher Lorenz of the *Financial Times* reported a KPMG Management Consulting survey of change management. 'Most of its 250 corporate respondents are running four or more different types of cross-functional change programmes. With ample justification, KPMG doubts whether many of them are being properly integrated.' It warns of the need for co-ordination and prioritisation, 'so that the change machine does not get out of control.' Lorenz also cites Boston Consulting Group's report that in many large US companies, up to 15 process improvements are under way, 'But these seldom added up to a coherent programme' (*Financial Times*, 27 July 1993). When Heraclitus and Gaius Petronius made their comments on the ancient world, they were also making wonderful predictions about twentieth-century business!

Michael Beer, Russell Eisenstat and Bert Spector tell of the major US bank which announced a company-wide change effort in the mid-1980s. The new CEO carefully reviewed the bank's purpose and culture with his top executives. They produced a mission statement and hired a new Vice-President, Human Resources, who established company-wide programmes to push change deep into the organisation; a revised organisation structure, performance appraisal, reward system, attitude surveys, and so on. Two years later, nothing had changed. What went wrong? Just about everything. Say our trio of authors, 'Every one of the assumptions the CEO made about who should lead the change effort, what needed changing and how to go about doing it was wrong' (Beer *et al.*, 1990). Maybe Mick Crews' story was not a joke!

A paradox of the change process, for those who believe it has to start at the top of an organisation, is that the chief executive will usually have reached that position as the result of success in an environment which values strength measured by decisiveness, direction, the ability to take the tough decisions and by short-term results. (As we have seen when discussing teamworking, the top executive group is the most difficult to develop as a team.) Such a person may see the need for change but will have great difficulty in establishing anything other than a centrally directed, top-down process. And the problem is that most people like the established way, whether it is always sitting at the same table in a restaurant or conducting their business in their accustomed fashion. They will resist change that is thrust upon them.

The most difficult organisation to change is the one which is large and comfortable, well established, making good profits, often in a monopolistic position; 'Why should we change?' Such organisations, whether in the private or public sector, became fat and complacent Managers have their perks and staff their ever-rising salaries, shareholders have their dividends and suppliers their profits. The customer may complain about lack of choice but if there is nowhere else to go they cannot do very much about it. There is little need to worry about competition. The organisation may even think that it *is* responding to customer needs. It has what it believes to be a good product development programme but it determines the pace of innovation, for each product must achieve full profitability before the successor comes on to the market. It has established ways of doing things which, although at one time may have been innovative, have become so embedded in the organisation, so accepted, that no one even considers challenging them. This applies not only to the products or services actually offered to the customer but also to the way of providing them. In fact, all the ingredients making for future disaster! Two examples of comfortable organisations were BP and IBM.

BP

An example of a change programme that did not work as well as planned is the experience of BP, the petro-chemical company, employing in 1990 some 120 000 people world wide. Robert Horton, with a highly successful track record with BP in the USA, took over the top job in 1990. He inherited a large, comfortable, matrix organisation, multi-layered and bureaucratic, with a headquarters organisation of 2200 people (which had risen by 200 during the tenure of the previous chairman) and nearly 90 committees. A questionnaire sent to 150 top managers in 1989 and subsequently to 4000 other staff, had revealed widespread ignorance of BP's strategy and strong criticism of its multi-layered committee structure and review process, which virtually institutionalised second guessing. Horton was determined to change the culture and initiated a programme which formally was called Project 1990 but within BP came to be known irreverently by some as 'Horticulture'.

Building on lessons learned from the USA, Horton sent out a three-page 'vision and values' statement to all employees, *Project 1990.* It aimed for a new, slimmer headquarters, no longer working in large, hierarchical departments but in small, flexible, cross-functional teams; and instead of a formal organisation, the emphasis was to be on informal networking with open and informal communication. 'Managers are there to support and empower their staff, not to monitor or control their activities.' Horton sought 'Openness, care, teamwork, empowerment and trust' and said that the current appraisal system was wholly deficient in coping with teamworking and should focus more on interpersonal skills and the ability to motivate staff.

Along with this, the matrix organisation was changed to give business streams (divisions) primacy over the old, geographical regions. The headquarters staff was cut to 400 (except that 800 of the operational headquarters jobs were retained but relocated) and about 70 of the committees were abolished. Throughout the organisation BP cut some 8000 jobs.

BP therefore had both hard and soft objectives. A £750 million per annum cost-cutting programme was to be accompanied by a programme aimed at making the company more open and caring. But in December 1991 a top management review said, 'As we remove complexity in our organisation and reap the benefits of Project 1990 job security becomes an increasing concern.' One aspect of the project, personal development plans, was redefined by staff as 'personal departure plans'. If people do not feel secure, their commitment is difficult to achieve.

The great problem was not in seeking to combine hard and soft objectives, but that Bob Horton allegedly did not walk like he talked. At the pre-launch conference, a senior executive was reported as saying, 'Do we really believe that Bob is going to stop second guessing his top colleagues. That's the only way all this change will work: if the top managers behave differently, managers will take their cues.' Another said, 'I don't believe he'll really change his spots. If he trusts you, you get delegated authority heaped upon you. But he will want to be involved in every significant decision . . . he instinctively wants to be seen as hands on. But he also wants to be seen as an innovative leader' (*Financial Times*, 30 March 1990).

Project 1990 declined as a programme not because its objectives were wrong, but because of the failure of the people at the top to walk like they talked. A personnel officer said, 'Open, empowered – great. But when we saw that the company was not living by that credo, scepticism grew and now has turned to cynicism' and a consultant added, 'Throughout the two years staff have consistently said there was talk but little action. This must reflect on the wisdom of such grand schemes' (Miller, 1992).

Despite all his efforts to cut costs, BP remained under considerable financial pressure – but Horton, an advocate of the primacy of the shareholders, insisted on maintaining the dividend. Four months later, he resigned.

The other directors made it clear that the resignation was not entirely voluntary and that it was about personality rather than policy. His replacement, David Simon, said, 'This is about the style of running the company at the top. It is not about changes in strategy'. Under Horton, BP has refused to cut its dividend in spite of falling profits and rising debt levels – a short-sighted policy, jeopardising 'the company's long-term future just to maintain the dividend' (*Financial Times*, 26 June 1992). In August 1992 BP cut its dividend for the first time since the First World War and said it was reducing staff by 11 500 worldwide. In December of that year it announced a further 9000 job losses. 'Horticulture' was over.

IBM

IBM was long held by many to be the epitome of success. In 1984 profits after tax exceeded $7 billion and in 1990, $6 billion. By the late 1970s, 70 per cent of the world's computer applications were centred on IBM mainframes and mini computers and by 1980 it had 38 per cent of industry revenues and 60 per cent of its profits. As IBM moved into the 1990s, Sir Edwin Nixon, Chairman of IBM UK, was able to say 'IBM United Kingdom Holdings Group experienced its 37th year of growth.' In 1986 IBM ranked first in the *Fortune* magazine ranking of the best-managed companies.

IBM was committed to change. Founder Tom J. Watson Jnr. said in 1962, 'I believe that if an organisation is to meet the challenges of a changing world it must be prepared to change everything about itself except its basic beliefs.' These basic beliefs are, 'Respect for the individual, the best possible service to our customers and the pursuit of excellence.' According to Len Peach, then IBM's UK Personnel Director, 'Respect for the individual' meant, 'Full employment, promotion from within, equal opportunity, pay for performance and single status.' Common factors included, 'Drawing out the best of individuals' energies, talents, skills, creativity and adaptability.'

In 1989 when visiting IBM's main UK operation in Havant, Hampshire, I was told that 90 per cent of staff were involved in improvement activities, that simultaneous engineering had been introduced to reduce product lead time; and that they were moving from 140 suppliers to 40 and from 2000 parts numbers to 120 over the next five years, with suppliers becoming responsible for designing the parts they supply. They had an extensive programme for recognising individual and team achievements and in 1989 achieved 779 improvement projects, with a £14 million saving. Many other initiatives were in place and everyone was genuinely proud of their success.

In that very year of 1989, however, IBM's *Fortune* ranking had slipped to 45th and in 1992 the company lost $4.97 billion. In July 1993 IBM said that some 50 000 people would have left the company by the end of the year and a further 35 000 would go by the end of 1994. The group took an $8.9 billion pre-tax charge in its second-quarter results to cover the payouts to people leaving the company and the closure of factories and offices around the world. What went wrong?

Basically, the computing world changed more rapidly than IBM. Its success in the 1960s, 1970s and 1980s was due to its System P60 series of large mainframes, based on solid-state memory chips, each costing millions of dollars with profits to match. It was the low-cost silicon microchip leading to low barriers to entry, few real product differences, vigorous price wars and slim profit margins, that ended IBM's dominance. Open systems, allowing customers to integrate equipment produced by a variety of manufacturers, had taken over from the proprietary system, and the new companies were able to develop technology more quickly and respond to customer needs more effectively.

When John Akers took the helm at IBM in 1985, he recognised that the products were lagging behind the competitors' and were grouped in families which could not connect to each other. He saw that the company was technology-driven rather than customer-driven and decreed that this must be reversed. Five years later Jack Knehler, IBM President, said:

> The new IBM is market driven . . . IBM aims to offer information technology solutions . . . IBM will bundle computer hardware, software and support service to provide turnkey systems designed to meet the specific needs of individual customers and industry sectors . . . IBM has not made major investments in applications software in recent years . . . it has had to turn to third party software developers in recent years . . . IBM recognises that its field sales force is ill equipped for solution selling. (*Financial Times*, 27 April 1990)

But the reforms were too little, too late. In 1984, IBM's revenues were $46 billion and it was building a company capable of handling a predicted $180 billion revenue by 1994, which simply did not materialise. In May 1991 IBM was forced to cut the price of its high performance workstations by 60 per cent to compete with Hewlett Packard, Sun and the myriad of other competitors appearing in the market place.

In April 1991 one of the most infamous meetings in IBM history took place. Akers attended what was thought to be a routine meeting of high-flying middle managers at IBMs New York headquarters, and told it to them like it is. He repeated what he had said to his top corporate management team two days earlier. He said that he believed that the messages from the top get 'filtered' on their way through the organisation and that, 'I'm sick and tired of visiting plant after plant to hear nothing but great things about quality and cycle times, [no doubt presented on the high quality slides which are a feature of any IBM presentation] – and then to visit customers who tell me of problems. If the people in labs and plants miss deadlines tell them their job is on the line . . . the tension level is not high enough in the business, everyone is too damn comfortable at a time when the business is in crisis.' Revenues in the first quarter of 1991 were down by 5 per cent over the previous quarter and profits were down by 50 per cent.

Akers directed his diatribe across all of IBM's geographic divisions. Of the USA he said, '20 000 people four years ago delivered $26 billion dollars . . . now [we] have 25 000 people who in 1990 delivered $27 billion . . . unsatisfactory . . . Where's my return for the extra 5000 people? Where's the beef? What the hell are you doing for me?' On people management he said, '[Its] not good enough. Our people have to be competitive and if they can't change fast enough, as fast as our industry . . . goodbye . . . half of one per cent MIA'd [sacked through management-initiated attrition] from laboratories and we have the nerve to think this is performance based? [We] need a forced march on the MIA problem.'

IBM was managerially inflexible. In the thirty years to 1986 it had the same top-down functional organisation in every country, with fourteen layers of management. In 1989, 55 per cent of non-manufacturing employees in the UK were in the support sections with only 45 per cent in the front line.

Despite IBM's efforts to change during the second half of the 1980s, it had clearly not done enough, it had not *led* the change process and for too long behaved as though the years of success would continue. I remember being frustrated towards the end of each year as the special offers came out. 'Buy now and we can knock 25 per cent off the price' or, 'Our prices are going up on 1st January – if you get your order in now I can let you have it at this year's price even though it won't be delivered until next year,' or, 'We're updating the model shortly, we can't tell you exactly what the improvements will be, but if you order now you'll be near the head of the queue.' All indicative of the monopolist who does not really have to try.

But change continued – substantial job cuts (voluntary, but usually on the basis of generous offers which were difficult to refuse), restructuring into thirteen highly autonomous business sectors each measured by their individual revenues and profits, the elimination of much of the corporate bureaucracy, reducing management layers (in the UK from seven to four) and spinning off activities such as property services and professional training into new companies. In 1992, IBM split off its personal computer division, eliminating the boundaries between development, manufacturing and distribution to speed product development time, and reducing the bureaucracy needed to achieve a price change – allowing decisions to be made at division level in days rather than at corporate level in weeks or months.

On 26 January 1993 John Akers announced he would step down and the company slashed its dividend from $1.21 to 54 cents, the first time it had cut the payout to shareholders.

The lesson of the IBM story is not that of failure to change but of failure to change in the good times before the need to change was thrust upon it. The time to implement major change programmes is when the organisation is able to be pro-active rather than reactive, when people do not feel threatened. As the gardener once said, 'If you weed before you need to weed you never *need* to weed.'

JAGUAR

Another lesson is to have regard to the whole organisation, not just part of it. Ford found this out when it acquired Jaguar in 1990. The previous chairman, Sir John Egan, had done a marvellous job on the sales and marketing side, projecting an image of a high-quality, high-prestige product, and had dramatically improved distribution (particularly in the USA); but he did not fundamentally change Jaguar's manufacturing, which Bill Hayden, previously Ford of Europe's Vice-President, Manufacturing, subsequently compared to a Russian car plant in Gorky. In early 1990 Jaguar was experiencing 2500 defects per 100 finished cars coming off the assembly line. Ford introduced a transition team, whose job it was to conduct an in-depth examination of Jaguar.

The transition team found that: 'People in Jaguar want to do well, building on the company's reputation for producing distinctively styled, luxury saloons and sports cars', but it identified many problem areas not conducive to producing good quality and high levels of customer satisfaction: 'Poor housekeeping, lack of measurement and data, incapable processes, sloppy discipline and poor material handling.' It found that throughout Jaguar there was a lack of adequate management. Specific criticisms included:

- compromised quality is being accepted by management throughout Jaguar – an inadequate and inconsistent approach in respect of the removal of the poor disciplines which compromise quality
- records and paperwork are in many cases dirty, unreadable, lost, poorly stored and filed
- there are many examples of processes which are not capable of providing consistent, good quality
- insufficient data is being collected, analysis is poor and dissemination is inadequate

In short, poor leaders and managers were neither able to motivate the workforce nor control the processes. The change process had barely impacted on manufacturing and this prejudiced the chances of success in those areas that Egan had genuinely improved.

IMPOSING CHANGE – FORD

Ford put in a major change programme in its traditional way – very much a top-down imposition of standards – and sometimes that is necessary. Sometimes an organisation has to act decisively to sort out its problems through draconian action before it can become constructive and creative. In 1975, in the Ford Dagenham Metal Stamping and Body Plant, there was no thought of being constructive, it was a battle which would be won or lost and which led in September 1976 to the riot which resulted in the dismissal of many left-wing activists and later to the dismissal of some of the Trotskyite ringleaders. After that it was possible tentatively to begin to be constructive. It is no way to run a manufacturing operation and fortunately times have changed, but as we shall see when discussing the general principles of change, very often major obstacles have to be removed, whether they be militant activists or reactionary top management!

The results of those battles took a long time to come to fruition. An internal document in 1990 recognised that by the late 1980s:

> Dagenham had become unreliable and almost out of control. Combined labour disruption, poor quality and adverse cost performance were the product of an operation that required dramatic change if it was to survive in the 1990s. The survival of this plant depends totally upon achieving improved quality, reliability of supply and productivity.

However, the report said there had since been a:

> marked improvement in employee relations in most areas of the organisation. We have been able to achieve changes to production shifts, work allocation and levels of employment without major conflict. These changes have been brought about by a combination of actions ranging from a more open management style, a willingness to involve all personnel in the changes, and of course the realisation that the future of this plant is uncertain unless significant changes are made.

In April 1994, when announcing its intention to raise Fiesta output from 940 to 1000 cars a day, Ford of Europe's Chairman, Jacques Nasser, said that Dagenham had reduced the time taken to build a car by 45 per cent between 1989 and 1993, with costs down by 23 per cent. 'Dagenham has made huge improvements in productivity and cost effectiveness and has become a competitive manufacturer of top-quality products.' The change process had taken nearly twenty years!

Ford's problems in promoting change were many. It had institutionalised conflict, but perhaps as important was that when the need for change was seen, following Bill Hayden's visit to Japan in the early 1980s, the subsequent AJ programme (After Japan) failed to establish a totally clear, shared strategic vision and Ford, as it always did, made a meal out of the process. The AJ programme became a series of targets to be negotiated with the trade unions, a part at a time, during the formal pay and conditions negotiations. The unions and employees were lectured as to the dire consequences if things did not change but there was no attempt to win hearts and minds. Even as late as 1992, Lindsay Halstead, then Chairman of Ford of Europe, said when speaking of the two planks of customer focus and lowest cost producer, 'I have no intention of closing plants in Britain. They will close themselves if they are not competitive.'

THE ROVER GROUP

Michael Edwardes' job with British Leyland in the 1970s was to implement the blood-letting process and though both demanding and exhausting such a process is not that difficult; the narrow focus concentrates the mind. But in the late 1980s and early 1990s The Rover Group (to give it its new name), having learned much and made steady progress with its then Japanese partner and shareholder, Honda, decided that a change of gear was needed. They developed a strategic vision aimed at repositioning the company for success in the late 1990s. This vision included moving the product upmarket, growing in Europe, reducing its break-even sales level, increasing employee involvement and commitment, improving its image with greatly enhanced customer satisfaction and moving to a business unit focus.

To achieve such objectives Rover recognised that it needed to act on many fronts at the same time, but also that each was dependent on the other. With regard to the people issues, it would be seeking considerable improvements in the flexibility, mobility and teamwork activities which had already begun in 1987, when the Board and executive committee were trained in total quality and had launched a Total Quality Improvement programme. Team and cell working had been introduced, but this was not enough. Rover sought to move away from what many still called their 'megaphone management' style, towards an open and honest style which treated people with respect and dignity.

Rover recognised that if it was to succeed, the trade union role was critical and union leaders were brought into the thinking process at a very early stage, before anything was formally published. They even brought together 400 shop stewards to discuss the issues, an arrangement previously considered impossible. They recognised that job security was of critical importance. All the preliminary work culminated in September 1991, when Rover management formally presented to the unions a document *Rover Tomorrow – The New Deal* with the headline 'We need a workforce distinguished only by individual's/teams' contribution to the company.' Not exactly the stuff of tabloid newspapers, but meaningful to those who needed to know.

Of central importance to the subsequent discussions was the fact that Rover and the unions did not seek to tie them into the bi-annual pay and conditions negotiations. Management laid out its long-term vision, recognising that it could not get there in one step, and invited middle management, the trade unions and employees to share that vision. The subsequent agreement in March 1992 was very little different from the original document, which was, in fact, based on the type of package initiated by Nissan (Rover had visited Nissan as part of its researches). It introduced single status, which it perceived as fundamental to eliminating 'them and us', payment by credit transfer and a commitment to no lay-offs: 'In the event of a problem which disrupts production, all employees will be engaged in worthwhile activities and be required to co-operate with efforts to maintain productive output.' Continuous improvement was built in as 'a requirement for everyone'. 'There will be maximum devolution of authority and accountability to the employees actually doing the job.' Productivity bonuses were to be progressively phased out and, most critically: 'Employees who want to work for Rover will be able to stay with Rover. Necessary reductions in manpower will be achieved in future with the co-operation of all employees, through re-training and re-deployment, natural wastage, voluntary severance and early retirement programmes.'

Things did not go smoothly. The deal, advocated by the trade unions, was accepted by 11 961 votes to 11 793, a majority of 168 out of 23 754. When I visited Rover at the end of 1993, it was clear that at shop floor level much remained to be done; some shop stewards, and no doubt some managers, still speak of the 'good old days' of Red Robbo (Derek Robinson) the convener of shop stewards eventually dismissed by Michael Edwardes. The level of knowledge of the control processes remains limited and its application at shop floor level irregular. But it is a five-year programme, the product is excellent, quality dramatically improved and motivation greatly enhanced. Rover is now one of the success stories of the European automotive industry.

Rover, and many others, have shown that you do not need a greenfield site to make major changes. Indeed, those who point to the advantages of a greenfield site or a Japanese parent as the reasons for success are often simply seeking excuses for their own inactivity. They point to the favourable circumstances of one company and because they do not enjoy such advantages argue that they are a condition of success. They are not.

The key to success is not a greenfield site but a greenfield mind!

HOW TO BECOME AN ASCENDANT ORGANISATION

Readers of this book will now have a fairly good idea of what an ascendant organisation is, and, perhaps, will know how not to implement a change programme if they wish to achieve and sustain a commitment to the concept. They will also realise that if a revolutionary change is needed there will not have been enough evolutionary change in the past. They may know that they must *not*:

- begin before achieving some understanding of what they wish to achieve
- believe they have a monopoly of wisdom and know the full results and impact in advance – they will not even know all the questions, let alone the answers
- impose a 'big bang' new concept from the top
- concentrate on short-term results, either financial or non-financial
- bring in an outsider to take responsibility, or remove responsibility from accountable managers in favour of 'facilitators'
- talk in vague terms of 'culture change'
- use off-the-peg panaceas
- produce a written statement and think they have done all that is necessary
- simply concentrate on the vision and strategy and then lose interest in the 'doing', believing that saying it means achieving it
- talk one way and act differently, or give out inconsistent messages
- ignore the key implementors until late in the process
- believe that by changing the structures and processes they will achieve the objectives
- negotiate a little at a time without a perception of the long-term plan

As I have consistently stated, leadership can exist at all levels in any organisation and, indeed, one of the tasks in moving to an ascendant organisation is to provide the environment in which such leadership can flourish. In moving to the 'how', I speak for simplicity of the whole organisation. 'The top team' means the chief executive, immediate reports and other key individuals respected for their capabilities and influence. But the process can start at any level, division, location or geographical area, although in a centralised organisation, without corporate commitment, freedom may be limited and the ability to spread the word restricted. The process is much the same wherever you start. However, to omit steps in the process, without good reason, could result in a weakening of commitment and make it more difficult to sustain any advances made.

At all times it is important to remember that the old has to continue alongside the new – it must continue to operate effectively while change is going on around it. Concentration on the harvest due in five-years time may result in this year's crop being neglected and if this happens too frequently there may not be a five-year harvest!

Understand the concept

As a result of a catalyst, perhaps someone in the top team has read this book, the top group needs to begin to achieve a true understanding of what the concept means. But reading one book is, by itself, insufficient. Read many of the other references. Visit companies you feel have something to contribute. Go away to a country house or similar retreat to thrash through the issues and ensure the top team has a common understanding. Begin by trying to write down what you wish to achieve. Perhaps even use an outside agent to help you through this process but, if so, remember the agent is the servant, not the master. This process may even allow the top team to gain an understanding of the type of organisation they currently are, even 'why we are in business'. There will, in fact, be different levels of understanding of the present, let alone different views of the future. Seek to gain 'knowledge' as well as 'know how'. Assess what your competitors are up to and what might be the impact on your products or service or on your suppliers. Begin to define specific business needs that should be addressed, but keep it broad at this stage. Remember Ivor Vaughan's 'stand'. If you have to prove every detail in advance (which in any case you will not be able to do) then it is not a 'stand', not something in which you passionately believe.

Hopefully, this process of gaining understanding will lead to the conclusion that it is not possible to be precise about the future, that it may be unclear and subject to many complex, conflicting and changing pressures, both internal and external; that future progress will depend on gaining ownership throughout the organisation, so that people are motivated by diagnosing problems for themselves and initiating action rather than by vague talk of 'culture change'. Behaviour is shaped by the way people are managed. As we saw when discussing the integration of quality, it is practice which convinces, and the great thing about moving towards an ascendant organisation is that the process through which people go is a living example of the concept in action.

Some argue that trade unions and/or middle management should be brought in at this very first stage and in some circumstances, particularly at plant level, this may have validity. However, there is also strength in the argument that top management needs a period of internal contemplation and most organisations will choose this option before deciding to extend the process.

There is a paradox, however. If the top team is convinced, the great danger is to fall into the trap of wanting to direct the change, whereas what is really needed is for the people in the organisation to find out for themselves what the top team want them to find out. 'But', the CEO may argue, 'isn't that like re-inventing the wheel?' Yes it is, but there is no harm, in fact there are positive benefits in people finding out for themselves. And their conclusions may be different, for views change depending on your position – but I guarantee that, provided the process is followed, there will be a high level of agreement as to the broad direction.

Leadership and example will still be required – do not assume that things happen by themselves. Leadership must be continuous and consistent. The great danger is for the top team to produce the concept or written document and think it has done its bit. Until the ascendant organisation is a reality, the top team must be there to support, reinforce, cajole, assess and to be a sounding board – but not overtly to direct. It is the day-to-day running of the organisation that really counts, not the sudden surge of enthusiasm for a new concept, and it is by its day-to-day leadership that the top team will be judged.

Before moving to the second step, the top team *may* decide that it wants to do something affecting *it* that sends out a signal. Ralph Stayer, of Johnsonville Sausages fame, said, 'Just start, don't wait until you have all the answers. Start by changing something visible. I stopped tasting sausages!' (Stayer, 1990). But beware of empty gestures – if the rest of the organisation is not ready or not in the know, then such action may be premature and treated with cynicism. Above all, do not prematurely change things which affect other people, but remember that when the rest of the organisation is changing, nothing is better than specific examples from the top.

Determine the strategy

The essential task for top management is to determine the broad vision, strategy, perception, whatever term is appropriate. They must determine where they are today and where they wish to be in, say, five years from now and write it down, but not in tablets of stone. Only if they have this perception is there any point in starting on the journey. The road of change is rocky. Those rocks can include militant trade unions, inflexible senior management, demoralised supervisors or a poorly educated workforce. Therefore, perception alone is not enough – the determination to see it through is also needed. Top management must create the climate for change, determine the broad destination and the approximate route. If they do not, they may as well not start on the journey, for they will then be blown around by whichever wind happens to be strongest and when the rocks appear, they will either founder or stop or turn back. They must determine what they will do about the rocks – go round them, smooth them or even blast them away. Do you bring them into the process, keep them out until later or tackle them head on? Only the people in the company can make the decision. But they must also realise that the destination will change as they go along. Nothing stands still and if, in five years time, they arrive where five years before they said they wanted to be, they will be out of date. Part of the process is to become a learning organisation, one in which the people create the climate that facilitates the continuous development of all members, who as a result are able to transform the organisation.

Some 2500 years ago, Sun Tzu, a Chinese military strategist wrote, 'All men can see the tactics whereby I conquer but what no one can see is the strategy out of which great victory is evolved', a statement as relevant to the top management team today as it was to the Chinese military of 500 BC. The top team is concerned with the strategy – the dynamics of the process, not the detail – but it has to understand how the elements of that process fit together and react upon each other. This is true whether they are seeking revolutionary or evolutionary change.

Involve the people

The next steps depend partly on the size of the organisation. Dowty Seals, a small manufacturer with a 320-strong workforce, diagnosed at top level that it was getting smaller, losing out on business and that there was a lack of direction and enthusiasm. Change was needed and the top management group decided that the best way for them was to talk directly with the whole workforce, reasoning that change would not be accepted if the staff felt their future was secure. By taking staff into their confidence, a programme was initiated which resulted in a change from a centralised structure to focused business units, manufacturing cells and a reduction from eight to four levels between the MD and the shop floor.

As a result, order to delivery time was reduced from sixteen weeks to two, work in progress was cut by 40 per cent, profits rose and motivation was much higher. This was not a move to an ascendant organisation and the implied threat challenges my argument emphasising the need for security, but unfortunately life is not simple. All any organisation can do is what is right for it in its circumstances and there will always be examples of organisations which break all the rules and succeed.

The essential point, however, is that this step begins (and perhaps in small organisations ends), with the involvement process. In large organisations it simply is not possible for everyone to be involved in the strategic debate but equally you will not achieve long-term ownership if communication is restricted to a one-way information session – the very antithesis of the concept of communication in the ascendant organisation. You will fall at the first hurdle. People in the middle of an organisation and those at the periphery, both core and non-core, want to be able to contribute to forming the new way. How can you expect them to develop infectious enthusiasm if they have not been part of the process? 'Sharing the vision' can only be achieved if it is an interactive process.

It is critical to remember that this may well be the first time that many in the organisation have had anyone seek to 'share' anything with them. The top team often fails to realise that people at lower levels do not have their perspective. Because senior executives spend a considerable proportion of their time meeting people from other organisations and are frequently away from the four walls of their own business, they fail to realise that many people are restricted in both their contacts and their movements. Ask senior executives if they gain from their external perspectives and the answer will clearly be, 'Yes'. Ask them if they would lose by being restricted to their four walls and the answer will also emphatically be, 'Yes'. They cannot therefore expect everyone else immediately to share a perspective which they will have developed over many years of both internal and external experience. This is why people respond to actions not words, by seeing things for themselves rather than by being told about them.

At this point of 'going public' the top management team will have to decide whether or not to give the process a title. Some decide on a grand sounding name, for example, BP's 'Project 1990' or British Telecom's 'Project Sovereign'. Such titles have the advantage of focusing attention but, equally, can be dangerous if seeking to move to becoming an ascendant organisation. Commitment cannot be commanded. Better to leave it until you have some successes, if you want a title at all. Then maybe a positive name will emerge – no 'Horticultures' please!

The ways in which people can share in the process are many and varied. There is no single right way. When discussing 'culture', I emphasised the sharing of a written document. When discussing quality, I emphasised the approach of bringing together the diagonal teams. Such an approach can also work when tackling broader issues. Some organisations may choose to cascade the discussions vertically through the organisation, others may wish to involve middle managers or supervisors as discrete groups, some may permutate any combination. Yet others, with strong trade unions, will seek to involve them at this stage. One example was in the General Motors Cadillac Engine Plant in Livonia, USA. When starting their change programme, Irving Bluestone, then the UAW director of the Union's GM department, said:

> Truly successful endeavours in employee participation in decision-making are not developed by management and simply handed down to the union and workforce. A successful improvement programme derives from mutually agreed upon understanding in which the union and management are co-equal in planning, designing and implementing the employee involvement process. (Nora, Rogers and Stramy, 1986)

Although not all managers would entirely agree with Bluestone, his personal track record was such that he was listened to carefully by GM management.

Whatever the actual structure of the groups handling this stage, similar golden rules apply as when seeking to integrate quality into the organisation and for the same reasons:

- members must have high personal credibility and be trusted
- members must be innovators, achievers and effective communicators
- members must represent all parts of the organisation and retain full normal responsibilities

'Ownership' is paramount and, particularly in large organisations, the group or groups must be able to contribute actively to the thought processes and refine the broad strategy and draft documentation of the top management team. They will know far more about the nuts and bolts of the organisation and top management will learn much from this. This is the beginning of the process of sharing the vision and each organisation will have to decide how many people are involved. Too many and it will become a glorified talking shop; too few and the result will be nothing more than handing down the tablets of stone. Some organisations may wish to involve some doubters in the groups. There are advantages – the doubters may become early converts and/or their questioning will challenge the values of the majority; and disadvantages – they may weaken the group. On balance, a small number should be involved. If the concept is so weak or the majority so uncommitted as to be unable to withstand criticism, it is better to find out sooner rather than later.

If, in a multi-location organisation, it is decided to establish a series of groups based on divisions or location, the results will differ from location to location. This does not matter. Provided the analysis is properly done, it is inevitable that the history, market circumstances and personalities will lead to different answers. Indeed, if everyone came up with the same answers, that would be the time to worry; the top team would have been too prescriptive. Some may even decide it is not for them. Again, this does not really matter. After a few months, they will either be shown to have been right, or they will decide to learn from others and follow behind, or their conclusion will be proved wrong, in which case they will, one hopes, change.

This process seeks to achieve a shared understanding of the strategy, the involvement of key implementors, the placement of the initiative in the hands of people in places where the practical issues manifest themselves, and a diagnosis of the detailed change requirements. It can help prepare the organisation for the change process by questioning and weakening commitment to the existing way of doing things. It can also help to build the essential critical mass within the organisation. How large this needs to be is a question for debate. Myron Tribus, who is now the prime proponent of Deming, has suggested it is the square root of the number of people employed. Although it is impossible to be precise, there can be little doubt that a comparatively small group of people who know what they want can greatly influence a large group who, initially, do not mind what they get.

The groups should *not* at this stage seek to make changes to the overt structures, systems, rewards or procedures of the organisation. They are the tip of the iceberg, and only in very exceptional cases will such changes have any impact at this stage except to confuse. Good people can work together, if allowed, irrespective of the organisation and to seek to force them into the straitjacket of premature organisation change will result in mistakes that later will need confusing revision. Better to let any changes result from a subsequent need, rather than to predict.

Implement the change

Involving and implementing are not discrete steps. They overlap and combine; often they will be simultaneous, and are separated here only for descriptive convenience. Remembering that the ascendant organisation achieves the right balance between commitment and control, implementation eventually involves everyone in the organisation in doing practical things differently.

It can take many forms. George Stalk and Thomas Hout, in *Competing against Time*, speak of pilots and breakthrough teams. 'Pilots are a good way to energize those parts of the organisation where good people are ready to go and where local trial and error experimentation is the right way to get solutions'. They advocate sheltering the pilots both physically and politically, particularly keeping, 'senior people with turf issues out of the pilot itself'. Pilot activities work best when an organisation wants a demonstration of what can be achieved and knows that it will achieve early success. Breakthrough teams are multi-functional managerial teams, brought together for a period to achieve radical goals, 'like collapsing time in half', substantially challenging the organisation's assumptions, for example, 'How to establish an around the clock global short-term money management function in the company.' Say Stalk and Hout:

> In this way, the change process is neither top-down nor bottom-up, but really driven from the middle and co-ordinated at the top by those who settled on the vision. The able middle managers are in the best position to do the cutting-edge learning that will reshape the company's practices. (Stalk and Hout, 1990, pp. 217–22)

Involving the key middle managers in 'doing' is clearly correct, but the great danger is isolation: Stalk and Hout's 'breakthrough teams' can easily become 'special' and work for short periods *because* they are different. If the lessons are applied widely, that is fine, but the ascendant organisation uses the talents of *all* the people, gives to all the freedom to do their own thing, to re-invent the wheel, to make their own mistakes and learn from them. By definition, the ascendant organisation involves everyone as the normal day-to-day way of doing business. It achieves its shared values by using the talents of everyone, not by imposition or by peering over the fence at what someone else is doing.

Having said that, it is vital that goals are set and performance against those goals measured, but within the overall framework these goals must be determined by the groups themselves, perhaps on a cascade basis. At an operating division an introduction goal may be nothing more than, 'Within one year involve 50 per cent of the people in small group activities', thus concentrating solely on the process, leaving that 50 per cent to define their own specific improvement objectives. Alternatively, the divisional objectives may be performance-related within a framework of achieving them by involving the people. Some may seek to combine the two, making the decision either as the result of a top-down directive or following a consultative process. In summary, unless you achieve genuine employee commitment to change in an organic way, then no amount of management theorising or pontification will achieve anything that will last beyond the flavour of the month panacea. We must remember that directors and managers actually deliver very little. It is the people in the front line, the sales people, operators, teachers and their immediate supervisors, who deliver. Some leaders may inspire, but unless they achieve the hearts and minds conversion of the front liners and have the capability to make that inspiration last, the benefits will be but short-lived. Eventually even the forces of inertia will arouse themselves to resist change!

Then, get on and do something, though not everything at once. In 99.9 per cent of cases that will be both impossible and undesirable, but keep an eye on the vision, seeking to ensure that all elements are integrated. I am a great believer in involving the people in setting goals and targets to act as motivators, and in going for early success. There is nothing like a sense of achievement to enhance self-esteem and spur further efforts. What is achieved, within reason, does not really matter as long as it is something that is meaningful to that group. As with the specific issue of integrating quality; training and development needs will quickly become identified as will necessary support from other functions. The organisation must be aware that this will happen and be ready to respond speedily to the demand, otherwise frustration will quickly set in. Supervisors will need to be trained in facilitating and coaching and in problem-solving techniques, but such training must be against a background of an understood need. There is nothing worse than a comprehensive training programme set up in advance with nothing to do thereafter except wait for the rest of the organisation to get ready.

It is here that the top team *must* be seen to be making its very visible contribution – perhaps abolish the executive dining room or remove reserved car parking spaces – or stop tasting sausages! In Nissan we take great pride that directors park outside the gates along with everyone else, on a 'first come first served' basis and when it is raining *everyone* gets wet;

everyone uses the same canteen and important visitors queue for their food along with shop floor operators – they delight in it and anyone who suggests you cannot talk business in such an environment has never tried it. (It also has the advantage of keeping standards high – a director walking into the kitchen to complain on the spot is far more effective than any catering committee!).

Create indicators of progress: not, 'How far we have progressed to becoming an ascendant organisation' – that will be impossible to measure – but visible recording of achievement against specific targets. Gradually it may be possible to make these measures common across the groups, sections or divisions or even the organisation, but be patient: this could take years. Or the organisation at the top may decide that a small number of highly important corporate measures of performance should be made known quickly so that people will understand how the total effort is progressing. Top management must never be successfully accused of failing to tell it to people like it is.

It is important to take away feelings of insecurity, because if people feel threatened by change, they resist it. In Chapter 3 we saw that the behavioural scientists put security as a base need which has to be satisfied before an individual can move on to a 'higher' need. But we have also seen that flexible organisations are moving to flexible employment practices and the traditionally defined type of security is no longer the automatic expectation. However, within the revised definitions and practices, we also know that it *is* possible to achieve a different type of security and that includes equipping people to be able to cope with change.

There is however a 'first time', the beginning of a new set of experiences, and if an organisation has yet to make the step change transition brought about by the restructuring needs described in Chapter 2, it would be irresponsible to guarantee existing employment levels. It may be necessary to go through the restructuring process *before* seeking to move to an ascendant organisation type of culture, for to attempt both at the same time will, to say the least, send out confusing signals. Confrontation and construction normally lie uneasily together.

However, when the first traumatic step is under way, it is important not simply to take away the feeling of insecurity but to give a feeling of security, remembering of course that security is a hygiene factor and in the end we are all subject to the vagaries of the market place. But in seeking a culture change to becoming an ascendant organisation, I advocate that no one, except top managers, should compulsorily lose their employment because they cannot make the transition from the old to the new way. It is not their fault. They have been hired and trained to behave in a different way and why should they be punished if management wishes to change the style? Some may have to change their job within the organisation and if others wish to go voluntarily, this option can be made financially attractive if the organisation can bear the cost – but seek to avoid dismissals. That takes away the threat, the insecurity, and makes acceptance easier.

It is easy to argue that if people cannot adapt, 'We'll fire them anyway'. That is not the way of the ascendant organisation, which seeks to treat people properly and with respect, including those who leave. Those who remain observe how those who leave are treated and to believe that their attitude is not affected is to suffer a delusion.

Sustain the gain

Launching any programme is easy, sustaining it is extremely difficult. Once achieved, even in the ascendant organisation which should be self-sustaining, it is not easy to maintain. The easy thing is to revert to type, especially when the going gets tough. It is for this reason that top management must stick in there all the time, not just at the vision and strategy stages. It must be aware of all the stakeholders – the employees, investors, customers, suppliers and the community. John Neill, the innovative chief executive of Unipart, who turned a sickly British Leyland subsidiary into an independent world-class automotive component supplier, referred to all having the same destiny:

> If you run a traditional Western model which is a power-based, short-term relationship between a company and its stakeholders, those businesses will fail. If you put the interests of one group continuously above the interests of another you will hit the wall when you come up against companies that build high quality and enduring relationships with all their stakeholders. (*Works Management*, September 1992)

This does not mean that everything remains unchanged. As I stated earlier, if in five years time we are where we aimed for five years before, we will be out of date, ossified in a time warp.

However, in order to sustain the never-ending change process of an ascendant organisation, a number of guidelines for top management are evident. Top management must:

- maintain its long-term commitment to all aspects of the change process and ensure by its behaviour and requirements that everyone recognises this
- ensure that the environment is maintained, support provided, lessons spread and people developed, so that at all levels throughout the organisation good people are held accountable and enabled to make good decisions and do good things
- regularly review progress against the strategy, adjusting as appropriate, recognising when desirable, cajoling when needed and acting when required
- as the needs become evident, facilitate changes to the structure, reward systems, working arrangements, development programmes, processes and procedures, and so on, to ensure the organisation responds positively and consistently and encourages further initiatives
- ensure that career progression is based on success in the new way
- continuously communicate the principles and objectives to all stakeholders: the shareholders, suppliers, customers, unions and staff and ensure that their interests are properly balanced
- benchmark the competition, not forgetting the need continuously to improve the product and service and to remain profitable or achieve financial objectives
- never cease to learn, not be impatient, take the tough decisions at the right time to remove the rocks, and pray that sufficient progress is made in the good times so that it will see you through the next recession!

Living through a total change process is perhaps one of the most demanding, most exciting and most rewarding of all business activities. Machiavelli called it difficult, doubtful of success, and dangerous. The three d's of Japanese manufacturing were dirty, dangerous and difficult, and that is a reason *for* change, not an excuse for inaction!

16 Two Sides of the Coin Lead to an Edge

Globally, the greatest challenge to the most successful Japanese firms is, the more successful they are the less Japanese they have to become.

(Dan Jones, 1992)

Both the sword and the chrysanthemum are part of the picture. The Japanese are to the highest degree both aggressive and unaggressive, both militaristic and aesthetic, both insolent and polite, rigid and adaptable, submissive and resentful of being pushed around, loyal and treacherous, brave and timid, conservative and hospitable to new ways.

(Ruth Benedict, *The Chrysanthemum and the Sword*, 1982)

In Chapter 3, I referred to William Ouchi's *Theory Z* in which, by concentrating mainly on the people management areas of Japanese management practices, he sought to build a model which demonstrated an American version of Japanese practices and showed that Western companies could learn much from Japan. In this he was correct, but his analysis of the reasons for Japanese success was extremely simplistic, omitting many of the 'hard' reasons for that success. Neither did he consider the lessons Japan could learn from the West.

The purpose of this chapter is to pull together and identify not only those areas in which the Japanese have made a special contribution, but also those in which the West, at its best, can also specially contribute. But in addition to these special areas there are the overlaps – areas in which both the oriental and the occidental can contribute, where, in the title of this chapter, the two sides of the coin lead to an edge.

THE SPECIAL CONTRIBUTION OF JAPAN

There are numerous influences on the culture and behaviour of people. The Japanese ethical system built on the teaching of Confucius clearly has an influence, but so too does the fact that historically the Japanese formed a nation of mutually dependent farmers with the person who disrupted the village harmony being ostracised. The long period of isolation, during which there developed the practice of interdependent allegiance between servant and master, no doubt played a part. The code of the warrior – *bushido* – emphasised winning, but also honour in personal relationships. The first true constitution of Japan, promulgated by Prince Shotuko Taishi in AD 604, stipulated that the principle of all societies and communities was *wa*, harmony. The desire to emulate Western standards without losing Japanese values was the guiding spirit of the Meiji Restoration in 1867, which began the emergence of the nation from isolation. No doubt the fact that Japan is one of the most homogeneous industrialised nations in the world helps achieve an intuitive understanding within a unified culture; so that *Ishin Denshin* (feelings conveyed without words) is a powerful tool of communication. The practical manifestation of the Japanese aphorism 'Silence is expression' is extremely difficult for voluble Westerners to handle.

The Japanese tend to value group harmony more than individuality and it is not surprising, therefore, that group-oriented ideas have been adopted in corporate management practices. The Nissan publication, *Things you want to know about Nissan and Japan*, puts it neatly:

> There is a belief in Japan that a person who works diligently will gain social recognition and work is regarded as something of a virtue . . . an integral part of a person's life and consequently that it should be enjoyable; this leads to independent efforts on the part of workers to improve their jobs and to upgrade the quality of their work. In addition since changing jobs is relatively rare in Japan the work that an individual does within the framework of a single company takes on a great deal of importance in his personal life. Therefore, there is a strong feeling that if one contributes to his company by working hard, his efforts will be rewarded and his private life will be enriched accordingly.

Although, as we have seen, elements of these sacred treasures are under strain, the deeply-embedded culture has a lot of life left in it.

These deep-rooted social and cultural values clearly impact on Japanese behaviour in the workplace and in particular on those areas in which they have been able to make a special contribution. Most of these have been discussed throughout this book and include:

- the primacy of the group
- the commitment to security of employment for the core workers in the blue chip company
- the prime importance of the quality of the product or service
- always achieve the required schedule
- absolute control of the process
- continuous improvement
- the elimination of waste in all its forms
- rapid product development from concept to market
- simultaneous engineering
- long-term view of investment

The West had little to contribute in these areas and much to learn. To its credit, it *has* learned.

THE SPECIAL CONTRIBUTION OF THE WEST

The Anglo–American tradition traces its origins back to the liberal traditions of Adam Smith, who regarded government as a necessary evil which should be restricted to the minimum functions necessary to maintain law and order. In continental Europe, Max Weber argued that the prime influence was the growth of the Protestant ethic and its influence on the pursuit of individual wealth (Weber, 1930). The American frontier thesis based on the individual pushing forward, responsible for only himself and his immediate family, did nothing to encourage a group mentality except for short-term defensive alliances. The cultural development in the West has been centred upon the individual and from this the special Western contributions flow:

- the primacy of the individual
- structured development
- the importance of clearly-defined leadership
- financial control
- market research and product planning
- understanding of diverse customer needs
- software development and use
- innovation

The Japanese had little to contribute in these areas and much to learn. However, because of the complacency which built up during the successful years, it is only in the mid-1990s, when faced with a crisis, that they are beginning to realise what they lack.

THE TWO SIDES OF THE COIN

These listings are of course subjective and none more so than in those areas in which there are overlaps. By this I mean that both Japan and the West have something to contribute. I illustrate this in Figure 16.1.

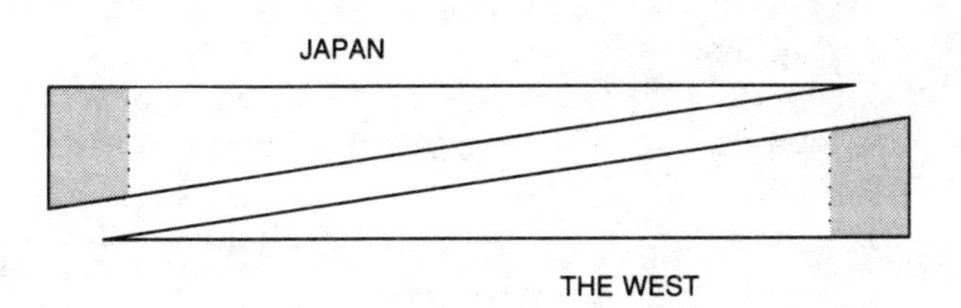

Figure 16.1 The Occidental/Oriental Synergy

This is a spectrum. At the outer limits there are the special contributions but the overlaps are significant. For example, both Japan and the West continuously improve and technologically innovate so they cannot be said to be unique, except that at the extremes the difference is pronounced enough to be special.

While subjective, the listing shown overleaf is based on much experience and observation. Perhaps there will be some surprises!

Some of these appear contradictory – and they are. Unfortunately, life is never simple. It is not my intention to give a detailed explanation of each area, much has been covered elsewhere in this text, but some explanations are warranted.

The most confusing group is that related to *status*. The Japanese, despite a superficial appearance of egalitarianism, are one of the most status conscious nations in the world, with the most overt symbol being the company for which they work and the position attained. Being a salaryman in a blue chip company or in one of the more prestigious Ministries is the apex. If they have left school at age 18 or have attended one of the lower-level universities, they will only very rarely attain such a position. Once employed, it is very clear where they are in the pecking order; the position of the desk, the depth of the bow, the honorifics of address; whether or not they are allowed in the executive dining room or

The Two Sides of the Coin

	Japan	*The West*
The market place	Market share	Profitability
	Emphasis on producer	Emphasis on customer satisfaction
	Product variety	Product concentration
	Supplier integration	Partnership sourcing
Internal processes	Minimum stock	Buffer stock
	Eliminate waste	Live with waste
	Just in time	Just in case
	Standard operation	Flexible practices
	Continuous improvement of product and processes	Technical innovation
	Evolution	Revolution
Internal processes	Implicit control	Explicit control
	Measure systematically	Judge intuitively
	Measure effort and progress	Assess results and achievement
	Long-term planning	Short-term objectives
	Problem avoidance	Problem solving
	Work hard and smart	Operator care
	Low salary differentials	High salary differentials
Motivation	Begins with group	Begins with individual
	Duty to colleagues and company	Duty to self and family
	Teamworking	Individual initiative
	Co-operation and harmony	Competition
	Consensus	Individual responsibility
	Meetings are to share information	Meetings are to make decisions
	Commitment to company	Commitment to profession
	Strong status differentiation	Single status
	Workplace egalitarianism	Workplace authority
	Respect for authority	Challenge authority
	Concern for whole person	Concern for individual at work
	Accepts reduced benefits in the tough times	Seeks to preserve benefits

Career development	Career track (for example, salaryman or operator) fixed by education level	Career flexibility – depends on personal performance
	Non-specialist careers – broad experience	Specialist careers before general management
	Single company careers	Multi-company careers
	Slow burn development, late responsibility	Fast development, early responsibility
	On-the-job training	Off-the-job training
Leadership/ Management	Decision-evolving	Decision-making
	Consensus	Inspirational
	Listens	Speaks
	A continuum	Discrete
	Needs to know details	Interested in the 'big picture'
	Must be accepted by and harmonise with the group	Leads from the front

have a reserved car parking space or a chauffeur, are all clearly defined. Senior executives even have separate entrances to their office building, which no other people are allowed to use.

There is tremendous respect for authority based on age and seniority and though *consensus* may operate, it usually forms around the wishes of the senior person, whose views are rarely challenged. However, in the workplace, while mindful of the difference in rank, the senior person, because he will have a broad experience based on the slow burn development and can practice his knowledge as he progresses, will have a far deeper understanding of what is actually happening than his Western counterpart does. I have already told how Toshiaki Tsuchiya could relate to shop floor people and problems far more readily than any Western executive I have ever met.

One area that has not been previously covered is that of dedication to the company. While to the Japanese both the job and the family are important, the salaryman in particular is still obliged to spend a disproportionate amount of time at his work. Ask a Japanese what his job is and he will tell you that he is with Nissan, Toyota, Mitsubishi, and so on. He will not say that he is an engineer or salesman. Japanese companies compete vigorously with each other and managers constantly remind staff of their rivals' achievements. One of the reasons for enterprise trade unions is the perceived unity between people at all levels in a single company. That unity of purpose within an enterprise is stronger than the unity between the working classes from different enterprises.

That dedication is also apparent in the concept of *giri*, the indebtedness a worker has to colleagues. This means not outshining their contribution nor falling significantly behind. I have seen, literally, black marks put against the name of an individual on the information board and signs put over his workplace indicating that the person has let the team down in some way. The individual has to work well for a considerable period before that sign is removed, and in the meantime everyone knows that he has erred in some way. On the other hand, devotion to one's colleagues means that you never forget your peers; if you are promoted you will look after them and always assess them well if they are perceived as having contributed to your success.

One of the most frequently mentioned Western traits is *the exercise of initiative by individuals*. At the highest level this may be manifested in the relative number of Nobel prizes won by each nation, but at operational level the Japanese are always amazed at the attitude of British and American workers who spend time working with them on the shop floor. Tom Peters is fond of telling companies to hire a few weirdos, a few real headcases, curious people who will spark the organisation. Most people step back from this advice and generally they are right to do so, because we want everyone to contribute, not just a weird few. But to the Japanese, the curious, challenging Westerners who do not accept the rules of the game *are* weirdos.

The Japanese are great at taking something and making it just that little better – that is the great strength of *kaizen* – but they are not so good at fundamentally challenging the accepted way. When British and American workers first went on to the Japanese shop floor, the Japanese expectations were, to put it mildly, low. It did not take them long to realise that the Westerners questioned everything and were prepared to break out of the framework as well as grow within it. As with all nations the Japanese have concerns about their education system. One of their big complaints is that Japanese children are never taught to analyse or question; they are taught to listen and absorb. This is reflected in the workplace, so that although their level of knowledge is invariably higher than the Westerners', their ability to take individual initiatives is considerably less.

This manifests itself in the improvement activities. I visited an electrical harness manufacturer and was regaled with the usual listing of the number of suggestions submitted by the staff. I asked if they could show me something that had changed as a result of a suggestion and after a considerable period I saw the unwinding room in which the spools of many different types of wire were de-coiled. The improvement was a redesign of the spools and facilities so that there was no interruption between the end of one spool and the beginning of the next. Although this was of considerable benefit, it was an engineering task; it could easily have been designed that way in the beginning and the change had, in fact, come about as the result of an engineering project rather than from an operator's suggestion. To the Japanese, small-group activity is about learning from each other and teambuilding rather than actually making improvements. Suggestion schemes are about involvement rather than change, and involvement and commitment are ends in themselves. To the Westerner *achievement* through individual initiative is what counts and this manifests itself through the desire to have something to show for one's efforts.

Initially, I spent a lot of time being confused at meetings with Japanese colleagues. There was no agenda, discussion ranged freely, few decisions seemed to be made and no formal minutes were kept (although the Japanese would write copiously in their notebooks). The British came away not really knowing what had happened and were amazed to see further 'Japanese only' meetings going on. We eventually realised that the purpose of a Japanese meeting was to share information, to allow all opinions and perspectives to be heard, so that the eventual decision, which might not have been discussed by the meeting, was fully understood by all. Their view is that, regardless of how obvious the solution might be to the proposer, others need to understand, and by discussion they may be able to assist in providing a better solution. The Japanese also came to value the Western precision, organisation and ability to make clear decisions with defined responsibility.

One factor assisting Japan's rapid product development is its relative lack of market research, particularly in consumer electronics. To them the ultimate market research is to develop a product quickly, develop many minor variants and get them into the stores. Pure market research takes time and slows the process. Applied market research is the customer buying the product. If it sells well, more will be produced; if it does not it will be withdrawn. Akio Morita, Chairman of Sony, said:

> Our plan is to lead the public with new products rather than ask them what kind of products they want. The public does not know what is possible but we do. So instead of doing a lot of market research, we refine our thinking on a product and its use and try to create a market for it . . . I do not believe that any amount of market research could have told us that the Sony Walkman would be successful. (Morita, 1988, pp. 79–82)

This approach clearly worked in the growth era but in the recession companies are having to rethink. MITI has said that consumers are no longer fooled by gimmicks and has warned manufacturers that frequent model and product changes are an unnecessary waste of resources and labour time. The pace is now being set by Europe and the USA and lack of market research and product planning capability is, in many instances, leaving the Japanese trailing.

The Japanese concept of slow burn career development is something which is frequently mentioned as a plus point, but in comparisons between Japan and the West contradictory trends are emerging. In Japan, the slow burn development is being challenged. The traditional, seniority-based progression system resulted in the majority of salarymen progressing up the hierarchy to the general manager level almost irrespective of their ability. Not only did this allow people with comparatively low capability to reach senior positions, it also resulted in swollen ranks of managers, many with few real managerial responsibilities, and high salary costs. Whereas this was acceptable in the good times, they have realised that they can no longer afford their surfeit of managers. They are the first to go in early retirement programmes and progression is now very much more based on merit. In fact, if a graduate has not made it to the manager level by the time he is aged 35, he will never make it and will in some companies be 'encouraged' to look for alternative employment.

The opposite trend is evident in Western companies. Today's top executives, in their fifties, are part of a comparatively small age cohort, born in the late 1930s and in the war years. Their career progression took place when organisations were numerous, multi-layered and labour intensive, there were few opportunities to progress to higher education and women had not begun to enter the managerial ranks. Today's 25-year-olds are part of a larger age cohort, and organisations have dramatically slimmed down, both in layers and numbers of people employed. Women are entering the managerial ranks and in many countries are effectively competing for senior positions. As a result the attitude that 'If I'm not promoted every three years, I'm a failure' no longer is sustainable. Thus when Japanese career progression is speeding up, Western progression is slowing down.

What is happening is that the West, in seeking to emulate Japan, is seeking a target that in many areas is moving towards it. The West has learned from Japan, and the USA, after getting over the trauma of realising that it will not always be number one in everything, has put much of its house in order to an extent that the doomsayers of the 1970s would have thought impossible.

The resurgence of the American automobile industry in the mid-1990s is but the most prominent example. The USA has continued to develop in its areas of comparative advantage – cost control, product planning, top level drive, the ability to respond rapidly and has learned from those areas in which the Japanese had comparative advantage – quality, simultaneous engineering, commitment to achieving schedule, control of the process, involvement of the people, and so on. However, since the initial surge of the 1950s and 1960s *the Japanese have not learned from the West*, and this is of tremendous significance. They became comfortable, confident and complacent. They did not subsequently change when they needed to change. Now that they *need* to change they are beginning to realise it is a little, but not too, late!

17 The End of the Beginning

This is not the end. It is not even the beginning of the end. But perhaps it is the end of the beginning.

(Winston S. Churchill, 10 November 1942)

If this book is to have any impact, this final summary chapter must be the end of the beginning. Part I concluded with a chapter titled 'Conclusions – and Beginnings' and defined the ascendant organisation:

> The ascendant organisation combines high levels of commitment of the people and control of the processes to achieve a synthesis between high effectiveness and high quality of life leading to long-term, sustainable business success.

It is not my intention to repeat here what I called the emerging conclusions from Part I, for Part II has been concerned with the practicalities and has attempted to show 'how to' progress to becoming an ascendant organisation. This final chapter will pull out some of the key requirements.

THE CULTURE

- All organisations, even those which have never heard the word, have a culture, either implicit or explicit. It does not have to be written down, but doing so can assist the definition of the shared values. True commitment has, though, to be earned and it is earned when the culture is 'lived'.
- Strong cultures can contribute to decline, because that very strength makes it difficult to change when needed. Only cultures which encourage flexibility and adaptive behaviour can achieve long-term success.
- The ascendant organisation recognises that it is people who make things happen and the culture is as much, if not more, about how people relate with each other as it is about the objectives.

- The people employed by the ascendant organisation are just as much part of it as are other stakeholders. They are not 'our people'. The greatest asset of all the people in an organisation is customers.
- It is concerned with treating all people with respect, trusting them, valuing their individual contributions and providing opportunities for them to grow throughout their lives.
- It permeates all relationships, processes and objectives and encourages flexibility and adaptive behaviour. Only such cultures can achieve long-term success.
- A culture must integrate with all expressed values and support, and be supported by, the business strategy.
- If the organisation has an expressed mission that, too, must integrate with the culture. It must not be a 'motherhood and apple pie' statement. It must inspire and require effort to achieve.
- Although it forms the bedrock of the organisation, it is valuable at lengthy intervals (maybe five years) to involve people throughout the organisation in reviewing it. 'Are we behaving as we ought?' 'Do we need to modify anything in the light of changing circumstances?'

LEADERSHIP

- Leadership in the ascendant organisation is about getting people to do what you want them to do because they want to do it for you. It sets the tone, part of which is responding to the needs of all stakeholders, and is about working through and with people.
- Leadership is not just about transformation. It exists at all levels and it is a key task of the top leadership to create the environment in which leaders can grow and flourish throughout the organisation.
- At the top, the leaders have to *align* the organisation, that is to make sure that everyone and every unit are working together within the same broad principles and business strategy to achieve shared objectives.
- Leaders seek to ensure that the organisation structure is such that it focuses on the essential flows of the business processes but they are not hidebound by them. They hire good people, and genuinely devolve responsibility and accountability and allow headroom, recognising that good people can work effectively within most structures; but if these structures need modifying to accommodate them, then they make sure it happens.

- Key attributes of leaders in the ascendant organisation include an intuitive empathy with the needs and desires of people at all levels, respect for all and the ability to inspire and motivate. They are members of the team as well as leaders of it. Such leaders set high standards and lead by example. They are concerned with the 'how' as well as the 'what'. They constantly challenge, seeking both continuous improvement and, periodically, fundamental change. They are both intuitive and logical. They have a vision of where they want the organisation to go and the ability and passion to take it there.
- Some people are 'born' leaders; most leaders are made by experience.
- Leaders, and managers, exist in a time continuum. They must build on or redirect the work of their predecessor, undertake their own initiatives and prepare the ground for their successor. In the ascendant organisation they do not seek short term success at the expense of the long term.
- Management is about the organisation and development of resources. Managers are more concerned with doing things right than doing the right thing, with a shorter time-scale than the leader. But a manager who cannot also lead is, in the ascendant organisation, a waste of space.

LEADERSHIP IN THE FRONT LINE

- Supervisors, if carefully selected, well-trained, highly motivated and given the status and pay appropriate to being the professional at managing the processes and the people, can make more difference to the long-term success of an organisation than any group other than top management. And even here, it is the supervisors who deliver top management's policies in the workplace.
- Appointment to the position of supervisor is seen as the beginning of a career, not the end of it.
- In the ascendant organisation, the supervisor exercises technical leadership (can understand the current technology and appreciate and deploy the new); applies modern techniques and processes; creates a positive environment for the people and identifies development needs and ensures they are met.
- The supervisor takes on many of the responsibilities which in other organisations have been assumed by functional specialists including cost control, team selection, communication, training and process control, achieving schedule and quality, inputting into new products,

and so on, and must therefore be regarded and paid as the professional at managing the production process. The supervisor is at the same level as all other professionals.

- The supervisor is a member of the team as well as leader of it.
- The high-calibre supervisor – like all leaders – devolves responsibility, thus achieving commitment, and creates the environment in which the prescribed tasks and processes are properly performed.
- By increasing the influence of the staff, the role of the supervisor changes and grows. The 'influence pie' expands.

SINGLE STATUS

- You do not get a first-class response from people who are treated as second-class citizens.
- Common terms and conditions of employment are a necessary but not sufficient condition for achieving that first-class response. Nevertheless, the ascendant organisation begins to eliminate, as a pre-condition for behaviour change, illogical differences in the way people are treated; and aims for total elimination of such differences.
- The ascendant organisation does not give 'perks' to senior executives that are denied to others.

TEAMWORKING

- Teamworking begins with individuals whose contributions are recognised and valued and who are motivated to work together to achieve clear, understood and stretching goals – which they have helped develop, and for which they hold themselves accountable, and which are bigger than they could achieve by working separately. Such teams have positive leadership. In this they are different from work teams or groups which are based on organisational and/or physical structures.
- In the ascendant organisation the leader of the team is fully accepted as a member of the team.
- The team in the ascendant organisation works together for the success of the enterprise.
- The ascendant organisation comprises numerous interlocking teams – the day-to-day work groups, the project teams, task forces and *ad hoc*

groups. Teamworking is the norm on a day-to-day basis and special 'teambuilding' activities are rarely needed.

- Teamworking operates just as successfully in an office environment. The physical layout, with genuine open areas can greatly help.
- The ascendant organisation works very hard at creating teamworking among the top executives, recognising that this is the most difficult group in which to achieve success.
- Successful task or project teams comprise good people who learn together, explore their tasks, develop their own way, establish their goals and measure their progress. Often their families are involved in social events.

COMMUNICATION

- We all communicate all the time. Verbal communication is but one aspect. The ascendant organisation sends out messages when it eliminates illogical benefits, when the senior people are approachable, when distinctions of dress are removed and when, for example, the toilets on the shop floor are to the same standard as those in the offices. It has a 'no door' not an 'open door' policy.
- The ascendant organisation distinguishes communication from information. Communication is about a genuine multi-lateral exchange of views, or occurs when a senior person can speak directly to anyone without anyone else feeling threatened.
- If something is worth communicating, it is worth communicating quickly and the only way to do this is every day, face to face. If it can wait for the monthly magazine or the corporate video, it is information, not communication.
- 'The communicator is king' and it is a top management responsibility to equip all managers and supervisors to be able to communicate effectively, not simply through meetings and discussion, but also by their demeanour in the morning and participation in social activities in the evening.
- The ascendant organisation communicates at all times – in the bad as well as the good. Most communication is about matters affecting the group, and the ascendant organisation is not concerned that everyone should get exactly the same message at exactly the same time: the important point is that the group shares what is important to it in its way. When the process is in place for the small issues, it then becomes easy to communicate about the big issues.

- Because it trusts the people and believes they have a right to know, the ascendant organisation communicates more than is necessary, rather than less.
- The top executives ensure that they get out to where the action is. They are available at regular intervals to communicate face-to-face with all the workforce, to give the 'global' picture in the way only they can, and to allow anyone to question them directly. This is not by-passing the immediate management, but adding a different dimension.

INVOLVING PEOPLE

- The ascendant organisation does not speak of 'empowerment' but of genuinely ensuring that responsibility, authority and accountability are held in the most appropriate part of the organisation. Rather than the centre 'giving power' to the business units, the business units 'take power' from the centre.
- The ascendant organisation understands the difference between involving people and Employee Involvement. Employee Involvement involves the representatives in a formal process. Involving people ensures that all people throughout the organisation are fully involved in those aspects of the business they can influence and are fully informed about those aspects they cannot.
- Involving people at their place of work includes genuine multi-lateral communication, ownership of the standard operation by the people doing the job, full participation in the change processes, definition of the objectives, problem-solving and improvement activities. It takes people beyond the prescribed tasks into the discretionary, and values individual contributions.
- The ascendant organisation creates the environment in which such involvement is part of every-day life. It recognises, therefore, that if it is to have a philosophy which involves people, it has to involve people in determining that it will involve people. Once it becomes the norm, it ceases to be 'voluntary'.
- By involving people in 'local' issues, the ascendant organisation develops the people so that they are able to contribute effectively on the key issues. It includes both core and non-core employees in the processes.
- If the organisation has trade unions, it encourages their representatives and officials to contribute in a constructive way recognising that they will represent the collective view, that they will bring a different

perspective and that if this challenges management's conventional wisdom, this is no bad thing.

- The ascendant organisation is not greatly concerned about big presentations, but recognises that in some circumstances they are valuable. The important point is to ensure that people know that their contributions are valued. Such recognition is developed in a myriad of ways appropriate to the personalities and the people.
- The ascendant organisation does not theorise, discuss, debate or negotiate about involving people. It just does it – at all levels all the time.
- The ascendant organisation believes passionately in *kaizen*, continuous improvement, recognising that the people doing a job know more about that job than anyone else. The managerial responsibility is to create the environment in which that knowledge is brought out and is used for the benefit of the organisation. It aims to achieve an environment in which all staff are motivated to contribute those hundreds of 0.01 per cent improvements – and then modify the standard operation. It recognises that contributing small improvements greatly improves the chances of large improvements being generated and accepted.
- As *kaizen* develops, it can become increasingly sophisticated, but in so doing, it can generate more enthusiasm, not less.

FLEXIBILITY

- The ascendant organisation aims for flexibility within a consistent framework.
- It has a framework which does not restrict what people do. Therefore it eschews rigid organisational structures, fixed employment patterns, unchangeable processes, immutable rules, detailed job descriptions, analytical job evaluation and precisely defined job titles and 'grades'. It recognises that people grow and develop their skills and competencies and that the organisation must adapt to them, rather than they to the organisation.
- The organisational structure is an outcome of good management, not a substitute for it.
- Flexibility in the ascendant organisation is about being able both to have an impact on the business environment and to respond to changes in that environment. It is about pro-active, evolutionary

change and continuous improvement which avoid the need for violent, reactive change.

- People have the freedom to make decisions and, particularly in service organisations, it is recognised that it is at the face-to-face level that this freedom can make a significant difference.

COMMITMENT IN AN INSECURE ENVIRONMENT

- The ascendant organisation, through effective management, seeks to offer security: not simply through long-term employment but by valuing everyone, by ensuring they know where they stand and by developing transferable skills so that employability as well as employment become important.

CONTROL OF THE PROCESSES

- The starting point for control of the manufacturing processes is the standard operation, the currently known best way of performing a task so as to achieve the required quality and productivity levels in a safe manner.
- The ascendant organisation seeks to ensure that the standard operation is always followed – until it is improved, usually by the people doing the job.
- In the ascendant organisation the standard operation is, then, the 'property' of the people doing the job. It is not imposed on them from the outside. The operational team, instead of being controlled *by* the standard operation, has control *of* the standard operation.
- The actual manufacturing process, whether it is cellular manufacturing, batch production, or line paced volume production has to be right for the organisation but the ascendant organisation recognises the needs of the people and ensures that they are able to influence and control. There is proper integration of machinery and people and not domination by the former of the latter.
- Manufacturing cells are a particularly effective method of improving production, allowing simplification, increased productivity, an improved environment, more responsibility and greater involvement.
- The ascendant organisation simplifies before automating and then only automates at the appropriate level. It does not believe in automation for automation's sake, recognising that too complex a

system is unreliable and expensive to maintain and that it is only people who can make further improvements to the processes and products. Machines, by themselves, improve nothing.

- The ascendant organisation devolves responsibility to the work groups, whatever the structure of the manufacturing processes. This can extend way beyond quality and productivity into team selection, purchasing decisions, work scheduling and the very structure of the group. There are many levels of the autonomous work group and each organisation has to make its own decisions as to how far to go.
- Total productive maintenance recognises that the people using equipment have a better 'feel' for it than anyone else and involves them fully in the maintenance of their facilities. Maintenance then becomes a partnership between the operators and the professional maintenance teams. The objective is not simply to ensure the facility operates to its specification but also to improve it.
- The ascendant organisation seeks to eliminate waste in all aspects of its work. It removes buffer stocks, eliminates non-value adding work, minimises changeover times, reduces inventory and controls its logistics. It concentrates on doing 'just' what is necessary 'in time', but recognises that such systems can easily become fragile. Therefore it aims to achieve the right balance between security, flexibility and waste elimination.
- In particular, the ascendant organisation aims for the right balance between its JIT minimum inventory philosophy and the appropriate logistics control systems. It recognises that, as with physical automation, it must simplify before introducing complex systems and must involve the people who will use the system.
- The ascendant organisation regards housekeeping as a fundamental aspect of workshop management. It is systematic about it, places responsibility where it belongs – with the people doing the job – and establishes control processes to ensure the high standards are maintained.
- Visible management is vital. This means managers being visible and relating to the people throughout the organisation, not just by 'walking around' but with purpose. It also means ensuring that the performance of each group is known to everyone by the visible display of information prepared by the group in a relevant way. QCVP boards – quality, cost, volume and people – are a vital element.
- The ascendant organisation recognises that the elimination of waste potentially increases the intensity of work and therefore concentrates enormous efforts on the ergonomic aspects of job design, seeking to

eliminate problems at source through product and facility design. It then assesses the tasks and, as always, it ensures that those people directly affected are fully involved in subsequent modifications.

INTEGRATING QUALITY

- In the ascendant organisation quality is not voluntary.
- The ascendant organisation regards high quality as the norm and does not need initial capitals like TQM. It does not give a competitive advantage. It is the price of staying in business and therefore is fully integrated into the business. It is no longer special.
- Quality focuses on customers, who are often irrational, illogical and whose views are constantly changing. Therefore, the quality of a product or service is the customers' perception of it, taking into account their total experience of those features they consider important. These are many and varied.
- Therefore, the ascendant organisation gets close to its customers, seeks to understand their needs and forms partnerships with them.
- It recognises that its front liners are key links in this partnership.
- Internally, the ascendant organisation trains the staff and controls its processes to ensure delivery of consistent high quality, and determines internal performance measures which correlate strongly with customer requirements.
- The ascendant organisation designs for quality, and through the simultaneous engineering process integrates customer needs, suppliers, production and marketing. In the process it reduces the time from conception to delivery and also concerns itself with disposal and resurrection. It recognises that top management does not have a monopoly of wisdom as to what is a good product or service, and devolves responsibility to those directly involved.
- The ascendant organisation does not rely on a few mavericks, but spreads innovation and commitment to quality throughout the organisation. It recognises that without everyone's commitment, the formal systems do not work for long.
- Within the ascendant organisation there are no change agents, but everyone is an agent for change. The standard operation is the starting point for quality improvements.
- The internal customer is vital. You never knowingly pass errors to the next person. Staff are encouraged to flag up their mistakes and are never criticised for so doing.

- Recognising human fallibility, the ascendant organisation seeks to 'foolproof' the physical process as much as possible.
- Quality circles are the cherry on the icing on the cake. They work when there is already a commitment to quality, and it is the total commitment to involvement and improvement that is important. The process is as important as the results and the organisation benefits from the experience the participants take back to their normal job.
- The ascendant organisation speaks not of the cost of quality but the price of poor quality – that price is to go out of business.
- Bureaucratic systems, such as ISO 9000, do not in themselves set quality standards. They determine detailed procedures and rules which may help those who already have a commitment to quality but will make those with bureaucratic inclinations even more so inclined. The ascendant organisation uses such standards positively and learns from them.
- Benchmarking is a valuable tool – but in addition to making comparisons with competitors, the ascendant organisation seeks to understand the 'best in class', whatever the business in which it occurs, and uses that information to help determine where it wants to be.
- The ascendant organisation determines its key measures of externally assessed quality success and establishes key internal measures which correlate with the external. It fully involves the staff in this process.
- Change to processes, structures, and so on, result from a perceived need, not precede it, and may require fundamental challenges to the established way of doing things.
- Techniques for improving quality are tools, not a religion.
- Top management attention has to be maintained for ever.

PARTNERSHIP SOURCING

- The ascendant organisation is interested in the quality of its relationships with its suppliers and therefore develops long-term, mutually supportive partnerships.
- Partnership sourcing is a whole company philosophy which depends on relationships throughout both organisations and in which both are stakeholders in the other. The supplier knows that in all normal circumstances the business is secure.
- Because of the depth of the relationship, partnerships can only exist with a comparatively small number of suppliers, the vast majority of whom will be the single source for a component or service.

- The customer will assign people specifically to work with its suppliers to develop their capabilities in design, manufacturing, quality assurance, delivery, management and any other areas relevant to the relationship – but will not usurp their authority and responsibility. Ascendant suppliers will assign people to work with their customers.
- The financial relationship changes from Cost + Profit = Price to Price – Cost = Profit. Rather than continuous inflationary increases, the target is real price reductions due to increasing effectiveness and volumes.
- The ascendant organisation measures the performance of its suppliers and sets demanding improvement targets. In so doing it avoids complacency. The ascendant supplier will measure its customers!

KNOWLEDGE WORKERS

- In the ascendant organisation every worker is a knowledge worker.
- The ascendant organisation continuously develops all staff. Continuous development is a continuum in which, in a structured way, all people learn, are challenged and motivated so that they can grow and develop as individuals throughout their lives.
- The ascendant organisation builds on performance management – a partnership between managers and staff in which the business strategy, objectives, organisation requirements and individual evaluation and needs are integrated.
- All young people receive thorough training both on, off and near the job. They work for formal qualifications in specific skills but also develop broad competencies in teamworking, innovation, flexibility, problem-solving, and so on.
- In the ascendant organisation many of the attributes once regarded as the prerogative of managers become the natural currency throughout. All people use their brains as well as their hands. Therefore the development of these attributes begins as soon as people join the organisation, at whatever level – and all subsequent development builds from the bottom-up.
- The development of managerial skills and competencies is not reserved for people at or approaching management positions, but identifying those who are likely to progress through the managerial ranks is vital. Such people will be given the opportunity to develop and broaden their competencies and skills. High-potential people are placed in challenging positions.

- The ascendant organisation does not spoonfeed people. They take on much responsibility for their own development and line managers regard it as part of their responsibilities to facilitate this process. Often it is only line managers who are able to provide the necessary knowledge, and therefore a key part of everyone's training is being trained how to train. All staff participate in developing other staff.
- The ascendant organisation seeks joint agreement on roles, accountabilities, objectives and competency requirements as a means of measuring performance and on development and performance plans.
- The ascendant organisation encourages learning of all types and provides the necessary resources.
- Skills training is systematic and assessed. It seeks to answer the question, 'How do you *know* the staff are properly trained?'
- The ascendant organisation seeks to define in all people the 'magic powder' element, that elusive 'something' peculiar to an individual which will enable the person to perform better than he or she had thought possible.
- Non-core, as well as core, staff are properly trained and developed.
- The ascendant organisation both learns and forgets. People create the climate that facilitates the continuous development of all members who, as a result, are able continuously to develop the organisation.
- As a result, the ascendant organisation seeks to avoid the need for the traumatic paradigm shift but from time to time recognises that such a shift is necessary, but without the trauma!

CORPORATE FINANCES

- The ascendant organisation has a long-term horizon. Although it values good short-term results, it does not risk the long term for the sake of the short term. It invests in people, product and facilities for long-term success.
- It values organic growth and development and though it may acquire other organisations, it is not a 'predatory Viking'.
- It takes into account the interests of all stakeholders, not just the financial investors, but seeks to communicate effectively with the financial investors to ensure they understand and support the principles and objectives.
- The ascendant organisation makes good use of genuinely independent non-executive directors, particularly in assessing the overall

performance of executive management against pre-determined indicators.

- It values non-financial as well as financial indicators, particularly when seeking to determine future performance. Judgements are made on the basis of long-term performance.
- It does not have an obsession with the numbers. The task of the finance people is to provide a service which helps the direct people do their job better. They are not there just as inquisitors.
- There is total openness about directors' remuneration and options. Their contracts are not substantially different from those of other staff.

REWARD

- The reward structure is an outcome of good management, not a substitute for it.
- In the ascendant organisation the reward structure is integrated with and supports the culture, business strategy and objectives.
- The ascendant organisation does not pay people extra for achieving what they are paid to achieve. It takes account of intangibles as well as tangibles, aims for transparency and seeks the commitment of everyone, not just a favoured few.
- Short-term payment by results systems have no place and skill-based pay is questionable.
- Performance-related pay (PRP), if introduced in the ascendant organisation, is designed to reinforce the culture, is clear as to the targets and standards, enables performance to be tracked, and ensures that people are able to impact on that performance. It is clear about the benefits to be gained.
- In the ascendant organisation a common form of PRP is salary progression. It is part of an overall performance management system and is based on a performance assessment which is as objective as possible. This assessment incorporates achievement against previously agreed goals and the individual's contribution to the team. It is a genuine two-way process, not a top-down evaluation.
- The performance assessment is fair and seen to be fair. Mechanisms are in place to avoid favouritism and to control costs.
- Linking individual performance with the overall business performance is management's job 365 days of the year, not a bonus payment's job one day of the year.

- Performance bonuses are based on measured achievement against defined mid-term performance goals, both financial and non-financial, which are integrated with the long-term goals of the business.
- The ascendant organisation relates its performance bonuses as closely as possible to the business unit in which people work. It may even let them have a say in how the bonus should be structured. It extends the bonus to all employees, not just to those at the top, and ensures that it is equitable.
- The ascendant organisation makes no secret of pay levels, being confident that they will be seen to be internally and externally fair. The top executives do not receive 'excessive' pay in relation to others and if there are share options they are available to all.
- Any performance-related pay system at the top is related solely to measured outputs against previously agreed objectives.
- The ascendant organisation payment system does not include more than three elements. Any more serve only to confuse.

TRADE UNIONS

- The relationship that *really* counts in the ascendant organisation is that between individuals, not that between the representatives of trade unions and the representatives of management.
- Trade unions can have a constructive role in the ascendant organisation provided that they are committed to the success of the enterprise and they consider carefully their changed role. They ask, 'Can we provide a service which our members want?' and seek to become involved in the 'new way' where it matters to their members – on the shop floor – ensuring that there is no abuse and that the benefits are equitably distributed.
- They seek to represent both core and non-core employees.
- The new agenda for trade unions in the ascendant organisation is about the quality of outputs as much as the price of inputs.
- Trade unions retain their traditional roles but in a modern way, while at the same time accepting that teamworking, employee involvement, flexibility, and so on, have resulted in employees recognising that their only real security comes from working for a successful enterprise.
- The ascendant organisation does not resist constructive trade unionism but opposes those who attempt to be destructive. It recognises that it is what employees, not management, want that counts.

- In the ascendant organisation what unites people because they are all employees of the same organisation is stronger than what divides them because of their different levels and roles.

THE CHANGE PROCESS

There are many different change processes depending on the area of the organisation to be changed – the whole culture, quality, teamworking, reward system, and so on. However, running through the 'How to' sections there have been common threads:

- At the top level, analyse what you have now and seek to establish a common understanding of where you want to be. Benchmark the opposition and 'best in class'. But do not be precise: you will not get it right because you will not really know what goes on throughout the organisation. It is top management's job to create the framework which liberates people throughout the organisation to determine the detail. Writing down the first thoughts is a great discipline, but make sure it *is* first thoughts and not 'tablets of stone'.
- Appoint the best people to develop the concepts but ensure that they do not think they have a monopoly of wisdom. Make sure they consult widely and involve all the stakeholders, including non-core workers and trade unions if appropriate, and particularly the middle managers who will often feel the most threatened but who will be the key deliverers of change.
- Allow gun jumping – provided the people concerned have thought it through. 'Ownership' is critical. Do not worry about the wheel being re-invented. Let people do their own thing and make their own mistakes, but ensure they learn from their mistakes and from each other.
- Perhaps send out signals from the top. Change something which is visible and symbolic but choose the timing carefully, otherwise it may be seen as a cynical exercise.
- Take away insecurity – but in some organisations you may have to go through the traumatic 'downsizing' before you can even begin to think this way. Although no one is protected from the market place, remember that it is not individuals' fault if they are unable to make the change. They have been hired and expected to behave in a particular way and it is management's responsibility if a change takes place. They may have to change their job or may choose to go with

generous financial payments, but do not dismiss them. If people think that they will lose their employment if the changes go through, they will make sure that nothing happens.

- Trust people. You will get surprises. It will not happen the way you thought, but it will be all the better for that.
- Encourage experiments, provide training.
- List critical success factors and, where possible, measure, but often this will be a 'stand'. If you have to prove it, you do not believe in it; and do not forget that what is measurable is often not important and what is important is often not measurable. Do not start by changing the structures or processes. Leave them alone. If the need arises it will become obvious to everyone. Maybe you will be able to abolish many of the previous bureaucratic systems which inhibited flexibility – but this can only come at the end. Too early and you will make some horrible mistakes.
- Top management interest must be sustained throughout. It is no good setting the train in motion and walking away. It will be a long haul.
- Outsiders can help, they can ask the difficult questions but they must never take over. Ownership must rest within the organisation.
- Remember that the old must continue for a considerable time to operate beside the new. Not everything can change at once.

THE FINAL MESSAGE

Remember that we all have a part of our organisation we can influence. We do not have to wait for the change process to start from above us. Do not miss out the planning and understanding, but avoid paralysis by analysis.

There comes a time when you have to make a stand and just do it!

Today is a great time to begin!

References

Note: This listing contains some references which are not specifically quoted but which have been used in the preparation of this book.

A. T. Kearney (1992)	*Total quality management: a business process perspective*	A. T. Kearney Inc.
Adler, P. S. (1993)	'Time and motion regained'	*Harvard Business Review* (Jan.–Feb.)
Advisory, Conciliation and Arbitration Service (1993)	*Issues in reinforcing and developing teamworking – interim report*	QWL (Winter)
Anderson Consulting (1993)	*The lean enterprise bench marking project*	
Armstrong, M. and H. Murlis (1994)	*Reward management* (3rd edn)	Kogan Page, London
Arnold, D. (1992)	'The dawn of a brand new empire'	*Ashbridge Management Review* (Spring)
Atkinson, J. and M. Spilsbury (1993)	*Basic skills and jobs*	Adult Literacy and Basic Skills Unit, London
Barnett, C. (1986)	*The audit of war*	Macmillan, London
Beer, M., R. Eisenstatt and B. Spector (1990)	'Why change programmes don't produce change'	*Harvard Business Review* (Nov.–Dec.)
Belbin, W. M. (1981)	*Management teams – why they succeed or fail*	Heinemann, London
Bell, D. W. and C. G. Hanson (1987)	*Profit sharing and profitability*	Kogan Page, London
Bennis, W. (1992)	*On becoming a leader*	Century Business, London
Bentley, J. (1990)	*Competitive manufacturing strategies*	Financial Times Conference: 'Manufacturing strategies', 23 May
Benyon, H. (1973)	*Working for Ford*	Allen Lane, London
Berggren, C. (1993a)	*The Volvo experience*	Macmillan, London
Berggren, C. (1993b)	*Volvo, Uddevalla – a dead horse or a car dealer's dream*	Royal Institute of Technology, Stockholm

Berggren, C., T. Bjorkman, and E. Hollander (1991)	*Are they unbeatable?*	Royal Institute of Technology, Stockholm
Binney, G. (1992)	*Making quality work – lessons from Europe's leading companies*	The Economist Intelligence Unit, London
Blumenthal, W. M. (1988)	*Countdown to the future*	A. T. Kearney Inc. (Fall)
Bolwyn, P. T. and T. Kemp (1990)	'Productivity, flexibility and innovation'	*Long Range Planning Journal* (vol. 23, no. 4)
Bonfield, P. (1993)	*Building a resilient company*	Management Centre Europe Conference (25 May)
British Institute of Management/ Manpower (UK) Ltd (1992)	*Survey of Long-term UK employment policies*	BIM, London
Brydon, D. (1990)	*Short termism and industrial innovation*	Department of Trade and Industry Conference, London
Burns, P. and R. Savers (1988)	'Participative management and employee involvement'	Ford Motor Company
Carlzon, J. (1989)	*Moments of truth*	Harper & Row, New York
Centre for Alternative Industrial and Technical Systems (1988)	*Teamworking – employee involvement but worse*	
Chadwick, P. (1993)	*Supervisory roles, responsibilities and training in British industry*	Peter Chadwick Ltd
Churchill, J. H. (1988)	*Doing business with Japanese companies in the UK*	Institution of Mechanical Engineers (24 March)
Confederation of British Industry (1991)	*Partnership sourcing*	
Conference Board of New York (1993)	*Does quality work? A review of relevant studies*	Conference Board of New York
Cross, M. (1990)	*Changing work practices in UK manufacturing 1981–1990*	Paper given at Durham University, 19 June
Darling, P. S. (1990)	*Short-term fund management*	Mercury Asset Management, London
Deming, W. E. (1982)	*Out of the crisis*	Cambridge University Press

Development Council of Sweden (1984)	*Volvo, Kalmar revisited – ten years of experience*	
Drucker, P. (1993)	*Post-capitalist society*	Butterworth–Heinemann, London
Ebel, K.-H. (1989)	'Manning the unmanned factory'	*ILO Review* (vol. 128, no. 5)
Employment Department (1992)	*New developments in employee involvement*	Research Management Branch, London
Employment Department (1994)	*Teleworking: the way forward – or is it?*	Skills and Enterprise Briefing (May)
Epps, T. (1987)	Untitled	European Metalworkers Federation Conference, 14 April
European Metalworkers Federation (1988)	*Six propositions on the future of work in the European automobile industry*	
Fayol, H. (1916)	'General and industrial management' in Pugh, D. S. (ed.) *Organisation theory* (3rd edn) 1990	Penguin Books, London
Feigenbaum, A. (1983)	*Total quality control* (3rd edn)	McGraw-Hill, Maidenhead
Ferdows, K. (1992)	*New mandates for global manufacturers*	European Manufacturing Management Conference, Genevea, (Jun.)
Fisher, J. (1992)	*Notes for Seminar on Lean production and European trade union co-operation*	TGWU (Dec.)
Fisher, J. (1993)	*Notes for Ford European Works Council Seminar*	TGWU (Sept.)
Foster, M. and S. Whittle (1989)	'The quality management maze'	*TQM Magazine* (vol. 3, May)
Fucini, J. J. and S. Fucini (1990)	*Working for the Japanese*	The Free Press, New York
GMB/UCW (1992)	*A new agenda – bargaining for prosperity in the 1990s*	GMB and UCW, London
Gregg, P., S. Machine and S. Szymanski (1993)	'The disappearing relationship between directors' pay and corporate performance'	*British Journal of Industrial Relations* (vol. 31, 1 March)
Guest, D. (1984)	'What's new in motivation?'	*Personnel Management* (May)

Guest, D., R. Peccei and P. Rosenthal (1992) — 'Management training and development and career success' in K. Bradley (ed.), *People and Performance* — Ashgate Publishing, Aldershot, UK

Gulowsen, J. (1971) — *Autonomous production groups on the road to industrial democracy (1971)* cited in Berggren (1993a)

Hackman, J. R. and G. R. Oldham (1985) — 'Motivation through the design of work: test of a theory' — *Organisational Behaviour and Human Peformance* (vol. 16, no. 2) in T. Robertson and M. Smith, *Motivation and job design*, Institute of Personnel Management

Hamada, M. (1984) — *Twelve questions regarding Japanese management style* — Centre for Organisational Research and Education, Tokyo

Hammer, M. and J. Champy 91993) — *Reengineering the corporation* — Nicholas Brealey, London

Handy, C. (1987) — *The making of managers* — National Economic Development Office, London

Handy, C. (1993) — 'What it takes to make a manager' — *Director* (Dec.)

Handy, C. (1994) — *The empty raincoat* — Hutchinson, London

Harbour, M. and J. Brown (1993) — *Customer driven quality* — National Franchise Dealers Association, Rugby

Her Majesty's Inspectorate (1991) — *Aspects of vocational education and training*

Herzberg, F. (1959) — *The motivation to work* — Wiley, New York

Hibbert, A. (1991) — 'Employee involvement; a recent survey' · — *Employment Gazette* (Dec.)

Hitchens, D. A. and K. Wagner (1985) — *Productivity, machinery and skills in a sample of British and German manufacturing plants* — NIESR, London

Holloway, J. (1987) — 'The red rose of Nissan' — *Capital and Class*, no. 2

Hopson, B. and M. Skally (1989) — *Twelve steps to success through service* — Lifeskills Publishing Group, Leeds

Howard, G. (1993) — 'Design for assembly' — Automotive Vision

Hutton, W. (1991) — 'Why Britain can't afford the City' — *Management Today* (Sept.)

Huws, V. (1993)	'Teleworking in Britain'	Employment Department Research Series (no. 18, Oct.)
IG Metall, RKW and VDW (1992)	*Nine principles: Towards an innovating and social; industrial culture in the machine tool industry*	
Imai, M. (1986)	*Kaizen: the key to Japan's competitive success*	Random House, New York
Ingersoll Engineers (1991)	*Change: the good, the bad and the visionary*	Ingersoll Engineers Ltd
Ingersoll Engineers (1993)	*The quiet revolution continues*	Ingersoll Engineers Ltd
International Institute for Management Development (1993)	*World competitiveness report*	IIMD, Lausanne
International Labour Office (1993)	*World Labour Report*	ILO, Geneva
International Motor Business (1993)	*Face to face with the President of Saturn Corporation*	The Economist Intelligence Unit (2nd Quarter)
International Survey Research Limited (1992)	*Employee satisfaction – achieving competitive advantage in the 90s*	ISR Ltd
Irish Congress of Trade Unions (1993)	*New forms of work organisation: options for unions*	ICTU, Dublin
Ishada, H. (1988)	*Case Study*	Keio Business School
Jacques, E. (1961)	*The measurement of responsibility*	Tavistock, London
JAMA (1991)	*Forum* (vol. 9, no. 3)	JAMA, Tokyo
JAMA (1993)	*Forum* (vol. 11, no. 3)	JAMA, Tokyo
Japan Auto Workers Union (1992)	*Japanese automobile industry in the future*	JAWU, Tokyo
Jevons, W. S. (1983)	*On industrial partnerships: methods of social reform*	Macmillan, London
Jordan, W. (1991)	'Working with Japanese investors: the trade union response', *Japan and the regeneration of British industry*	Anglo–Japanese Economic Institute
Kamata, S. (1983)	*Japan in the passing lane*	George Allen & Unwin, London

Kanter, R. M. (1989)	*When giants learn to dance*	Unwin, London
Kennedy, I. (1994)	*Prioritising company needs*	IBC Conference 'The learning organisation' London (May)
Kohn, A. (1993)	'Why incentive plans cannot work'	*Harvard Business Review* (Sept.–Oct.)
Kotter, J. P. and J. Heskett (1992)	*Corporate culture and performance*	The Free Press, New York
Lamming, R. (1993)	*Delivery-on-time initiative*	Institution of Mechanical Engineers/Chartered Institute of Purchasing and Supply and EEF (South)
Lance, C. (1989)	*Management and labour in Europe*	Edward Elgar Publishing, London
Lazonick, W. (1990)	*Competitive advantage on the shop floor*	Harvard University Press
Lehndorff, S. and G. Bosch (1992)	*Working time and operating hours in the European and Japanese car industries*	Institut Arbeit und Technik, Gelsenkirchen
Levitt, T. (1983)	'The globalisation of markets'	*Harvard Business Review* (May–June)
March Consulting Group (1990)	*Managing maintenance in the 1990s*	EEC
Markides, C. (1984)	'Restructuring for competition' in R. Heller (ed.) *Managing 1994: the competitive edge*	Sterling Publications, London
Maslow, A. (1970)	*Motivation and personality*	Harper & Row, New York
Mayo, E. (1990)	'The social problems of an industrial civilisation' in D. S. Pugh, *Organisation theory* (3rd edn.)	Penguin Books, London
McGregor, D. (1960)	*The human side of enterprise*	McGraw–Hill, New York
Miller, P. (1992)	*Communications Review*	(no. 2, Apr.)
Millward, N., M. Stevens, D. Smart and W. R. Hawes (1992)	*Workplace industrial relations in transition*	Dartmouth Publishing, Aldershot
Mintel (1993)	*Quality assurance and the consumer*	Mintel, London
Mintzberg, H. (1975)	*The managers' job – folklore and fact*	*Harvard Business Review* (Jul.–Aug.)

Mintzberg, H. (1992)	Contribution to 'MBA. Is the traditional model doomed?'	*Harvard Business Review* (Nov.–Dec.)
Mito, S. (1990)	*The Honda book of management*	The Athlone Press, London
Monks Partnership (1993)	*Incentives for management*	Monks Partnership, Saffron Walden, Essex
Morita, A. (1987)	*Made in Japan*	Fontana, London
Muto, I. (1982)	'Class struggle in post-war Japan: its past, present and future'	*AMPO Japan–Asia, Quarterly Review* (vol. 14, no. 3)
Naisbitt, J. and P. Aburdene (1991)	*Megatrends 2000*	Pan Books, London
National Economic Development Office	*The roles, competences and training of supervisors*	NEDO, London
NEDC (1991)	*What makes a supervisor world class?*	NEDO, London
NEDC (1991)	*The experience of Nissan suppliers*	NEDO, London
Neumann, J. (1989)	'Why people don't participate'	*Industrial Participation* (no. 601, Spring)
Nikkei Research Institute (1990)	*Sixth annual survey on Japanese youth*	NRI, Tokyo
Nomura, M. (1992)	*The end of Toyotaism*	IG Metall conference, Frankfurt
Nora, J. J., C. R. Rogers and J. Stramy (1986)	*Transforming the workplace*	Princetown Research Press, New Jersey
Oakland, J. S. (1990)	'TQM: One way to delight your customers'	*Works Management* (May)
OECD (1994)	*The OECD jobs study*	OECD Publications, Paris
Ohno, T. (1988a)	*Workplace management*	Productivity Press, Cambridge, Mass.
Ohno, T. (1988b)	*Toyota production system*	Productivity Press, Cambridge, Mass.
Ouchi, W. (1981)	*Theory Z*	Addison-Wesley, Reading, Mass.
Parker, M. and J. Slaughter (1988a)	*Choosing sides: unions and the team concept*	South End Press
Parker, M. and J. Slaughter (1988b)	'Managing by stress: the dark side of the team concept'	*Industrial and Labour Relations Report* (fall)

Pascale, R. T. (1990)	*Managing on the edge*	Simon & Schuster, New York
Payne, R. (1991)	*Taking stock of corporate culture*	*Personnel Management* (July)
Pedlar, M., T. Boydell and J. Burgoyne (1989)	'Towards the learning company'	*Management Education and Development* (20.1)
Peters, T. (1988)	'Leadership excellence in the 1990s: learning to love change'	*Journal of Management Development* (vol. 7, no. 5)
Peters, T. (1992)	'Perfection is not enough'	*Works Management* (December)
Policy Studies Institute (1993)	*Employee commitment and the skills revolution*	PSI, London
Pugh, D. S. (ed.) (1990)	*Organisation theory* (3rd edn.)	Penguin Books, London
Quinn, J. B. (1990)	'Ford's Team Taurus 1988', in *International Motor Business*	*The Economist* Intelligence Unit (April)
Report of the Committee on the Evolution of Work (1994)	*The new American workplace: a labor perspective*	AFL–CIO (1994)
Rich, J. T. and A. Larson (1987)	'Why some long term incentives fail' in H. R. Nalbantian (ed.) *Incentives, co-operation and risk sharing*	Rowman & Littlefield
Robertson, D. (1992)	*New management techniques and the development of a trade union counter strategy*	TIE/Vauxhall Motors Shop Stewards Conference (30 Jan.–2 Feb.)
Roth, S. (1991)	*Analytik '91*	Hamburg (18 November)
Roth, S. (1992)	*Japanisation or going our own way*	IG Metall
Roth, S. (1993)	'Lean production in German motor manufacturing'	*P + European Participation Monitor* (no. 5)
Royal Society of Arts (1994)	*Tomorrow's company: the role of business in a changing world – interim report*	RSA, London
Sayer, A. (1991)	*Anniversary Review 1966–1991*	*Management Today* (October)
Schmidt, H. (1992)	*Skills for Europe: 1993 and beyond*	Conference, London (September)

Scholtes, P. R. (1987)	*An elaboration on Deming's teaching on performance appraisal*	Joiner Associates Inc.
Schonberger, R. B. (1982)	*Japanese manufacturing techniques: nine lessons in hidden simplicity*	The Free Press, New York
Schonberger, R. B. (1986)	*World class manufacturing*	The Free Press, New York
Secretary's Commission on Achieving Necessary Skills (1991)	*What work requires of school*	US Department of Labor
Securities and Investment Board (1993)	*Pension transfers*	SIB, London
Semler, R. (1993)	*Maverick*	Century, London
Sengenberger, W. (1992)	*Lean production: the way of working and production in the future*	International Institute for Labour Studies, Geneva
Shingo, S. (1988)	*Non-stock production*	Productivity Press, Cambridge, Mass.
Smilansky, J. (1992)	'How not to implement TQM'	Conference: Re-thinking Quality – *The Economist* Conferences, 4 December
Smith, Adam (1776; repr. 1980)	*The wealth of nations*	Methuen, London
Smith, M. (1990)	'The rise and rise of the NFI'	*Management Accounting* (May)
Sorenson, C. E. (1950)	*My forty years with Ford*	W. W. Norton, New York
Stalk, G. Jnr and T. M. Hout (1990)	*Competing against time*	The Free Press, New York
Stayer, R. (1990)	'How I learned to let my workers lead'	*Harvard Business Review* (Nov.–Dec.)
Steele, M., and A. Brown (1990)	*Leadership*	Cranfield Press
Tannenbaum, A. S. (1966)	*Social psychology of the work organisation*	Wadsworth, Calif.
Tannenbaum, A. S. (1968)	*Control in organisations*	McGraw-Hill, New York
Taylor, F. W. (1911)	*The principles of scientific management*	W. W. Norton, New York

Thompson, M. (1994)	'Paying for performance' in R. Heller (ed.) *Managing 1994: the competitive edge*	Sterling Publications, London
Thurow, L. (1993)	*Head to head*	Nicholas Brealey, London
Tichy, N. M. and S. Sherman (1993)	*Control your destiny or someone else will*	Currency Doubleday, New York
Toulson, C. and T. Coe (1991)	*The flat organisation – philosphy and practice*	British Institute of Management
Trades Union Congress (1993)	*The future of trade unions*	TUC, London
Trades Union Congress (1994)	*Human resource management*	TUC, London
Trist, E. L. (1981)	'The socio-technical perspective', in A. Van der Ven and W. F. Joyce (eds), *Perspective on organisation design and behaviour*	Wiley–Interscience
Trist, E. L. and K. W. Bamforth (1951)	'Some social and psychological consequences of the long wall method of coal-getting'	*Human Relations* (vol. 4, no. 1)
Tuckman, B. W. (1965)	'Development sequence in small groups'	*Psychological Bulletin* (no. 3)
Unterweger, P. (1992)	*Lean production: myth and reality*	International Institute for Labour Studies, Geneva
van Wolferen, K. (1989)	*The enigma of Japanese power*	Macmillan, London
Vroom, V. H. (1964)	*Work and motivation*	John Wiley, New York
Walton, R. E. (1985)	'From control to commitment in the workplace'	*Harvard Business Review* (Mar.–Apr.)
Weber, M. (1930)	*The protestant ethic and the spirit of capitalism*	Allen & Unwin, London
Weber, M. (1947)	*The theory of social and economic organisations*	The Free Press, New York
Weiss, H. (1992)	'The structure of the German company'	*RSA Journal* (Nov.)
Wickens, P. D. (1987)	*The road to Nissan*	Macmillan, London
Wilkins, T. (1991)	*Britax – continuous supplier development*	*Quality Today* (July)
Wilkinson, A., T. Redman and E. Snape (1993)	*Quality and the manager*	Institute of Management

Wolf, M. J. (1984)	*The Japanese conspiracy*	New English Library
Womack, J. P., D. T. Jones and D. Roos (1990)	*The machine that changed the world*	Rawson Associates, New York
Wyatt Company (1990)	*Performance management 1990*	The Wyatt Company/ *Personnel Today*
Zairi, M., A. Letza and J. S. Oakland (1994)	'Does TQM impact on the bottom line?'	*The TQM Magazine* (vol. 6, no. 1)
Zuboff, S. (1988)	*In the age of the smart machine*	Basic Books, New York

Index

Absenteeism 117–18
Acco Cable Controls 106
Adversarial supplier relationships 205–6
AFL–CIO 50–1, 278–9
Airlie, Jimmy 268
Akers, John 291–3
Albrecht, Karl 118
Alexander, Lord 239
Amalgamated Engineering and Electrical Union 273–4
Appraisal systems 230, 250–8
Attendance 117–18
Aufsichtsrat 241–2
Automated guided vehicles 53
Automation 39–40, 53, 67
Autonomous work groups 157, 160–2

Bacon, Francis 63
Behaviouralists 23–30, 66
Benchmarking 198–9, 330
Bendix, R. 115
Benedict, Ruth 310
Binney, George 193
Bluestone, Irving 303
Body Shop 78,128
Bonfield, Peter 236
Bonuses 259–62
Bowman-Shaw, Sir Neville 92–3
BP 288–90
Branson, Richard 100, 150
'Breakthrough' teams 305
British Aerospace 100, 263
British Airways 182
British Nuclear Fuels 78
British Telecom 249
Brooks, T. G. 106
Brydon, Donald 243
Burger King 144
Burt, David N. 205
Business process re-engineering 40–1, 93, 98, 203

Cahill, John 263–4
Callow, Peter 214
CAMI 45–8
Canadian Autoworkers' Union 45–8
Cantona, Eric 115, 120
Carlzon, Jan 94, 182
Cell manufacturing 157–60
Centre for Alternative Industrial and Technical Systems 275
Changeover times 164–5
Churchill, Winston S. 320
Citibank 86
Club Med 193–4, 198
Coca-Cola 194
Colbert, Jean-Baptiste 178
Commitment 3–7, 66, 71–8
  in an insecure invironment 154–6, 327
  see also behaviouralists, discretionary work, involvement, *kaizen*, teamworking
Communication 126–30, 324–5
  informal 128
  supervisors 108
  top executives 98
Confederation of British Industry 132–3, 208
Confucius 310
Connor, Danny 13, 120
Consensus 32, 69
Continental Can Company 151, 239, 241
Continuous development 227–35
Continuous improvement 12
  see also kaizen
Control of the processes
  autonomous work groups 160–2
  'controllers' 20–2, 64–5
  control v. commitment 3–4, 14, 17, 29–30, 135
  defined 73
  design process 184
  financial control 238–44
  housekeeping 171
  in Japan 31–51, 65
  ISO 9000 204, 330
  job evaluation 151–2

in leadership 92
logistics 167–9
Nine Alpha Organisation Map 71–8
poka yoke 189
prescribed work 70–1
rules 149–50
simple model 4–7
statistical process control 188
supervisors 105
Coopers and Lybrand 78
Core skills 232
Corporate finances 238–44, 332
Cost control 110, 239
'Cost plus' pricing 206
Courtaulds Textiles 248
Craven, John 241
Crews, Mick 286
Critics of Japan 40–51
Crosby, Philip 178, 180
Culture 81–90, 320–1
change 286–309, 335–6
Citibank 86
DEC 87
Federal Express 80
Honda 84
Sunrise Medical 83
written statements 83–90
Cushnaghan, John 109, 136
Customers 180–3, 321

Daiken Trade and Industry 227
Daimler-Benz 242
'Dark factory' 12
Darling, Peter Stormouth 240
DEC 87
Decentralisation 10
Deming, W. Edwards 37, 178, 245, 254–5
Design for quality 183–7
Discretionary work 71–2
Disney 264
Distribution systems 169–71
Dodge, Colin 111
Doolittle, General James 157
'Doubling-up' 22
Dowty Seals 301
Drucker, Peter 219, 264, 266
Dual system 223–5

Eastern Airlines 263
Edmonds, John 138, 274
Education 219–23, 316
Edwardes, Sir Michael 93, 246
Egalitarianism 315
Egan, Sir John 293–4
Eisner, Michael 264
Electronic transer of funds 11
Elimination of waste 36, 65, 68
EMI 264
Empathy 95–6, 129
Employability 18
Empowerment 15
Epps, R. Timothy 130
Ergonomics 174–7, 281
Ethicon Ltd 192
European Metalworkers Federation 276
Expectancy theory 27

'Fad surfing' 76, 148
Fagan, Gerry 192
Fayol, Henri 102
Federal Express 86, 93
Feigenbaum, Armand 178, 180
Fiat Motor Company 12
Fifield, Jim 264
Financial bubble 39
Financial Times 8, 38, 52, 53, 56, 57, 194, 227, 249, 264, 287, 289, 290, 291
Fisher, John 48, 277
'Five S' 171–2
Flexibility 147–54, 326–7
job evaluation 150
Nissan 152–3
Tate and Lyle 152–3
Flexitime 117
Flora Food Company 194
Ford, Henry 21, 65
Ford Motor Company Employee Development and Assistance programme 234
globalisation 10
imposing change 294–6
moving assembly line 21
product development 180
report on Jaguar 293–4
statistical process control 188
teamworking 119
trade union militancy 13, 120, 280
Freund, William C. 157
Futami, Masaharu 96

General Motors
capital investment 12, 38

General Motors (*cont.*)
employee involvement 130–40, 301–4
outsourcing 10
Saturn project 138–40
union agreements 274
German management 43–5
Gerstner, Lou 81, 89, 123
Gibson, Ian 97, 280
Globalisation 11
GMB Union 273, 279
Gompers, Samuel 238
Gow, Ian 55, 280
Gulowsen, Jan 160–1
Gyllenhammer, Pehr 58

Halstead, Lindsay 295
Hamer, Stuart 219
Handy, Charles 244
Harvard Business Review 3, 205, 253
Hatakeyama, Yoshio 103
Hayden, Bill 293, 295
Heractlitus 286
Herzberg, Frederick 25
Hewlett, Bill 93
Hewlett-Packard 93
Hierarchy of needs 26
Hirano, Hideaki 96
Honda Motor Company 53–4, 56, 84
Honda, Soichiro 54
Horton, Robert 288–90
Hoshin Kanri 230
Hughes, Louis 38
Hygiene factors 24

IBM 28, 81, 89
Akers, John 291–3
award mentality 145
change process 290–3
Knehler, John 291
performance measurement 245
salary progression 254
'speak up' programme 128
ICL 199, 236
IG Metall 44, 274, 276
Individuality 12–13, 16
Industrial Society, The 101
Institute of Manpower Studies 250
Integrity 95
International competition 8–11
International Labour Office 268, 270
International Metalworkers Federation 43
International Survey Research 140
Intuition 95
Inventory reduction 165–7
Involvement 130–47, 325–6
Irimajiri, Soichiro 54
Irish Congress of Trade Unions 271–2
Ishin Denshin 311
ISO 9000 204, 330

Jacques, Elliott 70–1
Jagawa, Tadaaki 53
Jaguar 293–4
Japan 31–62, 310–19
automation 39
changes in Japan 51–7
company size 43
consensus 315
continuous improvement 12
critics of Japan 40–51
egalitarianism 315
elimination of waste 36, 65, 68
kaizen 32, 34–6, 64, 140–4, 326
lean production 37–48, 67
lifetime employment 55–7
meetings 317
reciprocal obligations 68
responding to challenges 51–8, 68
small group activity 317
standard operation 32–4, 65
success factors 313–19
wages 43
working hours 41, 52, 68
Japan Airlines 56
Japan Autoworkers Union 41–2
Jeffries, Janet 132
JIT 165–67
critics 46
modifications 54
Job evaluation 150–2
Jones, Alun 225
Jones, Dan xiv, 310
Jordan, Bill 273–4, 283
Judge, Mike 23
Juran, Joseph 178

Kaizen 32, 34–6, 64, 140–4, 326
criticised 40, 44, 47
Kakimoto, Hideo 173
Kanter, Rosabeth Moss 267
Kawamoto, Nobuhiko 57
Keidanren 52
Keiretsu 238, 240
Kennedy, Iain 161

Kitamo, Mikio 53
Knowledge workers 219–37, 331
Kohn, Alfie 249, 265
Kwik Save 199

Labour costs 9
Lamming, Richard 167
Lao-Tzu 91, 93
Leadership xvi, 91–114, 321–2
  achievement 99
  aligning organisation 93
  communication 98
  devolving responsibility 94
  judgement 100
  personal attributes 95–7, 300, 322
  strategic perspective 97–8
  top leadership 91–101, 321
  transformational 91–3, 99, 101
Lean production 37–48, 67, 174–7
Learning organisation 149, 235–7
LeFauve, Richard 139
Level scheduling 169–71
Lifetime employment 55–7
Line balancing 110
Lorenz, Christopher 8, 287

Mackenzie, Neil 135
'Magic powder' 233
Management 15, 69, 102–3, 322
  by stress 50
  by walking around 129
Mandeville 20
Marks and Spencer 150, 199, 284
Marley 132
Mars 87
Maslow, Abraham 127
Material supply systems 167–9
Mayo, Elton 23, 73, 121
Mazda 53
Meister 104
Mercury Communications 254
Metallgesellschaft 241–2
Microsoft 78
Millward, Neil 49
Mintel 180–1
Mintzberg, Henry 102
Mission 81–90
MITI 51
Monks, John 284
Morita, Akio 317
MRP 168
Multi-skilling 154
Murlis, Helen 250, 253

Nasser, Jacques 295
National Economic Development Office
  supervision 106, 112
  suppliers 215
Neill, John 308
Nemawashi 55
Newbury, John 121
Nicholson, Frank 148
Nieuwenhuis, Peter 54
Nine Alpha Organisation Map 71–8
Nissan
  annual spend 203
  communications 127
  Company Council 136–7, 282
  construction 155–6
  flexibility 152–3, 284
  involvement 134
  JIT 167
  job evaluation 152–3
  Kaizen 140–4
  operator care 174–7
  performance assessment 257
  procurement policy 210
  Separation by Agreement 136, 280
  single status 115–16
  South Africa 121
  supervisors 106–11
  supplier assessment 212
  supplier development 213–16
  synchronous supply 168
  USA 82, 123, 280
  visible management 172–4
Non-financial indicators 244–5

Oakland, John 179
Ohno, Taiichi 6, 65
  debt to F. W. Taylor 21
  debt to Henry Ford 31
  inventory reduction 165
  single minute exchange of dies 165
Operator care 174–7
Organisation Development
    International xiv, 72
Organisation structures 148, 326
Organisation types 4–7, 71–8
Ovid 20
Ownership of change 22, 132, 140,
    161–2, 186, 195–204, 286, 298–309

Parkinson principle 124
Partnership sourcing 205–18, 330–1
Pattison, Mick 162
Pay systems 245–67, 333–4

Payment by results 218
Peach, Len 290
Pennington, Syd 150
Performance management 230, 254–8
Performance-related pay 249–67
'Perks' executive 118
Personal effectiveness 237
Personal pension plans 5
Peters, Tom 98, 180, 310
Petronius, Gaius 286
Piece rates 248
Pilkington Glass 251
Pirelli Cables 252
Poka yoke 189–90
Prescribed work 70–1
Pressac 215
Professional skills 232

Qualifications system in Japan 227–8
Quality 178–204, 329
  building for quality 187–9
  circles 190, 226
  definition 181
  designing for quality 183–7
  introducing integrated quality 195–204
  supervisors' responsibility 110
QWL 130

Ramsay, Rod 180
Rank Xerox 199, 245
Rearsby Automotive 158–9, 218
Recruitment 107
Roberts, David 111–12
Robertson, David 45–8, 174
Rolling contracts 263–4
Rothman 122
Roosevelt, Franklin Delano 81
Rover Group 93
  change process 296–7
  Edwardes, Sir Michael 296–7
  flexibility 153
  marketing strategy 180
  New Deal 275, 281, 296
  Robinson, Derek 297
  Rover Employee Assisted Learning Scheme 235
Ryder Distribution 168–9

Sadler, Philip 238, 263
Salary progression 253–8
Salarymen 42, 57
Salisbury store 181–2
'Save as you earn' 263
Schmidt, Herman 224
Schock, Manfred 44
Scholtes, Peter 254–5
Scott, David 249
Scott, John 164
Seaward Electronics 161
Secretary's Commission on Achieving Necessary Skills 219–22
Semler, Ricardo 91, 149–50
Seniority progression 56
Sengenberger, Werner 43
Shareholding patterns 240–4
Shell UK
  decentralisation 15–17
  globalisation 10
Shimada, Haruo 42
Shimanuki, Akira 155
Shimizu, Masamuchi 52
Shingo, Shigeo 6, 65
  Deming, W. Edwards 37
  Japanese overseas 49, 65
  single minute exchange of dies 165
Short-termism 238–44
'Simple Model' 3–7
Simpson, George 275
Simultaneous engineering 183–7
Singapore 9
Single minute exchange of dies 165
Single status 115–19, 323
Sissons, Keith 49
'Skunkworks' 186
Smilansky, Jonathan 195
Socio-technical system 26–8
Smith, Adam 20, 34
Sony 225, 317
Sorensen, Charles 21
Standard operation 32–4, 65, 135, 188
Statistical process control 188
Stewart, John 119
Strinz, Wolfgang 141
Sun Life Assurance 249–50
Sun Tzu xv, 301
Sunrise Medical 83–6
Supervisors 104–14, 322–3
Suppliers 206–18
  development 132
  measurement 212

Taishi, Prince Shotuka 311
Tannenbaum, Arnold S. 114
Tate and Lyle 152–3

Taylor, F. W. 20–2, 29, 31, 33, 50, 64, 105, 231
Teamworking 119–23, 323
  ad hoc 119
  assessed 250–1
  attacked 275–7
  'dark side' 50
  Hawthorne Plant 23
  introducing 123–6
  Nissan 107
  permanent groups 119
  supervisors 113–14
  top teams 121, 123
Technological change 11–12
Thatcher, Margaret 99
Theory X and Theory Y 24
Theory Z 28
3M 17, 87, 144
Torrington, Derek 249
Total productive maintenance 162–4
Total quality management 178–204, 329–30
Towers Perrin 264
Toyota 78
  automation 53
  criticised 41
  inventory 165
  pricing 210
  temporary contracts 56
  union approach 274
Toys R Us 264
Trade unions 268–85, 334–5
  future role 270, 283, 285
  lean production 41–51, 69
  membership levels 268–71
  militancy in Ford 13, 120, 280
  structure 269
  traditional role 277
Trades Union Congress
  on human resource management 48–9, 271
  legal representation 278
Training 219–37, 331–2
  Germany 223–4
  Japan 225–7
Transport and General Workers Union 46, 48–9
Tribus, Myron 304
Trigano, Gilbert 193–4
Trist, Eric 26
Tsuji, Yoshifumi 205
Tsuchiya, Toshiaki xiv, 109, 172, 315
Tuckman, B. W. 126

Union of Automobile Workers 130, 139
Union of Communication Workers 273, 279
Unipart 308

Vaughan, Ivor
  partnerships 218
  simplification 158–9
  'stand' 158–9, 299
Vaux Breweries 148
VDO 214–15
Venter, Barry xiv, 71
Veraldi, Lew 186
Virgin Atlantic Airways 100, 150
Visible management 172–4
Vision 81–90
Volkswagen 216
Volvo 53, 58–62, 65
Vorstand 242
Vroom, Victor 27

Walton, Richard 3–4
Webber, Michael 111–12
Weber, Max 312
Weiss, Heinrich 134
Welch, Jack 14, 126–7
Whybrew, John 16

Yawata Iron and Steel 191